Wordsworth and Feeling

By the same author

Wordsworth's Influence on Shelley: A Study of Poetic Authority (1988)
The New Shelley: Later Twentieth-Century Views, editor (1991)
Influence and Resistance in Nineteenth-Century English Poetry, coeditor (1993)

Wordsworth and Feeling

The Poetry of an Adult Child

G. Kim Blank

Madison • Teaneck
Fairleigh Dickinson University Press
London: Associated University Presses

© 1995 by Associated University Presses, Inc.

All rights reserved. Authorization to photocopy items for internal or personal use, or the internal or personal use of specific clients, is granted by the copyright owner, provided that a base fee of $10.00, plus eight cents per page per copy is paid directly to the Copyright Clearance Center, 222 Rosewood Drive, Danvers, Mass. 01923.
[0-8386-3600-4/95 $10.00 + 8¢ pp, pc.]

Associated University Presses
440 Forsgate Drive
Cranbury, NJ 08512

Associated University Presses
25 Sicilian Avenue
London WC1A 2QH, England

Associated University Presses
P.O. Box 338, Port Credit
Mississauga, Ontario
Canada L5G 4L8

The paper used in this publication meets the requirements
of the American National Standard for Permanence of Paper
for Printed Library Materials Z39.48–1984.

Library of Congress Cataloging-in-Publication Data

Blank, G. Kim, 1952–
    Wordsworth and feeling : the poetry of an adult child / G. Kim Blank.
       p. cm.
    Includes bibliographical references (p.   ) and index.
    ISBN 0-8386-3600-4 (alk. paper)
       1. Wordsworth, William, 1770–1850—Knowledge—Psychology.
2. Poets, English—19th century—Psychology. 3. English poetry--Psychological aspects. 4. Parent and child in literature.
5. Emotions in literature. 6. Family in literature. 7. Self in literature. I. Title.
PR5892.P74B53   1995
821.'7—dc20   94-43068
                                                                                          CIP

PRINTED IN THE UNITED STATES OF AMERICA

for Northfield:
an eternity of basements and backyards, forests and friends

> *Ah me, that all*
> *The terrors, all the early miseries,*
> *Regrets, vexations, lassitudes, that all*
> *The thoughts and feelings which have been infused*
> *Into my mind, should ever have made up*
> *The calm existence that is mine when I*
> *Am worthy of myself.*
>
> —Wordsworth (1805 *Prelude,* bk. 1, lines 355–61)

Contents

Preface / 9
Preamble / 11

Introduction: "The hiding places of my power" / 15
1. The Adult Child / 41
    A Mother / 47
    A Father / 55
    A Son / 65
    Penrith / 68
    Wordsworth's Health and the
        Composition of Poetry / 72
    The Abandoned Child and the
        Abandoning Father / 80
2. The Poet's Progress: Early Struggles,
   Early Gains / 91
    Wandering Lonely, 1793–95 / 93
    From Racedown to Alfoxden, 1795–97 / 98
    Towards the 1798 *Lyrical Ballads* / 114
3. *Tintern Abbey* Revisited; or, Aching Joys
   and Healing Thoughts / 125
4. Down and Out in Germany: Writing
   in Self-Defense / 140
    Off to Germany / 143
    The Letter to Coleridge, December 1798 / 149
    More Poetry from the Winter of Discontent / 167
5. Home Again in Grasmere / 174
    Towards the 1799 *Prelude* / 176
    Back in the U.K.: The 1799 *Prelude,* Book 2 / 184
    Longing for and Belonging at Grasmere / 189

6. The *Immortality Ode:* Back to the Future / 205

Appendix A: Wordsworth as the Lost Child / 216
Appendix B: Wordsworth, Trauma, and the Poetry
   of Dissociation / 218
Appendix C: Wordsworth, Recovery, and Writing / 220

Notes / 222
Works Cited / 248
Index / 263

Preface

How do we account for the kind of poetry Wordsworth produced?
 Since the moment I became interested in asking this question, I have never been completely happy with the many answers I have come across. Wordsworth, the figure of the man and the body of poetry, was something of a mystery to me. I was confused, even startled, not just by what he was writing about in some of his most famous poetry, but even more so by why this particular person was writing such poetry. Today I may be confused every now and then, but I am startled no more. I remain as impressed as ever by his poetry, and maybe even more impressed now that I have at least the beginnings of explanation with which I, at least, am satisfied—that is, for the time being.
 My worry is that the subject of my study is too narrow. My rationale, however, is that the subject is so prevalent. It's something like the corpse that keeps showing up in a detective story. By centering on the feelings or emotional content of Wordsworth's poetry, and in particular on the cluster of feelings that surround loss and grief, separation and endurance, guilt and fear, my hope will be to enrich the reading of the poetry and the understanding of the person behind the poet. Paying attention to feelings is a lesson that comes straight from Wordsworth, though it took him much work to come to terms with some of these feelings. Apparently many of us could benefit from his example.
 When I was first motivated to take up this study, I intended to do so by consulting and referring to only the primary sources—letters, journals, firsthand accounts, the poetry itself—and to scholarship that presented the facts of who, where, and when (for example, Reed 1967, 1975). I felt somewhat dissatisfied, perhaps even overwhelmed or intimidated, with the voluminous criticism on Wordsworth. In my sense of urgency, I thought this mountain of interpretation might get in the way of my molehill of a study. However, after reading Don H. Bialostosky's recent book, *Wordsworth, Dialogics, and the Practice of Criticism* (1992), I felt that I should, in the spirit of what is sometimes politely called academic socialization, enter the continuing critical dialogue that speaks

to and about Wordsworth. It seemed, after all, the professional thing to do. I am happy that I have done so, though of course there has been no way to take it all in, just as there has been no way to take in all of Wordsworth's poetry. Christopher Ricks writes, "There has been no greater poet in the last two centuries since he [Wordsworth] was born, and the best criticism does justice with as well as to him" (1987, 134). My somewhat immodest hope, then, is to do justice with and to Wordsworth as well as the best criticism. I have also been encouraged by Thomas McFarland's recent book on Wordsworth (1992), for, like McFarland, I find that, more than anything else, it is the emotional intensity in Wordsworth's poetry that distinguishes and characterizes the greatest English poet of the nineteenth century. My hope is to account for and follow the path of that emotional intensity in both the poet and the poetry.

As I look back upon what I have written from the position of a preface that is really a postscript, I see how very easily this study could have taken a Jungian turn and shown how the course of Wordsworth and his poetry was one of *individuation*: the struggle of a person to make himself or herself a whole being. What I have done, I think, amounts to the same, with enactment, healing, recovery, feeling, and thought as my signposts.

I would like to thank all those—students, colleagues, family, and friends—who have on occasion listened to me and have allowed me to listen to them about matters Wordsworthian. In particular, I would like to acknowledge Miranda Burgess, Robin A. Cryderman, Lisa C. Tarrant, and Jane Sellwood for their assistance at various stages of this project; Tara Ney for her psychological bent; Jocelyn Floyer for her very artistic insights; Patrick Grant for lending me his space; and A. B. England, Lisa Surridge, and Michael Cullen for reading parts of this study. And of course Jenner Lloyd Blank and Acia ("Ace") Charlotte Blank were always there, reminding me about childhood and feelings in the most direct and rewarding ways possible.

A note on the text

Whenever possible, and unless stated otherwise, I have used Stephen Gill's corrected edition of Wordsworth's poems (Wordsworth 1984). Gill presents the poems as they were first published. For poems from *Lyrical Ballads* that are not in Gill's edition, I have used *Lyrical Ballads*, edited by R. L. Brett and Alun R. Jones (Wordsworth 1965), because, like Gill's collection, it prints the poems as they first appeared. For *The Prelude*, I have used the Norton Critical Edition, edited by Jonathan Wordsworth, M. H. Abrams, and Gill (Wordsworth 1979). Besides excellence, these three texts have the advantage of accessibility.

Preamble

childhood shows the man, / As morning shows the day
—Milton, *Paradise Regained*

So what, or who, is the adult child?

The adult child brings the emotional baggage of childhood into adult life, influencing both personality and behavior in troubling ways. This bringing of the past into the present differs from ordinary memory and experience, for all of us, as adults, necessarily bring our past with us, and in this way our childhood is always there as an important part of our subjectivity and sense of self. We remember many of our feelings; we understand them or come to terms with them in the context of our development and identity. The difference is this: as adults we hope to be able to positively integrate the feelings of our childhood past into our adult behavior and personality, and we hope to be able to contextualize them; however, for the adult child, memory and experience and feelings originating in childhood are integrated in difficult and often detrimental ways, or they are not integrated at all. There is a gap, a stoppage, a holding back, a confusion. Feelings are displaced and mystified, and have difficulty being contextualized. Often they are internalized to such a degree that accessing them, or even being aware of them, is both difficult and painful. Because of certain circumstances, usually traumatic in nature and often involving family history and family dynamics, emotional growth has not fully taken place, yet intellectual and physical growth have continued. Childhood has not been played out, though this emotional burden of the past demands therapeutic reenactment. In order to grow up, the adult child needs to find appropriate ways to express those feelings. Thought and feeling must come together. Otherwise the child will never be father of the adult; the adult will forever be a slave to the unresolved feelings of the inner child.

Wordsworth and Feeling

Introduction:
"The hiding places of my power"

> We study the human person most fully when we take him as an individual.
> —Gordon Allport, *Pattern and Growth in Personality*

One picture of Wordsworth that emerges from the thematics of his poetry is predictable enough and has entered our received and cherished idea of "William Wordsworth": that of the restorative and stoic poet working steadily and in tranquility to control the overflow his imagination, certain in his uncertainty, conscious of his unconsciousness, finding the sublime in the banal, gracefully insightful even in his moments of profound blindness, and thoughtful in the presence of difficult feelings. From this perspective Wordsworth touches us all, because his poetry seems to be transformational; it often appears to transform all of the latter pairings into the former: personal blindness becomes general insight, inexplicable experience becomes meaningful in contemplation, the particularized banal becomes the universally sublime, the subjective unconscious becomes collective consciousness, individual uncertainty becomes shared security, difficult feelings become controlled thoughts. He is seen not as the poet of quiet desperation but of tranquil restoration. Moreover, and because of these apparent transformational acts, his poetry seems to supply what we often demand of powerful, canonical art: for most readers, including many attuned to the darker and uncertain side of Wordsworth's poetry, the universal is often privileged at the expense of the personal. Despite being concerned with the growth of an individual mind, Nature, in its largest sense, is preferred over nurture, in its private sense, even when, as for early Wordsworth, Nature is necessarily portrayed as both nurturing and authoritative, the source of and guide to self-acceptance.

We often prefer to view our meaningful connections as outward and transcendent rather than inward and arrested, especially when the objects of our attachment and concerns have to do with our emotional life, and especially when these are elevated in the name of art. Wordsworth himself says as much when he suggests that the truth of his kind of poetry is "not individual and local, but general, and operative," and that the ideal poet's "passions and thoughts and feelings are the general passions and thoughts and feelings of men" (Wordsworth 1984, 605–7). So even when Wordsworth nominates personal inner life as the goal of his meditated art, its validity and worth may only be as good as they pertain to "general" mankind. People do feel compelled to share experiences and feelings, and it does make them feel good to know that they are not alone. Freud notices as much when, in *The Future of an Illusion*, he points out that art heightens "feelings of identification" and provides "an occasion for sharing highly valued emotional experiences" (1989, 692). Some art may serve to confirm an individual's particular needs by airing them in a culturally accepted mode. Art can serve to valorize the artist's inner life while serving the needs of the community. Carl Woodring writes that Wordsworth "fought hardest of all to organize an individual interpretation of his own experiences into a complete whole" (1968, 5). Our own needs are something like Wordsworth's: we often prefer the "complete whole" over the detached, individual experience. In our desire, in our own need to share in those larger compensatory experiences, we prefer either to characterize Wordsworth's poetry as the expression of general, universal feelings; or, as an academic ploy, we situate Wordsworth in the more grand scene and scheme of other, external civilizing discourses—for example, literary criticism, critical theory, aesthetics, history, culture, philosophy, economics, politics. And even when Wordsworth is situated in the discourse of psychology or psychoanalysis, often the structure, concepts, or the lexicon of these discourses is used to render the text as if it were an end rather than a means, the proof instead of the pudding. That is, many readings of the poetry, in their ingenuity, become theory driven and overdetermined. Unfortunately, these days we often tend to privilege the product's discursive powers over the producer's subjective desires. Thus we are not quite so comfortable considering that the source of Wordsworth's universality, if indeed it is universal rather than eccentric or personal, might spring instead from hidden moments and confused motives. Our wonderful innocence as readers is ready to accept his profound experience as legislating poet. Where are the readers who see instead those hidden moments and confused motives of a someone whose view of his life and his inner self is divided and in conflict, who see much of Wordsworth's poetry as motivated by difficult, personal feelings that rise out of his history? And an impossible but irresistible question:

What are we left with when we take the art away from what Wordsworth was trying to express?

Language is a funny thing—funny peculiar, that is. Language both does and does not refer to people and places, feelings and thoughts. On one hand, language leads to that poststructural abyss where the signified waves farewell to the signifier as it falls away into the deconstructive darkness. Even this phrase—*on one hand*—reveals itself as a rhetorical rather than real gesture, and is therefore problematically nonreferential and limiting. (If only I had three hands . . .) On the other hand, language obviously and often efficiently serves a communicative function, so that plans can be made and carried out, pizzas ordered and delivered (without anchovies), situations explained and understood, and our subjective, private lives expressed to those willing and able to share the dictionary we were born into.

When I read and study poetry these days, I feel that my response, my positioning, is uncertain—and maybe even paradoxical. It is partly the two-hand problem: the rhetorical versus the referential, the sliding of the signified under the signifier. Can we *extract* from language—more particularly, radically self-conscious written language—the actual feelings and meanings of another person from another culture and another time? And whose story is history: that of the victors or the victims? Whose meaning counts: that of the actors or the audiences, the coders or the decoders, the authors or the readers? To borrow Freud's syntax: Where the Author is, the Reader shall be. Are producers of messages at one with consumers of meaning? Are we chameleon interpreters, capable of empathetically filling the body of any other, even a sparrow poet picking about in the gravel; or are we egotistically sublime readers, remaking the world in our own autobiographical or idealized image? Does language have its own independent reality? Should we respond to a text with our critical intellect or with our emotions? Can we even separate these two, or privilege one over the other? These are, in many ways, old questions, but they are also questions that will not go away with the birth or burial of a new theory of language, reading, or criticism.

William Wordsworth had his views on all of this, and he knew very well what he wanted his language to do. He was born into an age that began in earnest the arguments about phenomenology that continue today, arguments over experience, knowledge, and representation. But Wordsworth was clear about how he wanted his language to perform. He wrote in the Preface to

Lyrical Ballads that he wanted to keep his "Reader in the company of flesh and blood." The abyss of nonsignification could be bridged by thinking "long and deeply," by looking "steadily at . . . [the] subject," "by fitting to metrical arrangement a selection of the real language of men in a state of vivid sensation," by adopting "the very language of men," by bringing "language near to the language of men," by using "a selection of language really spoken by men." For Wordsworth, himself "a man speaking to men," language can express even "the spontaneous overflow of powerful feelings," so long, that is, as thought, the storehouse of "all our past feelings," is superadded to the process as a guide (Wordsworth 1984, 595–603).[1] In short, Wordsworth wanted to use natural language, and his theory of poetry was that it is expressive.[2] Whether this position is theoretically sound makes little difference. We have been reminded that the sign is, after all, arbitrary, and that there may be nothing outside of the text—well, except life, that is. But we should attempt to pay attention to what Wordsworth desired from language, and why. As far as Wordsworth was concerned, his life outside of the text determined what went inside of the text. We too should share this concern.

In the *Appendix to the Preface* (1802), Wordsworth rehearses a brief history of poetry in order to emphasize that poetic language had become "insensibly produced, differing materially from the real language of men in *any situation*." Wordsworth's nutshell reinvention of poetic history verges on the paranoid, or at least on the extremely hyperbolic. His descriptions make it sound like the spread of an unstoppable, insidious, and evil disease that must be halted in its tracks. Poets, suggests Wordsworth, had taken the "genuine language of Poetry," corrupted it, made it esoteric, and used meter to introduce "adulterated phraseology." The result was that "the taste of men was gradually perverted": "Abuses of this kind were imported from one nation to another, and with the progress of refinement this diction became daily more and more corrupt. . . ." (Wordsworth 1984, 616–19). It appears, then, that Wordsworth's poetic calling is one of redemption and salvation, to reclaim or deliver poetry and poetic language from damnation, to stop all this adulteration, perversion, abuse, and corruption. William Hazlitt, one of the first readers who managed to have some historical and literary perspective in assessing Wordsworth, but who was still close to the scene of production, noted as much in 1825, but he puts it in more reserved, literary terms: Wordsworth's "inartificial style gets rid (at a blow) of all the trappings of verse" (Hazlitt 1932, 87).

Wordsworth's strong belief that language can cut through to and connect directly with the real world of people, places, feelings, and thoughts is central to the Preface to *Lyrical Ballads*. Nothing, says Wordsworth, should be "standing between the Poet and his image of things" (Wordsworth 1984, 605). In summing up, he writes that had he more time, he might have "assisted my Reader in perceiving that the powers of language are not so limited as he may suppose" (614). This belief is central to his whole poetic project. In the 1815 *Essay, Supplementary to the Preface,* he acknowledges that "language" is "a thing subject to endless fluctuations and arbitrary associations," but the "genius of the Poet melts these down for his purpose" (660). As late as *Essays upon Epitaphs, III,* Wordsworth denounces the kind of poetry that is shallow artifice; he believes that words can be "an incarnation of . . . thought"; and "thoughts" can "assume an outward life without a transmutation and a fall" (Wordsworth 1974, 2:84–85). Without the belief in "the powers of language," Wordsworth could not write about his own reality.

Thus Wordsworth believed he could, in his poetry, overcome the failure of the word to measure up to the world, that he could give expression to experience, to feelings and thoughts. In the kind of poetry he would write, the gap between language and life would, he believed ever so deeply, be filled. So much depended upon putting real life, often his own life or poetic allegories of it, on the line, even if he gave those lines to other "characters." But at the same time, these claims he made upon his own style of poetry, to write in that "real language of men," can also, at particular points, be viewed as a front for the Personal acting as the Universal, the Universal posing as the Personal. Another way to put it: the naturalistic clarity that he wanted to communicate to us is the clarity that he needed for himself. Obsession for outer clarity, for the appearance of outer clarity, can, as we shall see, sometimes be read as an indicator for inner confusion or the desire to poetically vent swollen emotions. The Universal in Wordsworth may be a powerful deflector for the Personal. The feelings, nevertheless, remain just as real, except we might want to explore their origins in Wordsworth's particular history and emotional life. I believe his theory of poetic diction is grounded at least as much in his own personal history as it is in the literary history out of which he wrote. Wordsworth wanted to trust his words.

The important relationship between words and communicated feeling is also behind Wordsworth's *Note to "The Thorn"* (1800), which is both a defense of the style and diction of the particular poem and a precise expression of his belief in the emotive power of words and the emotive nature of poetry. Writes Wordsworth:

> Poetry is passion: it is the history or science of feeling: now every man must know that an attempt is rarely made to communicate impassioned feelings without something of an accompanying consciousness of the inadequateness of our own powers, or the deficiencies of language. (Wordsworth 1984, 594)

Wordsworth here points to much that is central to his own poetic project, but the big idea is the belief that his poetry has the power to overcome "the deficiencies of language" to express passion and feeling. He sees words (if they are the right words) as "active and efficient"—moreover, as part of the experience of feeling itself: "[T]he mind luxuriates in the repetition of words which appear successfully to communicate its feelings" (594). Over fifty years ago Wordsworth's vocabulary of emotion was so distressing for one critic that she was moved to produce a full-length study devoted to it (Miles 1942).[3] One important conclusion that has to be resurrected and reconsidered is not just that this lexicon of feeling is central to what was considered poetic by Wordsworth, but why emotional responses were fundamental to Wordsworth in the first place. The argument will be that Wordsworth needed natural language in order to have it measure up to his feelings and subjective life. Again: Wordsworth trusted his words to express what he thought and felt.

In the beginning of the 1802 *Appendix*, Wordsworth expresses his anxiety about whether the "Reader" would get his message about "poetic diction" right. In doing so, he states his desire for a return to a long-lost kind of poetry where language is both innocent and direct, where powerful feelings and elemental passions are voiced as original rather than mechanical, natural rather than artificial. Wordsworth sets this up as a kind of loss, a fall from innocence, and he laments the passing of a prelapsarian scene of poetic production. Evil has somehow entered the Garden, and Wordsworth, it seems, wants to return; he wants to write his way back to Paradise, to that vision of innocence, which for him (and here is the important turn) was often determined by the trope of childhood. Here the subject of innocence overlaps with the language of Innocence. As Thomas McFarland writes, "Wordsworth's paradise was the past" (1992, 135). But it is neither a general nor a mythic notion of childhood that emerges here—one, say, like Blake's. It is not universal childhood that he conjures up; rather, it is his own particular childhood that comes back to him. It is to the *idea* of his own particular childhood that he makes as his return to his own innocence, though not all of it may have been as paradisiacal as he wished. In truth, parts of this childhood may have been a bit of purgatory or limbo as well, especially when some of the feelings surfaced as confused and unresolved. In all of this I recall something that William Heath wrote about Wordsworth:

> The central problem is to discover the extent to which for Wordsworth, as an autobiographer, the composition of final truth about the self is the product of experiment with ambivalent feelings, improvised roles, within an environment which can sustain a tension between confession and justification, between the wish to Get on with It and the need to tell the truth. (Heath 1973, 91)

Wordsworth experimented with his childhood past in an attempt to create himself as an adult. What was frightening for Wordsworth was that the past he needed in order to fortify his present and future also "simultaneously threaten[ed] him with dissolution" (Heath 1973, 88, 99)—that is, with the fear he might not be able to recover, recreate, or heal the inner child. He needed to experiment poetically with ways of expressing those feelings that were most difficult for him. As I hope to show, this can be used to account for some of the more enigmatic poems in *Lyrical Ballads* that repeatedly address loss and separation, death and mourning—poems that tell, in effect, the same story. And so, to use Heath's words, Wordsworth did want to "Get on with It"; he wanted to get on with his adult life. It is just that, as an adult child, he found himself trapped by unresolved feelings.

The historical truth of the literary past that Wordsworth attempted to mythologize does not always matter, any more than it really matters whether the Garden of Eden actually existed. What counts is his invention of and desire for that innocent past. How much or how little the external facts of Wordsworth's own life enter his texts matters little. Once more, Freud is useful here: in a short paper entitled *Screen Memories*, he suggests that "childhood memories show us our earliest years not as they were but as they appeared at the later periods when the memories were aroused"; memories, he writes, do not *emerge*—they are *formed* as they are remembered: "And a number of motives, with no concern with historical accuracy, had a part in forming them, as well as in the selection of the memories themselves" (1989, 126). What is most important is the emotional reality of Wordsworth's words and the stories they form, and the functional power he invests in those words and stories as he finds himself necessarily having to come to *terms* with the meaning of his own life and experiences. What that innocence represents matters more. And most of all, for Wordsworth it matters that the feelings are real. The recollection of physical events may or may not be more reliable than the memory of psychological ones; but I believe that the psychological impressions (that is, feelings) are, paradoxically, both more reliable and more mutable. These days in psychotherapeutic circles it is recognized that traumatic childhood events do not even have to be remembered in order to be reenacted. Even if there are false memories, the emergent feelings remain the material to deal with. For Wordsworth, getting to the truth of feeling was more important, or more imperative, than getting to the truth of the event, though Wordsworth often strove to ground much of his poetry in his actual experiences.

This desire for and a fascination with a return to a prefallen state is important for our understanding of Wordsworth, not just as a poet but as a subjective individual.[4] This repetition compulsion, this desire for return, structures and determines not only his belief in a certain kind of poetic diction and style—that is, the use of a particular lexicon and syntax—but also points to his own needs and sense of self, and thus to a corresponding thematics that manifests itself in his poetry. (Recall above that Wordsworth promoted the idea that the translation of thoughts and feelings into language could be made without suffering what he called "a fall.") There are, both in Wordsworth's life and in his poetry, corresponding arrested moments that open up, as it were, gaps—as if he had two lives, two ways of being: before the Fall and after the Fall. And while some of his poetry addresses and seems to powerfully bridge those gaps, I will try to show in this critical narrative of Wordsworth's life into work that the material of the bridging moves between being reparative and retentive—poetically convincing and universally appealing, but revealing psychological motives and personal needs of the adult child. There were some difficulties in Eden.

In the opening of second part of the 1799 *Prelude,* Wordsworth himself confronts the gap between himself and his innocent, lost past. Once upon a time, out there in the "woods and fields," he played every day, from morning to evening, sleep being the only constraint for his "beating mind." From this recollection he suggests that no "one who has ever been young" could resist giving up the trials and tribulations of adulthood for the "eagerness of infantine desire," that every one would give up the wisdom and virtue associated with adulthood to reclaim childhood. He is in fact a little dumbfounded or stunned by the distance between himself and that child who was once he:

> A tranquillizing spirit presses now
> On my corporeal frame, so wide appears
> The vacancy between me and those days,
> Which yet have such self-presence in my heart
> That sometimes when I think of them I seem
> Two consciousnesses—conscious of myself,
> And of some other being.
> (1799 *Prelude,* bk. 2, lines 25–31)[5]

There is little sense of continuity here, of growth, of the child being father to the man. There is more a sense of irrecoverability, of loss, and of a potential for self-splitting. At this point he does not seem to be able to put those two lives together to make one. When he tries to think about himself, become aware of himself, one part splits off; the other part is, it seems, like a stranger, "some other being." Yet that "other being" within himself is both apart from and yet a vital part of his inner life, his "heart," which we must take to be the center of his emotions. What needs to be examined is that "vacancy" and the reasons for it. What needs to be examined is why that "other being" could not (at least at this point) be connected, liberated, and assimilated. This would be part of Wordsworth's great poetic project and is central to this present study.

There are identifiable subjects—interrelated subject clusters—that Wordsworth returned to over and over again in his poetry, and we have to make more than generic or stylistic observations about this fact, since these subjects appear in poems that differ considerably in genre and style. We have to, in other words, do more than bring an approach or theory *to his texts only*. The character of his life, of his poeticized incarnation of his life, must be made to account for the character of his work. For some literary scholars, these remarks must seem irrelevant, perhaps even crude. After all, we do have his words. What more do we need? I think we need—his texts need—much more than just our own professionalized intelligence. So, despite the creative or fictional nature of some of Wordsworth's narratives, I believe that in the pattern of Wordsworth's poetic responses can be found an expression of his inner life as he himself attempted to approach it; they are an expression of what happened to him, of what he felt or thought he felt. What often motivated Wordsworth's best poetry and what his poetry is all about is the desire to describe and admit to those particular feelings, especially negative feelings, such as fear, anxiety, loss, sorrow, grief, and guilt, and by such description and admission to attempt to transform those feelings and then leave them. I want to examine this process and to account for its necessity. The thematics of much of Wordsworth's earlier poetry is a product of his emotional difficulties.

Although it would make a great story to say that Wordsworth did finally become whole and at peace with himself, and that he did live happily ever after, we know better. He never got there. No one really does get there—get to a perfect end—though after 1800 Grasmere became a half-century resting place. And this study will not get there either. But the process of trying to get there matters, both for us and for William Wordsworth. As Alice Miller writes, "This process of deepening one's insights is never fully terminated" (1990b, 163). It is about endurance and the drive for self-recognition and self-acceptance, which are motifs that stand behind Wordsworth's best poetry. Getting there is what Wordsworth as a person was all about. By about 1802, Wordsworth was beginning to understand and contextualize most of his own negative feelings, while keeping feelings at the center of his poetic project. He was beginning to bring thought to feeling in profitable ways and not to privilege the former at the expense of the latter. In that year he could write, "[A] great Poet . . . ought to a certain degree to rectify men's feeling, to give them new compositions of feeling, to render their feelings more sane pure and permanent, in short, more consonant to nature, that is, to eternal nature, and the great moving spirit of things" (Wordsworth 1967, 355). This is almost as far as Wordsworth could come. His final step was to substitute his own mind for nature. He could now be nurtured by his own meditated history, which he could accept and with which he could connect. But he could only get this far by rectifying and making sense of *his own* difficult feelings. This, I hope, will show in the development of his poetry up until 1802–4. As Bateson points out, what always impressed the Wordsworth circle was the poet's strength to go on despite his extreme psychological difficulties: "So far from surrendering to the neurotic elements in his personality, . . . Wordsworth's early life was one long desperate struggle against them" (1954, 199).[6] From about 1802, Wordsworth began to understand the feelings associated with his split past, realizing that the strength he needed to go on depended on accepting the permanence of those feelings, their place in shaping his relationship to the world. Though much of that past became inaccessible to him over time, he could nonetheless find strength in what he could retain.

Joseph Campbell, in citing Karlfried Graf Durckheim, puts this to us: "When you're on a journey, and the end keeps getting further away, then you realize that the end is the journey" (1988, 230). I nevertheless have to make some gesture towards closure, and I will do so by formulating a stage, a point in a process, to which Wordsworth comes and then changes direction as he arrives at a different understanding of himself; the journey still goes on, but a new part of it begins. Literary history has sometimes chosen to read this as a loss of creative power on the part of Wordsworth, his so-called decline.[7] I see it as something closer to a personal healing process that changed the kind of poetry he wrote. An account of this change, then, will be an implicit aim of this study. Lionel Trilling in ending his essay on the *Immortality Ode* points out that anyone who wishes to speculate about Wordsworth's deterioration must be aware "that an account of why Wordsworth ceased to write great poetry must at the same time be an account of how he once did write great poetry. And this latter account, in our present state of knowledge, we cannot begin to furnish" (Trilling 1975, 167). True—the creative mystery behind great art will forever remain just that: a mystery. But in this book I hope to account for the circumstances motivating some of Wordsworth's poetry—its origin and substance—and why he ceased to write that kind of poetry. Why Wordsworth ceased to write "great poetry" is part of the same story as why he once did write "great poetry."

So here, then, is the big jump that I, as reader, will soon have to make. I believe that Wordsworth's words of worth (and occasionally the obvious lack of them, his gaps) do indeed express and communicate his sometimes displaced but always emergent feelings. Wordsworth's words and stories in question here cut through to the feelings and thoughts of a real person; I believe that they cut deeply into Wordsworth's subjective life, often showing the way past rhetorical and narratological defenses to real wounds and an extremely difficult personal uncertainty. Wordsworth's poetry is about Wordsworth's needs. These words and feelings do not necessarily correspond to the exact feelings in the original experience (can they ever?). But in Wordsworth's case he cuts as deeply as he can, knowing that present feelings and circumstances may, as he writes in *Nutting*, "Confound my present feelings with the past." But the bottom line remains: he does attempt to get in touch with his feelings. He attempts to bring thought to feeling, and feeling to thought, past to present. This is what he so strongly desired out of the kind of language he used. This is what interests me. And this, I believe, is what made Wordsworth write a certain kind of poetry. He wanted to bring feeling and thought together, just as he wanted to bring together past and present, loss and gain, the child and the adult, the personal and the universal.

To read much of Wordsworth's earlier poetry—that, say, written before 1802–4—is to become aware that he was after something other than interesting renditions of rustic tales and popular ballads, or even that he was interested in using nature in new ways to foreground aspects of moral philosophy or to generate social commentary from an examination of simple rural life. There are just too many instances of negative feelings and disturbing, unresolved subjects in the early poetry; and a large number of these subjects circle, sometimes evasively but always profoundly, around the notion of childhood, both in idealized and agonized versions, both in portrayals of his own childhood and in those of his imagined childhood characters. Childhood seems to be something that Wordsworth needed to approach and to understand. Thus there are a number of poems (especially in *Lyrical Ballads*) in which the adult and the child confront each other over subjects close to Wordsworth's own troubles. In the 1805 *Prelude* he posits that "simple childhood" is the mysterious foundation upon which man's "greatness stands," but he also adds that he is enigmatically prevented from coming to understand the source of his own "power":

> The days gone by
> Come back upon me from the dawn almost
> Of life; the hiding places of my power
> Seem open, I approach, and then they close;
> I see by glimpses now . . .
>
> (Bk. 11, lines 328–37)

My hope is to be able to examine both the source of the "power" and the reason for this closure as it relates to the source of his expressed feelings. His very early life comes back to him; he attempts to confront it, but then he is almost completely blocked. Yet he has come to know that the key to his "power" is hidden in those "days gone by." Thus the way Wordsworth's past returns to him is determined by the paradox of invitation and rejection, clarity and confusion, revelation and mystery, innocence and experience, desire and resistance. Between all of these pairs Wordsworth and his poetry must negotiate.

Wordsworth's poetic encounter with childhood could be called a dialogue with the self; and here we see Wordsworth develop a number of poetic and narratological strategies to maintain that dialogue. It could also be viewed as a personal or intellectual investigation. I see it as something closer to therapy— as being therapeutic and necessitated by the need to understand himself, in order, quite simply, to feel better about himself. For, psychophysiologically, Wordsworth was often unbalanced. And the evidence suggests he often felt worst during his compositional periods. The clarity, hope, bliss, happiness, and ecstasy that we sometimes associate with his poetry and the scene of production is overbalanced by the confusion, fear, pain, helplessness, sorrow, and depression in his life and poetry; and the joy in life is overshadowed by a concern for death. His adult concerns at this point in his poetry often centered around finding what nowadays we call the lost inner child.[8] He eventually formulated that recovery, ostensibly out of childhood, and we see that recovery voiced in what is perhaps his most powerful poetic gesture: the *Immortality Ode*. It is also anticipated in the act of meditation in *Tintern Abbey,* which works towards a kind of holistic vision and healing process. Thus one of the objects of this study is to trace his poetic tracks towards locating and healing the child within. The leap he made in his great *Ode* was that he moved towards integrating the cognitive and the emotional. While this was a significant point in his personal development, it also put a stop to an important aspect of his poetic development, or at least to the kind of poetry he had been writing, for little of what he wrote after the *Ode* has the kind of emotional intensity that drives his earlier poetry.[9] From this angle he appears to have become a better person and a worse poet, though this might be phrased otherwise: he became a different person and a different poet.

We have to admit and consider something that is so obviously striking about Wordsworth's poetry: that from the beginning of his most interesting poetry, Wordsworth spent a great deal of time thinking and writing about himself, his life, the meaning of his experiences, and especially the meaning of his preadolescent experiences. Richard J. Onorato, in his full-length study of Wordsworth's "I-speaking character" in *The Prelude*, refers to this as "Wordsworth's preoccupation with himself, his self-elaborating egoism," and he also notes that this is a compulsive act of "self-invention" (1971, 5–6). But this compulsion should not be confined to the later *Prelude*s; and, more importantly, it should not be confined to a "character" who wants to discover reasons to qualify himself as a philosophical poet. Neither should Wordsworth's "preoccupation with himself" be viewed as egotistical or an act of egotism. I read this compulsion as having to do with self-exploration and self-acceptance, necessitated by a troubled inner life. To make more complete sense of it, it needs to be taken over to the life Wordsworth lived and to the self he attempted to rediscover, understand, and remake. Thus a great deal of Wordsworth's other poetry is also about "self-invention"—but of a more fundamental, personal nature: it is about trying to pull together and reconstitute a dislocated personality, "Two consciousnesses," a split life, a life that calls out to see once more as it had seen before, to find the child who desires to be and can become father of the man.

Alice Miller's extensive and powerful writings on childhood trauma, child rearing, and psychotherapy prove useful in attempting to describe and understand Wordsworth and his poetry.[10] Throughout Miller's work, feeling and subjectivity are central for understanding any individual and important for any individual who wants to understand himself or herself. Subjectivity, writes Miller, is "revealed . . . in everything [a] person says, does, writes, dreams, or flees from," and in making her particular case studies, her method, she says, always "places *subjectivity* in the foreground" (1986, 8, 294). What I have also found to be especially useful to bring over to Wordsworth is an idea central to Miller's examination of adult behavior: the idea of *reenactment*, which, for those people who have had to endure a difficult childhood or traumatic events as children, involves "an essential, often dramatic, unconscious message about the early childhood situation" (1986, 15). Adults, then, necessarily reenact their negative, repressed feelings in various ways. I see much of Wordsworth's work as the *poetry of reenactment*, as communicating a "dramatic, unconscious message" about his feelings of loss, abandonment, and loneliness—and centering, quite often, around death. His poems are performative on an affective level.[11] They reenact these and other related feelings, and we can, with certain evidence before us, finally demystify much of Wordsworth's sometimes strange poems and idiosyncratic emotions. We can at last see more clearly not only what Wordsworth was writing about, but why he was writing about what he was writing about.

Despite the soft, nonthreatening touch that the notion of *interpretation* makes as a neutral, objective investigative gesture, the business of literary criticism has to do with formulating meaning *in other words*; and as we know, in these ideologically troubled dog days, when being politically correct is more important than following your bliss, meaning exists all over the place and serves multiple interests and purposes. Being conscious of this is a good thing. Sometimes approaches are invented and employed to situate or describe the meaning of a literary work so that we can be, so to speak, above it; texts can be made to follow an agenda; or, put less cynically, we can view texts via genres, traditions, histories, theories of language, conventions, philosophies, politics, or any "ism" or discipline or approach that pleases the momentary need for explanation and displays a shared lexicon or area of expertise. These kinds of readings are sometimes smarter than they are sensitive. We sometimes witness this in some New Historicist critical work, where in every poem the ideological dimension is central even when it is defaced, denied, deflected—that is, when it is *not* there.[12] At the same time, we have had to cope with deconstructive readings that suggest that no situated writing subject can say what he or she wants to say because language does not correspond with what it attempts to represent. And so it seems to me that, in their explanatory power, applications of these approaches sometimes end up going beyond the fact—that is, the fact of the existence of a text produced by a subjective, particular being who believed that his language could cut through the problems of referentiality to express feelings and thoughts. (The "being" I have in mind here is, of course, a dead poet whom we call William Wordsworth.) In short, these kinds of overdetermined approaches (I'd like to put them all under the umbrella of what I call Supplemental Criticism) do not often strive to account for the very being of the text at its most immediate level—that is, in the presence of a writing subject who has a history and a desire to express herself or himself as clearly as possible. Meaning is the product not just of perspective, of time and place, but also of subjective, individual needs. Time and place are the *when* and *where*; needs call to the *why*. Onorato writes that "Wordsworth's art is not easily explained by the facts of his life, nor does his art, even at its most confessional, satisfy one's curiosity about the life being transmuted into artifact" (1971, 406). I would like to satisfy this curiosity, for I believe that Wordsworth's art is indeed quite explainable by the facts of his life.

In this book, then, I quite unabashedly attempt to give just such an account of why some of Wordsworth's texts came into being, why they exist as the expression of a particular subject and subjectivity, and why they express certain feelings. I am looking at these texts in terms of their radical subjectivity—and by "radical" I mean essential and inherent. All behavior serves a function, and with Wordsworth we should attempt to address the function of some of his poetry—for him. Lionel Trilling points in the right direction when he writes, "His [Wordsworth's] finest passages are moral, emotional, subjective; whatever visual intensity they have comes from his response to the object, not from his close observation of it" (Trilling 1975, 152). Wordsworth's poetry demands that we pay as close attention to his responses as he paid to his own.

The greater part of this book will locate these feelings in the texts of the poems, and another part attempts to locate the origin of these feelings in his life. Thus I plan to reexamine some aspects and certain circumstances of Wordsworth's life as he remembered it. The ordering of this study is natural. I will first examine aspects of the life in order to understand the need for reenactment in the text as expressed feelings—as poetic affect. This does not necessarily mean paying attention to the poetry in the way that traditional psychoanalytic criticism does, which, in its emphasis on the oedipal structure, is beginning to appear both autocratic and bankrupt as a theory and practice. As Miller points out, rigid psychoanalysis in its applied methodology "reinforces intellectual resistance to feeling and reality; for as long as feelings can be talked *about* they cannot really be felt. And as long as feelings are not felt, the self-damaging blockages remain" (1990b, 183). This is an important point. Although a couple of centuries and clinical training prevent me from going back and fixing Wordsworth (in the sense of facilitating recovery through his expression of difficult feelings), I believe in approaching his work in an attempt to unblock some of his texts and to critically liberate our fixed idea of Wordsworth, given that the poet himself was attempting to liberate his own feelings. The force of Wordsworth's texts thus comes to be about this play between denial and acceptance, between blocking and liberation, between repression and expression, between rhetorical gestures and the language of his human heart—the language of feeling. Thus, while predating Freud in knowing that subjectivity and the past are the foundation of the self, Wordsworth also goes beyond Freud by paying close attention to feelings, by attempting to reconstruct his feelings in order to really experience and come to terms with the intense disquietude he held within himself. Coleridge, himself a firsthand expert on negative feelings and someone who certainly knew the complexity of Wordsworth's inner workings better than anyone else, jealously defers to Wordsworth's disposition when, in *Dejection: An Ode*, he admits he cannot connect with the elements surrounding him: "I see them all so excellently fair, / I see, not feel, how beautiful they are!"[13] In short, Coleridge was hyperaware that Wordsworth's genuine power resided in establishing the self by the ability to feel. We should be, too.

Then there is the poetry that is not ostensibly personal or autobiographical. In examining fairy tales and attempting to account for their problematical content, Miller writes that "there can be no doubt that someone who writes such a work must himself have gone through what he is presenting" (1986, 235); "The phantasies expressed in literature, art, fairy tales, and dreams often unconsciously convey early childhood experiences in a symbolic way" (315). This is helpful when brought over to Wordsworth, and especially for those more enigmatic poems where strong and difficult feelings like fear, grief, loss, and guilt are worked into rather thin narratives. These poems "convey" what Wordsworth "must himself have gone through," what he felt. The stories, incidents, and even the characters and narrators often may be fictionalized, but the predominant feelings and the experiences that are behind the creative reenactments are not. Geoffrey Hartman notices something like this in Wordsworth's *Lyrical Ballad* poems: "[E]ven when the loss is ordinary, the passion is extraordinary, and points to so deep and personal a sorrow that we call it natural only to dignify human nature" (1971, 143). Indeed, it is the extraordinary "passion," then, we should attend to. Hartman here also notices two other things that relate to the interests of this book. First, he recognizes there is the tendency to elevate the "passion" to a larger, more general context; and second, he finds that the "sorrow" being pointed to is utterly "personal." Unfortunately, Hartman says almost nothing about the source of such particular feelings. I hope to. Why is it that loss and sorrow are so passionately expressed by Wordsworth?

Here I might insert something anecdotal yet relevant to the function that some of Wordsworth's poetry may served for him. A few years ago I was talking to an acquaintance, a respected psychotherapist, who said that one quite successful technique for assisting persons to overcome emotional trauma is to have them write a story depicting the experienced trauma, the events surrounding it (even if they seem unrelated), and, if possible, the resolution to the trauma. The person is asked to read the story over a number of therapy sessions, revising when it felt appropriate, and, if necessary, even using imaginative capabilities to work towards a desired resolution. In effect, the same story was being written over and over again until, at last, a resolution was articulated. A direction often became clear, a kind of opening for expression and recovery and healing, and there was a good chance that the hindering feelings could be dealt with by making them active cognitions.[14] The idea behind this process is that, over time, the associated difficult or confused feelings would gradually be understood and accepted. There is seldom just one story that will tell of the trauma and its resolution; the different stories are all related by the same difficult feelings. In effect, the same story kept telling itself over and over *differently*. (See Appendix C: Wordsworth, Recovery, and Writing.) I believe that in certain circumstances and at certain times in his life Wordsworth felt a strong need to tell the same story over and over again, and that eventually, as he became cognizant of these feelings, they began to trouble him less frequently. He then had less need to write that kind of poetry. The thematics of this poetry is a product of his exploration of emotional difficulties. For Wordsworth, personal development can be linked to narrative strategies.

So how are the most significant feelings treated in Wordsworth? When are they expressed and when are they repressed? This is a tricky issue, for we must acknowledge that repression is also a form of expression. It is just not a very healthy one. For example, what takes place in those autobiographical passages that address what must have been the most traumatic events in his early, most formative years—namely, the death of his mother and father and the complete shattering of his family life? Are these same feelings expressed in his other poetry? I would argue that often they are; and I might even go so far as to suggest that while they initially tend to be played down in the autobiographical poetry, they tend to be played out in the imaginative poetry. I hope to show that there is a strong relationship between the two kinds of poetry, and that the terms "imagination" or "imaginative poetry" as they apply to Wordsworth should not necessarily suggest something not real. I think that in the case of Wordsworth, the imagination has to do with the difficult intersection of thought and feeling, and the transformation of one into the other. By 1803, Coleridge called Wordsworth "a thinking feeling Philosopher" (Coleridge 1956, 2:957).

Besides the cluster of feelings I have mentioned thus far, there is another feeling that is not so evident in the poetry examined in this book, though this feeling may stand behind some of the poetry and the other feelings—it is, as one might say, conspicuous through its absence. The feeling is anger. The repressed feelings in Wordsworth revolve around displaced anger.[15] To deny anger is to foster helplessness and to encourage other kinds of defenses. One gets stuck. With perhaps the exception of *Nutting*, a poem that is utterly unclear about its feeling, anger is what is missing in his imaginative poetry, though he does have a few important recollections of being angry as child. Even a poem like *Michael*, which takes a son from a father and destroys the idea of family continuity (by the loss of land), centers on feelings of loss and endurance, and ultimately leaves the old man helpless: he is stuck in quiet grief, his task incomplete, his feelings and actions blocked by his feelings of sorrow—and then he is dead. The son, appropriately, hides away. The father's actions (not completing the sheepfold) suggest a kind of catatonic denial attempting to disguise itself as acceptance. No positive emotions are mastered here. I would account for Michael (the character and the poem) as a reenactment of the pattern and, more importantly, the residual feelings surrounding Wordsworth's early family circumstances. This is where the poem comes from. No child, or even adult for that matter, can go through a difficult family life, the experience of having a loved one die, and then the dissolution of a family, without experiencing anger. Wordsworth's feelings of anger get expressed as or displaced by disproportionate guilt—guilt, that is, about feeling anger: *I shouldn't feel angry about my upbringing, the death of my most significant loved ones, and the loss of my family, but I do, and I feel guilty about my anger*. Anger turned inwards—that is, repressed anger—often turns into depression, and along with depression comes a host of other symptoms, behaviors, and feelings. While in the bulk of this book I hope to show how the feelings are apparent in his poetry, the symptoms and behaviors are just as visible in his life. I will devote some time to this in the following chapter, and there we will see how a child—abused, traumatized, and suicidal—became an adult struggling with psychosomatic and anxiety disorders .

A great deal about Wordsworth's life and work can be explained, then, by paying attention to these feelings, both as past recollection and present expression. One can expect to meet resistance from those who would deny feeling a place in poetry and literary criticism, just as they might in their own lives, but I would say that this is where Wordsworth's best poetry comes from. Some of the earliest negative criticism of Wordsworth dismissed such poetry simply because of its exploration of personal experience. For such critics, the subjective is hardly sublime. John Keats himself was, at times, extraordinarily resistant to this Wordsworthian style of poetry that dwelt on moods, but he also realized that Wordsworth's depth ("Wordsworth is deeper than Milton") was in exploring the "dark passages" that surround "Misery and Heartbreak, Pain, Sickness and oppression" (Keats 1975, 95). Given all of this, I can predict some resistance on the part of certain of my readers on four overlapping fronts. First, as mentioned, there has been, in our culture, a resistance to the kind of "truth" that resides in feelings and emotions. (This converges with the history of "poisonous pedagogy" as described by Miller in virtually all of her work, especially 1990c; Miller claims that in the name of righteousness, secrets are kept, feelings are disaffirmed, and children are reared in the name of social discipline rather than personal respect.) We should not trust our emotions; we should deny them; we do not need to know about them. We should especially resist acknowledging and expressing negative feelings. Second, feelings often (and unfortunately) suggest the realm of the feminine and ephemeral, and therefore are associated weakness and irrelevance. To fall prey to one's emotions is considered a sign of frailty. Big boys don't cry. Stiff upper lip and all that. Third, a study of feeling also contests the kind of empirical methodology and respectability that the critical business believes it must strive towards. As Freud points out in *Civilization and Its Discontents*, "It is not easy to deal scientifically with feelings" (1989, 723). Indeed, we know that feelings have a reciprocal relationship with personality, behavior, and health. Feelings dominate our lives perhaps more than anything else, and they certainly dominated Wordsworth's poetry more than anything else. Fourth, some minor resistance may originate out of a need for keeping the idea of Wordsworth, our sometimes sanitized poet-hero, intact. Canonization is a form of both mystification and idealization. In the past, the Wordsworth industry has contributed a little to this by keeping such things as the Annette Vallon affair and Wordsworth's severe health problems out of literary history—or at least making little of them.[16] Finally, Wordsworth's texts are themselves sometimes defensive and fearful when it comes to certain areas and events. Geoffrey Hartman's conclusion (1971) that for Wordsworth the growth of consciousness involved fear is correct. But therein lies the strength and individuality of Wordsworth's poetry, and I hope to be able to show that as Wordsworth's poetry develops, so too do we see an increase in the attention that gets paid to examining emotional responses rather than external circumstances. This begins in earnest at Racedown in such poems as *Lines left upon a Seat in a Yew-tree*. Given Wordsworth's difficult personal history, such consciousness would not be an easy gain. I would also add that the hidden source of his imagination, his imaginative powers, lies in his poetic attempts to address past emotions. I have not directly pursued this in my study, but I can no longer conceive studying Wordsworth's imagination without addressing his portrayal of feelings.

Wordsworth himself never denied the importance of feelings, especially as they related to his past and the need for restitution, reparation, and renewal. He says as much when he puts feeling at the center of both his poetic project and his personal needs, revealing, in fact, that for him the two are virtually the same:

> and I would give
> While yet we may, as far as words can give,
> A substance and a life to what I feel:
> I would enshrine the spirit of the past
> For future restoration.
>   (1805 *Prelude*, bk. 11, lines 338–42)

There are, finally, some interrelated literary-historical reasons why Wordsworth's feelings came to figure so prominently in his poetry. First, in the face of a faltering Europe and significant socioeconomic changes, subjectivity (or belief in self-depiction through introspection) had become an acceptable subject for aesthetic and philosophical investigation.[17] Quests sometimes turn inwards in times of outer despair; and thus emotions (instead of prayers or religious consultations) are turned to as a form of self-verification.[18] Goethe, seeing the negative effects of this, but more likely being tired of it, wrote in 1826, "Our whole contemporary period is a retrogressive one, for it is subjective. This you can see not merely in its poetry, but also in its painting and in many other things besides" (cited in Schenk 1966, 151). For Wordsworth, this also became a inner dialogue between self-consciousness and anti-self-consciousness.[19] Second, this turning to the subjective as a result of disillusion and discontent lined up with the confessional genre that was popular at the time, especially in continental Europe, and ended up in excess with Byron. Standing alone with his irreplaceable "free thoughts," Byron's persona tells us that, having suffered through what he considers the wackiest of all possible times, "now/ Even change grows too changeable, without being new" (*Don Juan*, bk. 11, lines 90 and 82). Third, feeling was valorized by the rise of the "romantic" version of individualism, where personality, individual differences, and self-reliance became central for any notion of selfhood. Fourth, surrounding

Wordsworth's time, there was an important epistemological shift: feeling, perception (experience), and imagination challenged the role of reason (rationality, ideas) as the primary way to "know" the world. Finally, there was the legislating authority that the age placed on the figure of the poet, that someone willing to explore private life through public performance validated that area of exploration. Here Wordsworth stood as the age's highest authority, and the rest of the century had to write with at least one eye on his very considerable accomplishments. In Wordsworth's hand, the solitary figure was the contemplative speaker himself—not more distant and unearthly figures like Cain, the Wandering Jew, Faustus, and the Ancient Mariner.

There is also a general question that has to be asked at some point, and it might as well be asked and answered here, although the answer is implicit throughout this study. It has to do with the belief that feelings, emotions, and subjectivity and their relation to the self are primary or foundational in how we in Western culture see ourselves and respond to the world. And the question is this: What is the primary determinant of art, even if art becomes a cultural possession? Society and social constructs (laws, tradition, community, politics, national identity, and so forth) influence the idea of family and how a family operates, and thus influence an individual's sense of self within the family and society. As a process, it is reduplicative: individuals, family, and society echo, reinforce, and reproduce each other in a kind of circular pattern, but it is also a spiraling one as the various elements—equal but interdependent—modify each other as they themselves are modified.

But "sense of self" is not quite the same as subjectivity or the subjective self. Sense of self is more of a social construct; it is, as it were, *out there*, to be projected and presented. It does things in the name of social and individual identity, and is outwardly narrated by the individual as he or she does things, including thinking. It says, *This is who I am and what I do. Recognize me as I present my self to you in the world.*

The subjective self moves differently and says different things. It is formed by how the immediate world has treated us as we grow into it, and we internalize this as it becomes our feelings. (What we do know nowadays is that the way one has been treated will determine the way one treats others.) Thus the subjective self operates psychophysiologically.[20] It is based on emotional activities, on affect. It too is projected (usually unannounced and sometimes to our embarrassment) *out there* in displays of how we feel, but it is inwardly voiced or narrated—and in terms that are often difficult to read, both by ourselves and by others. We do not always know how we feel, and sometimes it seems we do not want to know; we block and deny, and more often than not this can do us damage. The subjective self does not make the same overt demands for outwards acceptance, yet getting people to know how you feel can be one of the most agonizing and rewarding of human experiences, and herein lies Wordsworth's gift to our culture. So, unlike the sense of self, the subjective self is not just a statement of *who* we are, but *how* we are. And a degree of inner acceptance is what it needs first if we are to operate in a reasonably healthy way. While the sense of self necessarily tells its story openly, the subjective self often seems to need some encouragement. These days it may take the form of "Tell me how you feel," or "You should get in touch with your feelings." Feelings need to get *worked out*—that is, they have to be experienced inwardly, nonverbally, and then expressed and accepted outwardly, and this, surely, is the most difficult part of being a human being, yet often a part to which we pay little attention. Critics have not paid much attention to this as it operates in Wordsworth's poetry.

We must be absolutely clear in privileging the importance of early family life over all other formative influences. The complex circumstances of family life, of upbringing, of original close relationships, determine how we emotionally respond to the world. Events and interactions that take place within the family circle, not historical circumstances or economic conditions, shape our engagements with reality. How we respond to a revolution or to poverty or to other individuals—indeed, how we respond to ourselves—is powerfully conditioned by our early personal history. For some, like Wordsworth, the emotions associated with early circumstances are entrapping and difficult to escape from. They demand acceptance while also forcing denial. His poetry, I hope to show, displays as much. Wordsworth wrote less out of external history than internal history. Much of his poetry, the meaning of his poetry, derives less from conventions or history or social situations than it does from his inner life. I would like to return Wordsworth's words to Wordsworth.

The general approach used in this study is not altogether new, although what I am prepared to do with it is. Among my earlier predecessors who take what would have to called a psychological view of things, I would count George Wilbur Meyer (1943), F. W. Bateson (1954), and W. W. Douglas (1968). For more recent work I might add Richard J. Onorato (1971), Michael H. Friedman (1979), and David Ellis (1985). Thus, counting my study, we have what amounts to a rather well-spaced half-century spread. My approach might also be called "psychobiographical" in the sense defined by Richard E. Matlak—that is, in terms of creating "a personal historical context" and establishing "a corroboration among biographical data, psychological theory, and poetic text" (Matlak 1986b, 147). This study is not intended as supplemental to these others in the sense of correcting their deficiencies, though here and there in heated moments I may point them out. Every study is necessarily deficient and an act of exclusion. Rather, I hope the reader will find this work complementary yet continuing in the search for Wordsworth—in the spirit of Wordsworth's search for himself. Instead of attempting to see the subject in a certain way that is driven and thereby contained by a theory, I hope the endeavor is as open as it is realistic; for, as Don H. Bialostosky (1992) has shown, a great deal of theory has been spilt over Wordsworth's poetry, as if a particular theory is only as good as it can be applied to Wordsworth.[21] I think too of Mark Jones's conclusions: "[T]he works of Wordsworth invoke interpretation, while the interpretation *in* them provides a model and rationale for this activity that are indeed relevant to contemporary criticism" (1991, 566). Those poems that seem to have pervading answers usually, upon close inspection (caveat emptor), reveal wonderfully discursive cracks in the foundation. One reason for Wordsworth's canonized greatness is that his "great" poems appear to be a challenge to the academic profession and are thus made to be immanently educative. His texts are all things for all critic-teachers. Why Wordsworth's poetry became the focus for testing critical theory is uncertain, but my guess is that Wordsworth's strong voice of subjectivity challenges criticism's drive for objectivity.

Although this critical fuss confirms Wordsworth discursive powers, I do not want to apply a particular critical theory as much as I hope to be able to account for the kind of poetry Wordsworth found himself writing. This is not a case of good, bad, or ugly. It is, rather, a case of necessity. Wordsworth himself never adhered to any particular philosophy in a rigorous way, particularly after he rejected Godwinism in the early 1790s. He attempted to describe the world and formulate his beliefs in terms of his experience, and for Wordsworth experience ultimately centered around emotional responses. I hope to do the same here: formulate beliefs as I experience Wordsworth without holding rigorously to the tenets of any particular critical philosophy. I do not want my criticism to be smarter than his poetry. Here I might borrow some terms from social research: the approach I wish to evolve is *bottom up*; the kind of approach that comes to the object of study already armed with a critical model is called *top down*. With the top-down approach you always find your model; with a bottom-up approach you are guided by what you find. The latter is what I hope to do.

I believe that different poets (and even different poems by the same writer) demand different methods, different approaches. I am reminded of what Milton Erickson, perhaps the most influential psychotherapist of our time, says:

> Each person is a unique individual. Hence psychotherapy should be formulated to meet the uniqueness of the individual's needs, rather than tailoring the person to fit the Procrustean bed of a hypothetical theory of human behavior. (Zeig 1982, vii)

The same should be said of literary criticism, and here I will borrow Erikson's syntax and the spirit of his comment:

> Each poet and poem is unique. Hence literary criticism should be formulated to meet the uniqueness of the poet or poem's needs, rather than tailoring the poet or poem to fit the Procrustean bed of a hypothetical theory of literature or writing.

To hold on to one approach that does not evolve out of the material itself, and to drag it through the complex and extraordinarily diverse landscape of a canon or a period or an author, may be to violate the multitudinous communities or individuals or ideas that make up that landscape. It is top down. This kind of criticism sees neither the trees for the forest nor the forest for the trees, and there is only one way to deal with the subject in order to manufacture a predetermined product: clear cut. Often this kind of criticism is interested only in promoting its model; it is always already prepared to find its theory in the text. And so this clear-cut, top-down criticism sometimes willfully refuses to acknowledge or resists what are most powerful and singular in Wordsworth's poetry: his startling individual subjectivity, his particular history, and the expression of real feelings. For a significant period of Wordsworth's creative life, these were what he was most concerned with. Even in such a thorough and intelligent psychoanalytical study such as that by Onorato, we see precious little of that person called William Wordsworth and the personality belonging to him; instead, we most frequently see a text and a theory. Some kinds of overdetermined criticism (what might be called Nomothetic Criticism) often want a bigger "Wordsworth"—and bigger, for these kinds of approaches, is better. The kind of approach that I hope to employ in this study evolves out the material itself, and I would call it Process Criticism. I could also call this approach Idiographic Criticism, since it strives to understand individual and unique traits rather than simply looking to find general laws and principles. Patterns are recognized, but they are not imposed. And so the way I hope to approach Wordsworth comes out of Wordsworth and his poetry. I want to see Wordsworth's poetry in the spirit of what most powerfully motivated it: the reenactment of emotional life. Contemporary critical theory has displaced the subject; in the case of Wordsworth, and for the duration of this book, I would like to attempt to replace this displaced subject.

If there has been a history of resistance in turning directly to Wordsworth's emotional life as the source of some his poetry, it may have to do with a critical, pedagogical, and curricula history that marginalizes the personal. Until recently, very little real self-knowledge has entered academic discourse or the classroom. Knowledge (and especially knowledge about human behavior) has tended to follow nomothetic rather than idiographic models; that is, we tend to be interested in the gross measurement or what the mass of collected data tells us, rather than what the case study offers: general laws versus individual differences.[22] (This likely has to with the rise in status of the "social sciences.")

Knowledge is not built upon the foundation of personal history, despite the instruction "Know thyself." To teach Wordsworth in the way I will try to write about him here might even demand that students and teachers alike examine that which affects them more profoundly than anything else: their own history and personal emotional lives. As John Bradshaw puts it, "*[T]he primary motivating force in our lives is emotion*" (1990, 13; his emphasis). Until we learn about *that*, every other lesson may remain irrelevant and external. Wordsworth vigorously promoted the "self-conscious critical habit" or "self-critical consciousness" as an integral part of the educational process (Bialostosky 1992, 263–64). Everywhere in Wordsworth's early poetry one is struck by the habit of reflection, especially along emotional parameters. And I think that it is in this spirit that we should approach Wordsworth's texts. Reading Wordsworth is always more than an academic exercise. It makes you think *and* feel.

The attempt to transform individual experience into common experience through reflection is what a great deal of Wordsworth's poetry has as its goal, and Wordsworth, as teacher, asks as much from us. This, for Wordsworth, is the equivalent of aligning feeling and thought. Wordsworth needed to turn the personal into the universal in order to valorize (perhaps even exorcise) his own experience in the spirit of acceptance. But many of his poems resist closure not just because Wordsworth cannot come to universal conclusions (which is often the case), but because he invites us to engage in and participate with the text, to draw our own conclusions. Wordsworth is most challenging when he invites us in but does not always show us the way out, as is the case in the so-called Lucy poems. This must have to do with Wordsworth's treatment of the subject material in some of his poetry: he too does not always know what to do with what turns up.

I see Wordsworth's most interesting poetry as driven by a need to pay a great deal of attention to this personal, subjective, and emotional self; I see him attempting to articulate how he grew into his immediate world and how it treated him; I see him as attempting to voice these inward feelings and to work them out in his poetry, yet not always being aware of how he felt or the source of his feelings; I see his poetry as searching for a kind of inner acceptance through public performance, although during his lifetime he never gave the public *The Prelude,* his most deliberate attempt to confirm his personal growth and inner acceptance. I hear in Wordsworth's poetry not so much the voice of political, historical, or cultural discourse—or, perhaps more exactly, the voice I hear in Wordsworth cuts through these. Thus Wordsworth demands that his language talk to us as one person would intimately talk to another—or even to himself or herself. Despite certain kinds of criticism and critical theory, poems are more than just things; and they are products not just of time and space but of person and personality. Some of Wordsworth's poetry struggles with this tension, or even confusion, between personal experience and world history,[23] but the voice that speaks most eloquently, most profoundly, and sometimes desperately is that which springs from the emotions of personal experience. (At any rate, world history was to be Wordsworth's topic in *The Recluse*, which he never came close to completing.) And so the voice attuned to in this study evolves from an individual subjectivity, although the attitudes expressed in the poems or a particular poem (in various characters, moods, styles, and so on) may, in their dynamics, be dialogical: voices differing and competing in an effort to reenact difficult feelings both in the present and in the past, both in joy and in sadness.

William Hazlitt also made an observation about Wordsworth that is central to this present study: he wrote that in Wordsworth's poetry there is "an intensity of feeling" completely unique to Wordsworth (1932, 89). The source, nature, and poetic expression of this "intensity of feeling" is the subject of this study. We can approach the work of William Wordsworth in many ways—aesthetically, historically, and politically, for example—but these are, ultimately, determinants of the subjective self. How true this may be for other writers or artists I do not want to say. But if it is true at all for any writer, it must be truest of all for Wordsworth. If we cannot understand the formation and particularities of Wordsworth's emotional life, then we cannot claim to understand much of his greatest poetry.

I will end this introduction by quoting F. R. Leavis, a critic who these days is more often than not used as fodder for contemporary critical pronouncements. I myself have used him as such.[24] But unlike his overall disparaging opinion of the Romantics, in Wordsworth's poetry Leavis perceived a significant artistic achievement: "That Wordsworth is a great poet seems to me certain," Leavis said, though he sees this greatness in "a limited phase of his life" (1971, 323–24). He sees in Wordsworth a continuation of the inquiry into the relationship between thinking and feeling that began in the eighteenth century, yet at the same time he perceives a marked innovation in the style and expression of that inquiry. And Leavis likes the idea of continuity in literature. But equally as remarkable is that, first, Leavis sees this line of inquiry in Wordsworth poetry coming not just out of a tradition but out of Wordsworth's personal circumstances; and second, that Leavis is not offended by this:

> Behind, then, the impersonality of Wordsworth's wisdom there is an immediately personal urgency. Impelling him back to childhood and youth—to their

> recovery in a present state of tranquil seclusion—there are the emotional storms and disasters of the intervening period, and these are also implicitly remembered, if not "recollected," in the tranquillity of his best poetry. (Leavis 1972, 167)

This observation allows for speculation: Wordsworth turned to poetry because what he could control in language he could not control in his body. (This will make more sense in the discussion of Wordsworth's health in chapter 1.) Leavis only implicitly refers to the details of Wordsworth's life, those "emotional storms and disasters," but he nonetheless is convinced that the "personal urgency" in Wordsworth's poetry comes from the resulting emotions of what happened to the writer as an individual. He also sees in Wordsworth the desire to transform such emotional turmoil into wise or controlling cognitions. Finally, he believes that in attempting such transformations, such recovery, Wordsworth wrote his "best poetry." Unfortunately, I could hardly agree more. Unlike Leavis, however, I will attempt to consider some of the details, and I will attempt to describe how, in the development of his poetry and subjectivity, Wordsworth attempts to integrate feeling and thought; for, as Leavis recognizes, it was impossible for Wordsworth, at least in the early poetry, to think of general human sorrow and grief "without profound emotional disturbance" (1971, 336). It was impossible for Wordsworth to think without feeling—and that, for the poet in question, was a problem. Wordsworth in his most productive phases was a poet of feeling attempting to become a poet of thought.

1
The Adult Child

> For the majority of sensitive people, the true self remains deeply and thoroughly hidden. But how can you love something you do not know, something that has never been loved? So it is that many a gifted person lives without any notion of his or her true self. Such people are enamored of an idealized, conforming, false self. They will shun their hidden and lost true self, unless depression makes them aware of its loss or psychosis confronts them harshly with that true self, whom they now have to face and to whom they are delivered up, helplessly, as to a threatening stranger.
> —Alice Miller, *The Drama of the Gifted Child*

Some of the finest scholarship in the English critical canon has been dedicated to the details of William Wordsworth's life. It ranges from George McLean Harper's thoughtful work (1916; 1921) and Mary Moorman's wonderfully fair-minded biography (1957; 1965), to Mark L. Reed's remarkable chronology of Wordsworth's life (1967; 1975), to Stephen Gill's accessible coverage of the poet (1989); and with the steady arrival of the volumes making up *The Cornell Wordsworth*, the poetry, with its plethora of attendant biotextual paraphernalia, has received tender loving care of the highest academic order. So while the details of Wordsworth's life may not need rewriting, the way parts of his life relate to his poetry does.

Yet Wordsworth did not want his own examined life to be examined by others. Publicly, he did not approve of literary biography. In 1816, he published his *Letter to a Friend of Robert Burns,* which defends Burns's "injured reputation" against those who would reveal the poet's personal "infirmities" to the world.[1] In it Wordsworth makes it very clear that he does not approve of the "coarse intrusions into the recesses, the gross breaches upon the sanctities, of domestic life" of authors, and, in particular, of poets: so long as a poet's work is "good," that is all we need to know (Wordsworth 1974, 3:117–22). He maintained that little had happened to him that was interesting or worthy of recording. When, in 1801, an acquaintance wrote to ask what events in his life "had an influence in forming [his] present opinions," he replied, "[T]he history of my life is very short," and he proceeded to sketch out his past thirty-one years in about two hundred words. He mentioned where he was born, what school he went to, how he neglected his studies at university, that he had spent time traveling in Europe and England, and how he was now living in beautiful Grasmere with his sister, intending to devote his life to literature—if, that is, his health permitted him. He ended the sketch by returning to early events: "It may be proper to add that my Father . . . and my Mother both died when I was a Boy." In the following paragraph he apologized: "In what I have said I am afraid there will be little which will throw any light on my writings. . . ." (Wordsworth 1967, 327).

In some ways all of this might be viewed as more that just a little strange, since we know that Wordsworth put so much effort into writing about the growth of his mind and the meaning of his experiences. Thomas De Quincey called Wordsworth the "most meditative man of his own age" (De Quincey 1970, 155), and what he often meditated upon was the meaning of his experiences and the relationship between his present feelings and those of the past. Wordsworth, as the first modern poet, invented particularized subjectivity and self-history as a topic for poetic exploration. He made the egotistical sublime. In this he is also the last modern poet, for no one has gone beyond the mark he set. We cannot for one moment believe that the course of his life, the meaning of his life, was unimportant to him, and we cannot believe that he felt it was an unworthy project to communicate his experiences and the narrative of his life to others. After all, he wanted more than anything else to be remembered as a teacher,[2] and his teachings were, for the most part, his life-into-poetry. We might assume, then, that, not wanting others to write about his life, but writing about it himself, Wordsworth wanted some control over how his life was perceived, and so he perceived it for us as he wanted to perceive it for himself. This is a truly Wordsworthian maneuver, and, in its articulation, it is both defensive and heroic.

In 1805, when he was just completing the thirteen-book version of *The Prelude*, he wrote to Sir George Beaumont:

> I turned my thoughts again to the Poem on my own life, and you will be glad to hear that I have added 300 lines to it in the course of the last week. Two Books more will conclude it. It will be not much less than 9,000 lines, not hundred but thousand lines, long; an alarming length! and a thing unprecedented in Literary history that a man should talk so much about himself. It is not self-conceit, as

you will know well, that has induced [me] to do this, but real humility; I began the work because I was unprepared to treat any more arduous subject and diffident of my own powers. Here at least I hoped that to a certain degree I should be sure of succeeding, as I had nothing to do but describe what I had felt and thought, therefore could not easily be bewildered. This might certainly have been done in narrower compass by a man of more address, but I have done my best. If when the work shall be finished it appears to the judicious to have redundancies they shall be lopped off, if possible. But this is very difficult to do when a man has written with thought, and this defect, whenever I have suspected it or found it to exist in any writings of mine, I have always found incurable. The fault lies too deep, and is in the first conception. (Wordsworth 1967, 586–87)

Wordsworth is correct is pointing to the original nature of his poem—"a thing unprecedented in Literary history." And we believe him when he says that it is not "self-conceit" that motivates him but the need to work through his poetic uncertainties. But this is obviously quite different from the response he gave four years earlier when he said, "[T]he history of my life is very short." Now he finds himself visibly alarmed by how much he has to say about his "own life," not just as a history of events but as a deliberate reflection on how he "had thought and felt" about those events. The events are, in effect, secondary to the commitment he is making to describe his inner life. That he "could not be easily bewildered" in describing these thoughts and feelings may be a less convincing proposition once we get to certain spots in his life-into-text. That his emotional life is at the center of his obstinate questionings is clear:

> How shall I trace the history, where seek
> The origin of what I then have felt?
> (1805 *Prelude,* bk. 2, lines 365–66)

But in what ways or to what extent can Wordsworth's poetry be taken as autobiography, or at least as autobiographical? The root term seems clear enough: *auto* = self; *bio* = (human) life; *graph* = writing: the self comes into life through writing; or, the life of the self in writing. There is, admittedly, a rather cozy, idealized feel about it. It almost makes you want to run out and buy a diary in order to come to terms with yourself. But the deconstructive project does not have to be brought very strongly to bear on this portrayal of autobiography (loaded, as we view it now, with its logocentricity and the metaphysics of presence) to see that it is on extremely shaky foundations. By turning the term a bit from within we can say that in writing lives the idea of self—moreover, that writing creates the idea of self. And knowing the Saussurian breach between the signified and the signifier, between the world and the word, we must then admit we are in difficulties in considering how it is possible that language can unequivocally reflect experience. Is there a life outside of the text, a text outside of the life—and Wordsworth's life and text in particular? To repeat the question voiced in the introduction: Can a text even represent a life?

But the essential question to bring out the issues is this: Was Wordsworth's poetry written to qualify him as a poet or as person? My answer, in short, and for the life span of this present study, would be the latter, that Wordsworth often turned to poetry as a way to make and to understand himself. But it might be more useful to privilege the person over the poet, rather than using the "or" of the question ("poet *or* person") as a sign of exclusivity. Wordsworth himself would have wanted it both ways. Writing with the rhetorical detachment of the third-person singular, Wordsworth offers that *The Prelude* was written in order to record "the origin and progress of his own powers," and also to establish that his "faculties were sufficiently matured for entering upon the arduous labour [i.e., *The Recluse*] which he had proposed to himself" (Wordsworth 1936, 589). Wordsworth is, in effect, saying this: *I will prove my personal, subjective worth by writing poetry, and my poetic worth will be proven by writing about myself.* It should not be surprising that this sounds like the justification for the psychotherapist having to go through analysis in order to practice psychotherapy. There is an interesting logic here: to do psychotherapy you need to have had psychotherapy. We have to take this idea over to what Wordsworth felt he needed to do in order to become a poet.

We know that certain things happened to Wordsworth at certain times, but there is much we do not know, and biographers have often only had the poetry (and the ad hoc notes on the early poetry written forty years later)[3] to rely on. Of course, when we have the facts, we can use them as a form of evidence to contextually support the poetry. But we cannot always trust the details in the poetry—nor should we. As George Wilbur Meyer wrote half a century ago about a passage from *The Prelude* that describes a particular event in the poet's life, "This is excellent poetry. But it is misleading and therefore bad autobiography" (1943, 3). The point is well taken. Language, time, and memory are not the best mix for rendering the past—and all autobiography is, at least in Meyer's sense, "bad." Meyer's idea is that "Wordsworth, able rationalizer that he was, could not make all the facts of his youth fit [the] attractive mystical hypothesis," namely, "that all his youthful thoughts and experiences were portentous preparation for hard and high poetic duties" (4).[4] But Wordsworth nevertheless made strenuous poetic efforts to make it appear so, believing it himself. Reading the corpus of Wordsworth in order to find something out about Wordsworth's life is thus something like reading the Bible: it is ultimately an act of faith; there seem to be some general truths, but some of the historical details are untrustworthy; the pattern of events and their associations and commentary are at moments editorial and creative determinations rather than historical ones; and yet the faith, if it is there, is not diminished by the fictionalized or untrustworthy history; the faith, in fact, may even be stronger in the face of the uncertainty. What is struggling for articulation is an inner truth dressed in external circumstances. This, I believe, is the essence of Wordsworth's best poetry.

How Wordsworth originally experienced events is lost forever, as is the case with any experience that happens to anyone. Even if we write it down immediately, even if we have (as we do in excess these days) not just an instant replay, but an instant replay in slow motion, the event is transformed. The original is displaced by the "truth" revealed by *revision*—literally, seeing-again. Poetry is something like that. Time, language, and videotape ensure that all repetition is revisionary and follows conventions. Moreover, the framed repetition/replay as a spot of time seems to be considered more revealing or interesting than the originating experience (especially in televised professional sports), and hence our high regard for it. Our perception of what happened (and our reasons for that particular perception) is what matters. And that, we know, changes through subsequent experiences and over time. Every time one sees the replay, one sees something different. Stephen Gill says: "The biographer must conclude that, for all Wordsworth's attempts to tell us, we cannot know what the boy felt on 19 June 1779" (1989, 10). True: Wordsworth himself may have gotten neither the date nor the feeling quite right. But the feelings expressed in his poetry, in the act of composition, are what we have, and they are what matter. The point is this: he wanted to get something of it right, and we have to examine what he wanted to get right and why he wanted to get that particular thing right. Wordsworth revised and revised, and of course each revision cannot be taken to alter the original experience or even get closer to it; it may, however, get us closer to understanding why particular responses evolved. In fact, Wordsworth put so much into revising his poetry that it often made him ill—a fact that makes us question the emotional investment in the subject being worked on. It makes more sense, then, to give attention to the poetry as projections of his present feelings onto his past feelings, or, at the most, as conflated or even competing feelings: revisions, if made, necessarily represent a change in the present, in the present perception or understanding of the past. Revisions are not always a clearer portrayal of the past, although that may be the goal. And so we must pay considerable attention to *the desire to recover and poetically reenact something in that past that desires confrontation*. For it is precisely because of that desire for recovery and reenactment that we must look to the feelings and emotions struggling for articulation rather than to the particular details of, for example, dating or place. Some details may help to frame events and to get a sense of time and place, but *why* is ultimately more important than *what*. This, too, of course, helps us a great deal when we have to negotiate poetry that is not ostensibly autobiographical. It means we can deal with it in a similar way.

Wordsworth nevertheless wanted to believe, wanted us to believe, that, in composing poems, he could call up, cut through, and account for the originating and subsequent feelings, emotions, moods, and passions behind his poetry. In expressing this process and in attempting to convince us of his powers of poetic replay, it should not be surprising that Wordsworth comes up with his most memorable prose:

> I have said that Poetry is the spontaneous overflow of powerful feelings: it takes its origin from emotion recollected in tranquillity: the emotion is contemplated till by a species of reaction the tranquillity disappears, and an emotion, kindred to that which was before the subject of contemplation, is gradually produced, and does itself actually exist in the mind. In this mood successful composition generally begins, and in a mood similar to this it is carried on; but the emotion, of whatever kind and in whatever degree, from various causes is qualified by various pleasures, so that in describing any passions whatsoever, which are voluntarily described, the mind will upon the whole be in a state of enjoyment. (Wordsworth 1984, 611)

This passage is usually read as a description of Wordsworth's general process of poetic composition; but more importantly, it is also about recovery and emotional reenactment, and how these are a necessary and central part of *his* poetry. Most writers would not go so far as to delineate in such detail a model of creativity, but Wordsworth obviously felt an obligation, self-motivated, to account for what took place when he wrote his poetry—how the feelings evolved out of this proto-Hartlian associative process. It is also about experiencing "pleasure" and "enjoyment" out of this process, which, given the extreme physical distress that composition often actually caused Wordsworth, is worth noticing as a defensive ploy, as dissociative. These positive correspondent feelings are obviously idealized. But more than anything else, this passage clearly puts feeling and emotion at the center of Wordsworth's poetic concerns, and it points to how important it was for him to be able to separate them out and to distinguish one feeling from another. For Wordsworth, this is also the problem of reconciling feeling with thought that silently drives much of Wordsworth's best poetry. Once more, all behavior has a function, and I would argue that the function of a great deal of Wordsworth's poetry is to make this kind of distinction in order to come to terms with his problematical feelings. The act of writing about emotions was, for Wordsworth, the act of bringing thought to feelings.

For now, I want to turn to both certain aspects and episodes of Wordsworth's life and to portrayals of that life-into-poetry that I believe need revaluation; to a few of those people who shaped and shared his life; to certain events and to patterns of behavior; to his personality, his upbringing, and his health. And to his expressed feelings. There is a need to examine the origins of his thoughts on, for example, mind and nature, that are not purely cultural or philosophical in their bias. I want to understand where he came from and what he was like so I can attempt to understand where his poetry comes from and why it is like it is. The focus here may be predominantly on the darker side of Wordsworth, and for that reason I myself might be portrayed as the author of gloom and doom. So let me add this: Wordsworth did have many happy experiences; as a child, he often had the freedom to romp around the countryside; he did grow into a responsible adult; he did have close friends; he was loved, and he seemed capable of giving love. But I don't think his best art—that is, for me, his most interesting art—came out of this part of his life and personality. In fact, it might be said that some of his best poetry came about in his attempt to reconcile feelings of love and joy with those of confusion and loss. His regard for his past years, his childhood, is caught up in this paradox of emotional response.

William Wordsworth's parents, John Wordsworth (1741–83) and Ann Cookson (1747–78), were married in 1766, and they lived in Cockermouth, a small town on the edge of the Lake District in the county of Cumberland. William was born on 7 April 1770. He was preceded by a brother (Richard, 1768–1816) and followed closely by a sister (Dorothy, 1771–1855) and two more brothers (John, 1772–1805, and Christopher, 1774–1846). Ergonomically, they lived quite comfortably. They had the biggest house in town, which was owned by John's boss.

A MOTHER

Ann Wordsworth died of pneumonia at her mother's house just about a month before William's eighth birthday. She died suddenly, and any chance the children had of a reasonably stable family life and household died with her. Her husband, John Wordsworth, was not prepared for or, apparently, willing to assume a hands-on role as a single parent. In his later years, Wordsworth recalled that his father never really recovered from Ann's death (Wordsworth 1974, 3:371), which would have seriously thwarted the children's attempts to come to terms with the loss of their mother. If a husband cannot recover from the death of his wife, we can hardly expect the children to resolve their own grief in healthy ways. In effect, they would be tied to that death in ways that would filter through into other behaviors. Death, abandonment, loss, guilt, loneliness, and separation show up in much of Wordsworth's poetry with the kind of forceful regularity that must draw us back to considering its cause. Barbara Schapiro puts this plainly: "The experience of loss connected with the mother-child relationship lies at the core of much of Wordsworth's poetry" (1983, 101). For Thomas McFarland the bottom line about Wordsworth is similar: "He is certainly and above all the poet of loss" (1992, 73). McFarland explores something of how this came about. I would like to explore why it came about.

Wordsworth's mother may not have been completely in control of her household or even reasonably happy. Gill suggests that she may have "found the demands of her family overwhelming" (1989, 15). Within six years after she had married at age eighteen, she had given birth to five children. Her husband, who (we have good reason to believe) was unhappy in his job, worked long hours and was often away on difficult and unpleasant business. The children throughout their early years were frequently sent to the Cookson grandparents at Penrith, sometimes for extended periods, and perhaps to provide some relief for both parents and children (Reed 1967, 41–62); it is very possible that the mother suffered from bouts of depression. But as I will point out later in this chapter, Wordsworth and Dorothy's remembrances of and associations with being at their grandparents' place in Penrith were strongly negative, revolving around anger, suicide, death, and abandonment. But what was Wordsworth's mother for Wordsworth? What did she represent? With what is she associated, and why?

Wordsworth's actual memories of his mother were few. In his 1847 *Autobiographical Memoranda*, he says he remembers her pinning some flowers on him before an Easter service. He also recalls this incident in one of his Ecclesiastical Sonnets: the "happy hand" of his "Beloved Mother" fastening the flowers. But now

> Her countenance, phantom-like, doth reappear:
> O lost too early for the frequent tear
> And ill requited by this heartfelt sigh!
>
> (Pt. 3, stanza 22)

Wordsworth was still haunted by the image of his mother. But more important, it is evident that he never really understood or completely went through the grieving process, and for this he felt guilt. Even his "heartfelt sigh" is painfully inadequate. In short, he was troubled by his feelings of loss, and this emotionally pained and plagued him. In the *Memoranda* he also remembers being scorned by her for expecting a penny for being at church. Finally, he recalls "having a glimpse of her on passing the door of her bedroom during her last illness" (Wordsworth 1974, 3:372). After her death, he learned from one of his mother's friends that, of the five children, his mother was most concerned with him: apparently she said that Wordsworth "would be remarkable either for good or for evil" (372). Being singled out in such a way obviously stuck with him all those years. But despite the lack of actual memories and explicit references to her in extant letters, her presence was nevertheless poetically precious. She remained an idea and, more importantly, a feeling that, in his poetry, imaginatively connected him with his origins and the world around him.

A number of commentators have noticed that Wordsworth's mother's absence in his poetry is both conspicuous and strange. But her more subtle psychic presence, or at least various maternal images, is held to inform many passages (Onorato 1971, Schapiro 1983, Manning 1976 and 1983, Heffernan 1988). While much of this is valuable speculative criticism, often it seems to be theory-driven rather than text-driven, and it is seldom driven by the desire to consider the details of Wordsworth's life. And so I admit I am not always convinced by theory-driven readings of texts that disacknowledge the details of a real life and a particular personality, especially those that rather haphazardly resurrect the oedipal structure and fantasies or see wombs and breasts in too many activities and in aspects of the landscape.[5]

In the 1799 *Prelude,* Wordsworth's portrayal of his connection to his mother (and his general portrayal of the mother/child relationship) is framed by and conflated with his awakening to Nature's importance and influence. He mentions his mother in the context of the singularly important declaration: at a certain point in his life "Nature . . . now at length was sought / For her own sake" (bk. 2, lines 240–42). Until this point, nature was just "secondary" and "intervenient"—intrusive, that is (lines 240–41). It was just there. Wordsworth wonders how one can determine when and from where characteristics and ideas originate:

> Who knows the individual hour in which
> His habits were first sown even as a seed?
> Who that shall point as a with a wand, and say
> "This portion of the river of my mind
> Came from yon fountain?"
>
> (Lines 245–49)

This is a big moment—and it is a modern moment. It is self-examination of a new order. How does past experience shape an individual's thoughts and feelings? Wordsworth is searching for an understanding of beginnings, of the origin of individual consciousness and subjectivity itself. He wonders if the "boundaries" and "distinctions" that "we perceive" are artificial and imposed, and if they prevent us from seeing a Coleridgean "unity of all," for that is what the mind desires from the very beginning. He recognizes that it is an impossibly "Hard task to analyse a soul," and to discover the birth of "habits and desires" and "thought," especially when these things may have "no beginning" (lines 249–67). *Where does my subjectivity come from? What particular factors made me who I am?* It is at this point he turns to "the babe / Nursed in his mother's arms" and "who sleeps / Upon his mother's breast"; and who, when he discovers he is a separate being, "Doth gather passion from his mother's eye" (lines 267–73). Although Wordsworth is not openly referring to his own life in these gestaltian ponderings (he will a few lines later), the description of how someone comes into the world as an individual, as a part of and then apart from a mother, is necessarily a poetic reenactment of the idea of his own origins: his separation from one and his attachment to another.

What overflows into the child from positive maternal contact is called "passion," suggesting powerful feelings. (In fact, in the 1850 *Prelude*, the line "Doth gather passion from his mother's eye" becomes "Drinks in the feelings of his Mother's eye!," thus paralleling the affective intake with the breast-feeding idea.) A line later this is confirmed when "passion" is described as "Such feelings" (1799 *Prelude,* bk. 2, line 274). These in turn become the very origin of the powerful mind, which, as "an agent of the one great mind, / Creates, creator, and receiver both" of that "Which it beholds" (lines 302–5). Yet flowing along the "infant veins" is "the *filial* bond / Of Nature that connects him with the world" (lines 292–94; my emphasis). And it is *feeling,* in all its manifestations, both positive and negative, that is the all-important source of power connecting him not only with nature ("For feeling has to him imparted strength . . . "), but in turn leads ultimately to "the first / Poetic spirit of our human life." For some people, this originating "Poetic spirit" remains "suppressed"; for others, it is "Preeminent till death" (lines 295–310).

The world according to Wordsworth: Mother/love → passions/feelings → mind ↔ Nature. More precisely, this is the "progress of our being" by which Wordsworth sees himself reciprocally created by and creating in the "*active universe*" (line 296). The reverential idea that the mind has connective powers, worked through the ability to feel, is singularly important, since it appears that this is what he needs most to keep on going "till death." Again, *connection* and *continuity* are the master tropes here: the mind, made aware by emotions, is "eager to combine . . . all the elements / And parts of the same object"; it works in "alliance with the works / Which it beholds" and connects them with the "one great mind"; there is also a "virtue which irradiates and exalts / All objects through all intercourse of sense"; and there is the "filial bond / Of Nature . . . [that] connect[s] him [the growing child] with the world" (lines

274–305). Again, what the "poetic spirit" represents for Wordsworth is the idea of connection and continuity. And this is not a passing fancy. The desire manifest in these tropes stays with him at least until the *Immortality Ode*. The questions remain: Why are connection, interfusion, alliance, bonding, combining, and continuity so important for Wordsworth? Why is Nature sought after?

But now the generalized movement into the world and away from the "mother's breast" is explicitly brought over to a description of his own life. Wordsworth goes on to say that ever since his "early days" he has "held mute dialogues" with his own "mother's heart"; he has "endeavoured" to augment and sustain this alliance with the idea of the "poetic spirit," though it has been a difficult, muted dialogue. He sees this as a difficult "path" requiring both strength and inspiration (lines 310–20). But a testing disturbance enters the scene of connection and continuity, and a third element emerges as a central Wordsworthian feature:

> For now a trouble came into my mind
> From obscure causes: I was left alone
> Seeking this visible world, nor knowing why.
> The props of my affections were removed,
> And yet the building stood, as if sustained
> By its own spirit.
>
> (Lines 321–26)

This too is a singularly important moment for Wordsworth to articulate. So to connection and continuity we can also add the trope of solitude (and, along with it, loss, endurance, and separation). This too will remain problematically central to much of Wordsworth's poetry, and it will represent more than just a romantic convention or a physical posturing for dramatic purposes. The reasons for finding himself in this circumstance were, for him, in 1799, not completely knowable. Children, traumatized children, do not know why such events happen to them; with support, they come to terms with it; without support, they are often doomed to carry the burden within them for a very long time.

What we are heading towards is this: for Wordsworth, his emotional life (despite often being somewhat repressed nonverbally—that is, in his manners and projected personality) was the determinant for all other concerns, including, most importantly, the kind of poetry he would write. And so solitude would be an emotional condition necessitated at that very moment: because of the inexplicable death of his parents, he was, as he says, "left alone." But keep the lone-standing building metaphor in mind here. It suggests some kind of emotional fortress—impersonal, impregnable, independent—and it is also somewhere one can live. It is a defensive structure necessitated by circumstances beyond his control. It will need some sensitive yet determined analysis from within if it is to survive—and this is the kind of renovation that Wordsworth's poetry often performs. If we fail to understand the powerfully affective and conditional use of solitude and loneliness in Wordsworth's poetry, we may fall short of comprehending what he really felt and needed when, for example, he wandered "lonely as a cloud."

Despite the loss of all emotional support, and, much more importantly, because of it, he created himself as this kind of lone edifice, "sustained / By its own spirit." What other choice would he have? Where else might he turn? What else could he lean on? Of course he would go on to have other "props" for his emotional life, like Coleridge and his sister, Dorothy, but they would largely be supplemental and reflective rather than foundational. He was henceforth alone, and in his monumental solitude he turned to poetry with its restorative and creative powers. And in his poetry he would have to fashion or create something else to both foster and reclaim his emotional life; he would have to open himself up to some other need-projected idea that would see him through "till death." He has already told us what this is, and he tells us again immediately after telling us about the loss of his parents, those "props of his affection":

> All that I beheld
> Was dear to me, and from this cause it came
> That now to Nature's finer influxes
> My mind lay open. . . .
>
> (Lines 326–29)

Nature was nominated to take over as the emotional support for his life, perhaps as a replacement for aspects of what he could no longer receive from his mother; and he would have to formulate Nature in such a way that it would satisfy his emotional needs. Nature in this sense, at this point in his life, was thus made to fill the gap in Wordsworth's emotional life. He needed something to turn to, to hold him up, to reflect his identity and subjectivity. That is, in some of his poetry, we find that nature is a complex figure for and a reflection of what he desired most from his emotional life.[6] Later, when he was able to look within and synthesize thought and feeling, Nature was replaced by the mind as the trope for the all-in-all.

What has this to do with Wordsworth's real mother? Everything and nothing; for everything was what he needed her to be and nothing—an empty, solitary building—was what she left him with. But he needed to formulate that what his mother left him with—or, perhaps more properly, what she could not give him because of her absence—led him towards a particular view of Nature. Recall: it was the "*filial* bond / Of Nature" that connected him "with the world" when those others "props" had left him homeless and alone. If his regard for Nature is indeed a determinant or projection of his feelings towards his mother, then we would expect the kind of ambivalent response that I am promoting here. He loved her, but she left him. He lost her, but he remade or found her in Nature.

In later, expanded versions of the *Prelude*, Wordsworth says more about his mother and her death. He reverentially describes the superabundance of her homely, Christian virtues: she is gentle, kind, humble, honest, patient, and trusting (1805 *Prelude*, bk. 5, lines 260–90, 260–93). (Not surprisingly, this is similar to Wordsworth's description of his wife in *She was a Phantom of delight*.) Wordsworth comes to this idealized portrayal of his mother via a description of "the parent hen" who, with "tenderness and love," is the moving center for her brood. Even though her young ones are "fledged and feathered"—suggesting a degree of maturity and independence—she nevertheless cares for and is held to them by the "maternal bond" (lines 246–56). In this context Wordsworth turns to his own mother:

> Early died
> My honoured mother, she who was the heart
> And hinge of all our learnings and our loves;
> She left us destitute, and as we might
> Trooping together.
>
> (Lines 256–60)

"*She left us destitute*. . . ." This is more than just dim sadness recollected in the spirit of tranquil acceptance. Wordsworth nominates her as the esteemed foundation of the children's development and emotional life—as a "heart," the center of all their feeling; as a "hinge," the point around which everything turned. Without their leader, they had to soldier on, "Trooping together." There is thus a clear feeling of desertion and the loss of hope—and, certainly along with this, some residual resentment, or even anger. But it is denied, and will necessarily be displaced. He would be compelled to reenact the loss of a loved one, especially in the parent/child relationship—through death, desertion—in his poetry. Suffering and endurance come naturally to many of his characters. But the resentment involving the death of his mother goes even deeper:

> Little suits it me
> To break upon the sabbath of her rest
> With any thought that looks at others' blame,
> Nor would I praise her but in perfect love;
> Hence I am checked. . . .
>
> (Lines 260–64)

Wordsworth uncomfortably articulates his struggle to keep the idea of his mother anything but complete and exemplary. But he clearly alludes, somewhat mysteriously, to "others' blame" in the circumstances associated with his mother's death. R. D. Havens (1941; referred to in Wordsworth 1979, 164 n. 9) suggests that these "others" may be Wordsworth's grandparents, the Cooksons at Penrith, with whom Wordsworth had to spend much time both before and after the death of his parents. And Wordsworth's feelings for his grandparents was extraordinarily negative, as they certainly emotionally abused him.[7] Thus the result of and associations with the death of his parents, and particularly with the death of his mother, are emotionally tainted by the cruel treatment by his mother's parents.

This is an important indication of Wordsworth's emotional condition, both as he writes this text and tries to recall what he felt, and we must stop and look at it. The feelings for his mother, the "perfect love," are crossed through with both the desire to "blame" others and to repress saying any more about these negative feelings—"Hence I am checked." This kind of emotional double bind is anything but a healthy psychological state. Such unresolved anger will necessarily be turned inwards and will become manifest in negative reenactments of one sort or another. Poetry will be one. *Mother, because of you, I have had to endure the horrible treatment of your parents. After your death, I had to endure this and more. Mother, I love you.*

Moorman writes that Ann Wordsworth "bestowed upon her brood . . . the priceless gift of a peaceable and tranquil love, that sustained and cherished them without ever interfering with their pleasures or dominating them with schemes and activities of her own." She goes on to say that it was Wordsworth's mother who "first introduced him to 'Nature'—and when her own presence was withdrawn, he stood safely, though a little solemnly, in that universe which she had trusted and in which she had felt so perfectly at home. Soon he learnt to transfer to Nature the affection, the faith, the 'religious love' which he had felt for his mother" (1957, 2, 3). This is moving stuff. But it is also a romantic gloss of what Wordsworth says about his mother (1805 *Prelude,* bk. 5, lines 246–90) taken at face value. Moorman does at least as much idealizing of the mother as Wordsworth does—maybe even more. No doubt Ann Wordsworth loved her children, and no doubt they loved her. But child-parent love is largely unconditional; it will exist despite anything that comes its way. When she died, his position in the universe was anything but safe. It was extraordinarily precarious and sad, and Wordsworth struggled with her loss and the attendant feelings for a very long time. Not until writing this text is there any indication that he dealt even just a little openly with how he felt. And he did not "transfer to Nature" his feelings for her because she taught him to appreciate it; he projected onto Nature what he needed from her but never received. Nature begins for him as a manifestation of his emotional gaps. He created that capital-*N* Nature so that it might love him back. He created nature as a guide and guardian to sustain him when his mother and his family circle could not. Nature is thus in many ways his affective image of her; it is a show of his needs for connection and continuity in his subjective encounter with feelings of loss and loneliness. At the center of Wordsworth's emotional life stands his mother, but she is as much a figure of discontinuity and pain as she is a figure of support and purpose.

The flowing of mother's milk that connects the child to the mother and gives him life, the flowing of the River Derwent that opens the 1799 *Prelude* as the origin of his thoughts and his connection to Nature, and the blood flowing through the child's "infant veins"—these are part of the same flowing as Wordsworth traces the source of who he is. Mother and Nature, Nature as Mother, flow into him, poetically and emotionally conflated as one; that, at any rate, is how Wordsworth once needed to see it as he began to unravel his personal history. Where the actual mother leaves off, a "prop" inexplicably "removed," the other begins. But Nature, as beautiful and vital as it is, is not the same as a real parent, and it cannot do the same things. It can, however, like any object or idea, be made to supply what it is not nor can ever be. And that is what Wordsworth has it do. Any reader of Wordsworth must be impressed with the poet's powerful and sensitive portrayals of nature, and if we might wonder about the source of such attachment and emotional intensity, I believe we have to look at least in part to his displaced feelings for his mother.

For Wordsworth, childhood can be divided into two: before the death of his mother and after the death of his mother. As Don Johnson writes, "The death of his mother marks the division of experience into the bliss of childhood and the alienation that comes with advancing years" (1988, 287). But there is also a finer split within his childhood between the years before she died and the years after. Wordsworth had the imaginative luxury of transforming the time before her death into a kind of Eden, a time that did not admit thinking, only feeling and being.

Having been abandoned by his mother, Wordsworth became the responsibility of his father.

A FATHER

For almost twenty years, John Wordsworth was steward (law agent, bailiff, coroner, political aid) to Sir James Lowther (1736–1802), earl of Lonsdale, Cumberland's most influential citizen and one of the most wealthy men in England (Beckett 1981, 3). This would have been an extraordinarily demanding job, knowing what we do of Lowther's ruthless desire for power and how much he was disliked by those in the area (Bonsall 1960, Dann 1980). Thomas De Quincey records that he was known as "the bad Lord Lonsdale" and that "he used his power in an oppressive way." He was perhaps a little mad, and De Quincey likened him to "a true feudal chieftain" (De Quincey 1970, 149–52). Carl Woodring says that "He was without exception the most unpopular" political figure in that part of England (1968, 1). Lowther's real estate and coal mining interests were massive, and he "owned" nine seats in the House of Commons. There were always scores to be settled, some of them very nasty. There were rents, mortgages, and taxes to collect, and political strings that needed pulling. John Wordsworth's job was to act upon Lowther's wishes while attempting to appease those who had to be dealt with. John Wordsworth's neighbors would have to be careful what they said around him and his family. The Wordsworth family's place in the community was very likely uneasy.

Of John's position Gill writes: "That their father was the arm of a man hated as much as he was feared would hardly have troubled the infant children [viz., Wordsworth and his siblings]" (1989, 14). But this could not be so. Just at the time of William's birth, John Wordsworth was involved in rather shady electioneering activities that would have alienated him and his family even more from the locals. The children would have been very troubled by the family circumstances and the resulting dynamics. As Joanne Dann puts it rather safely, "The existing evidence suggests that William Wordsworth, born in 1770, arrived at a time of some stress to his parents" (1980, 82). Parents under stress necessarily put their children under stress. We know that John Wordsworth worked long and hard hours. We know he was often away on business. And, as Moorman tells us, John "served his strange master with zeal and fidelity" (1957, 6)—a fact that says a great deal about John Wordsworth. So we must assume that his position *did* affect his disposition and the style of parenting, and that the pressures exerted by Lowther via John's position would get expressed in one way or another in the Wordsworth household—and expressed to the children.[8] We know from family systems theory that the various moods, behaviors, and personalities of parents, both positive and negative, necessarily get communicated to children in diverse and indirect ways, and children, even at a very young age, do pick up on this family dynamic and internalize it, making it a part of their personality and behavior. We have to question how available he was to his children, what kind of influence he had on them, how distracted he might have been by his work while at home, and how he and his family were perceived in their immediate community.

We have to consider John Wordsworth's personality. He was someone who could bow down to a tyrannical boss, and he appears to have been without confidants sympathetic with his situation. Perhaps he had neither the time nor the disposition for such intimacy. He was apparently without close friends. As a teenager, Dorothy records a startling discovery made by her and her brothers. She writes to her best friend, Jane Pollard: "I, (young as I am) flatter myself that Halifax contains several real friends to me, but it is indeed mortifying to my Brothers and me to find that amongst all those who visited at my father's house, he had not one real friend; would you think it Jane?" (Wordsworth 1967, 7). There is both astonishment and hurt here, as if some supportive truth had suddenly been found out to be a lie. They in all likelihood did not fully understand the kind of job their father had and how he was perceived in the community. Yet the kind of man their father was would greatly influence their personalities and life choices.

The father must have developed something like a pathological perseverance in his position for Lowther, for, as Moorman points out, "There is no evidence that he [John] ever received any payment for his services to his employer" (1957, 7). (The family managed to live on money generated from some inherited property.) These unpaid expenses, close to five thousand pounds, and the accompanying resentment, were passed on to the children after their father's death in 1783. He was just forty-two years old. Ten years later, with the settlement of the debt still in the courts, we witness Dorothy's enduring bitterness: "We [her and her siblings] in the same moment lost a father, a mother, a home, we have been equally deprived of our patrimony by the cruel Hand of lordly Tyranny" (Wordsworth 1967, 88). The money owed to John Wordsworth continued to plague the children, causing Dorothy much anxiety and eventually generating some angry exchanges between William and Richard, who, being the eldest brother, handled his father's estate.[9] Lowther himself died in 1802, and when in 1803 assurance came that the account would be settled, more than two decades after the death of John, a great burden fell from the children. Perhaps not coincidentally, we shall see that it was at this very time that both Wordsworth and his poetry changed. But of this we can be certain: the twenty years of bitterness and anxiety left many scars in the name of the father[10] A considerable amount of confused, negative feelings surfaced during those years, and much of it surfaced in the kind of poetry Wordsworth would write during that time. Disparaging his father's boss, in 1795 Wordsworth could write in an *Imitation of Juvenal:* "Must honour still to Lonsdale's tale be bound?" (Wordsworth 1940, 302). But one irony in all of this is that, within a few years of Lonsdale's death, Wordsworth would become close friends with the next Lord Lonsdale, Sir William Lowther. He would even campaign for him,[11] and he would go on to dedicate his longest public performance, *The Excursion* (1814), to him:

> —Now, by thy care befriended, I appear
> Before thee, LONSDALE, and this Work present,

> A token (may it prove a monument!)
> Of high respect and gratitude sincere.

Although the terms of the relationship were different, in serving this master Wordsworth could not only carry on where his father had left off but also succeed where his father had failed.

A few years after the death of his father, Wordsworth wrote a passage in *The Vale of Esthwaite*[12] that mentions his feelings about the death of his father and how it severely isolated him and turned him to intimations of his own death wish (lines 416–37). Wordsworth tells us that this was the first poem he had written from "the impulse of my own mind" (Wordsworth 1974, 372–73), and so part of it might be read on a more personal, subjective level. The poem itself, pieced together from various manuscripts, is for the most part of the evening graveyard genre of Gray, Collins, and Cowper—with a dash of the gothic (à la James Beattie's *Minstrel*) and a pinch of the pastoral thrown in. It is a poem unsure about what it wants to do. Moorman writes that at this time Wordsworth could not "describe, as he did later in *The Prelude*, what he himself was going through" (1957, 64).[13] True enough. But, as mentioned, embedded within it in clearer terms are some striking personal touches that suggest important and difficult residual feelings revolving, ostensibly, about the loss of a loved place, his beloved vale of Esthwaite. More to the point, it is a poem about the inability to come to terms with loss. Wordsworth singles out one cold, windy, winter evening, when, with the sheep, a hawthorn, and a naked rock as witness, "Alone, [he] bore the bitter shock" of his father's death. But it is a confused passage with confused feelings. He wonders of what use the tears may have been, yet he claims they "eased" him of "a heavy load." He also says he received emotional relief

> To pay the mighty debt of grief,
> With sighs repeated o'er and o'er,
> I mourn because I mourned no more.

The language of emotional exchange put in financial terms—"pay . . . debt"—is especially fitting given the circumstances of his father's estate. Yet is he sad because he didn't feel sad enough for long enough? But again, he says he has had his emotional "load" lightened by expressing his sorrow. What the father's death meant to Wordsworth comes in form of a realization: he did not "foresee" that he "lost a home" in "losing" his father, and that with that loss "little more than Heaven was left." By "Heaven," Wordsworth means death, for in the immediate lines that follow, he rather morbidly and with self-pity writes, "I soon shall be with them that rest": "may my weary body sleep / In peace beneath a green grass heap" (lines 445, 455–56). His feelings are painful, and it is from this that he seeks relief, almost in a Keatsian way, with sleep, death, poetry, and forgetting poetically conflated. But he has not finished with his personal situation yet:

> For I must never share
> A tender parent's guardian care;
> Sure, from the world's unkind alarm,
> Returning to a mother's arm;
> Mist-eyed awhile upraise the head
> Else sinking to Death's joyless bed,
> And when by pain, by death, depress'd
> Ah! sure it gentler sinks to rest.
>
> (Lines 514–21)

Showing up here are Wordsworth's unresolved feelings, his losses, and his needs, and, in their sadness and grief, they don't have to be spelled out here in any more detail. It is nevertheless worth noting that he wants to be taken care of by a parent. He wants to return to his mother's sheltering embrace. He wants protection. And if he can't have it, then he may as well surrender to death. This is anything but the security-in-the-world that Moorman associates with the mother's legacy. It is sadness and self-pity.

Wordsworth's descriptions of fathers in some of his other work suggest a struggle to address what this figure meant for him. They are, for the most part, unsympathetic portrayals. As William Gordon (1972) notes about *The Borderers* (completed in 1797), it is a play in which Wordsworth attempts to work through ambivalent but primarily negative feelings revolving around his father and his past. Other father figures, like those in *Lyrical Ballads*, also suggest some difficulties. Lawrence W. Mazzeno gives a composite of this father:

> He is a man concerned with worldly affairs. He sees nature only as landscape. He responds to the material needs of his family, but cannot comprehend imaginative or spiritual needs. Consequently, in moments of crisis, he is incapable of functioning as a stabilizing influence with a world made chaotic either by circumstance, by nature, or by other people. At the moment of crisis he is literally absent or imaginatively empty. The father figure is without exception a character much like the one Wordsworth himself may have struggled against in his early attempts to gain psychological independence. (1977, 423)

Wordsworth's idea of the father figure is particularized in such a way as to point to his own experience—that is, to his own father. And why shouldn't it? When we turn to other portrayals in poetry that are more explicitly autobiographical, they are more complex and emotionally charged; but these other father figures are, in their inability to touch the emotional side of the children and in their lack of support for the children, reenactments of Wordsworth's own emotional history of his relationship to his father.

One of the most impressive episodes in *The Prelude*—impressive in its startling and stark nature—expresses Wordsworth's confused feelings about his father, and those feelings are guilt, hurt, and rejection. These feelings meet, not surprisingly, over punishment and death. It is a scene, Wordsworth writes, powerfully "Implanted in my mind,"[14] and its precursor passage comes out of lines discussed above from *The Vale of Esthwaite* (lines 418–27). He is thirteen years old. It is the day before Christmas break, about a week before Christmas, 1783. When school is out, he goes into the fields, and he is drawn to a place where he surveys and anxiously thinks about the route the horses will take that will bring him and two of his brothers home, but he cannot see far enough into the distance (which might be interpreted as a projection of his inability to see into an uncertain future). It is "Stormy, and rough, and wild"; Wordsworth, correspondingly, is "Feverish, and tired, and restless." He ascends a "crag, / An eminence" from which he can better survey the roads. There, "half sheltered by a naked wall," and huddled between a sheep and a wind-swept hawthorn, he sits "on the grass," "eyes intensely straining" through the mist and against the elements, looking towards his home. The horses must have eventually arrived, and Wordsworth and his brothers did make it home, but the poem does not record that particular journey. We know that on the last day of the year Wordsworth's father died, and we know that he died because he had been out on Lowther's business and got lost on the way home, and he ended up having to stay outdoors for a cold winter's night (Reed 1967, 58). Wordsworth does, however, leave us with the feeling of being cheated by time, and the journey he substitutes for the ride to a secure, warm home leads elsewhere, to the cemetery:

> Ere I to school returned
> That dreary time, ere I had been ten days
> A dweller in my father's house, he died,
> And I and my two brothers, orphans then,
> Followed his body to the grave.
> (1799 *Prelude*, bk. 1, lines 349–53)

For young Wordsworth, or for any child in his position, there can be no reason for a death like this, for being robbed of a possession desired so badly but never really owned; for we cannot say that Wordsworth's relationship with his father was close or nurturing, which, paradoxically, makes it more difficult to cope with in this particular circumstance of loss. But the profound feeling, reinforced by his particular Christian background,[15] usurps the memory of his father's death and turns on him as an admonishment for self-improvement and as a guilty feeling:

> The event,
> With all the sorrow which it brought, appeared
> A chastisement. . . .
>
> (Lines 353–55)

When Wordsworth recalls this and the paradoxical "anxiety of hope" he experienced on that bleakest of all days, the elements come tumbling back to him as a catalog of particular detached images, piling up as snapshots from the poetic psyche that are forever associated with the circumstance of unannounced abandonment and the feeling of loss:

> the wind and sleety rain,
> And all the business of the elements,
> The single sheep, and the one blasted tree,
> And the bleak music of that old stone wall,
> The noise of wood and water, and the mist . . .
>
> (Lines 361–65)

And yet this necessarily negative experience and these embedded images from the landscape, associated and enmeshed as they are with the death of his father and the stifled feelings of loss and abandonment, are subsequently transformed into a positive source of satisfaction and future sustenance, something to which Wordsworth would return and "would drink / As at a fountain." There is, so to speak, no admitted or explicit bad taste left in his mouth. But at the same time he acknowledges that he cannot escape these images and their associations, and that they may indeed work away at him, moving, as they might, in mysterious ways:

> And I do not doubt
> That in this later time, when storm and rain
> Beat on my roof at midnight, or by day
> When I am in the woods, unknown to me
> The workings of my spirit thence are brought.
>
> (Lines 370–74)

Unannounced and unacknowledged, but located in the sense and circumstances of solitude, the "event" and these triggered associations return, being wrapped up in his confused and discomforting feelings for his father, feelings of hurt, rejection, loss, and guilt. Wordsworth's logic at his point is not (as it will be later) clearly restorative, but fixated. His poetic power and personal strength are founded on holding back this flood, in attempting to replace the parental loss with a punitive gain, in knowing that these feelings are "unknown" but inescapable. They represent one center of his being: a place, he writes, to which "The workings of my spirit thence are brought."

This passage that evolved out of the death of his father obviously represents one of Wordsworth's shaping and indelible experiences, a (re)turning point, a crossroad,[16] appearing, as it does, as the last "spot" in the first book of the first version of *The Prelude*. One moment he was a child with great holiday expectations; the next he was an orphan—abandoned, and with an uncertain future. Now he was alone. His father's death differed from the death of his mother a few years earlier, in that at least then he still had one parent left.[17] Now his solitude was absolute. The idea of death, now turned towards himself as someone who was victimized by death's cruel hand, became for him something difficult to come to terms with; it is denied: "Nothing was more difficult for me in childhood than to admit the notion of death as a state applicable to my own being" (Wordsworth 1963, 286). Death and abandonment, dominating his own personal history and emotional life, remained prevalent elements in his early poetry.

Like his mother's death, his father's death forced the formulation of one of Wordsworth's many beliefs about childhood, and in this case one of the most important ones: the belief in a time when innocence, his own complete, uncluttered innocence, actually existed, when his relationship to the world was direct, when the rain was just rain, a tree just a tree—and when a parent was a parent and not a hopeful projection onto nature. Wordsworth recalls that once he could look to the mists, waters, clouds, and crags with that unthinking innocence. There was a time, he writes, when he could hold "unconscious intercourse / With the eternal beauty, drinking in / A pure organic pleasure" from the landscape, a time when "images like these" had "No body of associated form" (1799 *Prelude*, bk. 1, lines 391–412). But evidently that time was gone: trees were not just trees, and winds brought more than rain. (We note too that in terms of composition, this passage belongs to the remarkable but distressed Goslar period, to which I will devote a later chapter.) The problem was not just how to return to that Edenic time before the Fall, but also how (by using images, by using imagination) to meet unfulfilled needs. It was nurturing that he missed out on and was cheated of, and, conditioned, as it were, by the experience of his mother's death, it was Nature he now turned to. As an act of both substitution and retention, Wordsworth again turned to nature for nurture. The head of the family was gone, and now instead Wordsworth looked to "the face of Nature" to *speak* to him of and connect him with "things" from the past, both remembered and forgotten; and most importantly, those "things" had to do with the realization that feelings, "affections," were the "invisible links" holding together the distant scenes from the past—in short, holding him together (lines 418–42). This is the yearning force behind much of Wordsworth's poetry, when, for example, he connects his solitude with the quiet of the sky or recovers joy from every meadow, grove, and stream. It is the need to replace one form of authority and guidance with another in order to construct the idea of growth and continuity. It is writing motivated by self-defense.

When we read Wordsworth's impassioned invention or formulation of Nature, we must keep in mind the impulse and the association as they work via projection, from both mother and father onto Nature.[18] We might then be in a better position to understand the origin of his feelings about himself and his intense regard of nature. As Wordsworth writes this poetry, he begins to realize this, although he fears that even with "such inquiry" he might not be "taught / To understand myself" (lines 455–56). Again, this is why he is writing such poetry: to "make our infancy a visible scene / On which the sun is shining" (lines 463–64). This innocent happiness in its hope for clarity may be a idealized vision, but it does not decrease the desire to reclaim it. It makes it an agonizing necessity, since to get to it there are troubled waters that must be crossed.

The lines that continue to stand out in this passage remain those which express the most discomforting feelings:

> The event
> With all the sorrow which it brought, appeared
> A chastisement. . . .
>
> (Lines 353–55)

Alice Miller writes that one of the key issues in understanding childhood and trauma is the "need to distinguish more clearly between feelings of guilt and feelings of sorrow" (1990c, xvi). This seems to be an uncanny reference to these very lines, for it is clear that Wordsworth has not made this distinction, though he seems to be striving to do so. Indeed, I would argue that the creative impulse behind this episode and some of his other poetry comes out of the need to resolve and correct this kind of affective confusion—or at least to rationalize it. Elisabeth Kübler-Ross notes that "Guilt is perhaps the most painful companion of death" (1970, 161), and for Wordsworth, this appears to be so. He felt that he must have done something wrong, that he was somehow responsible, and the death of his father came as a punishment for this wrong-doing; hence the guilt. Miller goes on to say that when the "child within is not allowed to become aware of what happened to him or her, a part of his or her emotional life will remain frozen" (1990c, xvii)—not unlike a spot of time, we could add. Wordsworth, through powerful acts of rhetoric and mind, attempts to transform such moments into supportive or rehabilitating instants. He wants to become aware of what happened to him. He wants to be able to move on and do great things, perhaps not knowing that his great thing was giving poetic expression to the desire to move on.

Why Wordsworth chose poetry as his vocation is a question that is impossible to answer completely or with complete certainty. It certainly was not the choice for the vast majority of persons in similar social circumstances. One answer, or part of an answer, may be connected to John Wordsworth. When we think of what his father meant to him and what embedded associations he had for him, beyond the feelings of guilt and loss, we should not be surprised to discover that it was the father who, in a program of indoctrination, instilled a very young Wordsworth with his very first and obviously lasting acquaintance with poetry, forcing him to memorize and repeat significant passages. This is recorded by Christopher Wordsworth in his 1851 *Memoirs* of his uncle: "[T]he Poet's father set him very early to learn portions of the works of the best English poets by heart, so that at an early age he could repeat large portions of Shakespeare, Milton, and Spencer [*sic*]" (C. Wordsworth 1851, 1:34). This rather romantic portrayal of the father/son relationship unfortunately carries with it the feeling that Wordsworth, and we along with Wordsworth, should be thankful for the father's gift of poetry to the son. After all, the English literary tradition would be unimaginable without Wordsworth. But in fact the father robbed the son. As Richard Matlak writes in the context of the "spot of time" discussed above, the passage represents Wordsworth's "response to the loss of the parent he need[ed] most to assist him in becoming a man" (1978b, 396). We could, in the positive spirit of gift giving and family romance, say that Wordsworth owed his deep and lifelong love of poetry to his father. But the point may be to *not* take for granted the source of Wordsworth's dedication to or feelings about poetry, as if it were some natural vocation or means of expression. The father's presence acts belatedly but powerfully in Wordsworth's attraction to poetry. The need to come into being through poetry is what his father left him as a substitute inheritance, but this legacy did not at first liberate him as much as subjugate him: poetry as imprisoning patrimony.[19] As Michael H. Friedman (1979) argues, even Wordsworth's failure to negotiate political ideals, the social order, and the sense of community, both earlier on in France and later on in the Lake District, resulted from the paternal authority that he internalized.[20] Yet, as Matlak concludes, "[T]he love and presence of an adult male . . . seems to have been Wordsworth's most pressing adolescent need" (Matlak 1978b, 396).[21] Thus the agonizing double bind: the father is needed, yet stands in the way.

We cannot say that Wordsworth loved poetry. We can only say that he needed it, and that he needed to master himself through it, as he needed to master his father's abandonment and the feelings of loss and separation. This would not be an easy mastery. For Wordsworth, embodied in the idea of poetry were some difficult associations. After all, and as I will show later, writing poetry sometimes gave Wordsworth extreme physical distress. Father/Death/Poetry/Sickness: this is indeed a disturbing cluster within which to situate a significant portion of Wordsworth's creative motivation and artistic achievement. That the idea of unresolved death, and, in particular, the death of a family member, stirred deeply in Wordsworth's psyche became apparent when Wordsworth's favorite brother, John, died in 1805. As McFarland notes, this event represented a "reawakening of the losses of his father, and especially his mother, in childhood" (1981, 161). The event has even been viewed as the beginning of Wordsworth's decline (McAdam 1962),[22] and if it is so, it only demonstrates that Wordsworth never completely recovered from or healthily came to terms with the events and feelings that had dominated his youth. His father never taught him how to grieve appropriately or to accept loss. Little wonder that Wordsworth's emotional life and much of his poetry circle around such feelings.

A SON

I quoted the following sentence in the introduction, but I want call it up again to remind the reader that even the most careful, extended treatment of Wordsworth's art from a psychological perspective seems to be blinded by theory: "Wordsworth's art is not easily explained by the facts of his life, nor does his art, even at its most confessional, satisfy one's curiosity about the life being transmuted into artifact." Thus writes Onorato (1971, 406). Again, I believe that much of Wordsworth's art can be explained by the facts of his life. We, like Wordsworth, just have to face up to them.

In this section of the chapter, I will not attempt to retell Wordsworth's life, but I will attempt to reevaluate certain moments and patterns of behavior that demand new attention. This, I hope, will return us to the source of his personality and to his poetry, which, as I've said, has a center that is emotional and based not on the *idea* of subjectivity but on Wordsworth's individual subjectivity.

Often these are events that are underplayed or misinterpreted by other commentators and are not made to account for the kind of poetry he wrote.[23] What emerges are the cluster of feelings that are reenacted in the poetry. We have already seen something of Wordsworth's family circumstances: his young mother seemed to have had trouble managing the household; the children were often sent to abusive grandparents (this will be looked at again, below); the mother died when he was barely old enough to remember her; his father was an overworked, underpaid loner whose dealings with the children seems to have been cursory; the father never recovered from the death of his wife; he too died when Wordsworth was still a youth; the siblings were split up, causing significant distress; and they had to suffer extended financial worries. The predominant feelings that he must have experienced were loss, grief, guilt, anxiety, confusion, and endurance. No wonder, then, that in describing his early years he recalls

> The terrors, all the early miseries,
> Regrets, vexations, lassitudes, that all
> The thoughts and feelings which have been infused
> Into my mind . . .
> (1805 *Prelude*, bk. 1, lines 356–59)

These were reinforced by further factors. These infused feelings and thoughts would eventually be reconciled in the form of recovery, however, and this passage ends with a kind of confidence that all of these early problems will go into making up "The calm existence that is mine when I am worthy of myself" (lines 360–61). Past difficulty is reconciled by the positing of an integrated, individuated self.

The negative side of young William's disposition and personality seems to have been set at least in part by circumstances predating the death of his mother. In his *Autobiographical Memoranda*, dictated in 1847, Wordsworth is not easy on himself, although he has had almost three-quarters of a century to distance himself. The reason his dying mother was very worried about him was that, as he says, "I was of a stiff, moody, and violent temper" (Wordsworth 1974, 3:372). This is not a picture of your average child. Wordsworth was also somehow in his early years pushed into himself, into his own ego, by the circumstances of his life. He himself apologetically points to this characteristic as it developed in childhood: "And I was taught to feel—perhaps too much— / The self-sufficing power of solitude" (1805 *Prelude,* bk. 2, lines 77–78). The phrase, "perhaps too much," is revealing; in this context it hints strongly of regret and uncertainty, as if he was forced into fending for himself. Solitude was not a choice; for this young person, solitude was a defense, not a luxury.

We have to examine the source of this disposition, why he had to find safety in solitude. Trauma of the kind Wordsworth experienced has two well-known effects: withdrawal and/or acting out. In Wordsworth, we see both.

Wordsworth lived a significant portion of his life in a world of confused feelings and emotional turmoil. Bateson's reason for Wordsworth's behavior is as romantic as it is typical: "The boy's naughtiness, it is obvious, was a sheer superfluity of animal spirits" (1954, 45).[24] This is complete nonsense. Wordsworth's "naughtiness" was the product of his upbringing, of factors and circumstances that formed his character and emotional problems. His solitary self-sufficiency evolved out of an inability to turn elsewhere, just has his "stiff, moody, and violent temper" must have had its source in his family circumstances. It was not nature; it was nurture—and part of Wordsworth's development, based on his emotional needs, was to make the former out of the latter.

Many people who knew or met the adult Wordsworth—such as Coleridge, Benjamin Robert Haydon, Henry Crabb Robinson, Charles Lamb, William Hazlitt, and John Keats—noticed that he sometimes had problems understanding the feelings of others. Often his egotism is expressed as insensitivity or the inability to accept criticism (McFarland 1981, 137). This insensitivity is likely the reenactment of the kind of treatment that was dished out to him in youth: doing to others as he had been done to. And most recognized Wordsworth's need to bring everything within the orbit of his own emotional sphere. Shelley had heard of it from persons who knew the older poet quite well, and certainly, as one of Wordsworth's closest readers, he had beheld it the poetry. Here, in Shelley's *Peter Bell the Third*, a satire mainly on Wordsworth, we see it described with some critical and poetical panache:

> All things that Peter saw and felt
>   Had a peculiar aspect to him;
> And when they came within the belt
> Of his own nature, seemed to melt
>   Like cloud to cloud, into him.
> . . . .
> He had a mind which was somehow
>   At once circumference and centre
> Of all he might feel or know;
> Nothing went ever out, although
>   Something did ever enter.
>   (Lines 273–77, 293–97)

But Shelley, like the others, also recognized that this characteristic was also Wordsworth's strength and the source of his inspiration:

>   Yet his was an individual mind,
>   And new created all he saw
>   In a new manner, and refined
>   Those new creations, and combined
>   Them, by a master-spirit's law,
>
>   Thus—though unimaginative,
>   An apprehension clear, intense,
>   Of his mind's work, had made alive
>   The things it wrought on; I believe
>   Wakening a sort of thought in sense.
>   (Lines 302–12)

All of this is very perceptive criticism.[25] Shelley recognizes the intensity of Wordsworth's feeling and thought as Wordsworth animated the world around himself as a form of self-projection. There is an acknowledgment of Wordsworth's depth of feeling through introspection. As Haydon put it in 1817, "Wordsworth's great power is an intense perception of human feelings regarding the mystery of things by analyzing his own. . . . Wordsworth's feelings are exclusive, because his intensity of purpose is so strong" (Haydon 1960, 2:171–72). What we have been attempting to determine is why Wordsworth was driven to analyze his feelings with such intensity, which amounts to an examination of the source of such feelings.

Penrith

Wordsworth tells us in the *Memoranda,* "The time of my infancy and early boyhood was passed partly at Cockermouth, and partly with my mother's parents at Penrith, where my mother, in the year 1778, died. . . . " (Wordsworth 1974, 3:371). As Reed's research makes clear, these visits were numerous and often extended.[26] The Wordsworth children may have spent as much as half their time at Penrith (Gordon G. Wordsworth 1920, 414–15). The physical ties to his father's house at Cockermouth became less and less. One commentator puts it this way: after the mother's death, Wordsworth's father's house "was simply a place he periodically visited until his father died" (Heffernan 1988, 258). But the emotional ties to his place of origin, problematic as they were, remained with him. In some ways, the death of Wordsworth's mother was also the death of his father.

As mentioned, aspects of life at Penrith were not happy, since he seems to have suffered from significant emotional abuse. In the *Memoranda*, he recalls just a few particular events from his early childhood. Two recollections that refer to his mother have already been mentioned. But the two most striking childhood memories are from those Penrith visits: "I remember going once into the attics of my grandfather's house at Penrith, upon some indignation having been put upon me, with an intention of destroying myself with one of the foils which I knew was kept there. I took the foil in my hand, but my heart failed" (372). We do not have to know the specific circumstances to at least note that his treatment there must have been heavy-handed, and that his response, that of suicidal child with sword turned towards himself, was desperate. He appears to have been shamed in some significant way. The other incident he recalls is also revealing. He dares his brother to strike one of the family pictures with the lash used to start up a spinning top. His brother refuses, and so he does it himself: "[N]o doubt, though I have forgotten it, I was properly punished. But possibly, from some want of judgment in punishments inflicted, I had become perverse and obstinate in defying chastisement, and rather proud of it than otherwise" (232). The resentment, anger, and the feeling of being treated unfairly by his relatives (note that they were "family pictures" that he wanted to disfigure) seem to have been internalized and fortified by the perceived strength of his character. His inner strength had to come about as an act of defense. Sadly, at Penrith, Wordsworth seems to have been without emotional support from any adults in his family. These, then, were the bare memories that stayed with Wordsworth after all those years, and they were memories of anything but happy occasions. Other kinds of memories seem to have been displaced by these unpleasant recollections.

Dorothy Wordsworth paints an extraordinarily severe picture of the Penrith household and her relatives after the death of her parents. In place of affection, she was dealt alienation: "the cold insensibility of my Gmr and the ill-nature of my Grandfr" (Wordsworth 1967, 9). These children were obviously a burden, and the relatives seem to have gone out of their way to make life miserable for both Dorothy and her brothers. And William was singled out as the object of their bad feelings.

As a teenager, in late July 1787, Dorothy wrote to Jane Pollard, about the "ill nature of all [her] relations" and how much it meant to be reunited with her brothers, even though it was temporary. She writes that all of the conversations she has with her siblings "generally take a melancholy turn, with wishing we had a father and a home": "Many a time have W[illia]m, J[ohn], C[hristopher], and myself shed tears together, tears of the bitterest sorrow, we all of us, each day, feel more sensibly the loss we sustained when we were deprived of our parents...." (2–5). Remember, this was five years after the death of the father and nine years after the death of the mother, and they were still having great difficulties dealing with the loss.[27] Their feelings of loss had in no way been resolved. Dorothy continues describing the abuse the Wordsworth siblings had to endure: "[E]ach day we do we receive fresh insults, you will wonder of what sort; believe me of the most mortifying kind." But the cruel mistreatment did not stop with the grandparents and the uncle: even one of the servants, "James," seems to have been given a free reign to treat the children in the most degrading and condescending ways, by calling their attention to their poor circumstances. She notes too that her Uncle Kit (Christopher Crackanthorpe Cookson) had "taken a dislike to my Br. Wm." (3); and in Dorothy's next letter to Jane, written just after her brothers had left, she is depressed again, and she adds: "I absolutely dislike my Uncle Kit who never speaks a pleasant word to one, and behaves to my Br Wm in a particularly ungenerous manner" (8). Six years later, Dorothy was still recording for Jane the way that William had been singled out:

> You must know that this favorite brother of mine happens to be no favorite with any of his *near* relations except his Brothers by whom he is adored.... I have not time or room to explain to you the foundation of the prejudices of my two Uncles [Mr Cookson and Crackanthorpe Cookson] against my dear William; the subject is an unpleasant one for a letter, it will employ us more agreeably in conversation, then, though I must confess that he has been somewhat to blame, yet I think I shall prove to you that the Excuse might have been found in his natural disposition. (100)

We do not know with complete certainty why these "*near*" relations" were so much against Wordsworth and why Dorothy perceived her brother as part of the problem, but it would not be surprising to find that his moody disposition and resentment about his family circumstances were directed to these relatives. They, in turn, were not prepared to empathize with or tolerate him. There seems to have been plenty of pent-up anger in young Wordsworth. It would be naïve to think that this would not effect the adult Wordsworth.

Wordsworth and his siblings were not just without parents. They were without a home (that is, the secure feeling of a home) and without the kind of adult/child love needed to nurture and develop their emotional lives. We can talk all we want about good teachers and kind landlords; they can help, but they are never substitutes for the unconditional positive regard that the continuous presence that parents or parent figures can offer. The truth is, the evidence we have says that these children were ignored, resented, and abused by those to whom they were entrusted. William and Dorothy seem to have been especially created in and caught by these unfortunate circumstances, and certainly their closeness resulted from these circumstances. His anger and moodiness and her melancholia were manifestations of the same conditions. And these conditions created a kind of intense and often hindering co-dependency[28] that has been the subject of much speculation about the style and healthiness of their relationship.[29] That Dorothy's life was completely wrapped around Wordsworth's was not a healthy situation, and it says a great deal about how the children were brought up. In 1791, years before they lived together, when asked, Dorothy confessed that she was "partial to William"; and two years later, she apologized for expressing, at length and with some guilt, excessive affection for this special brother of hers (Wordsworth 1967, 51, 98). More than ten years later we read in Dorothy's own journal her pathetic obsession while her brother was away for a few days:

> Since he has left me (at 1/2 past 11) it is now 2 I have been putting the drawers into order, laid by his clothes which we had thrown here and there and everywhere.... Now for my walk. I *will* be busy, I *will* look well and be well when he comes back to me. O the Darling! Here is one of his bitten apples! I can hardly find in my heart to throw it into the fire. . . . I walked round the two Lakes crossed the stepping stones at Rydal Foot. Sate down where we always sit. I was full of thoughts about my darling. Blessings on him. (D. Wordsworth 1973, 97–98)

We must imagine what went into these feelings of being utterly lost without Wordsworth, and we must think about their source. Consider too Dorothy's extraordinarily confused emotions when her brother was married in 1802. In her own words, she approached the event with "half dread" (Wordsworth 1967, 377). The night before the event she slept with the wedding ring on her forefinger, and when she gave it to William in the morning he slipped it back onto her finger (D. Wordsworth 1973, 154). She was in such a state that she did not even attend the wedding. And then we have Wordsworth, in *The Vale of Esthwaite*, wondering why he feels such deep love for his sister and concluding that it is because she represents "all that Heaven has claimed"—in short, his dead mother and father.[30] Dorothy embodied the family life he never had.

We do not know if the relationship between Dorothy and William overtly admitted the actual act of incest. I think not, although there would obviously be some incestuous undertones in their actions and in some of his poetry simply because of the intensity of their relationship. They were intimately bound by what they did not have and by what they wanted to share; they were bound by what they shared and by what was missing in their inner lives. Each represented for the other the idea of family, and for both this was a troubling yet hopeful idea. Their emotional bonding was perhaps even stronger than that of two lovers. We should not be surprised by this. Dorothy's history was largely expressed by her unusual character and mannerisms.[31] Wordsworth's history was largely expressed in unusual poetry.

Wordsworth's Health and the Composition of Poetry

The extreme degree to which Wordsworth's emotional life worked away at him is evident in the record of his health, especially in the first part of his life. This needs to be reviewed in some detail, since I hold that it can be related to and substantiated in much of what shows up in his poetry. We should, then, simply and honestly acknowledge that Wordsworth's subjectivity needs to be understood in terms of his individual history—the difficulties in his immediate family, the abusive grandparents, the traumatizing loss of both his mother and father long before emotional maturity, the loss of a home, the splitting of the family. As a youth, he also had to endure the loss of the two most significant father figures for him; Hugh Tyson in 1784 (husband of Ann Tyson, with whom Wordsworth boarded while at school), and William Taylor in 1786 (the young headmaster at Hawkshead).[32] For Wordsworth, the manifestations of such circumstances, or times when he was working on difficult poetic material, produced serious chronic health problems that were clearly psychogenic: headaches, stomach problems, chest pains, anxiety, and insomnia. Further, the extreme moodiness he used to describe himself when he was a child was still evident at least up into his early and middle adulthood. The lost inner child clung to him and made claim to both his all too human heart and to his poetry.

In Dorothy's letter of late July 1787 cited above, she mentions that William will probably go on to be a lawyer "if his health will permit." She repeats the exact phrase in a letter written a week later, and she adds, "he is troubled with violent head-aches and a pain in his side, but I hope they will leave him in little time" (Wordsworth 1967, 4, 7). In fact they did not go away for some time. In December 1794, when reasoning a "further circumstance" that would prevent him from taking a position of parliamentary reporter, he refers to suffering from "nervous headaches, which invariably attack me when exposed to a heated atmosphere or to loud noises and that with such an excess of pain as to deprive me of all recollection" (Wordsworth 1967, 138). Wordsworth himself seems to be aware that the cause of his extreme difficulties is emotional, that certain conditions, especially stressful circumstances, created in him a kind of dissociative or amnesic state. This is not typical behavior. We can only suggest that these conditions with their "excess of pain" recall something of earlier situations in which he also felt emotional duress; these feelings return to him in similar circumstances.

They are many more passing references to Wordsworth's health, and at the risk of overstating the case —given that until now it has been understated— I will list many of the particular instances in order to open the case file on Wordsworth's condition.

We find from Dorothy that in the first week of March 1798 Wordsworth was "very unwell," "oppressed with languor, and weakness" (200). On 3 September 1799 Dorothy writes to her brother Richard that "William has been unwell lately he is sadly troubled with a pain in his side" (270), and within a few days of this, Wordsworth writes to Coleridge that he is unwell (Reed 1967, 273). Coleridge relays this back to Richard Wordsworth on 10 September: "I received this morning a letter from William & was agitated to find that his Health is in a State which I should deem alarming," and he repeats this to another correspondent: "I have heard from W. Wordsworth—he is ill—& seems not happy" (Coleridge 1956, 1:526–27). On 8 June 1800 Wordsworth writes to Josiah Wedgewood, "ill health has for some time rendered literary labour not adviseable for me" (Wordsworth 1967, 284). Dorothy also reports on the pains in his side and stomach in September 1800, May 1801, and February 1802 (Wordsworth 1967, 301, 335, 343). In June 1802 and March 1804, Wordsworth says that due to a "weakness in my stomach and digestion and partly from certain habits of mind I do not write any letters unless upon business," and refers to "a kind of derangement in my stomach and digestive organs which makes writing painful to me" (353 and 453).

As these last quotations show, Wordsworth claimed that writing letters, or even thinking about writing letters, caused him much distress. He actually gave this a name: "Letter-Phobia" (436). His health difficulties became even more psychologically pronounced when he turned down an invitation from Sir George Beaumont because his "nervous system [wa]s so apt to be deranged by going from home" (516). There is something vaguely agoraphobic in this feeling of derangement. Being fixed to a place meant a great deal to him beyond merely sentiment.

Dorothy's Alfoxden and Grasmere journals are by far the most detailed record we have of the day-to-day goings-on of the Wordsworths, although they only cover the period from January 1798 to January 1803. There are also many large gaps in this record (for example, the months spent in Europe, September 1798 to April 1799), and we can be certain that Dorothy did not report all of the times Wordsworth was ill, and that Wordsworth did not report to Dorothy all of the times he was ill. There were also the many times when he was away and she could not report; and there are also missing parts of the journals. Nevertheless, we have left to us numerous references to Wordsworth's bad health that make it evident that his illness was chronic. (Dorothy herself was often sick, going back to the times when she was separated from her brothers; her sickness often sounds more like depression.)[33]

On 14 February 1798, Dorothy records gathering sticks "with William in the wood, he being unwell and not able to go further," and five days later, on a walk, "Wm unable to go all the way" (D. Wordsworth 1973, 6–7). On 16 March, she writes, "William very ill" (10). When the Grasmere journals begin in May 1800 after the trip to Germany, Wordsworth is not there with Dorothy, but the journal is motivated, we know, to give "Wm Pleasure when he comes home again" (16–17). The same pattern of bad health continues. On 25 August 1800 she records, "Wm not quite well" (35); on 7 September, "Wm poorly" (39); on 5 October, "Wm went to bed very ill after working after dinner," and later in the evening, "Wm still in bed and very ill" (43); 18 October, "He lay down in the afternoon till 7 o'clock but could not sleep . . . .he unable to work" (46); 31 October, "W. very sick and very ill" (49); 5 November, "Wm not well" (49); 7 November (in the morning), "Wm still unwell," and later in the day, "Wm still unwell [and melancholy]" (50);[34] on 22 November, "Wm not quite well," and the next day, "Wm not well" (52); 6 December, "William was not well had laboured unsuccessfully," and later on, "William tired and not well" (54).

The notebook containing the Grasmere journal that picks up after December 1800 is missing, and we don't have any further entries until October 1801. On 13 November, after a "restless night," Dorothy notes that "Wm better than I expected" (58), and on 16 November, "Wm somewhat weakish, but on the whole pretty good" (59). During an evening walk with Mary Hutchinson two days later, she writes, "Wished for Wm, he stayed at home being sickish," and on the 21 November, "William out of spirits," (60); on 23 November, "Wm unwell and did not walk" (60); and on 28 November, "William having slept ill lay in bed till after one o'clock" (64). On 1 December Dorothy writes, "William was not well and staid at home reading after having lain long in bed," and later in the day, "Wm poorly and out of spirits" (64); on 5 December, "Wm not well" (66); on 9 December, "William slept well but his tongue fev[er]ish" (67); on 13 December, "William had been very unwell but we find him better" (69); on 28 December she reports that both she and William "had bad head aches" (74).

On 24 January 1802 Dorothy writes, "Wm could not beat away sleep when I was gone" (79); two days later he is "ill" (81); on 28 January he is "out of spirits" and cannot sleep, and on 29 January, "William was very unwell" (81); on 30 January, "Wm slept better but he thinks he looks ill" (81); and on the 31 January, "William had slept very ill—he was tired and had a bad headache," and later on, "William's head bad" (82). On the first day of the next month, February, she writes, "Wm slept badly. . . . He could not fall asleep, but I found in the morning he had slept better than he expected" (83); the next day, "William not quite well"; and the next day, "He went to bed and could not sleep" (84); on 6 February, "William had slept badly" and "William had a bad headach; he made up a bed on the floor, but could not sleep" (86); on 8 February, "William was very unwell," and the next day he was "unwell" (86–87); 11 February, "William still poorly" and "went to bed unwell" (88); 22 February, "William . . .

went to bed in bad spirits" (94); 27 February, "Wm was not very well," and the next day, "Wm very ill" (96). On 14 March she writes, "William had slept badly," and "William rose without having slept" (101); on 21 February, "William was very unwell this evening," and the next day, "William very poorly" (105). On 20 April 1802 Dorothy records, "William was not well" (113), and on 28 April, "he was ill and tired" (116); on 30 April, "he had a bad head ache owing to his having been disturbed the night before with reading C[oleridge]'s letter which Fletcher had brought to the door" (118). On 4 May, William "went to bed nervous and jaded in the extreme" (120); 11 May, "He complains that he gets cold in his chest" (124); on 15 May, "William lay very late because he slept ill last night" (125); 23 May, an erased entry, "William was very nervous" (127); the next day, "William slept not till 5 o'clock," and the next day, "again no sleep for Wm" (128). On 2 June she writes, "After dinner William was very unwell," but she erases the last four words (130); on 4 June, "William had slept miserably . . . he got some sleep but was much disordered" (132); on 7 June, "he had slept miserably for 2 nights past" (133); on 9 June, "Wm slept ill"; 10 June, "William very poorly"; 11 June, "William had slept very ill" (p.134); on 13 June, "William had slept better but not well" (135); on 15 June, "William has not slept all night" (136); 19 June, "William has no sleep" (138); 20 June, "he was far from well all day . . . . he could not fall asleep." The next day, "he had slept so miserably" (139); on 25 June, "Wm had not fallen asleep till after 3 o'clock" (142); 30 June, "William slept ill, his head terribly bad" (143). On 6 July Dorothy writes, "William had slept ill" (145).

The entries for the next few months are neither detailed nor continuous, but on 19 October we find "William was much oppressed" (162), and on 2 November, "he was not well" and "William was not well this evening"; on 8 November, "William has been ill in his stomach but he is better tonight" (163); on Christmas Eve she mentions his "poor chest," and on 11 January 1803, a few days before the journal ends, she mentions his "poor chest" again (164 and 166).

Again, we must keep in mind this record is very limited. We can take it that there is much more that was not recorded or was lost. There is much more before and after this period. But the bottom line is that Wordsworth suffered from health problems that have an emotional basis. More interestingly, *Wordsworth's health problems also have a history that relates directly to the composition of poetry*—as if, somehow, the act of writing poetry, or a particular kind of poetry, produced such psychological distress that physiological symptoms showed up; as if, somehow, the feelings put into and set off by the poetry caused a disturbing reenactment of the difficult emotions, causing the kinds of illness cataloged above and making writing difficult. In chapter 4, I will discuss in more detail how this showed up in the intensive, distressing, and productive

German period, in which Wordsworth wrote about writing in "self-defence" and the "uneasiness and heat" in his "stomach and side" that hindered his writing, and Dorothy reported that her brother's industriousness was causing "pain and weakness in the side" (Wordsworth 1967, 236, 247). But after the German period the difficulties persisted. Wordsworth wrote to Coleridge, "Composition I find invariably pernicious to me" (277).

Dorothy makes absolutely clear in early September 1800 the relationship between Wordsworth's health and the production of poetry of feeling:

> William's health is by no means strong, he has written a great deal since we first went to Allfoxden, namely during the year preceding our going into Germany, while we were there, and since our arrival in England, and he writes with so much feeling and agitation that it brings on a sense of pain and internal weakness about his left side and stomach, which now often makes it impossible fo[r] him to [write] when he is in mind and feelings in such a state that he could do it without difficulty. (Wordsworth 1967, 298)

Dorothy's syntax may be a trifle confusing, but what she sees Wordsworth investing in his poetry is not. The emotional experience with "so much feeling" literally cripples him and makes him sick, and we cannot put down such recollections in agitation as simply due to hard work. Three years later Wordsworth himself abundantly confirmed his writing and health problems in explaining his state of health to Sir George Beaumont:

> Owing to a set of painful and uneasy sensations which [I have] more or less at all times about my chest, from a disease which chiefly affects my nerves and digestive organs, and which makes my aversion from writing little less than madness, I deferred writing to you, being at first made still more uncomfortable by travelling, and loathing to do violence to myself. . . . I have now been more than [a] fortnight at home, but the uneasiness in my chest has made [me] beat off the time when the pen was to be taken up. I do not know from what cause it is, but during the last three [y]ears I have never had a pen in my hand for five minutes, [b]efore my whole frame becomes one bundle of uneasiness, [a] perspiration starts out all over me, and my chest is [o]ppressed in a manner which I can not describe. [T]his is a sad weakness, for I am sure, though, it is chiefly owing to the state of my body, that by exertion of mind [I] might in part control it. (407)

The struggle between mind and body apparently comes down to holding a pen in his hand; and holding a pen in his hand comes down to what comes out of that pen. The "cause" of the physiological suffering that Wordsworth troubles to understand is, I believe, the emotional turbulence that is being channeled through the pen: the repressed, the internalized, the forgotten, the unresolved—all struggling for articulation. His body resists and reenacts the pain; his mind and the need for expression push him on. And these difficult years, the "last three [y]ears," roughly 1799–1803, are, arguably, those in which Wordsworth produces his most intensively personal poetry exploring those difficult feelings closest to him.

There is more evidence confirming, to coin a term, the *psychosomapoetics* operating on and in Wordsworth. At the end of April 1801, Dorothy writes to Mary Hutchinson: "William is better than he was a while ago—he is taking a stomachic medicine which I hope will do him good but his digestion is very bad—he is always ill when he tries to alter an old poem—but new composition does not hurt him so much. I hope he will soon be able to work without hurting himself" (332). About a month later she writes to Coleridge: "Poor William! his stomach is in bad plight. We have put aside all the manuscripts poems and it is agreed between us that I am not to give them up even if he asks for them" (335). It is difficult to imagine this situation: Dorothy taking away Wordsworth's poems because they are giving him physical pain, but, as they say, desperate ills call for desperate remedies.

In Dorothy's journal there is much evidence linking the composition of poetry with Wordsworth's bad health. On 23 December 1801 she writes, "William worked at The Ruined Cottage and made himself very ill" (D. Wordsworth 1973, 73). A little over a month later, "Wm wrote out part of his poem and endeavoured to alter it, and so made himself ill" (80). On 2 February 1802, she records the obsessional side of her brother: "William wished to break off composition, and was unable, and so did himself harm" (83). Five days later, the same thing: "William had had a bad night and was working at his poem. We sate by the fire and did not walk, but read the pedlar thinking it done, but lo, though Wm could find fault with no one part of it—it was uninteresting and must be altered. Poor William" (85). And two days later: "He fell to work, and made himself unwell" (87). This continued on for a few more days (88). It thus appears that when Wordsworth began to write, he sometimes experienced a general malady that was a kind of nervous exhaustion. On 18 February 1802: "Then William got to work and was the worse for it" (93); on the 28th, "Wm very ill, employed with the pedlar" (96); and on 4 March, "Wm got to work and was worn to death" (97). Later in the same year, in early May, when working on *The Leech Gatherer*, Dorothy writes that he "went to bed nervous and jaded in the extreme" (120). Watching her brother work on the poem a few days later in fact made her sick: "William worked at the Leech gatherer almost incessantly from morning till tea time.... I was oppressed and sick at heart for he wearied himself to death"; and the next day, "he will be tired out I am sure.

My heart fails in me" (123). And on 14 May she writes, "William very nervous—after he was in bed haunted with altering the Rainbow" (125). Again, her co-dependency is noticeable.

Coleridge, himself greatly interested in unusual psychological disorders and the relationship between emotional and creative states (Mail 1991),[35] and also being a very keen observer of Wordsworth, noticed the problems of his friend's condition. For example, in July 1800, Coleridge writes that it is impossible for Wordsworth to write for a newspaper because of health problems; on 17 September, he writes, "Wordsworth health is but *so so*"; at the end of the month he notes, "Wordsworth's health declines constantly"; and some days later, "Wordsworth's Health is very indifferent" (Coleridge 1956, 1:603, 623, 627, 635). He is aware of the precariousness of Wordsworth's state. Like Dorothy, he also sees the relationship between Wordsworth's health and his writing: "He [Wordsworth] is well, unless when he uses any effort of mind—then he feels a pain in his left side, which threatens to interdict all species of composition to him" (608).

But what Coleridge tried to figure out was the unusual association of ideas and feelings with pain: "In Wordsworth's case . . . you will see a curious instance of ideas, linked with feeling habitually, at length forming blind associations with a particular pain, probably in the right hypochondrium—so as immediately to excite that pain" (606). Aided by the vague application of Hartlian psychology, Coleridge was, in a general sense, quite right. Wordsworth, in thinking about his feelings, manifested by associations those feelings with physiological pain—in particular, that area of the right, upper stomach just below the ribs which is associated with melancholia (this, I take it, is what was meant by the "right hypochondrium"). Coleridge was also onto something else that figures importantly in this study, and that is Wordsworth's grappling with feeling and thought, and he saw its origins in Wordsworth's psychosomatic health problems and what precipitated them. We too, then, should pay attention to Wordsworth's desire to have feeling and thought somehow reconciled, and to see it in the context of his poetry and personal development. We will have to wait until *Tintern Abbey* to see the two fully integrated.

Coleridge, in short, was certain that Wordsworth's physical pains originated in his mind. Wordsworth, he said, was a hypochondriac. In October 1803 he wrote to Thomas Poole about Wordsworth being "benetted in hypochondriacal Fancies," and in January 1804, Coleridge wrote of Wordsworth's "hypochondriacal *Graft* in his Nature," "occasional Hypochondriacal uncomfortableness—from which more or less, and at longer or shorter Intervals, he has never been wholly free from his very Childhood" (2:1013 and 1032). Coleridge, who knew and understood Wordsworth in a profound and personal way, recognized the lifelong battle Wordsworth had with that part of his nature and history. That the onset of these kinds of problems goes right back to Wordsworth's "childhood" is extremely significant, for, as we have seen, it was in Wordsworth's childhood that his emotional life became troubled. It was in his childhood that he experienced trauma and abuse; it was in childhood that he had to turn into himself. The poetry of his early adult life would often reenact these confused emotions as he attempted to discover who he was.

Two broad ranges of mental disorders fit with Wordsworth's history and the pattern of his behavior (though I have to admit it saddens and discomforts me to have to bring clinical labels over to our dead poet when common sense should suffice): one is classified as somatoform/somatization (or psychosomatic), and the other is anxiety. Particular manifestations of Wordsworth's internal turmoil are clearly somatoform disorders. In fact, it was during the age of Wordsworth, in the work of J. Christian Reil in 1803, that the interactional relationship between psychological and physiological events began to be understood and deemed treatable (Wahl 1964, 9–10). (The term "psychosomatic," seems first to have been used in 1818 by Johann Christian Heinroth, though some Coleridgeans suggest that it was Coleridge himself who coined the term.)[36] Today somatoform disorders are accepted forms of mental disorders where there is no overt or demonstrable physical origin for physiologic symptoms (such as abdominal pain or headaches) and are sometimes associated with other behaviors (such as insomnia or depression), yet such symptoms persist; sometimes such physical pain develops following psychological trauma; the person experiences no control over the symptoms, but, significantly, they can be linked to psychological factors.[37] The strong psychosomatic indicators suggest that Wordsworth was at times depressive,[38] and it is also the case that the loss of parents at an early age can also lead to depression (Heinicke 1973).

The second mental disorder that I believe Wordsworth experienced is an anxiety disorder: post-traumatic stress disorder. This results from experiencing a distressing event or events (such as "bereavement" or the "loss of home"); often there are "recurrent and intrusive recollections," and sometimes "dissociative states"; a person "may complain of feeling detached or estranged from other people"; often symptoms are "intensified or precipitated when the person is exposed to situations or activities that resemble or symbolize the original trauma"; "Children may exhibit various physical symptoms, such as stomachaches and headaches"; sleeping problems also often occur.[39] Again, we should not take these kinds of diagnoses to charge Wordsworth with having a completely dysfunctional personality, or to make out that he was some kind of oddball; these kinds of disorders work in degrees rather than as absolutes; and both, over time, and with changing conditions and self-understanding, can fade away. This, I believe, was the case with Wordsworth.

My thesis, then, is not so much that Wordsworth experienced emotional difficulties and the kinds of symptoms outlined above. That much is absolutely clear from the evidence presented. More important is that the feelings associated with these difficulties persisted up to and through his most creative period, and that there is a strong relationship between Wordsworth's history and the production and quality of his poetry.

After 1803–4, the references to Wordsworth's health are considerably less frequent, but they do show up occasionally. For example, in 1809 Dorothy writes to De Quincey: "My brother was indeed very poorly, his head having been continually tormented, and especially upon his pillows at night with those dreadful head-aches (which, you know, he in his gloomy way, calls apoplectic)" (Wordsworth 1969, 292). There may be a number of reasons for the dropping off. Perhaps they are not recorded; certainly there is nothing later on quite as detailed as Dorothy's Grasmere journals for 1800–1803 giving the intricacies of Wordsworth's daily life. Or perhaps his bad health was being taken for granted, and was considered nothing out of the ordinary. I don't believe this was the case. I believe his health changed after, say, 1803–4. These psychogenic illnesses began to fade away because he was, in some significant ways, getting better. The intense and difficult feelings articulated in his poetry were beginning to be resolved by their detailed expression and emotional reenactment. Certainly this is the course that psychotherapy—the talking cure—takes in its progression toward mental health and psychological stability. These days psychotherapists prefer to call it being healed. And as Alice Miller notes throughout her writing, it is the feelings that must be addressed and reenacted in the process of psychotherapy—and this, I hope to show, is what Wordsworth does in his poetry as he works towards unblocking his emotional recollections. This would also, I should add, account for the "decline theory": Wordsworth's poetry changed because the problems that earlier inspired the material of his poetry were no longer there. It may be not the case that Wordsworth's genius failed him or that he experienced a loss of power. The style of his poetry changed with the kinds of changes that were taking place within him as he moved from feeling to thinking, loss to gain, uncertainty to faith. We can look forward to seeing this first in *Tintern Abbey* and later in the *Immortality Ode*, the two halves of which were written at different times.

THE ABANDONED CHILD AND THE ABANDONING FATHER

Late in November 1791, when he was twenty-one years old, Wordsworth went to France to improve his French; he had the vague idea of becoming a tutor.[40] Certainly in the year he spent there, mainly in Blois, Orleans, and Paris, his French must have improved. The plan to become a tutor was not much more than a passing fancy. What cannot also be overlooked is the profound influence that the French Revolution and its aftermath had not just on his politics but on his worldview. He was there at an extraordinary time: in April 1792, France declared war on Prussia and Austria; in August, Louis XVI was dethroned and jailed (and executed in January 1793); September witnessed the Paris massacres and a victory over the Prussians at Valmly; and at the end of October, just about the same time Wordsworth was returning to England, Robespierre was being accused of abusing his power, thus setting the stage for the Reign of Terror. This was quite a different experience from the two months he had spent traveling through France and Switzerland in the summer of 1790 with his college pal, when sightseeing and keeping up a good walking pace seemed to be the most important concerns (Hayden 1983). He recalls this in *The Prelude* as "the glad time when first I traversed France, / A youthful pilgrim" (1805 *Prelude,* bk. 10, lines 449–50). In *Descriptive Sketches*, which was also based on this first tour, Wordsworth portrays himself as a slightly more melancholic solitary wanderer, but his sorrowful state is likely a recollection of how he felt during the composition of the poem in the summer and autumn of 1792 rather than when, as we shall see, his personal life was much more troubled. What happened to him in that second visit, besides his education in revolutionary politics and human nature, must be examined in the context of his past personal life.

A few months after arriving in France, Wordsworth and a French woman a few years older than himself conceived a child.[41] This child was born on 15 December 1792, a week or two after Wordsworth's departure for England. Before he left, he made arrangements for the child's baptism, and in following years he took on some responsibilities to keep in contact with the mother, Annette Vallon, and the child, Anne-Caroline Wordsworth.[42] But despite Annette's clear expectations of being reunited with her "husband" that are expressed within a few months of the birth, this was not to be.[43] We do not know whether this hope was unilateral, but from the letters it appears that Wordsworth had indicated to her that he would see to it that in the not too distant future this family would come together.

Wordsworth's relationship with Annette seems to have been based on more than just a passing fancy. It was not a one-night stand. Although they likely met in Orleans, they also certainly spent much time together during the spring and summer of 1792 in Blois, which was the home of Annette (Reed 1967, 127 n.16). The issue that has to be addressed is why Wordsworth left her. And here we deal with the protective gloss that, unfortunately, has been put on the incident.

One would not expect this kind of protection from Mary Moorman, but it is there. In short, Moorman, quite remarkably, lays the blame on Annette for the failure of this relationship. She suggests that Annette was overemotional and "unsophisticated," and that her only interests were "pure womanly" (1957, 180), as if, somehow, these things would have made her unattractive and would have prevented Wordsworth from fulfilling his spousal and paternal obligations—that is, from wanting a long-term relationship. Her background and connections suggest although her family might not measure up to the solidly middle-class Wordsworths, she nevertheless came from an established but humble family with established ties. Both her father and stepfather were surgeons at a venerated charitable institute, she had brothers who would also become surgeons, she had cousins who were priests, and the family seems to have been politically informed. That later in her life she became directly involved in underground politics (helping people escape from Napoleon's France) also points to a woman of more than usual interests and conviction. There were, admittedly, language and religious problems that would have made it difficult for his potential in-laws to approve of her, especially considering how Wordsworth was thought of by his own relatives. As Wordsworth knew, they were apparently waiting, "with a title," for Wordsworth to enter the clergy (Wordsworth 1967, 76). Annette's few existing letters indicate that she was indeed sensitive, but given the context of those letters, that of a young mother desiring to be with her estranged mate whom she loves deeply, we would expect an outpouring of tenderness and a desire to be reunited. Moreover, we would expect that her sensitivity might have been an attraction rather than a detraction for Wordsworth. Would Wordsworth be attracted to someone not sensitive? To suggest that her interests were "pure womanly" is to reduce Annette to an unfortunate stereotype, which she was not. And even if her interests were "womanly" (whatever that might mean), this would not necessarily make her an unattractive or inferior person in the eyes of Wordsworth. She was, in March 1793, a young woman hoping, waiting, to establish a home with her beloved "husband" and baby: she writes, "Come, my love, my husband, and receive the tender embraces of your wife, of your daughter" (Moorman 1957, 180). Her feelings and expectations are perfectly understandable; Moorman's are not.

Moorman further suggests that "probably the attraction was felt at first more on her side than on his," and that, after a time, Wordsworth saw "some flaw, unrecognized at first, in the beloved object which time and absence gradually revealed" (181). How Wordsworth would come to know her better by absence is a little unclear. Annette's *"flaw,"* according to Moorman, was that she *"undoubtedly lacked* certain qualities which were essential if his love for her was to be permanent" (181; my emphasis). She was, according to Moorman, not in tune with "his exploration of the human spirit, . . . his visionary experience of the natural world," and, unlike other people to whom he could apparently give his love, she was not capable of inspiring him in "the great business of life"—"indeed, . . . she had no conception that such a world even existed as that in which he lived and thought" (181–82). In short, no matter how we put it, from Moorman's perspective she did not have the right stuff to be Wordsworth's soul mate: she had a "flaw," she "lacked certain qualities," she did not have the necessary capabilities to measure up to the man who would be Poet. In not being with Annette, Moorman claims, Wordsworth somehow learned something about her that we are in no way capable of assessing. This assessment is, unfortunately, biased and speculative in the extreme.

Blame is not the way to view any such event. It tends to make people right or wrong, better or worse, and prevents a clear understanding of what takes place. Blame in such circumstances is clearly judgmental, and Moorman unfortunately passes a judgment on Annette that protects Wordsworth. Stephen Gill touches upon the more appropriate way to understand the episode when he describes Annette's letters to Wordsworth as "the cries of a woman who is beginning to fear that she has been abandoned" (1989, 66), but Gill goes no further than this. The word that has so much worth here is "abandoned." So how could Wordsworth abandon this woman and her child? An answer: because abandonment was a powerful determinant in his own life. He was capable of abandoning because he himself was abandoned. It fit with him in ways he was barely capable of grasping. As will be seen in some of the following chapters, in his poetry he repeatedly returns to various reenactments of abandonment that pulls families apart. Many of his most memorable characters are victims of and defined by abandonment and loss, from the vagrant wanderer in *Salisbury Plain* and Martha Ray in *The Thorn,* to Michael in the poem of that name, to both Margaret and the Solitary in *The Excursion*. Wordsworth was, unfortunately, very familiar with this circumstance and the difficult feelings that accompany it. Over time he was very capable of writing about it out of his own experience and subjectivity.

Many commentators point out, quite rightly, that Wordsworth's relationship with Annette gets aired, very obliquely and with little poetic force, in the story of Vaudracour and Julia in the 1805 *Prelude* (bk. 9, lines 556–935), and later in a poem of that name published in 1820.[44] Wordsworth could not or did not want to bring himself to express the incident openly and directly, despite writing at length about his French experiences in books 9 and 10. As Gayatri Chakravorty Spivak writes, "Wordsworth the autobiographer seems more interested at this point in transcending history or coping with it rather than declaring history—in producing a poem rather than a child" (1981, 326). That is, Wordsworth attempts to displace his story with history, but nonetheless the father, mother, and child make an appearance. Perhaps on a public level too much was at risk, and on a private and emotional level the incident was too difficult to come to terms with. It was better, perhaps, that it be blocked out of his poetic discourse of self-growth. The passage was written more than a decade after the actual episode, but it could be argued that in the narrative Wordsworth attempts to at least retrospectively approach the experience and the emotions he felt—in particular, the passion, loss, and the guilt—while at the same time imagining what he might have done or what might have prevented him from acting as he did. The story becomes both a shield and a looking glass. As a sad, even pathetic, romantic tale, the poem conflates his present feelings with those of the past, while, in the spirit of allegory and displaced feelings, his actual guilt works awkwardly towards resolution by a convoluted plot and weak narrative outcome. The tale as Wordsworth tells it is extraordinarily uncertain and confused about what it wants to do and where it wants to go, yet the depths of his feelings are still implanted within the text. In this way it reenacts Wordsworth's state of mind during this episode in his life as he attempted to understand it.[45]

In the 1805 *Prelude*, Wordsworth gives an account of his autobiographical experiences in France, but then he suddenly, and, it seems, arbitrarily, swerves away from this in order to tell of the two "youthful lovers" from different backgrounds: Vaudracour is a young aristocrat, while Julia is "a bright maid from parents sprung / Not mean in their condition." But while he loves everything about Julia, his father "spurned the very thought / Of such alliance." Vaudracour wants to marry her and is "prepared to turn aside / From law and custom" to gain happiness with Julia. With such passion, she becomes pregnant, carrying "about her for a secret grief / The promise of a mother" (105 *Prelude,* bk. 9, lines 556–612). Julia is secretly taken away by her parents to a "distant town" to have the baby, but Vaudracour finds and rapturously meets with her. They part, and resolve that Vaudracour should return to his home to obtain some money; then they could go to "some remote and solitary place" to retire in undisturbed love and happiness. At home he openly declares that "nothing less / Than death" would prevent the hope of being "A blessèd husband of the maid he loved" (lines 612–63). The father threatens to use legal means to stifle Vaudracour's desires, and he hires three ruffians to seize him. Vaudracour kills one, wounds another, but in the end gives up and goes to prison. Julia, meanwhile, not hearing from her lover, contemplates suicide, but Vaudracour, having gained his liberty and breaking a promise not to see Julia, tells her that they can no longer belong to each other: "A murderer," he says, "cannot love / An innocent woman." They spend a few days together, but finding that there is a warrant for his arrest, he hides out until he is caught again while secretly meeting with her (lines 664–741). Once more he is without liberty, but again he is released on the condition that he return to his father's house. A few days before the child is born, Vaudracour and Julia are once more brought together. The child is born, and they pray that "he might never be / As wretched as his father" (lines 742–96). He stays with her two months, still wishing for "future happiness," and he hopes that as soon as his father sees the beauty of the growing child, he will permit their union. But this does not happen. Vaudracour has a further hope: that if he could be excluded from "the birthright of an eldest son," the father might then "sanction" the marriage, but this too is a "Vain request." Then Julia's parents decide that she must "retire / Into a convent" without her child. When Vaudracour hears of this, he falls into a state of "calm despondency" and does not show "even the least emotion" about losing his love forever. The child is placed with a nurse and is taken away. Vaudracour, twenty-four years old, returns "to his father's house," and "of his father beg[s], a final request" that is granted: that he might move to a lonely place in the country with his young child. But after a short time, "by some mistake / Or indiscretion" on the part of Vaudracour, the child dies. Henceforth "he never uttered a word":

> Thus lived the youth,
> Cut off from all intelligence with man,
> And shunning even the light of common day.
> Nor could the voice of freedom, which through France
> Soon afterwards resounded, public hope,
> Or personal memory of his own deep wrongs,
> Rouze him, but in those solitary shades
> His days wasted, an imbecile mind.
>
> (Lines 797–935)

The story ends here, plunked rather enigmatically in the middle of a poem about the growth of Wordsworth's poetic mind and his personal history, and, more particularly, in the middle of his account of being in France. There is nothing else quite like it in *The Prelude*. But keep this in mind: by the 1850 *Prelude*, that is, by the time Wordsworth makes the final revisions to his poeticized life story, the tale of two lovers is more or less edited out of existence—censored, reduced to only the vaguest sketch of an "ill-fated pair" (1850 *Prelude*, bk. 9, lines 553–85). But this swerve away from his experiences in France is, as I have suggested above and will say more about below, the result of a third-person narration troubled by first-person feelings.

If my seesaw sketch seems to provide justification for passing a negative judgment on the literary worth of this tale, it is in good company, for even Ernest de Selincourt, perhaps the most knowledgeable of all Wordsworthians, places the poetry among Wordsworth's worst, and he finds the outcome "ludicrous" and "a climax of absurdity difficult to parallel in our literature" (Wordsworth 1926, 574). De Selincourt nonetheless sees the tale as a compromised reenactment of Wordsworth's "passion for Annette," and he also suggests that the experience changed the poet in ways he himself might not have been able to perceive: "That it had more influence upon his mind and art than he believed it to have is probable; it can hardly be doubted, for example, that he owed to it that sympathetic penetration into the heart of the deserted woman, and the relations of mother and child, which is a marked feature of his poetry from 1795 to 1805" (573). Paul Sheats with a slightly narrower focus writes that Annette "must be recognized as a contributory cause of the psychological crisis that did shape the poetry of 1797 and 1798" (Sheats 1973, 272–73 n. 10). I would agree with these observations, adding that the experience sadly confirmed the emotional world in which Wordsworth was nurtured.

Onorato views the tale as expressing Wordsworth's unconscious obsession with the death of babes, his unresolved "grievance against his own unnurturing father," his tendency for "psychic withdrawal," and the trauma of maternal separation. He also finds in the tale Wordsworth's conflict between personal love and social commitment (Onorato 1971, 327–32). While I believe aspects of these observation are true—more particularly, that Wordsworth held within him his family troubles and circumstances—Onorato does not fit his reading strongly to Wordsworth's actual experience. The tale intersects with Wordsworth's personal history in being the account of a child separated, first of all, from his mother, and then, in death, from his father; and Wordsworth seems condemned to reenact this history in his relationship with Annette and her child. The tale, then, bridges Wordsworth's own family circumstances with what happened to him in France.

We can locate in the story parallels with Wordsworth's own situation and his experiences with Annette. First, it takes place it a respected town "in the heart of France" (1805 *Prelude,* bk. 9, line 563); second, the two lovers have different social backgrounds, with Vaudracour/Wordsworth in the superior position; third, in the story there is strong family disapproval, which certainly would have been the case from Wordsworth's relatives; fourth, there is the pregnancy and birth out of wedlock; fifth, as in the case with Caroline's birth, it takes place away from her hometown; sixth, there is the resolution to be together, which seems to have been the plan of Wordsworth and Annette; seventh, the age of Vaudracour, given as twenty-four at the end of the tale coincides closely (if not exactly) with Wordsworth's age; eighth, the story centers around Vaudracour's perspective and feelings; and finally, the relationship fails. There are obviously numerous differences, but the frame of reference and the structure of the situation make it clear that in the tale of Vaudracour and Julia is the vicarious representation of Wordsworth's feelings about the Vallon affair. As it is told, it may be out of synch with the style of *The Prelude*, but it reflects the kind of emotional trauma Wordsworth suffered both at the time and later, in poetic retrospection.

In Wordsworth's incarnation of Vaudracour we can see the attempt to do in narrative what might have been tried in life: against all odds the father does all he can to be with his wife and child to keep the family unit together, the hope being to live with them in solitary happiness. As Spivak quite rightly puts it without referring to the details of Wordsworth's life and personality, "The possibility of his being a father is handled in the Vaudracour and Julia episode" (1981, 326). But we are shown how Vaudracour is broken "down in heart and mind" (1805 *Prelude,* bk. 9, line 751) by the situation and emotional pressures. The story is based around the idea of *promise* and Wordsworth's apparent difficulty in understanding if Vaudracour did the right thing (Caruth 1987), as Wordsworth certainly wondered in his handling of his own affair. In the end, Vaudracour is the abandoned figure, the figure, of course, that Wordsworth knows best; he is a figure of uncertainty and confusion. The ideal family that is imaginatively constituted in the tale remains a potential negated by hostile and unfortunate circumstances. Everyone loses—including Wordsworth, who is obviously befuddled by and entangled in the unhappy family romance he has put on the page.

Despite Stephen Gill's opinion that "None of this biographical material [i.e., the Vallon affair], perhaps, demands inclusion in an account of the growth of a poet's mind" (1991, 78), I believe that the tale of two lovers does indeed deserve a place in the story of his life as the sadly allegorized representation of his relationship with Annette Vallon, even if we have to painfully reconstruct it out of a bad plot. Should it be left out just because it does not meet with certain critical standards, or because there is a flaw in Wordsworth's attempt to poetically unburden himself? It is not the kind of experience that can be brushed aside as unimportant in anyone's history or inner life. Wordsworth had to deal with it in the best way he could, though to some it may appear lacking. So although it is important poetry, it is not, artistically speaking, Wordsworth's best poetry. In what he un-wrote into the story of Vaudracour and Julia we nonetheless detect feelings too deep for tears.

But some of the poetry written on his visit to see Annette and Caroline in August 1802, in the Calais sonnets,[46] is, artistically speaking, among his best, and it too, like the tale of Vaudracour and Julia, can be read as embedded with his confused feelings over Annette and Caroline, just as some of Wordsworth's inner turmoil is expressed in *The Borderers*, written 1796–97.[47] For detailed readings of the sonnets I defer to Judith W. Page, who sees in some of these poems Wordsworth's reflections on marriage and paternity as they relate to Annette and Caroline. Page views Wordsworth in *It is a beauteous Evening* as "distancing" himself from his child by making her an abstraction, evading "his particular responsibilities to his illegitimate daughter Caroline," using "patriarchal religious language to sanction his actions" which release him from responsibility, and placing "Caroline in the hands of God—a substitute father for the father Wordsworth knows he will never be." Moreover, at the end of the sonnet, when the "Girl" / Caroline is mde to lie "in Abraham's bosom," this can be read as symbolically killing the child—"a father willing to sacrifice his child." Page's conclusion about Wordsworth's investment in this poetry: "Although Wordsworth might try to submerge or disguise this private self and its anxieties, his sonnets are more revealing and powerful because he fails to do so" (Page 1988, 198–201).

At this point in his life, in the summer of 1802, Wordsworth was at a crossroads, and he might have been looking for emotional liberty, for in just over a month he would be married to Mary Hutchinson, an act that would allow him now to visit his child and her mother with some feelings of safety. Was he there in order to break this news to Annette? Was it guilt, honor, curiosity, love, or a combination of these that took him back to France?

In her journal, Dorothy beautifully describes that month in France—the long walks along the beach under black and gloomy skies, with the coast of England across the dark seas ever present, like a beacon summoning them home (D. Wordsworth 1973, 152–53). The weather in that August of 1802 seems to have been as brooding as Wordsworth must have been. Dorothy made another copy of this part of her journal, but in it she omitted the last sentence, which described a little girl's response to the sparkling ocean on one hot, calm night in the summer of 1802: "Caroline was delighted" (153 n. 4). This was in many ways a cruel cut, symbolic, perhaps, of the sadness that sometimes comes closest to Wordsworth's very deepest feelings in his moments of crisis.

These days we know that in experiences with profound loss, there is often an initial suppression of feelings. As two of the leading consultants on loss, grief, and recovery put it, "the time bomb ticks softly," and there are clear signs of trouble that show themselves in sleeplessness, confusion, fear ("of the future and fear of the past"), and in feelings of isolation (James and Cherry 1989, 47–48). Wordsworth's life, from the death of his mother to the separation from his child, was dominated by loss, and hence the kinds of symptomatology displayed in his health, his action, and, in terms of subject material, the kind of poetry he would write.

In *The Prelude*, Wordsworth describes revolutionary France, like his once-Edenic childhood, as paradise lost. "Bliss was it in that dawn to be alive" when, like the "budding rose" (an image from "Paradise itself"), the time held so much "promise" (1805 *Prelude*, bk. 10, lines 692–705). But it was not to be. His personal and political ideals fell as one, and his childhood feelings of loss, confusion, meaninglessness, and abandonment are repeated and conflated.[48] It can only be his past experience that predisposed his intense response to the present, otherwise his devastating response to the failure of the Revolution would be difficult to account for; and that past, with its agonizing confusion and irresolution, now came flooding back to him. History reenacted his story—or at least he made it seem to do so. He did not know how to feel or what to think: "all passions, notions, shapes of faith" were called into question:

> now believing,
> Now disbelieving, endlessly perplexed
> With impulse, motive, right and wrong, the ground
> Of moral obligation—what the rule,
> And what the sanction—till demanding proof,
> And seeking it in every thing, I lost
> All feeling of conviction, and, in fine,
> Sick, wearied out with contraries,
> Yielded up moral questions in despair. . . .
>
> (Lines 889–901)

Wordsworth saw France's war with England (declared by France in February 1793) as threatening to destroy his happy childhood experiences and the chance for these memories and experiences to mature naturally:

> I, who with the breeze
> Had played, a green leaf on the blessed tree
> Of my beloved country—nor had wished
> For happier fortune than to wither there—
> Now from my pleasant station was cut off,
> And tossed about in whirlwinds.
>
> (Lines 253–58)

The threat of discontinuity was something that Wordsworth found hard to bear, and as a problem it motivated a great deal of his poetic intimations.

In the years between his French experiences up until about the summer of 1796, Wordsworth was unsettled and, for the most part, unhappy. We might picture him as a sensitive young man, solipsistically inclined, confused about his past and uncertain about his future, wandering about England and Wales, projecting his feelings onto the forsaken figures and landscape he encountered. He was, as it were, a lost child.[49] In September 1795, he settled at Racedown with Dorothy, and there he took on the role of foster parent to a two-year-old child whose father had trouble taking care of him; it was an act no less kind for being perhaps motivated by his own past feelings and more recent experience with family separation.[50] The child taken on might have assuaged his guilt for having just deserted his own child.

Wordsworth moved slowly but surely towards an intense crisis late in 1795, a crisis that spilled over into 1796. Almost all commentators refer to this as a moral or spiritual crisis,[51] as if somehow this virtual breakdown had to do with philosophical problems of belief or some such thing. In truth he was depressed and likely moving towards a nervous breakdown.[52] He did not write much poetry: "Reluctantly to England I returned, . . . well assured / That I both was and must be of small worth. . . . A poet only to myself, to men / Useless" (lines 188–201). Ultimately Wordsworth's story of experiences in France will not do. Our poet at this point was not sure whether Godwinism, the certainties of mathematics, nature, or even his own mind could see him through. Who he was and the meaning of his experiences had to be approached, and this called for a new kind of poetry that would begin to express his deepest feelings.

2
The Poet's Progress:
Early Struggle, Early Gain

> Unfinished business from the past doesn't simply disappear. If it is not dealt with, it remains buried inside. Then the wounded inner child resurfaces later in unexpected and troubling ways.
> —Covington and Beckett, *Leaving the Enchanted Forest*

Time to take stock: Now that aspects of Wordsworth's life have been worked through, it can be suggested that both his development and some of his poetry tend to follow a pattern something like that outlined by Elisabeth Kübler-Ross in her landmark studies on death, dying, and grief. She sees five stages of grief and loss that have to be negotiated or experienced in order to accept the notion of death: 1) denial and isolation; 2) anger; 3) bargaining; 4) depression; and, finally, 5) acceptance (Kübler-Ross 1970). While her observations are focused primarily on the dying person, these sequential though not absolute stages are often paralleled in the behavior of the bereaved. Except for bargaining (which has to do with postponement, making final promises, or being given one last chance to do or complete something), these are defined here clearly enough by Kübler-Ross's simple terms. While I do not intend to apply Kübler-Ross's observations in any rigorous or direct way in this study, I believe it may be useful to keep in mind the general process she outlines—the movement from denial and isolation to acceptance—as we examine Wordsworth's personal history, the subject matter in his poetry, and his development as a individual. After all, loss, and especially loss associated with death, is the most prevalent subject in Wordsworth's early poetry.

Wordsworth's bereavement was extended and delayed by the circumstances described in the previous chapter. The mother's and father's projected presence into nature can be seen as a form of *denial*. His promises to be true to nature were also a forms of *bargaining*, of attempting to trade off loss for gain. In fact, much of his poetry might be read as a poetry of emotional bargaining, of negotiating loss and gain. Wordsworth's sense of *isolation* was continuous, and began, perhaps, even before the death of his mother, within family circumstances that might not have always nurtured positive emotional growth. Wordsworth himself tells us of his *anger* and moodiness as a child (and we have seen how this showed up psychosomatically). At this moment in the story of Wordsworth, we find him in the middle of a kind of lingering *depression* that weighed him down over a number of years. We might hope, then, to find intimations of *acceptance* in Wordsworth's subsequent poetry, keeping in mind that it might be the point his poetry and personal development were working towards.

These stages and terms, then, might be helpful in attempting to understand Wordsworth as an individual who tried to find his way through loss and grief to maturity, both as person and a poet. At this moment in the story, as a new chapter begins, he was beginning to discover that being one might depend on becoming the other.

When Wordsworth returned from France in December 1792, he must have been emotionally stunned by all that had happened to him. He had left his lover and child, and he had no professional prospects, almost no money, and no home. He was without any constant companions, and even more at odds with his relatives because of his French affair and political views. His relatives seemed determined to keep Dorothy and William apart. The brother and sister had to make secret plans to meet each other. Within a few months of his return to England, Louis XVI would be executed, and France and England would declare war on each other, and this, as Wordsworth put it in *The Prelude*, caused him to feel "the ravage of this most unnatural strife / In my own heart" (1805 *Prelude*, bk. 10, lines 249–51). Wordsworth would not have been, at this time, on the right side of government or popular opinion—or of his relatives. Sitting in church with his countryman while they prayed for victories over the French, he recalled: "I only, like an uninvited guest / Whom no one owned, sate silent" (lines 268–73). This is an epiphany of alienation. In such a circumstance, confused by the hope of the Revolution and with an abandoned child in France, he felt like an outsider within his own country—and within himself.

Wordsworth stayed in London for more than half a year after his arrival from France. He stayed with his brother, Richard, for most of this time, but it is unlikely that it was a happy living situation, since of Wordsworth's siblings, Richard was perhaps the least like Wordsworth. The two never seemed to share the same views or interests. But at least while he was in London he managed to have *Descriptive Sketches* and *An Evening Walk* published. Wordsworth must have felt a little satisfaction in seeing the results of the emerging poet within himself.

De Quincey records in his essay on Wordsworth (published 1839) that during this time in London, Wordsworth experienced a "crisis of his fate" and "became a martyr to some nervous affliction." To keep his mind off his "sense of distress," nightly his friends played cards with him (De Quincey 1970, 191–92). It is, in some ways, very hard to imagine Wordsworth sitting around a card table, night after night, with his London friends, but that is apparently what he did to fill his time. What else did he have to do? But more important, this may be the first public mention of the poet's "crisis," a "nervous affliction" that began early in 1793. It was obviously something more than mild stress, and it was not a kind of spiritual crisis. In a few years Dorothy would delicately note that her brother lived in an "unsettled way" in London that was "altogether unfavorable to mental exertion" (Wordsworth 1967, 149). Wordsworth was lost, alone, and he did not really know where to go or what to do.

Wandering Lonely, 1793–95

By late June or early July 1793, Wordsworth left London with an old school friend, William Calvert, but after a carriage accident, a month later, they split up. Wordsworth, alone and on foot, traveled across the Salisbury plains, stopping at Stonehenge, passing by Tintern Abbey and Goodrich Castle, and finally making his way to North Wales to visit Robert Jones, who had been his touring companion during his walking trip through France and Switzerland in 1790. He arrived at Jones's sometime late in August. Wordsworth may have made a very brief return to France in early October (Reed 1967, 147 n. 14; MacGillivray 1930), which, given the hostilities between England and France at the time, would have been extremely dangerous. If he did go, it was likely motivated by a desire to see Annette and, for the first time, his daughter Caroline. That he could not stay, or bring them back, must have been at least as agonizing as the first time. He would now be able to picture an actual young child, his own, as a figure of abandonment. His own feelings of abandonment may have come back to him.

Wordsworth, then, remained unsettled, uncertain, and unhappy. During this same time, Dorothy was very concerned about her brother's welfare, and she too felt very much alone. She wrote to Jane Pollard in the summer of 1794 when Wordsworth was wandering about by himself: "I often hear from my dear Brother William, I am very anxious about him just now as he has not yet got any settled Employment." Dorothy expresses her love for "William my earliest and dearest Male Friend," and she imagines her brother leading her to the most perfect of all cottages, a retreat they might call their own. She admits she is blinded by her fondness for William, but her need to be with him is obsessive and overwhelming: "You can have no Idea of my Impatience to see this dear Brother" (Wordsworth 1967, 95–104, 109). We do not have Wordsworth's letters to Dorothy during this time, but we can assume that his feelings corresponded with her sense of anxiousness and isolation. It would be a few years before her wish would come true.

In February 1794, William and Dorothy met again, but they did not have the means to permanently stay together. To her relatives at Penrith she had to justify her desire to extend her visit with William, and there was both resentment and determination in her tone as she wrote to them: "I am now twenty two years of age and such have been the circumstances of my life that I may be said to have enjoyed his company only for a *very few* months. An opportunity now presents itself of obtaining this satisfaction, an opportunity which I could not see pass from me without unspeakable pain" (117). Dorothy would not be denied.

But things had not yet settled for Wordsworth. He was still without purpose. In February he wrote to William Mathews:

[S]ince I had the pleasure of seeing you, I have been do[ing] nothing and I still continue to do nothing. What is to become of me I know not: I cannot bow down my mind to take orders, and as for the law I have neither strength of mind purse or constitution, to engage that pursuit. (112)

Three months later, in another letter to Mathews, he responded to plans about starting up a modest periodical, but he did not have enough money to get it going: "I am so poor that I could not advance any thing"; however, he also wrote that he had plenty of time on his hands (118–19). At the end of the year, in December, when the suggestion was made that he become a reporter, he wrote back that when exposed "to a heated atmosphere or to loud noises" he became subject to "nervous headaches" (138). There seems to be little at this time that Wordsworth could face up to. The letter continues:

I have no news to communicate; and not liking to send you so much blank paper as is now before me, I have paused for a moment to reflect in what way I must fill it up. . . . I have no apology to make; I have lately undergone an uneasiness of mind; but I have had sufficient *time* on my hand to write a folio Vol:! I am therefore without excuse.... I fear you will be unable to decypher this scrawl. I must learn to write a better hand, before I can earn my bread by my pen. (138–39)

Wordsworth would need more than good handwriting to become a successful writer. He would have to poetically tap that "uneasiness of mind" and explore the source of those "nervous headaches." He would have to find subjects that, in the spirit of both catharsis and self-exploration, would reflect his own emotional condition. I believe that it took him about ten years to clear himself of these feelings; emotional healing is not a quick fix. At this point in his life, Wordsworth's sense of self was very fragile. But at least in his sister Dorothy he had found someone to transcribe his "scrawl"; it is just about at this time that she took on the lifelong job of custodian of his writings.

During the final months of 1794, Wordsworth watched over Raisley Calvert (William's younger brother) as he slowly moved towards death. Months before Raisley's death in January 1795, Wordsworth knew he would be receiving a substantial legacy (nine hundred pounds), and he made sure that the money would not be taken from him and used to pay off his debts. Not until he began to receive some of this money in early 1795 and he rented a place at Racedown with Dorothy in September of that year were there even any vague feelings of prospect or purpose. A poet yet he would be. As Wordsworth put it in *The Prelude*, Calvert's support "cleared a passage" for him, giving him some amount of freedom to make choices (1805 *Prelude,* bk. 13, lines 349–67).

While crossing the Salisbury Plain in 1793, Wordsworth's poetic identity as we now conceive it began to form. In his recollection of this lonely walk as described in *The Prelude*, he claims to have experienced a "reverie," a vision of a primitive past and of human sacrifice (bk. 12, lines 312–53). More interesting, however, is the poetry we now refer to as the Salisbury Plain poems: *Salisbury Plain* (which is the core text for these others), *Adventures on Salisbury Plain, Guilt and Sorrow;* and carved out of these, *The Female Vagrant.*[1]

In the earliest of these poems, *Salisbury Plain* (composed, roughly, between the summers of 1793–94, but not published), Wordsworth moves towards the subject of individual human suffering and a more direct examination of the feelings of isolation and hopelessness.[2] A peripheral social consciousness frames the poem, but what he most of all projects into the surroundings and into the history he relates are feelings that have been working on him, feelings that have filtered through his own circumstances and personality. When the poem opens, Wordsworth pictures for us a homeless and lonely traveler moving across a shadeless, uninhabited wasteland—"And vacant the huge plain around him spread" (line 62). Something like Shakespeare's Lear, he appears to be "the only creature in the wild / On whom the elements their rage could wreak" (lines 66–67). He wanders lonely through the storm until he comes to a shelter where he encounters a sleeping female vagrant. She wakes in terror, thinking that the traveler might be a murderer. But they discover that they are bonded by their despondent circumstances, and she tells her history. She was (like Wordsworth)[3] brought up beside the Derwent; her father was a fisherman. Her mother died when she was born. The pastoral happiness in which she was nurtured offered "thoughtless joy" (line 231), but, as a teenager, this ended abruptly. Rights to their fishing grounds were denied, and they were forced to leave their land. A young friend took them in; she married him, and within four years had three children. War put demands on their land, and when her father died, she and her family were forced to go to the New World, but within one year her husband and children were dead. Traumatized, forlorn, her spirit broken, she returned to England, wandering hopelessly, waiting for death. Interspersed with her tale as they move from their shelter and into the morning, the sun shines through, downs glisten, larks warble, and they see herds of cattle moving in lush green meadows. But the tale ends without any prospect for this "friendless hope-forsaken pair" (line 415), and Wordsworth as narrator steps outside of the story to bring in the point of injustice.

The poem should be considered very important in understanding the history of Wordsworth's poetic development.[4] It marks the beginning of his break from the loco-descriptive or topographical tradition that had, until this time, drawn upon his poetic talents. Equally important is that he simultaneously attempted to formulate a kind of contemplative stability in the midst of, and because of, the suffering, isolation, hopelessness, and homelessness that he encountered in the reflective landscape, though in *Salisbury Plain* he did not yet have the imaginative power or state of mind to abundantly redress or counter the loss. Soon he would be closer to expressing and meeting these needs. Positive intimations in face of negative feelings become a repeating pattern in Wordsworth's poetry, and it was born out of the necessity, on Wordsworth's part, to find compensatory meaning in what he felt and experienced. And often, as in the female vagrant's tale, there is a structure of a past paradise, a fall, destitute circumstances, and an uncertain future, though eventually he would be able to point to a philosophic mind to see his troubled feelings through. Eventually he would be able to transform that uncertainty into hope, and that hope into faith. One of the places, then, to find Wordsworth's originality and power is in those clashes of moods and voices and characters, for it is this area, in the dialogue of emotions where thought and feeling attempt to meet and transform and work on each other, that Wordsworth is, paradoxically, most troubled and articulate. Here is his transformational poetry. He knows what he is talking about, even in his confusion. In the production of art, this is a surely a good thing. We just have to look carefully at the kinds of characters and situations that Wordsworth sets up in his poems to see what makes Wordsworth work. His poetry is not based on a studied sympathy for others; it is based on poetically expressed feelings for himself. The lonely wanderer and the despondent vagrant both embody qualities and circumstances close to Wordsworth's condition. And if they are credible characters at all, it is not so much because Wordsworth had creative empathy for them as because he was moving towards expressing feelings and circumstances that were beginning to touch and draw upon his own inner life.

But even while the strength and immediacy of the feelings in *Salisbury Plain* are evident and a kind of poetic agenda is set, these feelings do not seem fully realized. They are in some ways awkward, insufficient, and partially held off, but not because they are stiflingly uncertain; indeed, as mentioned, Wordsworth, of all poets, was capable of making the most out of emotional uncertainty. Moreover, all the important Wordsworthian topics are there: inexplicable death, individual suffering, loss, and separation; parents die, a child is abandoned, and a home is lost; innocence ends abruptly and faith is questioned; a landscape is washed over with both hope and despair. These are all very close to home for Wordsworth, and we can say that the generalized subject material and the attendant feelings are rooted deep within Wordsworth's own history and subjective self. But the overt wandering he makes into the realm of social critique (especially towards the end of the poem) may demonstrate that he does not know what to do with those emotional wounds he has opened, and what caused them, or that he cannot firmly place such emotions in a social context. It is relatively easy to say, "Well, here is a social injustice, it is wrong, and it must be changed." This is not so easy to say about individual human suffering and persistently troubling emotions, especially when they are your own: "Well, here are my problems, they are difficult, and I must change." How can one change one's feelings or escape from them? Wordsworth made a first step by laying them out on the page before him. He would need more time—and many more pages.

In the next few years following his start on *Salisbury Plain*, Wordsworth composed very little poetry. He was still not so sure of his calling. Others, however, like his sister and Raisley Calvert,[5] firmly believed in his gifts, and they kept the hope alive. During these crucial years he would become acquainted with Coleridge, William Southey, Joseph Cottle, and William Godwin, and these four would also figure importantly in fostering his poetic career and ideas.

The years between France and a more settled time were described by Wordsworth in vaguest terms, as if they constituted a kind of limbo in his life. In the last book of *The Prelude* he writes:

> Since I withdrew unwillingly from France,
> The story hath demanded less regard
> To time and place; and where I lived, and how,
> Hath been no longer scrupulously marked.
> Three years, until a permanent abode
> Received me with that sister of my heart
> Who ought by rights the dearest to have been
> Conspicuous through this biographic verse—
> Star seldom utterly concealed from view—
> I led an undomestic wanderer's life.
> In London chiefly was my home, and thence
> Excursively, as personal friendships, chance
> Or inclination led, or slender means
> Gave leave, I roamed about from place to place,
> Tarrying in pleasant nooks, wherever found,
> Through England or through Wales.
>
> (1805 *Prelude,* bk. 13, lines 332–49)

This is an extraordinarily vague gloss on these times, arguably his most difficult adult years. Wordsworth obviously cannot find some sense or particularized order in what he was doing for these "three years" when he was down and out in England and Wales—depressed, homeless, with "slender means," alone, and confused. We already know that when he writes, "I withdrew unwillingly from France," he is speaking volumes about a traumatic experience he does not directly confront in this, his "biographic verse." He only recalls that in approaching this period in his life, as he "roamed" aimlessly about here and there, "time and place" themselves seem to have been misplaced. He cannot come up with any real excuse for this three-year blur. It is not like Wordsworth to apologize for passing over the details of his life. *The Prelude* is supposed to be rationalized by Wordsworth as an effort to find and qualify the poet in his life. What he did, how he felt, is buried deeply within this passage. But we see here that this very important time is more or less a personal and poetic gap, a twilight zone, conspicuous in its vagueness and remarkable by its understatement.

From Racedown to Alfoxden, 1795–97

The "permanent abode" in which he finally settled at the age of twenty-six was Racedown, in Dorset. In September 1795, Wordsworth, Dorothy, and young Basil Montagu went to live there rent-free and in relative isolation. Besides ordering six pairs of shoes, including four heavy-duty pairs for walking (Wordsworth 1967, 155),[6] one of the first things he did was radically revise

Salisbury Plain. But the revisions make abundantly clear that Wordsworth did not know what he wanted to do with the poem. As Reed puts it, Wordsworth's "troubles" with the poem "appear to have stemmed from his inability to draw the poem into [a] final state from this point" (1967, 333–36). He did not even really know what kind of "final state" he wanted from his poem. Wordsworth himself was without any notion of finality, completion, and certainty. There may have been too much in the poem—or at least too much going in too many directions. Paul Sheats suggests that in 1795 Wordsworth's feelings of "fear and guilt" began to show up, perhaps as a result of his French affair (1973, 114), and we have to add this to the other stressful factors of the time. The MSS for *Salisbury Plain* suggest that Wordsworth was fuzzy about what he wanted to be central to the poem (Wordsworth 1975, 6–16), and this uncertainty is a reflection of his state of being. Wordsworth would have been at a loss in his own personal priorities. Likely he was intimidated by what found its way into the poem, and was not quite ready to face it. Poetically, he could not find a form to accommodate what needed expressing. He would eventually have to invent one.

After about a year at Racedown, Wordsworth began a play, first called *A Tragedy* and later titled *The Borderers*. The bulk of it was composed between autumn 1796 and spring 1797, though Wordsworth added to it and refined it significantly after this time.[7] It was not the kind of play that was well suited to the popular stage, and after it was submitted by Coleridge to an acquaintance at Covent Garden it was rejected. In its outer appearances it is simply too wordy, too abstract, and too didactic. Even more so than *Salisbury Plain*, it is very dark work, but in the substance and expression of what it communicates, it is often very powerful. The emotions in the play are stark. In part, this may have had to do with Wordsworth's discovery and use of blank verse, rather than the more constricting Spenserian stanza that is found in *Salisbury Plain*. One of the other main differences between *Salisbury Plain* and *The Borderers* is that the political, legal, and social dimensions are even more secondary to an examination of individuals in crisis (Stoddard 1980, 93).[8] The plot, in which an evil character (Rivers) convinces a naïve character (Mortimer) to commit a murder, is almost incidental to the kinds of psychological subjects that dominate the play: personality, motivation, blame, guilt, suffering, sorrow, victimization, betrayal, loneliness, isolation, desperation, pride, death, and evil. As mentioned in the previous chapter, Moorman suggests that the play is a study of "criminal psychology" (1967, 302), but she is closer to the truth when she also sees in the play reenactments of Wordsworth's own "mental conflicts during the past three years" (304). Even the setting for the play, which evokes the area around Penrith (Osborn 1976), is unsettling and significant in terms of Wordsworth's experiences with the Cooksons. For very brief moments the play seems to find some light and redemption as Mortimer, the object of Rivers's manipulations, tries to understand what he has done and to find some peace, but they do not stay for long. It is in the person of Rivers,[9] the play's unrelenting central character, that Wordsworth may have gone his furthest into the heart of darkness and seen the horror within. As Rivers says in the most memorable lines in the early version of the play:

> Suffering is permanent, obscure and dark,
> And has the nature of infinity.
>
> (Wordsworth 1982, 214)

Mortimer is left at the very end of the play to feel and live with what he has done. He will "wander on" in his "uncertain way" without hope in the silence of his own "pain," "Living by mere intensity of thought" until he dies (294).

Up until this point in Wordsworth's life, all of this would have been close to his own experience. Here his own bleak outlook and the confusion about the origin, duration, and endurance of his own guilt-ridden sufferings get expressed by both Rivers and Mortimer. It has been suggested that the way Marmaduke cannot have his lover parallels the way Wordsworth could not have Annette (Erdman 1978, 16–17). There was so much in Wordsworth that needed expressing. Without his art, without poetry, he certainly would have found other ways to act out his feelings, and some of them might have led to an indefinite continuation of his unhappiness. Poetry, as writing therapy, allowed Wordsworth an active voice in the possibility of recovery. As Alice Miller points out, unless the truth of feelings are met and confronted, healing cannot take place (see especially Miller 1990b, 147–66). Wordsworth's poetic voices often sound such personal confrontation.

The Borderers, despite its sprawling gothic nature, perhaps reflects Wordsworth at his lowest point. But this is good, for only by hitting the bottom does the bottom become something real, something from which to work. Wordsworth began to see himself in this dark time. That this low point appears in this, his only play, where acting out can take place on a literal level, is significant. Wordsworth does not so much visualize aspects of the landscape; he is much more interested in trying to come to terms with the darker side of personality components and problems of motivation and responsibility. Wordsworth wanted to know about himself and what made him act. And we see in the characterizations in the play both the power and determination to explore and enact, in a frightening way, these kinds of questions. We will not see a character quite like Rivers again in Wordsworth's poetry, though up until the Solitary of *The Excursion* we will encounter many softer versions of him. Through the figure of Rivers, Wordsworth exorcised some of the demon in himself, and he could foresee where embracing Rivers might take him. He could use his powers of articulation and his determination, but not his direction.

Book 10 of the 1805 *Prelude* gives in outline the dimensions of Wordsworth's crisis after France and his movement towards recovery during this time at Racedown. But events long before France predisposed him to this moment, giving him both strength and vulnerability. Intellectual confusion and conflicting emotions put him in a state of paralysis and complete discomposure; and he believed that only the abstract certainties of mathematics offered him any future and consolation (1805 *Prelude,* bk. 10, lines 889–904). But now, at Racedown, he records that his sister reminded him of "a saving intercourse / With my true self"; she preserved in him the name of Poet; and finally, and most important, with nature's help, "the feelings of my earlier life" were revived (lines 907–24). If he is to find the strength anywhere, it will be in these "feelings" that remain behind but are always there with him. At the very least, the direction of his poetic calling would have been made more clear.

The completion of a first draft of *The Borderers* in the spring of 1797 would have given Wordsworth both some psychological relief and professional confidence—he had completed a work of significant scope that tapped, albeit somewhat uncomfortably and at a distance, into his emotional life. Other poetry was being composed this spring, but it was taking a different direction and was demonstrating the kind of clarity in diction and style that can be found in his most characteristic work. So too in subject matter we begin to see an attempt to open a dialogue with particular issues and problem. Carl Woodring describes Wordsworth's position at this point: "At 27, Wordsworth stood on the edge of great poetic power; he had not yet achieved it" (1968, 19).

Lines left upon a Seat in a Yew-tree (composed while completing the play) offers a kind of postscript to the thinking that dominates *The Borderers;* the poem suggests that pride and contempt for life are ultimately self-defeating. We have here one of the first suggestions of Wordsworth as the transformational poet, controlling himself both as narrator and object of narration as he attempts to formulate restoration from depravation, gain from loss. He uses the third person, but it is Wordsworth situating his feelings via the license of artistic retrospection and introspection. He opens the poem claiming to "well remember" who it was that once sat in the desolate landscape in which he now finds himself. Indeed! He recalls the young solitary idealist with "lofty views" who went forth into a hostile world that could not meet all of his expectations; who, after being caught in the mire of "his own unfruitful life" and saddened to tears "to think that others felt / What he must never feel," died, leaving behind the place where he sat as "his only monument" (lines 1–43)—not including the poem itself, of course.

This depressed "lost man" (line 40) with his oxymoronic feelings—his "morbid pleasure" and "mournful joy" (lines 28, 39)—is an ambivalent construction. He is exemplary in his individuality, talents, and motives, as well as in his dissociative capabilities to "gaze / On the more distant scene . . . till it became / Far lovelier" (lines 30–33), although this kind of dissociative behavior (common in Wordsworth) might also be suggestive of past trauma. Likewise, his suffering is perceived as noble, even natural, in its humility. He does, after all, fit rather unobtrusively into the landscape among the sheep, birds, rocks, and plants. But his development is blocked by his own solipsistic and dispirited behavior, and he cannot go beyond dwelling upon what has been an "unfruitful life" (line 29). He is stuck in it. He needs and gets, as it were, a kick in the butt from the narrator, being reminded that despite "lowliness of heart" (line 60), knowledge and dignity can be maintained by self-esteem, if he can "revere himself" (line 59). Although the feelings of regret and loss as experienced by the idealist can, according to the narrator, be countered by "inward thought" (line 57), that this morbidly introspective figure dies suggests Wordsworth has not taken control of his own present condition. But he can see it.

Lines left upon a Seat in a Yew-tree acts all of this out, and, most importantly, recognizes and articulates it as a problem with a possible solution. The details of what happened to this "lost man" that put him in such a condition are not as important as his *response*: what he did and how he felt. This is a significant point in Wordsworth's development. Again, how it happened deserves some attention, yet at the same time it is incidental. The attendant feelings are where Wordsworth best displays his expressive talents: on one hand the trauma, isolation, helplessness, and feelings of loss; on the other hand, hope, direction, and a belief in the self. There is now, in the form of the speaker's teacherly overview, a desire to go beyond this trapped figure or to liberate him from tracing and retracing the pattern of his "unfruitful life" that he seems, at least in part, to be denying. Wordsworth wanted to connect him(self) to what "others felt." This determination can be seen in other poems, as can the cluster of difficult feelings that have been exhibited and explored. So can the three-stage narrative pattern of 1) centering on a spot and/or time, 2) exploring its significance in the form of a story that gives it significance, and 3) a withdrawal from the spot or time to gather a philosophical truth. But the means and the motivation seemed now, at Racedown, to be promising, despite the nagging and elaborate financial problems that continued to plague the Wordsworths (see, for example, Wordsworth 1967, 182–85, 188). There was at least some stability that would enable Wordsworth to begin working out such feelings through a discourse of recovery in his poetry.

Beginning in this spring of 1797, Wordsworth was also connecting more intimately with Coleridge, and the two had begun to mutually cheer and encourage each other, while at the same time providing critical feedback about each other's work. Late in March, Wordsworth briefly visited Coleridge at Nether Stowey. At the time of the visit, Coleridge was not in very good spirits. He had grown tired of reviewing gothic novels, his finances were troubling him, and he felt that he had lost something of who or what he once was. He wrote to a friend, "Wordsworth's conversation, &c roused me somewhat," but he still had feelings of "hopelessness" (Coleridge 1956, 1:319–20). But working hard on his play, *Osorio*, roused him, as did correcting the proofs to his *Poems*. He could also look forward to sharing his work with Wordsworth.

A few months later, in early June, when Coleridge came to visit the Wordsworths at Racedown, the two poets' enthusiasm and admiration for each other confirmed their alliance. Almost fifty years later Wordsworth would remember Coleridge's arrival as his visitor jumped over a gate and bounded up across a field to the cottage (Wordsworth 1988, 719). This meeting meant a great deal. Within a few days of his arrival, Coleridge passed judgment on his fellow poet in a letter to Joseph Cottle:

> Wordsworth admires my Tragedy *[Osorio]*—which gives me great hopes. Wordsworth has written a Tragedy *[The Borderers]* himself. I speak with heartfelt sincerity & (I think) unblinded judgement, when I tell you, that I feel myself a *little man by his* side; & yet do not think myself the less man, than I formerly thought myself.—His drama is absolutely wonderful. You know, I do not commonly speak in such abrupt & unmingled phrases—& therefore will the more readily believe me.—There are in the piece those *profound* touches of the human heart, which I find three or four times in "The Robbers" of Schiller, & often in Shakespere—but in Wordsworth there are no *inequalities*. T. Poole's opinion of Wordsworth is—that he is the greatest Man, he ever knew—I coincide. (Coleridge 1956, 1:325)

A few days later to another correspondent he repeats, "Wordsworth is a great man" (327). And he says it once more, a few weeks later, to Robert Southey: "Wordsworth is a very great man—the only man, to whom *at all times* & in *all modes of excellence* I feel myself inferior. . . . " (334). Although all of this rings of rhetorical hyperbole on the part of Coleridge, it is nonetheless a remarkable appraisal because Coleridge was so very self-conscious of what he was saying—"I do not commonly speak in such abrupt & unmingled phrases. . . ." Relative to Coleridge, Wordsworth's public literary voice was virtually unheard, yet it was Coleridge who felt overshadowed. What Coleridge saw in *The Borderers* were the "*profound* touches of the human heart," the depth of feeling that Wordsworth had at his artistic disposal. He perceived a kind of sustained power in his friend rivaling and even surpassing that of Shakespeare and Schiller, and literary history suggests that Coleridge was not altogether wrong. He had great expectations for this poet from the north, and he let him know it. Again, we must keep in mind how relatively little Wordsworth had done at this point, making Coleridge's estimation all the more remarkable. But important for Wordsworth would have been that someone like Coleridge, who was already connected with the literary scene and intelligentsia, felt this way about him. It would have been the kind of confidence to help set Wordsworth's poetic course.

About Coleridge's June visit Dorothy writes, "The first thing that was read after he [Coleridge] came was William's new poem *The Ruined Cottage* with which he was much delighted; and after tea he repeated to us two acts and a half of his tragedy *Osorio*." The next morning William read his tragedy *The Borderers*" (Wordsworth 1967, 189). The extraordinarily complicated manuscript history of *The Ruined Cottage* does not make it clear whether Coleridge heard a completed 1798 version of the poem (MS B), or if he heard a few passages. Most likely it was a completed 1797 version somewhat shorter than MS B (528 lines) and the better-known MS D, 1799 (538 lines) that centered on the tale of Margaret. Unfortunately, an earlier completed version (earlier, that is, than MS B) no longer exists.[10]

The changes that *The Ruined Cottage* went through in its many versions reflect Wordsworth's own uncertain and changing position as he attempted to view the poem's subjects and various perspectives to find, as Leavis put it, "equipoise" (1971, 338–41), a balance between thought and feeling. Wordsworth was never quite certain what to bring together or pull apart, when to add comments to or to leave well enough alone. But of one thing we can be clear: it forcefully continued the exploration into the realm of particular emotions that began earlier; but now, along with this, there was also an marked advancement in Wordsworth's artistry, in his style. As Herbert Read noted, *The Ruined Cottage* "really contains the germ of all his subsequent development" (1930, 133). And for Leavis, "Wordsworth becomes a great poet here" (1971, 338).

In the earliest versions (which date from 1797, MS A), the most striking features of the poem are the bleak sufferings and endurance of Margaret. The tale is about as dreary as can be told, with the complete dissolution of a family. The poem ends, quite abruptly, with Margaret's solitary death (MS B). There is no moralistic mopping up. But MS B (and MS B2, which rapidly expanded upon MS B, adding more about the Pedlar) does give some background about the Pedlar that is not in MS D. We are told he came from a humble Cumbrian background, and in his wanderings,

> much had he seen of men,
> Their manners, their enjoyments and pursuits,
> Their passions and their feelings, chiefly those
> Essential and eternal in the heart,

> Which 'mid the simpler forms of rural life
> Exist more simple in their elements
> And speak a plainer language.
> ....
> To every natural form, rock, fruit, and flower,
> Even the loose stones that cover the highway,
> He gave a moral life; he saw them feel
> Or linked them to some feeling.
>
> (MS B, lines 59–65, 80–83)

This first passage quoted here is a remarkable harbinger of Wordsworth's central idea about his poetry as expressed in the Preface to *Lyrical Ballads*: "Low and rustic life was generally chosen, because in that condition, the essential passions of the heart find a better soil in which they can attain their maturity, are less under restraint, and speak a plainer and more emphatic language...." (Wordsworth 1984, 597). This effectively gives us a strong connection between Wordsworth's view of poetry and the role of the Pedlar as a poetic negotiator of affect. The Pedlar comes to be the link between the Poet and Margaret; more interestingly put, the Pedlar is the link between the feelings Margaret represents—grief, sorrow, abandonment—and Wordsworth's thoughtful attempt to come to term with those feelings. In the second passage we see, quite plainly, Wordsworth's other important strategy, that of projection, where feelings are projected onto aspects of the landscape, where they can be considered at a distance and then reinternalized in loving nature.

As *The Ruined Cottage* evolves, however, so does the attempt to give some moral or philosophical meaning to Margaret's sufferings, so that, in the 1799 MS D, the Pedlar is not given the extended passages about his background that appear in MS B2. But now he is provided with a compensatory gloss on the sorrow, despair, and grief (lines 508–25). The changing role or positioning of the Pedlar did not go unnoticed. By March 1798, Dorothy writes to Mary Hutchinson, William's future wife: "The Pedlar's character now makes a very, certainly the *most*, considerable part of the poem," and she transcribed a great deal of the poem for Mary (this would have been from MS B2; Wordsworth 1967, 199). James Butler observes that Wordsworth's "focus shifts from the unadorned account of Margaret's tragedy to the Pedlar's philosophic ideas—and how they developed—which cause the Pedlar to react in a peculiar way to that account" (Wordsworth 1979a, 15). Again, my view is that the Pedlar's positioning relative to the tale of Margaret parallels Wordsworth's attempts to understand his feelings of grief, loss, and sorrow—and the circumstance of death—that structured his history and emotional life. *The Ruined Cottage* can be read as Wordsworth's imaginative reenactment. It strives to move, perhaps too quickly, from denial to acceptance, for the Pedlar's role is to supply a discourse of reconciliation and recovery, and the history of his own life becomes exemplary. Wordsworth himself may have realized the danger in such a speedy recovery, for he ended up striking out two endings for the poem, likely geared for MS B2, that give the poet an overly secure grasp of Margaret's tale: "to myself / I seemed a better and a wiser man"; "And for the tale which you have told I think / I am a better and a wiser man" (Wordsworth 1949, 400). We might be thankful that Wordsworth stepped a little back from such an easy mastery of grief; otherwise, he might not have gone on to make other attempts to master his emotional life.

From 1801 to 1804, the Pedlar's presence begins to more or less take over Margaret's tale, and he is made to have his own poem, *The Pedlar* (MS E, 883 lines). Details about the Pedlar's early life and disposition take up most of this expansion. Moreover, there is an earlier and much shorter separate poem (356 lines) about the Pedlar that goes back to perhaps 1798 (printed in Jonathan Wordsworth 1969; 1982). Finally, a few years later, Wordsworth's editorial decision was to recombine Margaret's tale with the expanded history of the Pedlar in a two-part poem, and to entitle it *The Pedlar*. And it was this poem that found its way into the first book in *The Excursion*, 1814, where the Pedlar was now called the Wanderer. As late as 1845 Wordsworth was still adding lines to the gloss on Margaret's sufferings (*The Excursion*, bk. 1, lines 934–40).

Two further relevant features about this poem's development need to be brought out. First, we know that working on the poem over the winter and spring of 1801–2 caused Wordsworth significant stress and poor health. We know this from Dorothy's journal, some of which was cited in the previous chapter: "William worked at The Ruined Cottage and made himself very ill"; "William tired with composition"; "Wm wrote out part of his poem and endeavoured to alter it, and so made himself ill"; "William worked at the Pedlar all morning. He kept the dinner waiting until 4 o'clock—he was much tired"; "William worked hard at the Pedlar and tired himself"; "William wished to break off composition, and was unable, and so did himself harm"; "William had a bad night and was working at his poem. We sate by the fire and did not walk, but read the pedlar thinking it done but lo, thought Wm could find fault with no one part of it—it was uninteresting and must be altered. Poor William"; "He fell to work, and made himself unwell"; "After Molly went we read the first part of the poem and were delighted with it, but Wm afterwards got to some ugly places and went to bed tired out"; "William sadly tired and working still at the Pedlar"; "I almost finished writing The Pedlar, but poor William wore himself out with labour. We had an affecting conversation"; "Wm very ill, employed with the pedlar. . . . Disaster pedlar"; "I was so unlucky as to propose to rewrite The Pedlar. Wm got to work and was worn to death" (D. Wordsworth 1973, 73–97). Moreover, during all this time, Dorothy recorded that her brother was suffering from insomnia.

Of course this is a partial record, since we do not have a complete daily account for the compositional period—earlier or later—of *The Ruined Cottage/ The Pedlar*; neither can we assume that everything relevant was recorded. But from what we do have, it is clear that this poem deeply troubled Wordsworth. There was something he desperately had to get right, and it obsessed him to the degree of making him ill. I would speculate that the subject material Wordsworth was attempting to artistically master was emotionally problematical. Via the Pedlar, a figure of maturity, he was attempting to create a distance from or find a perspective for the difficult originating feelings embedded in the poem. And these were feelings right out of Wordsworth's own history and subjectivity: desperate hope; solitary suffering; the meaning of death, solitude, loss, and grief within family circumstances; psychological endurance without self-esteem. He was having trouble integrating thought with feeling, the Pedlar's gloss with Margaret's suffering. We have the poet-narrator's, or Poet's, own confused responses to witness this.

The story of Margaret in its barest form (MS B) overflows with inexplicable sadness and sorrow. Even the sagacious Pedlar who tells her story to the narrator at moments finds the grief irresistible (lines 118–19, 188–98), yet he knows that in this "tale of silent suffering" must be found something of virtue (lines 227–36). Margaret and her husband Robert work their land hard, but with war and bad growing seasons things begin to fall apart. Robert becomes ill and never quite recovers. One day he disappears, and we learn that he has sold himself into the army for some money, which he leaves behind for his family. Margaret, now responsible for their two children, is stunned, and in the trauma of loss she, like her cottage, slowly falls to ruin. She loses her oldest child, and she is even capable of leaving the remaining child "helpless," alone, and crying (line 354) as she wanders the countryside; she says, "what I seek I cannot find" (line 351). Her only hope is to be able to "endure" (360) the overpowering grief. The Pedlar himself is unable to shake away her sorrow (lines 361–74), suggesting that he knows all too well how she feels. The Pedlar's portrayal of Margaret shows her as a severely depressed person (lines 374-87, 396); like the Yew-tree poet (27), she too casts her eyes downward. Unfortunately, her emotional disposition is passed on to her child: "Her infant babe / Had from its mother caught the trick of grief" (409–10). There are remnants of false hope around her, and even when her child dies and her grief-ridden solitude is absolute she clings to her spot and looks into the distance for the return of her Robert. And there, a ruined woman beside her ruined cottage, she dies.

The second point to be made about the poem's development is related to the first, and has to do with Wordsworth's investment in the Pedlar. Wordsworth gives the Pedlar a history and, in particular, a childhood based upon his own. As Butler notes, the passages about the Pedlar's past are Wordsworth's "first autobiographical work" (Wordsworth 1979a, 17). This is an extraordinarily important moment, for in trying to formulate how the Pedlar came to have his views by returning to his own background, Wordsworth discovered (or uncovered) his own life, his own history, as a subject for poetic inquiry. Through using the Pedlar as a way to understand his feelings and his past, he made his first gestures toward *The Prelude*, which began in 1799 as the two-part version. Wordsworth apparently wanted to become like the Pedlar and collapsed his own past with a projected figure that might be his future. (This becomes a characteristic move in Wordsworth's poetry, anticipating, among others, the figure of the Leech Gatherer.) The negotiating voice, that of the Poet himself, stands between, as it were, the past and the future: he begins the poem irritated and uncomfortable, and we are not told why. He is hot, tired, listless, and bothered by the pesky insects flying around his face (MS B, lines 17–25; MS D, lines 18–26; MS E, lines 4–9); but by the end, through the Pedlar's meditated discourse of accepting "sorrow," "despair," and "grief" (MS D, lines 520–21; MS E, lines 865–66), he is visibly changed: he feels aligned with and quietly comforted by his surroundings; tranquilized, he moves on. (Keep in mind that this discourse on acceptance is not in MS B.)

To repeat, some of the passages written for *The Ruined Cottage* ended up in *The Prelude*.[11] Perhaps the most significant *Cottage* passage that became a *Prelude* passage was that in which Wordsworth as a teenager emotionally corresponded to his surroundings, joyfully perceiving an indivisible "one life" in all things (1799 *Prelude*, bk. 2, lines 446–64). It is with this kind of belief that individual solitude, loss, and grief can eventually be overcome. Thus far it was Wordsworth's most profound attempt at accepting his past and building a future.

In recalling the Pedlar, Wordsworth himself wrote the following, and it represents a direction in the development of his poetry: "At all events I am here called upon freely to acknowledge that the character I have represented in his person is chiefly an idea of what I fancied my own character might have become in his circumstances" (1979a, 477). Wordsworth is owning up to something very important here. He admits he imaginatively constructed the Pedlar out of his own hopes and needs, and we do not have to add any more about what those hopes and needs were, but we can learn something about Wordsworth's view of his past and hopes for the future in the story of the Pedlar. He was one of three sons; his father died when he was young. He was a solitary, brooding child with an intense and lively imagination that took in and fastened onto images, making them the stuff of his own desires (MS E, lines 121–50). Through the generous "power / Of Nature" he was prepared for the "the lesson deep of love" (lines 180–85). By humility and patience he saw himself as part of all that he beheld—the infinite and the beautiful—and "did he *feel* his faith" so that his "being thus became / Sublime and comprehensive" (lines 192–233). Milton and geometry also occupied his "lonesome idleness" and "heavier hours of solitude" (lines 238–71). As he grew towards adulthood, a teaching career was a possibility, but because of his unsettled, wandering mind, he was ill-suited to perform this duty (lines 276–85). He decided that, like his older brother, he would become a wandering pedlar, a traveling salesman. And so, "In solitude and solitary thought," he traveled among his rural countrymen, observing all aspects of their lives and participating in their feelings: "Thus had he liv'd a long and innocent life," remarkable most of all for his uncluttered, unpretentious wisdom (lines 286–374).

In this sketch (some of which sounds like it could have been taken right out of the early books of the 1805 *Prelude*) we see the obvious re-creation of some of Wordsworth's past, complete with the dead father and the surviving children, the breakup of a family, the moody and solitary disposition, the nurturing in nature and the fostering of an intense imagination, the deep regard for Milton, the turning to geometry, the wandering, and the inability to decide what to do. This takes Wordsworth through the Alfoxden period. Where the Pedlar departs from Wordsworth is in having the capability to morally and philosophically master these kind of difficult feelings, to see them in a bigger context. As Leavis puts it, in the description of the older Pedlar/Wanderer we have "an idealized self-portrait" of Wordsworth, "what he would have liked to be" (Leavis 1972, 166). Elsewhere Leavis sees this as "the poet's strong impulse towards the Wanderer's state" (1971, 339). Leavis is right, especially since we have Wordsworth himself saying that the Wanderer "is chiefly an idea of what I fancied my own character might have become...." This is what his poetry was working on: hoping to be other than he was at the present, and thus fearing what he might become. He would soon be laying out such difficult emotions in the most unadorned ways possible (and in a way that would be new to literary history), and he would try to develop some understanding of the attendant feelings that haunted him. He would want to transform that loss into gain, fear into hope, feeling into thought. He would try to evolve a rhetoric of acceptance out of emotional dislocation. But we have to remember that at least in one stage of the poem, even the Pedlar, despite his "wiser mind," finds the "grief" of Margaret irresistible, and he finds himself "yielding" to it. But this may have been an understandable lapse on the part of Wordsworth, for these lines only appear in one version (MS D, lines 116–19).

Leavis makes one small but irresistible point. He is certain that the lines given to the poet upon hearing some of Margaret's tale—"I thought of that poor woman as of one / Whom I had known and loved" (MS B, 265–66; MS

D, 207–8)—mark the return of the repressed: "No doubt the particular memory of Annette asserts itself here...." (Leavis 1972, 168–69). We cannot be quite as certain as Leavis is (certainty is always Leavis's strongest suit), but Leavis reads the sources of Wordsworth's poetry as conflicts arising from the poet's past, and in this, I firmly believe, he is correct. And so Leavis is attuned to the "distancing" that the poem desperately tries to effect between the reality of Margaret's suffering and the Wanderer's invocation of tranquil acceptance. However, the Poet, as Wordsworth, seems not so undoubting of grief's subsumption.

Much of the critical work involving *The Ruined Cottage*, *The Pedlar*, and book 1 of *The Excursion* has centered around which version (and versions within versions) is artistically or narratologically superior, and most of this debate centers around the Pedlar's role relative to Margaret's tale and the poet's response to both the tale and the Pedlar's gloss. As I have attempted to point out, this too was Wordsworth's problem, and through these debates critics have, in effect, attempted to critically liberate what Wordsworth attempted to emotionally liberate; that is, our critical debates to a significant degree reflect Wordsworth's inner struggles. And so, while a number of critics and editors prefer Margaret's story without the history of the Pedlar,[12] others prefer versions where the Pedlar's words and history are viewed as complementary to or integrated with Margaret's story and the poet's response.[13] While much careful editorial work has given us distinct, individual poems to evaluate, I prefer to view the versions and revisions as a process, as a sign of Wordsworth's ongoing personal development, as the expression of his difficult emotional life through poetry. There is no best version. *The Ruined Cottage* is a collage of texts struggling for poetic balance, just as Wordsworth was a mix of emotions struggling for personal balance.

Perhaps the center of this text in all its forms and formulations can be found just after the Pedlar, having told part of Margaret's story, pauses to check his own emotions. The passage I have in mind has the Poet also attempting to resituate his own uncertain response, and then the Pedlar makes it clear that in the story of Margaret's misery there can be found something of sympathetic and congenial goodness. Significantly, these lines are found, in similar form, in all the main versions of the poem (MS B, lines 257–96; MS D, lines 199–237; MS E, lines 533–71, and *The Excursion*, bk. 1, lines 605–39). The Poet finds himself put so much at ease or mesmerized by the Pedlar's "easy cheerfulness," that he says the "simple tale / Passed from my mind like a forgotten sound" (MS D, lines 199–204). But when he snaps out of this amnesic state, he finds that he cannot resist thinking of Margaret as "one / Whom I had known and loved"; and such is the Pedlar's "power" to dramatize the story that the poet experiences "a heartfelt chillness in my veins" (lines 206–13). Attempting to comfort himself in the sun, and turning to the ruined cottage, he then begs the Pedlar to continue the story. But first the Pedlar wants to make it clear that the purpose of this kind of story is not to solicit a "momentary pleasure," a cheap thrill (lines 221–26)—and here Wordsworth may be setting his aim at those contemporary popular works that grossly sensationalize the suffering of others (Swann 1991). The Pedlar points out that in "mournful thoughts" there can often be found "A power to virtue friendly," and that this bare "tale of silent suffering" cannot be felt or comprehended by "him who does not think" (lines 227–36). Here there is a deliberate attempt to comprehend suffering. Something "heartfelt" has touched the Poet, and he has to hear more. The Wanderer wants to make it clear (to us and to Wordsworth, speaking to himself) that the Poet's reasons for wanting to hear more are the right reasons. The Poet *feels*; the Pedlar want him to *think*. This may be the crux of the poem. This is what we can anticipate Wordsworth himself wanting to do: transform feeling into thought, or to have the two accommodate each other in mutually profitable ways.

In trying to answer the question, "Why then did Wordsworth feel it appropriate or necessary to change the poem's focus?," James H. Averill suggests that no answers come out of Wordsworth's own life, other than "it would have been only natural that Wordsworth should begin to ask questions about the response to fictional suffering" and about imaginative sympathy (Averill 1976, 227). The question is a good one. The answer, however, is not quite right. The suffering may be in the fiction, but it was not, for Wordsworth, "fictional"; it was real; Wordsworth's interest was not so much in sympathy as in introspection. And, as I have shown, there is evidence from Wordsworth's life that explains and contextualizes the emotional tribulations with this text.

The main variables in this complex textual equation—Margaret's tale, the Poet's response, the Pedlar's history, the Pedlar's gloss on Margaret's tale—change with Wordsworth's attempts to view what is probably the essential feature in all of this: *Margaret's suffering*. Through Margaret, Wordsworth poetically reenacted his own grief, loneliness, and helplessness; through the Wanderer, he hoped to develop a position to understand and overcome these feelings; and as the Poet, he stood between and listened to the voices of hope and fear, gain and loss, thought and feeling. Very soon Wordsworth would not need the voice of the Pedlar to speak for his own needs. Soon he would be able to speak in propria persona rather than ventriloquize.

Racedown had been very important. It was Wordsworth's first real home since the death of his parents and the breakup of his family. Despite struggling with profound emotional uncertainty from 1795 to 1797, the stability of having a place, the less troubled financial situation, and the relationship with his sister all gave him the impetus to search out his inner life and to believe in himself as a poet. In his new circumstances he would actually become a poet.

Let us return to Wordsworth's new circumstances that began in the summer of 1797. Wordsworth had, with Coleridge's enthusiastic urgings, moved from Racedown to Nether Stowey in Somerset, so that the two could be close together. As Dorothy describes the reasons for their move, the "principal inducement was Coleridge's society" (Wordsworth 1967, 190). And so they left Racedown suddenly, in the same month as Coleridge's visit to the Wordsworths, June 1797, and by mid-July the Wordsworth's found themselves set up in new and very pleasant circumstances: a large furnished house set in extraordinarily beautiful grounds, complete with wandering deer, waterfall, woods, and expansive meadows. Wordsworth and Coleridge were now within relatively easy walking distance of each other, and Coleridge would especially take advantage of this, spending as much time as possible with the Wordsworths. Such was the pull of poet to poet, although we should not underestimate Dorothy's presence as a part of the relationship. Coleridge had very quickly grown to respect her opinion on all matters. A few years later Coleridge could write about himself, William, and Dorothy, "[T]ho' we were three persons, it was but one God" (Coleridge 1956, 2:775).

Their new place was called Alfoxden House. They would be there for just under a year. Their lease was renewable, but perhaps because of their seemingly French ways and sympathies, the Wordsworth Alfoxden circle was viewed with some suspicion by both the authorities and the locals.[14] In *The Prelude*, Wordsworth looks back to this time of wandering happily in the area with Coleridge, sharing their gifts of poetry with each other, Coleridge conjuring visions of old sailors and the "rueful woes" in *Christabel*, while Wordsworth offered murmurings from *The Idiot Boy* and *The Thorn* (1805 *Prelude*, bk. 13, lines 391–410). In late November 1797, Dorothy wrote to Mary Hutchinson, "William and Coleridge employing themselves in laying the plan of a ballad, to be published with some pieces of William's" (Wordsworth 1967, 194). The ballad, or course, was to be *The Rime of the Ancient Mariner*. Combined with other "pieces" by Wordsworth, these would form the basis for the 1798 *Lyrical Ballads*.

While at Alfoxden, Wordsworth also made plans for what would have been his magnum opus. On 6 March 1798, full of Coleridgean ambition, he writes to a friend that he has begun a poem, *The Recluse*, that "will give pictures of Nature, Man, and Society. Indeed I know not any thing which will not come within the scope of my plan" (Wordsworth 1967, 212).[15] Coleridge, referring to this project, a day later writes of "The Giant Wordsworth" (Coleridge

1956, 391). In fact, for more than a couple of decades, Coleridge and many of Wordsworth's friends would be harping on Wordsworth to get on with the great philosophical poem. For example, in September 1799, Coleridge wrote to Wordsworth: "I am anxiously eager to have you steadily employed on 'The Recluse.' . . . My dear friend, I do entreat you go on with 'The Recluse'" (1956, 527). De Selincourt, in summarizing the history of the poem, concludes that Wordsworth's "unfulfilled promise of *The Recluse* lay on his conscience and engaged the hopes of his friends for the rest of his life" (Wordsworth 1949, 367). It may have been that the more Coleridge and others wanted Wordsworth to write this great poem of the age, the more Wordsworth found the expectations impossible to live up to. The pressure would not have helped Wordsworth. *The Recluse* remains the greatest poem never written.

By March 1798, Wordsworth was also planning to go to Germany for two years with Dorothy, Coleridge, and Coleridge's wife, Sara, in order to learn the language and as much as possible about "natural science" (Wordsworth 1967, 213). He knew he would not be able to stay at Alfoxden. Without Sara, and shortened by about two-thirds for the Wordsworths, this trip would take place over the winter and spring of 1798–99, and for William it would not be pleasant, at least in terms of living conditions and mental health. In Germany the large poetic project would be put on hold—permanently, as it turns out—while Wordsworth would compose shorter enigmatic and emotionally packed poems, many of which would end up in the 1800 *Lyrical Ballads*. He would also begin writing explicitly autobiographical verse, which both he and Coleridge would consider preparatory or as an annex to *The Recluse*. And thus Wordsworth's great work would be that preparatory poem, *The Prelude*, not published until his death. The poem about *his* life would always stand in the way of his poem about life.

The remainder of this chapter will survey some of the poetry written while Wordsworth was at Alfoxden. In the spring of 1798, Wordsworth was especially productive, and it was in March that he and Coleridge began entertaining the idea of publishing a volume of poems that might help finance a trip to Germany later in the year.[16] This was the 1798 *Lyrical Ballads*. (Wordsworth added a number of poems for the 1800 edition, and he also omitted a few.) Both the emotional content of these poems, the feelings, and to significance of what the narratives reenact deserve close attention. Wordsworth said that "Low and rustic life" was chosen for his poems in *Lyrical Ballads* in order to better contextualize their emotional content, to communicate "elementary feelings" in the most uncluttered and free way possible. He wanted to show how thought can influence feeling ("I believe my habits of meditation have so formed my feelings"), though his poetry shows that this control of feeling by thought is not a victory so easily won. He wanted his language and the narrative circumstances as unobstructed and distinct as possible. He also wanted to make it clear that what distinguished these poems was that "the feeling therein developed gives importance to the action and situation, and not the action and situation to the feeling" (Wordsworth 1984, 597–99). That is, the feeling is the central or determining feature. And thus it is primarily to the feeling we should attend. We will see in these poems various formulations of Wordsworth's subjective self and his history. The range in the intensity and tone of these poems is wide, but they circle unrelentingly around a number of common features.[17] Literary history cannot in any convincing way account for these texts; Wordsworth's own history can.

Towards the 1798 Lyrical Ballads

Even a poem like *Goody Blake and Harry Gill: A True Story* must be questioned in terms of 1) why it was a subject demanding Wordsworth's poetic attentions, and 2) how he treated the subject. The "source" of the poem was a short winter's tale in Erasmus Darwin's *Zoonomia; or, The laws of Organic Life* (1794-96). We know that in late February or early March 1798, Wordsworth urgently desired that a copy of Darwin's book be sent to him at Alfoxden, and that shortly thereafter it arrived. As Dorothy wrote to the sender just after arrival, it "already completely answered the purpose for which William" had requested it (Wordsworth 1967, 199, 214–15). Years later, Wordsworth recorded a simple note on the poem: "Written at Alfoxden, 1798. The incident from Dr. Darwin's *Zoonomia*" (Wordsworth 1876, 3:182). What Wordsworth took from Darwin was a prose account of young farmer catching an old, poor woman taking sticks from his hedges in order to make a fire to warm herself. When caught, the old woman said to the man, "Heaven grant, that thou never mayest know again the blessing to be warm." Despite all efforts, the farmer henceforth could not make himself warm: "from this one insane idea he kept his bed above twenty years for fear of the cold air, till at length he died."[18]

Essentially, this is also the story of Goody and Harry as Wordsworth cast it. What did it hold for Wordsworth? Why was he so interested in it? First, and most obviously, there is the pure suffering and silent endurance of Goody Blake, which is the center of the poem. The coldness is utterly pervasive. Her hut, "on a cold hill-side" (line 30), is in a poor condition; she has little food and poor clothing; her solitude is absolute:

> 'Twas a hard time for Goody Blake.
> Her evenings then were dull and dead;
> Sad case it was, as you may think,

> For very cold to go to bed,
> And then for cold not sleep a wink.
>
> (Lines 44–48)

Like Margaret in *The Ruined Cottage*, she accepts her lot in life with a kind of benign virtue. Harry Gill does not. His fate, at the crucial moment of catching Goody with a bundle of his sticks, is to literally *embody* his emotional response to her: after hearing her little prayer that he might "never more be warm," and "icy-cold he turned away" (lines 100–104), "icy-cold" he becomes. Even with three riding-coats and numerous blankets pinned to himself, there is nothing he can do to warm himself: "His face was gloom, his heart was sorrow"—"as long as live he may, / He never will be warm again" (lines 107, 119–20). And this brings us to the second feature Wordsworth would have been interested in, namely, Harry's susceptibility to guilt and punishment. Both Harry and Goody end as solitary figures of suffering, but the subtle drama of the poem is to place these two side by side; for Wordsworth, in attempting of understand how best to deal with his own internal strife and the emotional suffering he has had to endure, would want to examine how best to respond. The older figure accepts her condition; the younger denies his. Harry is both helpless and responsible for his condition. His physical suffering is a result of his psychological disposition. Guilt is internalized. It is not the supernatural that acts upon Harry. It is closer to the superego.

Wordsworth was very interested in the effects that ideas and emotions have on physical health (in other words, psychosomatic illness), and this, in fact, was the context for the tale in *Zoonomia*.[19] In the Preface to *Lyrical Ballads*, Wordsworth says as much about what happens in his tale:

> I wished to draw attention to the truth, that the power of the human imagination is sufficient to produce such changes even in our physical nature as might almost appear miraculous. The truth is an important one; the fact (for it is a *fact*) is a valuable illustration of it. (Wordsworth 1984, 611–12)

In the Advertisement to *Lyrical Ballads* (1798), Wordsworth had already written that the poem was "founded on a well-authenticated fact which happened in Warwickshire" (592). Wordsworth seems to be protesting just a bit too much that someone becoming emotionally unbalanced due to the workings of his own mind is a "truth," a "*fact*." In effect he is saying, *Believe me, I know this kind of thing can really happen*. Turned inwards, a little "imagination" can be a dangerous thing. We must note too that, as in some of the other tales in *Lyrical Ballads*, Wordsworth attempts to construct a rather simple narrator who is held by—yet strangely a part of—the story being told. Stephen Parrish even suggests that "the poem verges on the dramatic monologue form" (1973, 97). *The Thorn*, too, has such a dramatic quality and a narrator who is strangely a part of what he relates.[20] But the poem is even more disturbing in its suggestibility and what it may be reenacting.

The Thorn is, quite literally, a poem overgrown with imagery of uneasy and unshakable death. The first stanza describes a thorn bush in uncomfortable, contradictory terms: the bush looks "old and grey" with "knotted joints," yet it is "Not higher than a two-years' child"; it also stands "erect, and like a stone / With lichens it is overgrown." It stands, that is, like a tombstone. This figure on the landscape, then, is old yet young, alive but dead, humanized and then dehumanized. When the narrator calls it "forlorn," suggesting its hopeless or abandoned condition, we have to remember that he actually calls it a "*thing* forlorn" (my emphasis), and once again we see the speaker's conflicting projections: bushes do not feel hopeless or abandoned (lines 4–11). People do. Wordsworth, for one, experienced such feelings.

The deathly personification continues into the second stanza, with the thorn, not unlike aspects of Margaret's cottage,[21] pictured as being choked and dragged into the earth by the creeping and clasping mosses, as if "To bury this poor thorn for ever" (line 22). The poem relentlessly narrows its focus on the measured features of the landscape until it settles on one spot: five yards from the path, and to the left, there is the thorn, and three yards to the left of the thorn there is "a muddy little pond" (two feet by three feet) and "a hill of moss" (half a foot high) (lines 30, 36).[22] The narrator suggests that the little hill of moss "Is like an infant's grave in size" (line 52), and for good measure he repeats this a few more times (line 61, 93). Given that we know the rest of the poem, we understand why he says this. Martha Ray, once blithe and happy, was to be wed to Stephen Hill, but she discovers he had sworn oaths to another woman. She is traumatized by this, and she is also pregnant. No one knows whether she had the baby and gave it up, or whether it died at birth; many believe she murdered the newborn child. But now, as a figure of self-imposed isolation, she returns to the thorn and to the pond, and to the hill of moss that may be the grave of her child. Here she can, in all weather and at all times, be heard to cry, in denial, her woes: "O misery! O misery!" (lines 202, 209, 252–53). Her fate seems hard to accept. But superstition keeps away those who want to know more. Some say that the moss is red with the blood of the child, and that the shadow of a child can be seen in the pond; some claim to have beheld the hill of moss and the ground around it shake when any sought to uncover the secret of Martha Ray.

We know a little about the circumstances of *The Thorn*'s composition. In the middle of March 1798 at Alfoxden, between the 18th and the 22nd, Dorothy in her journal records how very cold it was: "A cold, windy morning," "a very cold bleak day," "A very cold evening," "in the evening, very cold"; "spring," she writes, "continues to advance very slowly, no green trees, the hedges leafless" (D. Wordsworth 1973, 10–11). A few days earlier, on 16 March, she recorded, "William very ill" (10). On 19 she wrote: "Wm and Basil and I walked to the hill-tops, a very cold bleak day. We were met on our return by a severe hailstorm. William wrote some lines describing a stunted thorn" (10). This, then, must be the beginning of the poem as we know it. A month later Mary wrote, "Walked in the evening up the hill dividing the Coombes. Came home the Crookham way, by the thorn, and the 'little muddy pond.' Nine o'clock at our return. William all the morning engaged in wearisome composition" (14). It appears that during this month *The Thorn* was written and well known in the Wordsworth household. Wordsworth's own recollection of the poem's origin corresponds with what Dorothy recorded. Wordsworth wrote that the inspiration came during a walk on "stormy day" when he observed

> a thorn, which I had often past in calm and bright weather without noticing it. I said to myself, cannot I by some invention do as much to make this Thorn permanently an impressive object as the storm has made it to my eyes at the moment? I began the poem accordingly, and composed it with great rapidity. (Wordsworth 1876, 3:41)

The key idea here has to do with the notion of impressiveness. Seeing the solitary thorn on that bleak, cold day touched something in Wordsworth, and, with some urgency, he used poetry to capture the intensity of his response. For as his 1800 *Note to "The Thorn"* makes clear, the difficulty of communicating "impassioned feelings" is the real issue in this poem (Wordsworth 1984, 594). Wordsworth moves towards making this sound something closer to an artistic concern, but it is his feeling, his response, and the nature of his projection onto the landscape that is behind this poem.[23] He is asking: *How can I poetically transcribe what seeing this thorn made me feel?*

So what did this story, its subjects and emotional content, hold for Wordsworth? What did it reenact out of Wordsworth's history and subjectivity?

Mary Jacobus writes that *The Thorn* is "a poem not just about suffering, but about the difficulty of comprehending it" (1976, 244). Although she is going in a different direction than I am, no doubt the poem is grounded in "the difficulty of comprehending suffering"—but in particular, it is Wordsworth's own difficulty in comprehending the experience of suffering. We do not have to read very deeply into the story to see that what also dominates *The Thorn* is abandonment, articulation of loss, endurance, solitude, and death. Abandonment is perhaps the most pervasive element: the thorn is pictured as abandoned ("forlorn"); the child is abandoned (perhaps by the mother, perhaps by nature); and the mother is abandoned by her lover. So too do the thorn, the child, and the mother endure: the thorn is described as aged but also figured as ageless, enduring the elements; the child endures in the imagination of the people and in the painful emotions of the mother; and the mother endures her woeful feelings. The thorn, the child, and mother are all solitary figures, separated from the community or human touch of others. So too are these three figures of death. There is even a death wish made upon Stephen Hill by the speaker: "I'd rather / That he had died, that cruel father!" (lines 142–43).

The Thorn as a narrative may be incredible and apocryphal, but what surfaces in the poem are feelings that are powerfully credible and authentic. The essential history reenacted here, that of the broken family and the abandoned child, we have already seen both in Wordsworth's own childhood and later in France. But we do not even have to suggest that Stephen Hill is Wordsworth abandoning Caroline, or that he is Wordsworth being abandoned by his own father or parents.[24] Nor need we say that the death of Wordsworth's mother figuratively killed Wordsworth's chances for emotional stability. It might be more necessary to say that at this point in Wordsworth's poetry, the abandoned child does not quite yet have a chance to become father to the man. But Wordsworth is working on it. Like the thorn itself, which is a manifestation of both youth and age, he will endure. As an adult child, Wordsworth too is old and young; he too will endure.

It may seem unusual to now move to a poem that is ostensibly comic, but *The Idiot Boy*, written virtually at the same time as *The Thorn*, continues to explore, through emotional and situational reenactments, Wordsworth's subjective concerns. The two poems differ mainly in style, but not in the seriousness of how the subject matter is treated. J. F. Danby writes that in most of the poems of *Lyrical Ballads* "there is an essentially dramatic self-projection" (1960, 35), and we can appreciate Wordsworth's artistry in presenting, in dramatizing, that self. And thus the importance of the work by Stephen Parrish (1973) and Mary Jacobus (1976) in showing that without Wordsworth being able employ artistic judgments and skills, those expressed feelings would be shapeless.

The Idiot Boy is the story of a mentally handicapped child who, one moonlit evening, is sent by his mother by horse to the town to fetch a doctor for an ailing neighbor. But he never makes it. Neither does he return home at the expected time. Instead, on the faithful horse, he wanders joyfully through the night and into the forest until, just before morning, his mother finds him and brings him home.

The poem is striking in the purity and strength of the expressed emotions:

2 / THE POET'S PROGRESS: EARLY STRUGGLE, EARLY GAIN

the love of the mother for her child; her fear that he might be injured or lost or dead; her guilt that she sent him in the first place; his innocent contentment in wandering through the night; her joy in finding him. This easily might have become a poem in which we laugh *at* the protagonists. But Wordsworth's power of expression allows us to experience these emotions *with* the protagonists. The spontaneity of expression is reflected in Wordsworth's own words on the poem: he said that he wrote virtually all of the poem out straight, "not a word, I believe, being corrected, though one stanza was omitted" (Wordsworth 1876, 3:27). Perhaps the quirky tone he adopted and his unique employment of rhymed and unrhymed lines allowed him maximum freedom to distance his own self from his subject.

As we try to work this poem into the history of Wordsworth's own drive towards individuation or emotional well-being, using his poetry as a indicator of that drive, we can turn to a very long letter he wrote in response to a letter from John Wilson in 1802—that is, after the publication of a couple editions of *Lyrical Ballads*. Wilson must have, among other things, specifically criticized *The Idiot Boy* for its subject matter; as Wordsworth's paraphrase of Wilson goes, "nothing is a fit subject for poetry which does not please" (Wordsworth 1967, 354). Wordsworth answers with a wonderfully blunt question to Wilson: "Does not please whom?" (354). It appears that Wilson did not like the "Idiot" presence in the poem. In defending his poem, Wordsworth states: "I have indeed often looked upon the conduct of fathers and mothers of the lower classes of society towards Idiots as the great triumph of the human heart" (357). Parental love was obviously a subject close to Wordsworth's own human heart. But what Wordsworth reads back into the poem after a couple of years shows his developing sense of what he wanted to do with the feelings he was describing. He says that faithfully reflecting feelings is good, but he hopes that, with a poem like *The Idiot Boy*, he has gone beyond this:

> But a great Poet ought to do more that this he ought to a certain degree to rectify men's feeling, to give them new compositions of feeling, to render their feelings more sane pure and permanent, in short, more consonant to nature, that is, to eternal nature, and the great moving spirit of things. He ought to travel before men occasionally as well as at their sides. (355)

But remember, this is looking back from 1802, not 1798 when the poem was written. This rectification and purification of feeling, along with its compensatory function, is what Wordsworth wanted in 1798, what he was working toward. He was not able to clearly articulate this until (as I hope to show later) sometime after 1802, when thinking began to integrate with and perhaps even supplant feeling as the primary way of knowing and experiencing. The poem as it stands in 1798 serves a more immediate purpose for Wordsworth: it is the tale of an innocent child sent away because the father is away working; it is about a parent's guilt for letting a child go, when perhaps it was not the right decision. Again, these are close to Wordsworth's emotional center. We have a happy ending as the mother and child are reunited and return home, and that, perhaps, is what Wordsworth wanted most of all. As in *The Complaint of a Forsaken Indian Woman* and *The Mad Mother*,[25] other poems composed this spring and found in the 1798 *Lyrical Ballads*, Wordsworth is determined to show that the emotional bonding between parent and child endures all circumstances—even those as drastic as in *The Thorn*.

Although poems like *Goody Blake and Harry Gill*, *The Thorn*, and *The Idiot Boy* have overtly fictionalized narrators that might act to distance Wordsworth from the poems' subjects (though this distancing in facts draws our attention to his relationship to those subjects), *Lines written in Early Spring* introduces Wordsworth's voice directly. Unlike *Lines Written at a Small Distance from my House*, which was composed about a month earlier, in March, "I," "me," and "my" now figure prominently. The earlier poem is a "we," "our" and "your" meditation that centers on one point: "It is the hour of feeling" (line 24). Wordsworth wants his sister to experience the blessed and pervasive sweetness of this "One moment" (line 25) in which he finds himself connected to the earth and mankind through love. But in *Lines written in Early Spring*, though he similarly begins by hearing a bird song, we find him alone in his meditation. The earth remains connected with itself, as the flowers, birds, twigs, and air all interact with pleasure. Yet his "pleasant thoughts / Bring sad thoughts to the mind" (lines 3–4), and he grieves and laments "What man has made of man" (lines 8, 24). This is indeed something to trouble over. But here is the big point that goes in another, more personal direction: what troubles Wordsworth is that he cannot "prevent" the attendant feelings that accompany the thoughts (for *thought* and *thinking* dominate the poem)—the sadness, grief, and sense of loss. Once more we see that thought cannot encompass feeling.

Two other poems written at the same time and included in the 1798 *Lyrical Ballads* deserve to be mentioned together in that they explore how a child thinks and feels by having an adult relentlessly confront and interrogate a child: *Anecdote for Fathers Shewing how the Art of Lying may be Taught* and *We Are Seven*. (In all editions of *Lyrical Ballads* these two poems are printed consecutively.)

In *Anecdote for Fathers* the speaker is out walking with his five-year-old charge. According to Wordsworth, the poem is based on an experience with young Basil Montagu, who had now been with the Wordsworths for three years (Wordsworth 1876, 3:19). Unlike in *Lines written in Early Spring*, in which thoughts irresistibly lead to grief and sadness, it is emphasized almost ad nauseam that on this other day thoughts do not bring on any negative emotions. Instead,

> A day it was when I could bear
> To think, and think, and think again;
> With so much happiness to spare,
> I could not feel a pain.
>
> (Lines 13–16)

We get the impression that this "day" of emotional painlessness is somewhat precarious, or at least not usual. But it is a "day" when thinking in abundance can stifle feeling. He asks his young companion, quite out of idleness, whether he prefers the seashore or the farm. The child answers that he prefers the seashore. The adult gets no answer until, after being repeatedly questioned and held by the arm, the child gives an arbitrary answer, obviously a lie, just to silence the adult and free himself. Quite literally, the adult cannot let go until he hears an answer. But he has not had his way, for the answer does not reveal why the child prefers one place over another. He just does.

There is a similar narrative pattern in *We Are Seven*, though the subject material is arguably closer to Wordsworth as a poetic reenactment of an aspect of his own history and subjective self. An adult meets a little cottage girl, and he asks her how many brothers and sisters she has. She answers that she has seven, and in that number it is apparent that she is counting two who have died and are buried nearby. As in *Anecdote for Fathers*, the adult speaker is frustrated with the child's answer. He too cannot let go, and he keeps asking the question. In his inquisition, he persists in his mathematics of subtraction, whereas she insists upon the unity afforded by addition; he keeps counting five, and she keeps counting seven—and oh, the difference to him! In the end, he realizes he is wasting his time: "'Twas throwing words away; for still / The little Maid would have her will" (lines 68–69). He too does not get his way.

The irony in these two poems is that although the child seems trapped by the forcefulness and knowledge of a larger, smarter, and rather aggressive adult, the child is in fact free. It is the adult who is trapped by his limited and rigid sensibilities. The adult in no way seems to have grown out of the child, otherwise his questionings would not be so obstinate. He does not understand that the feelings of a child are foundational for an adult. So long as the adult maintains his chauvinistic (thinking) attitude, he will not be able to understand his inner (feeling) child. At this point, the possibility of the child being father of the man is not apparent.

And so once more we find poems where Wordsworth puts thought and feeling up against each other.[26] Where does this kind of adult come from?

Laurence Mazzeno suggests that this figure of the "hostile father" (1977, 431) in *Anecdotes for Fathers* is based on Wordsworth's emotional struggles with his own father, and he shows that revisions made much later to the poem portray a more gentler narrator.[27] The suggestion, then, must be that over time Wordsworth was able to work out such hostility.

These poems are internal dialogues in which Wordsworth attempts to confront childhood (in the case of both poems) and (in the case of *We Are Seven*) death. Wordsworth's problem was that he was locked into childhood by unresolved feelings and events that he experienced before adolescence. That child, and the feelings associated with the child, had to be confronted, otherwise Wordsworth would in part remain an adult child. But the naïvely determined child figure in *We Are Seven* is also an ambiguous figure, for it impossible to determine whether the eight-year-old child (who is just about the same age as Wordsworth was when he lost his mother)[28] represents the acceptance or denial of death. At any rate, it is clear where the adult is coming from: he wants the child to comprehend the idea of loss, and his determination, like his determination to force an answer in *Anecdote for Fathers*, is obsessive. But the child is not prepared to admit the idea of loss. Her song is one of innocence; his is one of experience. Between the two comes the metaphor of the Fall, which is placed by Wordsworth somewhere between youth and adulthood, feeling and thought, loss and gain, innocence and experience.

Wordsworth's own words about *We Are Seven* are revealing and extraordinarily important, and may help to clarify whether the solitary child's response to death is one of acceptance or denial. Wordsworth writes that *We Are Seven* is about "the perplexity and obscurity which in childhood attend our notion of death, or rather our inability to admit that notion" (Wordsworth 1984, 598). Wordsworth, of course, must be speaking from his own experience of losing both parents before adolescence, and thus this confusion about and denial of death: how it relates to feelings of loss and abandonment is central to his own history and emotional development. The death of the little girl's brother and sister might even be read as a projection of the death of his father and mother: they are in their graves, and Wordsworth, as the adult child, is never, in his mind, far from them. In short, *We Are Seven* is Wordsworth's attempt to articulate his own unresolved thoughts and feelings about death. With Wordsworth's statement, we can be more certain that Wordsworth is separated from his inner child.

I have suggested that, despite the range of characters and circumstances, and despite even the range in tone and style, most of the poems going into the 1798 *Lyrical Ballads* persist in tapping into and reflecting very specific aspects of Wordsworth's emotional life. In this sense the poems can be described as autobiographical. Wordsworth's personality would not, at least at this time, permit him to write about that to which he could not emotionally relate. Wordsworth had discovered that his process of imagination involved meditating on a subject or incident outside of himself until it led to an emotional connection with or reconstruction of that subject or incident, that is, until it led, in his own words, to a "spontaneous overflow of powerful feelings"—*his* feelings. Otherwise little sense can be made of many of the poems written at this time. Even readings of poems like *Simon Lee, the Old Huntsman* and *The Last of the Flock* can benefit from paying attention to what emotional circumstances Wordsworth sets up. Despite having very different central figures and incidents, these two poems also written this Alfoxden spring can be joined together and connected to the other poetry of the time by their attention to emotional helplessness and psychological endurance: Simon Lee is the "sole survivor" (line 24) of a happy past, but in his old age he is barely capable of looking after himself; the man in *The Last of the Flock* has no choice but to sell off the last his cherished sheep in order to feed his family, and the dilemma gives him guilt and "sore distress" (line 85), as well as thoughts of desertion and death. Both have an uncertain future—and that situation is something Wordsworth knew and would write much about. And, as in his other poetry, Wordsworth offers no solution to this kind of emotional limbo, this gap between two consciousnesses. He can only present it.

More playfully, in the companion poems *Expostulation and Reply* and *The Tables Turned*, Wordsworth invokes a kind a evaluative comparison between the brain and the heart, between intellect and perception, between books as teacher and nature as teacher. Once more, this comes down to an engagement between thought (brain, intellect, books) and feeling (heart, perception, nature). But the advancement Wordsworth makes in these two little poems is to hint of a new strategy, a new direction, to find some kind of inner peace:

> One impulse from a vernal wood
> May teach you more of man;
> Of moral evil and of good,
> Than all the sages can.
>
> (*The Tables Turned*, lines 21–24)

But the advancement intimated is subtle: the impulses from nature can somehow bring together thought and feeling, so that our emotional, physical lives can be one with our moral beings. It is hinted that mind and body, thought and emotion, can interact or be as one if you are prepared to "Come forth, and bring with you a heart / That watches and receives" (lines 31–32). The poet, it seems, is ready to make a step forward. A small step for mankind; a giant step for Wordsworth.

Geoffrey Hartman (1971, 141–62) suggests that the idea or theme of separation is central to much of Wordsworth's poetry in *Lyrical Ballads*. Hartman places it on a kind of spiritual stage. As the reader has seen, I would have Wordsworth's idea or theme of separation act out on a more personal or psychological stage. Accordingly, death, loss, solitude, endurance, and guilt, surfacing as they do from Wordsworth's subjectivity, accompany and surround it. But in a remarkable number of the poems discussed above—*The Ruined Cottage,* the poems that went into the 1798 *Lyrical Ballads*, and even *The Borderers* and *Salisbury Plain*—can be seen the suffering, sole-survivor figure. Wordsworth was clearly attracted to or, perhaps more correctly, attached to, this figure. We could say that this concern was motivated by philosophical, social, or historical interests; so too could we argue that this kind of subject was a popular literary convention.[29] But these do not fit strongly with the evidence thus far put forth. By keeping in mind Wordsworth's own history, and by paying close attention to the emotional content in these poems, we witness the remarkable self-examination of a suffering, sole survivor. There is nothing else quite like it in the English canon—and this is without including *The Prelude*. It was and would continue to be a difficult exploration. But Wordsworth's determination and strength gave him a kind of presence that impressed almost every one he met, even before he had done much to prove himself. In the spring of 1798, he was ready to produce something special that would prove himself and work towards connecting him with his self—*Tintern Abbey.*

But let me end with a speculation based on what takes place in the poems that went into the 1798 *Lyrical Ballads*. It is this: many of these poem strongly identify with the female suffering figure, and, in particular, the suffering mother figure. The father or male figures are often conspicuous by their absence (they are not there, they have left the scene) or by their rather stern qualities; the father figures are supportive of neither mother nor child. My suggestion can be put quite simply: Wordsworth emotionally identified with his mother, but he tended to act like his father. The psychodynamics of such a situation is not at all surprising, or even unusual. Should we have expected anything else given Wordsworth's history? But that it was reenacted with such force and artistic determination is surprising, and highly unusual.

3

Tintern Abbey Revisited; or, Aching Joys and Healing Thoughts

> Wordsworth's poetry has the strength to absorb thoughts that might unbalance the mind.
> —Geoffrey H. Hartman, *The Unremarkable Wordsworth*

In the last week of June 1798, Wordsworth, his sister, and young Basil left Alfoxden. It was, as Dorothy described it just after their departure, a "Dear and beautiful place" (Wordsworth 1967, 222). In terms of writing, it had been an extraordinarily productive twelve months for Wordsworth. He had experienced a kind of stability that showed up in the quality and quantity of his poetry, and also in his widened circle of friends, thanks largely to Coleridge. The Wordsworths had plans to go to Germany with Coleridge in a couple of months, but they would not be taking Basil. Dorothy expressed her sadness at leaving behind the child they had fostered for the last few years, but she was utterly convinced that he had been nurtured at Racedown and Alfoxden in the best possible way, and that physically and mentally he was a healthy young boy (lines 221–22).

The poems that would be going into the 1798 *Lyrical Ballads* had already been with the publisher, Joseph Cottle, for a few weeks—that is, all but two poems: Coleridge's *Nightingale* and Wordsworth's *Tintern Abbey*.

Between the time of leaving Alfoxden and the departure for Germany in the middle of September, Wordsworth and Dorothy stayed with a number of friends, including Coleridge at Nether Stowey and Joseph Cottle in Bristol. They also spent time in London just before departing. In between they did some traveling around, including a few days touring the Wye Valley on foot.

Five years before, in the summer of 1793, Wordsworth, alone and on foot, had traveled these same parts: from Bristol up the Wye, and passing Tintern Abbey on his way to North Wales. At that time he was uncertain of what to do with himself. He was without plans or prospects. Emotionally he was very low and at the beginning of his most unhappy period as an adult. It was also in the summer of 1793 when Wordsworth was deeply disturbed by the sights and sounds of the British navy readying itself for war against France: he experienced "thought of woes to come, / And sorrow for mankind, and pain of heart" (1805 *Prelude,* bk. 10, lines 304–5). Five years later it was different picture. Although leaving Alfoxden could not have been a happy occasion, much had happened to him. His finances were in better shape; he had written much fine poetry, some of which was about to be published; he was reunited with his devoted sister; he had become close friends with a number of supportive people who believed in him; and soon he would be off to Europe with his sister and his closest friend, and there, he believed, he would further his chances for a profitable future. Things were considerably better than five years ago.

Armed with a guidebook for the little tour (from which Wordsworth did some borrowing for his poem-to-be),[1] and by noting the Wordsworth's very energetic itinerary for this second short tour (walking perhaps over fifty miles while also doing much sightseeing), we note that he retraced at least part of his earlier way, and that Tintern was the focus of the trip (McNulty 1945). In four days he seems to have passed Tintern three times and stayed there twice.

On the way back to Bristol from Tintern by boat, Wordsworth likely composed most of *Lines written a few miles above Tintern Abbey, on revisiting the banks of the Wye during a tour, July 13, 1798,* and thus "above Tintern Abbey" in the title is slightly misleading, as is the suggested immediacy of the compositional circumstances. The short title posterity has given to the poem—*Tintern Abbey*—is itself misleading, since the poem really has nothing to do with the abbey itself. Later Wordsworth recorded, "I began it [the poem] upon leaving Tintern, after crossing the Wye, and concluded it just as I was entering Bristol in the evening, after a ramble of four or five days with my sister. Not a line of it was altered, and not any part of it written down till I reached Bristol" (Wordsworth 1876, 3:45). When he arrived in Bristol, the poem was almost immediately handed over to the publisher of the first edition, Joseph Cottle.[2]

Tintern Abbey is, on an essential level, Wordsworth's poetic evaluation of his altered emotional state over those "five long" years, a kind of comparative assessment of how he has been and how he is—moreover, how he hopes to be.[3] *What is the relationship between then and now? Have I changed, and if so, in what way? How did I feel, and how do I feel about how I felt and how I now feel?* With the landscape and his life before him, he opens up the problem of continuity and discontinuity in his life, and he attempts to articulate that what he has taken from those past moments is "food / For future years" (65–

66). But one problem has to do with whether he gathers personal and poetic strength by formulating the idea of a past that sustains him, or whether he actually rediscovers a real past that had always been with him. More importantly, he believes something positive can be taken from examining the relationship between his past and present. And then there is a further difficulty, for part of the past he writes of is void of thought, yet very formative in making him a contemplative individual. There is confusion or ambivalence about his past as we witness him subtly recording, revising, or even reinventing aspects of it in order to pre-*scribe* a future. Which past he is addressing is not completely clear: that of five years ago, when he was down and out, or sometime beyond that, going back to his childhood, itself a split experience. It may be that thinking about how he was five years ago triggers earlier emotional recollections. But most of all the poem expresses an attempt to establish emotional and intellectual maturity relative to how he once was and will never be again: "That time is past" (84) is a large and very determined pronouncement. And *Tintern Abbey* becomes thus far his most important personal and poetical achievement in his struggle towards individuation and recovery. It intimates both a break and an advancement, an acceptance and a prophecy.

Related to this is Wordsworth's desire to move from feeling to thought as the primary way of being-in-the-world, and one of the ways he does this in *Tintern Abbey* is by primarily associating feeling with the past and thought with the present and future. The ability to move from feeling to thought, or more importantly, the ability to fuse the two, is, therapeutically, an important one for Wordsworth, and we have already seen him struggling with this in much of his other poetry. The problem has to do with maturation and mental health, with growing up. Bringing the past into the present is a movement towards accepting the past and integrating it into the present. Being able to move from feeling to thought gives him both the distance and the sense of personal development he is working towards, and it puts him in a place where obstinate questions are answered by a "presence" (line 95) that seems to transcend him, yet can only be a product of his inner calm. That place he calls a "blessed mood" (lines 38, 42)—that is, a kind of emotional state that allows him to be at peace with himself; and that "presence" can be nothing else but a sense of his own connectedness with himself and the world around him. The "presence" around him is a projection that originates out of his needs. Seeing "into the life of things" (line 50) is seeing into an esteemed subjective self. We could properly call it self-presence. And this sense of self-presence takes place at the moment when feeling and thought seem to act together, move into each other, as one. In *Tintern Abbey*, a poem about being, about being empowered by seeing into the harmonious "life of things," Wordsworth manages to have feeling and thinking intersect while also transforming the former into the latter.

Not until the *Immortality Ode* does he articulate this as powerfully—and for perhaps the last time.

This coalescence between feeling and thought may also have other dimensions that are more wide-reaching but interrelated. Given that feeling traditionally represents the feminine (weak) and thought the masculine (strong), it might be suggested that in *Tintern Abbey* Wordsworth attempts to integrate the two parts of himself that were once separated (feeling, in fact, is denied or displaced; thought is desired because it intimates the more masculine idea of authority). That these two parts of himself are products of his relationship with his own parents also fits. We have seen that it is the figure of his mother that operates most strongly on his feelings of loss, while as a presence transferred into nature she is a connective presence. The father also has a presence that is transferred into nature, but he is associated with harder emotions, like guilt and anxiety; the mother's associations are with softer emotions, like sorrow and loss. The integration of Wordsworth's past into his present (and future) might also be viewed as constituting his efforts at balancing the feminine and the masculine, feeling and thought. Finally, there is the suggestion that the play of mind and nature in *Tintern Abbey* is the interaction of masculine and feminine (Wolfson 1988, 146-47). The mind/masculine is controlling; nature/the feminine is submissive. In the poem we see Wordsworth's attempt to correct this inequality, but it is not clear whether he is successful. Indeed, as James Holt McGavran Jr. suggests, Wordsworth in *Tintern Abbey* continues "to rank mind over nature, self over other, man over woman" (1990, 341). And so here, in this poem, we witness all of these dimensions (feeling/thought, past/present, feminine/masculine, mother/father, mind/nature) attempting to come together in a complex, perhaps even confused, interplay of images and associations. Because the larger rhythms of articulation are so powerful in *Tintern Abbey*, the logic of the poem also seems to sweep Wordsworth (and us along with him) toward a feeling of integration and individuation and permanence. But there are loose ends that make his accomplishment all the more remarkable.

That *Tintern Abbey* evokes a comparison between the then and the now based on continuity and repetition is explicit in the rhetorical and syntactical structure of the opening section: "Five years have passed; five summers . . . and again I hear. . . . Once again / Do I behold . . . I again repose. . . . Once again I see . . ." That these five years have been difficult is suggested through the five summers that have had "the length / Of five long winters" (lines 1–2). In this phrasing there also seems to be the need to return to this place, that waiting these five *"long"* years has not been easy. There may be something he now has to face up to. Now that he is here (at least rhetorically speaking), he can confirm that all he once saw and heard and felt can be seen and heard and felt once more, how the "secluded" landscape can again "impress / Thoughts of more deep seclusion" (6–7). As he looks to the woods and sees the "wreathes of smoke / Sent up, in silence," he imagines "vagrant dwellers" or solitary hermits sitting around their fires. It is as if he imagines those very self-projected figures who have populated much of his poetry over the last five years. That part of him which, as we've seen, strongly identifies with and reenacts the emotional condition of these lonely, suffering figures still seems to be out there, yet he is now somehow above and distant from it. This is how the first section closes, and where the poem takes its first breath: "The hermit sits alone" (line 23). When the end of the poem comes around, this solitude is counteracted by the inspirational presence of his sister. No longer does he sit alone. Even if he dies, he will live on in the epitaph of her memory, which he has written himself. At the risk of making it sound rather more mundane, Dorothy's powerfully articulated presence at the end the poem, when her voice and eyes take on and reflect his very being (lines 117–20, 149), represents Wordsworth's poetic life-insurance policy.[4] What he is, all that he has done, will be left to her when he goes. She will read his will as he reads it to her now. He wants to make sure that she will not "forget" him (lines 150, 156):

> Oh! then,
> If solitude, or fear, or pain, or grief,
> Should be thy portion, with what healing thoughts
> Of tender joy wilt thou remember me,
> And these my exhortations!
>
> (Lines 143–47)

But Wordsworth was not dying. He was not going anywhere without her. He was taking a dramatic—and poetic—step towards being a different person with a different understanding of himself and his past. In what he is going to leave behind yet retain, he will find a degree of inner strength. And the opening of the poem encourages a further progression: it quickly moves from hearing to seeing to thinking, but needs to get to feeling, as if locating feeling is the unacknowledged center of the poem's searchings. Only when he gets to articulating how he felt, or at least about how he perceives he felt, can he move on to those cognitions that offer compensatory healing.

Wordsworth claims that the particular "forms of beauty" he encountered five years ago have sustained him in "hours of weariness," in those moments of loneliness and "mid the din / Of towns and cities." We have to be reminded that this kind of sustenance works primarily in physical and emotional dimensions: "sensations sweet, / Felt in the blood, and felt along the heart." Only then does it become something vaguely cognitive, passing into his "purer mind

/ With tranquil restoration" (lines 23–31). But, as mentioned, it is this cognitive, thinking dimension that Wordsworth also wanted to work towards, and this would be the most difficult step, for *understanding feelings* is, for any of us, what might be called an oxymoronic act. Thinking and feeling seem to want to go together, especially for someone like Wordsworth, who was struggling to come to terms with his emotional life. But post-Cartesian Western culture has created a kind of dualism where they are conceived of as different functions or faculties, with feeling often considered as "lower" than thinking. Body and mind are separated in the Cartesian model, and Wordsworth needed to have them integrated if he was going to self-integrate. Jumping ahead a bit, one important contribution of Wordsworth was to have given thinking and feeling equal and dependent status, and in this way he anticipated a holistic model of the individual.[5] We cannot have one without the other, since one evolves from the other. But the question at this point remains for Wordsworth: *If I think hard about how I feel, how I felt, can I change how I feel?* Can thinking override feeling, or is feeling the undercurrent of thinking? How are the two related? There is a tough question here that still gets attention in psychological circles, though it has its origins much earlier: *Do I run because I am afraid, or am I afraid because I run?*[6] Fear may be an emotion, but it is the *idea* of fear that is most frightening: as they say, the only thing we have to fear is fear itself. And this even reminds us of Wordsworth's recollection in *Tintern Abbey* when he describes himself running

> more like a man
> Flying from something that he dreads, than one
> Who sought the thing he loved.
>
> (Lines 71–73)

Five years earlier, when he seemed more like someone being sought by what he "dread[ed]" rather than someone seeking "the thing he loved," he was not able to answer the question whether he was running because he was afraid or if he was afraid because he was running. He was just running, wandering, enduring. He could not bring his feelings to his thoughts. There was a gap between them. Now, as the poem evolves at this point in his life, he is more clear of his motives and the relationship between thought and feeling. He no longer has to run: once more, "That time is past."

Those internalized "forms of beauty" remind Wordsworth how his past, those "feelings . . . / Of unremembered pleasure," have influenced him. They help him carry "the weary weight / Of all this unintelligible world." Recollections of these "forms of beauty" put him in a "blessed mood," a state of suspension that quiets him and allows perception of and participation in the harmonious world around and within him (lines 31–50).[7] Despite Wordsworth's belief in this restorative function where emotions can be recollected in order to give him emotional tranquility and the feeling of transcendence, there is yet some doubt: what "If this / Be but a vain belief"? For the world is not always user-friendly—not only does Wordsworth refer to it as often burdening and "unintelligible," but he also notes that it is sometimes dark and "joyless," "Unprofitable" and full of anxiety. Wordsworth, we know, knew much of this side of life, but now he claims he is able to turn to these "forms of beauty" associated with the "sylvan Wye" in his times of need (lines 50–58).

Standing there (or at least picturing himself standing there) in the opening of the poem, seeing the river, cliffs, pasture land, orchards, and woods all spread out against the sky before him (lines 1–23), he now, almost halfway through the poem, sees something else quite different: "The picture of the mind revives again" (line 62), and the "again" here both aligns this new but repeated sighting with the "again" structure in the opening section, while at the same time going in a different direction. He sees himself again—and in particular, that part of him, the "mind," which retains and connects him with his past. Just as seeing "into the life of things" is a way into himself, a self-picturing, it is equally remarkable that the poem decidedly transforms *out there* into *in here*. A part of the effect of this dramatic transformation is to once more move from feeling (out there, the past) to thought (in here, the present and future), for it is in this section of the poem (lines 66–112) that Wordsworth is able to separate the two while also combining them. His sense of pleasure comes not just from what he now feels but from thinking about how he will feel in the future makes him feel now (lines 63–66). This is a rather complicated maneuver (vintage Wordsworth, mind you), but it demonstrates how thinking can use feeling, as opposed to dismissing it, projecting it elsewhere, or simply leaving it behind.

How is it that in *Tintern Abbey* Wordsworth now gestures towards and anticipates a condition of well-being? What new poetic strategy or creative technique or circumstances suddenly encourages this new style of self-reflection? Perhaps it should be asked the other way around: What new style of self-reflection now encourages this new poetic strategy or creative technique? Some of this can never be answered, since artistic inspiration and personal introspection are ultimately a mystery—and in the case of Wordsworth, these two, introspection and imagination, come close to amounting to the same thing. But part of the answer relates to what was mentioned a few paragraphs above when it was suggested that Wordsworth shows signs of reframing his view of himself—his past, present, and future, his conception of feeling and thought—through a holistic model that views the inner life as a part of the universal. One leading contemporary voice of holistic healing (or Ayurvedic medicine), a physician, actually cites *Tintern Abbey*, lines 42–50, as a powerful example of the meditational model, meditation being a powerful technique of participating in one's sense of being. Deepak Chopra, M.D., writes that when he has patients whose "physical and mental states have become severely disjointed," he often recommends mediation as a way of healing. (This problem of disjointedness is, of course, evident as part of Wordsworth's problems.) Chopra then refers to *Tintern Abbey* as "the classic description of a natural state of meditation" in English and quotes the passage mentioned. The kind of experience Wordsworth writes of, Chopra holds, with its attunement to the "breath" and "motion" of the body (lines 44–45), leading to feeling of "harmony" and "joy" (line 49) and the ability to "see into the life of things" (line 50), is what the meditational technique is all about. He adds that this process is "crucial for human development" (Chopra 1991, 143–45). My argument is that it is crucial for Wordsworth's development.[8]

Wordsworth's description of leaping around the mountains and rivers like a little deer is easy to misread as a memory of his childhood in the Lake District, but he claims to be writing about when he "first came among these hills"— that is, five years ago. And we know from the previous chapter what kind of confused and hopeless state he was in then. Thus it is his "hope" that he has "changed" (lines 66–71).[9] So too do we understand what he means when he recollects being unable to recognize nature as "the thing he loved." Five years ago he was "like a man / Flying from something that he dreads," and that feared "something" was within him: his lost inner child who did not know where to turn (lines 71–73). Wordsworth back then had no emotional anchors, and he was adrift. He could find little sense of responsibility or purpose.

The next twenty or so lines in *Tintern Abbey*, which are the physical center of the poem, are the most important and perhaps the most confusing:

> For nature then
> (The coarser pleasure of my boyish days,
> And their glad animal movements all gone by,)
> To me was all in all.—I cannot paint
> What then I was. The sounding cataract
> Haunted me like a passion: the tall rock,
> The mountain, and the deep and gloomy wood,
> Their colours and their forms, were then to me
> An appetite: a feeling and a love,
> That had no need of a remoter charm,
> By thought supplied, or any interest
> Unborrowed from the eye.—That time is past,
> And all its aching joys are now no more,
> And all its dizzy raptures. Not for this
> Faint I, nor mourn nor murmur: other gifts

> Have followed, for such loss, I would believe,
> Abundant recompence. For I have learned
> To look on nature, not as in the hour
> Of thoughtless youth, but hearing oftentimes
> The still sad music of humanity,
> Nor the harsh nor grating, though of ample power
> To chasten and subdue.
>
> (Lines 73–94)

There are three distinct times in the passage. First of all, there is the "then," five years ago, when "nature . . . was all in all";[10] second, further back, there are those parenthetical "boyish days"; and third, there is the ostensible "now" of the poem as it is written a few miles above Tintern Abbey on the banks of the Wye on 13 July 1798. By the end of *Tintern Abbey*, Wordsworth will intimate a further time, a future, "after years" (line 138) in which he hopes the "now" can be remembered and enshrined.

It would be a mistake to confuse the two distinct times from the past, the "then" five years ago when he "first came among these hills" and the "boyish days," presumably when he was much younger. There is some reason for such confusion, for the "coarser pleasures" and "glad animal movements" of those "boyish days" seem something like the "aching joys" and "dizzy raptures" of just five years before. There is an oxymoronic conceptualization in all four of these phrases. If any discrimination is to be made (given that Wordsworth was writing carefully here), it might be that in his "boyish days" he seems to have led a more instinctual existence, while five years earlier he worked on a more emotional level of existence. Yet as soon as this is suggested, we also note that five years ago aspects of nature were both an "appetite" and a "feeling," suggesting both instincts and emotions.[11] One further reason for confusing the two times is that the description of the haunting sounds of the cataract and "the tall rock, / The mountain, and the deep and gloomy wood" seem to invoke some of the "spots of time" passages that rise enigmatically from his childhood recollection recorded in *The Prelude*, but now they seem echoed in his adult life. Most important, however, is that both were times void of thought: these forms of nature "had no need of a remoter charm, / By thought supplied, or any interest / Unborrowed from the eye." Nature and actions were ends in themselves. Five years before he did not have any kind of perspective or purpose; what he got out of nature was limited by his physical experience and emotional perceptions. Wordsworth may be looking back at his condition five years earlier with slightly rosy glasses, but the loneliness, uncertainty, dread, fear, and lack of purpose persist in his description of how he was when he "first came among these hills" five years before. But, once more, "That time ["the hour / Of thoughtless youth"] is past." There may have been a "loss," but in the exchange he forces the belief that he has been abundantly compensated. For nature now is more, even if the landscape is the same. Nature does not, he believes, just give him some feeling of calm; neither is it just something to clamor over. In its power it is also expansive, connective, and (as we shall soon see) inclusive. And he is the center of it, if not the thing itself.

This new formulation of nature in *Tintern Abbey* promotes it as a trope for how feeling and thought (feminine and masculine) can, for Wordsworth, coalesce and correspond. This should not be surprising, since in the first chapter we saw how closely Wordsworth associated the loss of his parents (mother and father) with his turning to nature for support. That is, one part of this new formulation of nature suggests Wordsworth's growing acceptance of the loss of his parents as loved objects and the acceptance of himself as a capable and secure individual. So long as feeling and loss remain separate and contradistinctive, Wordsworth remains in denial, in a kind of split existence, which is a nonacceptance of both sides of himself and of his past. With thought now added and combined with feeling (with the present attuned with past, with the masculine integrated with the feminine), Wordsworth is now able to expand and fuse the two, between which there was once such a gulf:

> And I have felt
> A presence that disturbs me with the joy
> Of elevated thoughts; a sense sublime
> Of something far more deeply interfused,
> Whose dwelling is the light of setting suns,
> And the round ocean, and the living air,
> And the blue sky, and in the mind of man,
> A motion and a spirit, that impels
> All thinking things, all objects of all thought,
> And rolls through all things.
>
> (Lines 94–103)

That this "presence" occupies a position between feeling and thinking encourages the idea that *Tintern Abbey* is a poem of self-integration or self-actualization. The poem is on one important level an inner self-portrait. This may sound like an overdetermined observation, but recall the most dramatic, deliberate, and focused line in the poem: "The picture of the mind revives again." So now, even when that presence is externalized in the sunlight, ocean, air, and sky, it also inhabits (listed last) "the mind of man," thus recalling that earlier line picturing Wordsworth's own mind. This "presence," this "motion and a spirit" that sustains and exists in "All thinking things, all objects of all thought," also takes us back to that self-portrait of Wordsworth, for we have just seen him reshape his past in terms of going from "thoughtless youth" to thoughtful adult. Translation: *The recognition of this "presence" constitutes the new sense of myself as a whole person.* A gap has been filled. And Wordsworth's conclusion continues in the spirit of reasoned reconciliation:

> Therefore am I still
> A lover of the meadows and the woods,
> And mountains; and of all that we behold
> From this green earth; of all the mighty world
> Of eye and ear, both what they half-create
> And what perceive; well pleased to recognize
> In nature and the language of the sense,
> The anchor of my purest thoughts, the nurse,
> The guide, the guardian of my heart, and soul
> Of all my moral being.
>
> (Lines 103–12)

This is powerful stuff, and just about as good as it gets for Wordsworth. The world is no longer just out there. It no longer needs to be pursued yet never captured, as once it was. Neither is it any longer an end in itself, an "all in all." The "mighty world" is the balanced production of both itself and the senses, of perception and feeling and thought. This is less Wordsworth's commentary on the epistemological problems of perception than it is a strong statement of his own worth, a coming-to-terms with his own powers and sense of being through the meditative act: *I am part of the world and the world is part of me. We are each other.* Here he accepts himself in a new way that we might call holistic. Here his senses, thoughts, and feelings all come together. When he writes that "In nature and the language of the sense" (note that this is a very important "and"), he finds the "anchor of my purest thoughts" and "guardian of my heart, and soul / Of all my moral being"; he no longer pictures an individual adrift, lost in a sea of emotional troubles. The metaphors with which Wordsworth now situates himself are progressively personal, until they become the essential self-center: "The anchor . . . the nurse, / The guide, the guardian . . . and soul." He no longer just sees "into the life of things"; he is there, part and creator of "the life of things."

Up until this point in the poem, Wordsworth has written about small-*n* "nature" (lines 73, 90, 109); now, in the final section of the poem (lines 112–60), he writes about capital-*N* "Nature" (lines 123, 153). This capitalization represents the insertion, perhaps even substitution, of himself, his proper name, with—or for—his old conceptualization of nature. Now, at last firmly existing in the present, he can turn to the future, which is what happens in the final section of *Tintern Abbey*. The poet's progress is momentarily complete.

Wordsworth now, quite suddenly, and certainly unexpectedly, turns to his sister, who represents a reflected expression of his past emotional life: "in thy voice I catch / The language of my former heart." Her presence in the scene of writing is not anticipated by the poem's logic, but then again, she is not there for her own sake but for Wordsworth's.[12] That Dorothy represents an emotional presence is clear, and it may also be that her qualities—as one critic summarizes it, "her wildness, intensity, and fervidness"—were helpful to Wordsworth in his own recovery (Fadem 1978, 19).[13] She may even intimate the idea of Wordsworth's mother (McGavran 1990, 343), itself a cluster of buried emotions that move between love and loss, security and pain, continuity and disconnection. Yet at the same time, like Nature, she is the living embodiment and extension of Wordsworth's self-transformation. As such, she is also what one commentator calls "a self-object, a representation of the other in which the self is fully fused. The self-object is characteristic of early infancy, and behind most self-object representations hovers the figure of the mother, which here, as elsewhere, is implicit in Wordsworth representation of nature" (Kramer 1986, 402). Perhaps it is safest to say that Dorothy acts to capture Wordsworth's past, reflect his present, and intimate his future. Seeing into her eyes is seeing into himself, into his past and into his future. For the movement in *Tintern Abbey* is always a movement inwards: the "lofty cliffs, / . . . *impress* / Thoughts of more deep seclusion"; "forms of beauty" pass "*into* my purer mind / With tranquil restoration"; "We see *into* the life of things"; Nature can "*impress* / With quietness and beauty, and so *feed* / With lofty thoughts." And the movement inwards is always a journey of self-discovery.

Being with Dorothy now, as opposed to not being with her five years earlier, makes all the difference to him. It makes his presence absolute and unconditional. Without her there to listen, and to absorb and reflect his past, present, and future, and without her being there to be guided by him, the poem might never have expressed such authority. Her silence is filled by his presence.[14] And her presence now secures his possible absence in the future. Yet there is the suggestion that Dorothy is going to get left behind in the wake of Wordsworth's progress. But the text does not make it absolutely clear which "former heart" and "former pleasures" he is referring to as he looks upon her looking upon him; when he says he beholds in her "what I was once," it is most likely those five years ago that he has in mind, even though she was not there; it could also have been the time in between; so too could it be the more distant past of his "boyish days" (lines 117–21). Yet whatever she represents—and most of all she is the conflation of feeling and thought—when it comes down to what Wordsworth most of all wants out of this moment, it is that henceforth, in the face of all that might go against them, whether it be "evil tongues, / Rash judgements," "sneers," unkindness, or even "The dreary intercourse of daily life," they will with "lofty thoughts" retain their "chearful faith that all which we behold / Is full of blessings" (lines 129–35).

What is not said, but is so obviously implied, is that in the past such negative things must indeed have influenced their lives—and in particular, Wordsworth's life. His "prayer" (line 123) goes in the direction of feeling good about what they do have, rather than dwelling on what they may have lost. So too is there a feeling of maturation, for the "coarser pleasures" (line 74) of his distant past are reframed for the future as "sober pleasure" (line 140). The future needs fortification against whatever may come their way, and Wordsworth makes himself the object of such fortification for Dorothy: if she ever experiences "solitude, or fear, or pain, or grief," she can remember him and his words, and be healed: "remember me," he says, "And these my exhortations!" (lines 143–47). What takes place here is important in terms of Wordsworth's road to recovery: Wordsworth has projected onto his sister those very things that in the past have troubled him. That is, if in the future she experiences troubling emotions like those he has experienced in the past, but which he has now in the present reconciled by having feeling and thought attuned in a concept of Nature that includes his presence, she can call on his words. Wordsworth's eloquence is certainly superior to my paraphrase of his words here, but his logic needs to be pulled out. He has not quite, as they say, "dumped" on her, but the effect is to transform his troubled past into her possible future and, by his remembered presence, overcome those negative feelings.[15] Therapists sometimes call this kind movement of feeling transference—and it is an integral part of psychodynamic healing. Now, as a "worshipper of Nature," he is capable of both esteeming himself and healing his internal rifts.

More than any poem Wordsworth had thus far written, *Tintern Abbey* is based on various kinds of transformations and transitions: from external to internal; noise to silence; absence to presence; description to introspection; from seeing to meditating; from feeling to thought; from loss to compensation; from past to present and from present to future; from nature to Nature; from Wordsworth to Dorothy, and then Dorothy back to Wordsworth. Stylistically, the poem forms itself from within, beginning as a loco-descriptive and inscription poem and ending as an ode. Wordsworth himself points to something like this when he adds a note to the poem in the 1800 *Lyrical Ballads*: "I have not ventured to call this Poem an Ode; but it was written with a hope that in the transitions, and in the impassioned music of the versification would be found the principal requisites of the species of composition" (Wordsworth 1984, 692). Perhaps all of this might be another way of saying that *Tintern Abbey* is a sprawling, expansive poem, uncertain where it going to go and how it is going to get there—that is, until the poem makes its unexpected turn to Dorothy.[16] But it is held together by its own rhythms of growth as it makes those transformations and transitions, which seem to correspond with Wordsworth's own sense of growth. From a slightly different perspective, the poem does not come about just as a record of Wordsworth's discovery of himself; the composition of the poem—the scene of writing—is itself part of the discovery.[17] For the beginning of *Tintern Abbey* does not anticipate its middle or end. When we recall Wordsworth's description of the poem's compositional circumstances, how the poem more or less wrote itself out in final form without revision, we can understand more fully the nature of accomplishment sounded in the poem. The recollection and the tranquility create each other.

Yet so much of the dramatic power of *Tintern Abbey* depends upon a relatively simple notion: as the poem proceeds, *Wordsworth discovers that while the landscape has not changed over these five years, he has*. The nature of this change demands contextualization; and it cannot be contextualized adequately unless attention is given to reasons for Wordsworth's desire for self-change. At least for the moment the past is not denied. It is recreated in the spirit of acceptance.

Along with Shelley and Coleridge, John Keats was surely one of the deepest readers of Wordsworth. As a subtle psychologist of the imagination, he clearly recognized the accomplishment of *Tintern Abbey*. In early May 1818, he wrote of the "sharpening of ones vision into the heart and nature of Man—of convincing ones nerves that the World is full of Misery and Heartbreak, Pain, Sickness and oppression."

> We are in a Mist—*We* are now in that state—We feel the "burden of the Mystery." To this point was Wordsworth come, as far as I can conceive when he wrote "Tintern Abbey" and it seems to me that his Genius is explorative of those dark Passages. Now if we live, and go on thinking, we too shall explore them. he is a Genius and superior [to] us, in so far as he can, more than we, make discoveries, and shed a light in them—Here I must think Wordsworth is deeper than Milton . . . . (Keats 1975, 95).

Keats, then, sees clearly that if we are to get to where Wordsworth is, we too have to "go on thinking" about how we "feel" about those dark times that come upon us.

Just a few days before leaving for Germany, Dorothy wrote in a letter: "[William's poems are] printed, but not published. [They are] in one small volume, without the name of the author; their title is 'Lyrical Ballads, with other Poems'" (Wordsworth 1967, 227). Thus neither Wordsworth nor Coleridge's name would be on this first of the four editions of *Lyrical Ballads* that were published over the next seven years. (In the second edition, 1800, only Wordsworth's name appeared on the title page.) The stay in Germany turned out not at all as expected, and the Wordsworths significantly shortened their time there. Unfortunately, the kind of inner peace and healing in *Tintern Abbey* was, to a significant degree, temporarily negated or pushed aside by the kinds of feelings that resurfaced in Germany over the discontented winter of 1798–99. Much more of his troubled past would come flying back to him as he transcribed those feelings into the poetry of the cold Goslar winter. Now, at least, he was open to that past.

4

Down and Out in Germany: Writing in Self-Defense

> In a dark time, the eye begins to see
> —Theodore Roethke

The human being is an extraordinary animal. It can, by reflecting on its life, both on the most mundane and marvelous events in that life, transform those reflections into communicative acts that will then go on to touch others in important and meaningful ways. This is as wonderful as it is bizarre. For some individuals, communicating these reflections seems to be an imperative. There came a time in Wordsworth's life when it became especially imperative. It became, in Wordsworth's own words, a matter of "self-defence."

Wordsworth needed a place, even if he had to keep that place in his mind—even if he had to, like Milton's Satan, believe he could make the mind itself its own place.[1] He needed to feel connected because he feared disconnection and dislocation. He needed to hold on to things, real things, in the face of personal collapse.[2] He desperately needed to connect certain aspects of his hidden past with both the present and an intimated future. He needed the memory of objects and actions, often insignificant actions or arbitrary objects, to represent that place. When he was unable to be at one of those places that could give him meaning—when, for example, after leaving the relative serenity and security of Alfoxden, he felt abandoned and lost in Germany, or when he was away from the country, lying upon a couch in the city—his imaginative memory reenacted his forgotten needs and unacknowledged feelings in poetic form. The same might even be said of Wordsworth in the distancing between himself and his childhood. It may all amount to the allegorization of a displaced subjectivity; he needed to connect. Often at this point the confusing importance of his experiences in those places and with those objects enter the scene of poetic production, for the strong sense of place and things in Wordsworth's poetry, the apparent topophilia[3] or centroversion,[4] is only there to give a presence, a symbolic or associative presence, to experiences that demand emotional verification and thoughtful articulation. These objects and places are, in effect, props and backdrops for the drama of a poet attempting to pull together an otherwise discontinuous series of problematical experiences and the attendant feelings. And when the poems overtly fictionalize, creating stories and characters that cannot be located as part of Wordsworth's life, we must pay attention to the expressed feelings, for they tell us even more convincingly the story of Wordsworth. Poetry, then, for Wordsworth, was a continuing engagement with his inner life. Quite literally and quite tenuously, poetry held his sense of self, his continuous sense of self, together.

The German experience just alluded to (September 1798 to April 1799), and in particular his stay at Goslar, is perhaps the best and most important example of Wordsworth's use of poetry as a form of personal crisis management in the face of emotional dislocation. At Alfoxden (and shortly thereafter), we saw that Wordsworth was beginning to reconstruct his fragmented sense of self in poems that articulated his most difficult feelings. *Tintern Abbey* was decisive step forward. It opened up the possibility of bringing thought and feeling together, and thus the opportunity for personal recovery. While wintering in Goslar, Wordsworth once more confirmed that the source of his individual potential, his difficult and beautiful obsession, lay within his creativity as it was turned upon his inner life. He confirmed even more strongly that his sense of history was his sense of self.[5] But the nature of his stay in Germany made his poetic confrontation with his subjective self more precarious, and some of the poetry written there reflects this emotional intensity.

Emotionally, the German experience took him one step backward after having taken him two steps forward poetically.

The idea for a large, obsessively inclusive poem began to seriously work away at Wordsworth while he was at Alfoxden, just a few months before he left for Germany. *The Recluse; or, Views of Nature, Man, and Society* would take on just about everything. We recall that in March 1798 he wrote: "My object is to give pictures of Nature, Man, and Society. Indeed I know not anything which will not come within the scope of my plan" (Wordsworth 1967, 212). One of the ad hoc reasons for going to Germany in the first place was to get on with the poem. But despite the encouragement offered by Coleridge (perhaps nagging might be a better way of describing it), Wordsworth would never complete this obviously ambitious work, perhaps because he discovered something standing in the way of his external researches and general contemplation. Perhaps at this point he simply felt inadequate or unqualified for such an undertaking. As he said some years later through the idealism of hindsight, he believed that *The Prelude*, an autobiographical poem, was needed in order to "take review of his own mind, and examine how far Nature and Education had qualified him for such employment"—that is, for the writing of *The Recluse* (Wordsworth 1936, 589). But this is Wordsworth mythologizing the origins of *The Prelude*, and it sounds somewhat contrived and unconvincing. In 1798, Wordsworth had no definite plans to write about his life, although passages from *The Ruined Cottage* about the Pedlar's life were beginning to open up his personal history as a subject for poetic exploration. And so these origins in fact came upon Wordsworth unannounced and in bits and pieces—in the same way, that is, as his emotional life began to reveal itself.

In examining his reasons for not turning to the larger, more philosophical project and for never completing it, it becomes apparent that there were other uncharted territories, preeminent spots, that showed up in Goslar and demanded his immediate poetic attention. We have seen how he went through some of these at Racedown and Alfoxden, but he seems to have found something more lacking, some feelings unresolved, some journey incomplete, some form of a continuing quest for subjective authority.[6] This is what *The Prelude* comes to be all about, and why it comes about: compulsive self-substantiation and self-examination. And we have to ask why. Again, some other material now arose that needed analysis before he felt he could get on with the Coleridge-inspired magnum opus.[7] He needed to creatively explore the growth of his own mind via the development of his feelings to confirm the worthiness of his subjective self.

The symptomology of Wordsworth's bad health while in Goslar indicates that his illness was psychosomatic and that in its onset and origins it was posttraumatic. With this illness, and its association with the subject of the poetry he was beginning to write while he was there, we have to recall the reasons for his need to begin reconnecting himself with his past, which really amounts to Wordsworth attempting to understand his past and deal with the feelings that surfaced in the process of writing: writing as reenactment. Wordsworth, we saw, was the victim of trauma and emotionally challenging events that, until then, he had not worked through. They had been blocked. His story, his history, now demanded that he return to those instances that mysteriously impressed him with guilt and uncertainty, to those places and times in which associations of detachment left him open to dissociative moments. That is, his present negative feelings of separation were about to lead him to write about similar past feelings and accompanying experiences and places. And, corresponding with this, his style of poetry would also radically change from the poetry of *Lyrical Ballads*.[8] Wordsworth did not anticipate opening up what we might call the darker side—or, as mentioned in the introduction, what nowadays is sometimes referred to as the lost inner child. Surely he would have preferred to remember and reenact or even reinvent nothing but moments of childhood bliss, the kinds of moments closer to "the hour / Of splendour in the grass" that he would later be able to conjure up in the *Immortality Ode,* but instead he found himself necessarily opening up some painful and sometimes confusing feelings. Wordsworth's extraordinary creative impulse was, as we have seen, to be found in the psychological circumstances of loss, grief, separation, and endurance. A poetical reenactment of his past, a past that was enmeshed with feelings associated with those circumstances, was about to happen. It would manifest itself in the beginnings of the poem about his past: *The Prelude,* a poem ostensibly intended to rationalize his worthiness as a poet, but really motivated by the wish to establish his worthiness as a person.

Off to Germany

Late in June 1798, Wordsworth and his sister left Alfoxden. A few months before leaving, they, along with Coleridge, had made plans to go to Germany. The original idea was to acquire some working knowledge of German language and culture, which for Coleridge was especially important since he was greatly enthused with German philosophy and felt (as always) that his education was somewhat lacking. About a month before he left he wrote, "I think the realization of the scheme of high importance to my intellectual utility; and of course to my moral happiness" (Coleridge 1956, 1:414). (Some of his German enthusiasm would unfortunately end up taking the form of plagiarism.) The Wordsworths in turn felt they might be able to make money as translators. When Wordsworth anticipated the trip in March 1798, he had great expectations:

> We have come to a resolution, Coleridge, Mrs. Coleridge, my Sister and myself going into Germany, where we purpose to pass the two ensuing years in order to acquire the German language, and to furnish ourselves with a tolerable stock of information in natural science. Our plan is to settle if possible in a village near a university, in a pleasant, and, if we can a mountainous country; it will be desirable that this place should be as near as may be to Hamburg on account of the expense of travelling. (Wordsworth 1967, 213)

But it would not be putting it too glibly to say that the Wordsworths ended up being there for the ride, for the pairs soon split up. It was perceived, by at least one of Coleridge's friends, that the Wordsworths would have prevented Coleridge's German immersion.[9] For the Wordsworths, the planned two years turned into something less than seven months.

The trip began by boat from Yarmouth on 16 September, and it did not begin well for the Wordsworths. While Coleridge (who was accompanied by his friend, John Chester) was joyfully entertaining the various interesting passengers, impressing them with his virtuoso wit and intellect, Wordsworth and Dorothy were seasick. Dorothy was especially ill, and she remained in her cabin for almost forty-eight hours—that is, for virtually all of the voyage. Coleridge described it rather graphically and gleefully: "Chester was ill the whole voyage, Wordsworth shockingly ill, his Sister worst of all—vomiting, & groaning, unspeakably! And I neither sick or giddy, but gay as a lark" (Coleridge 1956, 1:416). But the trip did begin with enthusiasm for all things German. "We intend," wrote Wordsworth just a few weeks after arriving in Germany, "to apply with the utmost assiduity to learning the language when we are settled" (Wordsworth 1967, 232). It did not end that way.

After arriving at Hamburg on the afternoon of 18 September, the same pattern continued. Coleridge unexpectedly separated from the Wordsworths; and while Coleridge affluently wined and dined and studied (mainly in Ratzeburg and Göttingen), the Wordsworths, finding themselves in much more austere circumstances, with neither Coleridge's enthusiasm nor his funding, remained isolated in the country at Goslar near the Hartz Mountains, at which they arrived on 6 October. It just so happened that one of the most brutally cold winters on record was about to impose itself. And while Coleridge immersed himself in high German culture, the Wordsworths found themselves surrounded by low life, and they were not at all impressed. Goslar, Wordsworth wrote on 5 February 1799, was a residence of "a wretched race; the flesh, blood, and bone of their minds being nothing but knavery and low falsehood" (Wordsworth 1967, 249). And while Coleridge collected materials for writing a biography of Gotthold Ephraim Lessing and the history of Germany and German literature, Wordsworth, without even the company of books, found himself immersed in writing about some unusual feelings and aspects of his childhood. In more than one way he was bundling himself up against the cold that was to come.

In mid-November 1798, Dorothy and William reported to Coleridge that Goslar was "an old decaying city," and they complained that there was "no Society" there. Dorothy added, "William works hard, but not very much in German" (Wordsworth 1967, 233). Coleridge wrote to Wordsworth the same month trying to pinpoint the difficulties the brother and sister were experiencing: "You have two things against you: your not loving smoke; and your sister" (Coleridge 1956, 1:440). The Wordsworths apparently made plans to move more than once, and at least by the end of November, but the bad weather continued for the next months, as did Wordsworth's intensive work, and they did not go anywhere. Wrote Dorothy in early February: "For more than two months past we have intended quitting Goslar in the course of each week, but we have been so frightened by the cold season, the dreadful roads, and the uncovered carts" (Wordsworth 1967, 243). These words suggest that they felt more than stuck; they felt trapped, and they felt fearful. At Goslar they may have experienced something like cabin fever. In recalling his time in Germany many years later, Wordsworth romantically underscored his isolation and loneliness, remembering the daily walks he took out into the cold: "I had no companion but a kingfisher, a beautiful creature that used to glance by me. I consequently became much attached to it" (Wordsworth 1876, 3:160–61). Even the plan to learn the language came to nothing. At the end of February Wordsworth wrote to Coleridge: "My hope was that I should be able to learn German as I learn'd French, in this I have been woefully deceived. I acquired more french in two months, than I should acquire German in five years living as we have lived" (Wordsworth 1967, 255). True: Wordsworth did not have the kind of intimate connection that he had had in France. In Germany, the siblings must have been as disappointed as they were isolated. In a poem written in the middle of the stay, and tellingly entitled *Written in Germany, on one of the coldest days of the Century*, Wordsworth would write, "A fig for your languages, German and Norse," and he goes on to describe a confused, helpless, half-frozen fly stumbling about his stove. Wordsworth could very definitely relate to this lost, "disconsolate creature."

In an earlier letter to Wordsworth's brother Christopher, Dorothy noted, "William has been mixing with his German employments a good deal of english poetical composition" (Wordsworth 1967, 246), and in another communication she added, "William is very industrious: his mind is always active; indeed, too much so; he overwearies himself and suffers from pain and weakness in the side" (246–47). Coleridge repeated as much in a letter to his wife Sara and recorded his disappointment—and stern disapproval: "He [Wordsworth] seems to have employed more time in writing English than in studying German—No wonder!—for he might has well have been in England as at Goslar, in the situation which he chose, & with his *unseeking* manners...." (Coleridge 1956, 1:459). But it just so happened that Wordsworth was seeking elsewhere than in the German situation: he was seeking his English past and his subjective present. Coleridge added: "His taking his Sister with him was a wrong Step..... Sister here is considered as only a name for Mistress.... but W., God love him! seems to have lost his spirits & almost his inclination for it [i.e., making acquaintances]" (459–60).

The important connection between Wordsworth's writing and his illness, his "pain and weakness in the side," was made by Wordsworth himself. In the middle of December he wrote a revealing letter to Coleridge:

> As I have had no books I have been obliged to write in self-defence. I should have written five times as much as I have done but that I am prevented by an uneasiness at my stomach and side, with a dull pain about my heart. I have used the word pain, but uneasiness and heat are words which more accurately express my feeling. At all events it renders writing unpleasant. Reading is now become a kind of luxury to me. When I do not read I am absolutely consumed by thinking and feeling and bodily exertions of voice or of limbs, the consequence of those feelings. (Wordsworth 1967, 236)

This is an extraordinarily important and revealing passage; and as I will endeavor to show in this chapter, this letter, not coincidentally, also contains some of Wordsworth's most significant work-in-progress from the German period, revealing his emotional condition via both remembered scenes and creative reenactments. If we wish to understand Wordsworth at all, we will have to have to come to terms with the feelings expressed in the Goslar poems as well as the origin of these feelings.

Unlike Coleridge, who frequently indulged in articulating his various disorders, Wordsworth did not often write about his negative states so openly—at least not in his letters. But here in this passage we are supplied with insight into the difficult connection between his feelings and his sore need to write about "those feelings"—between, that is, feeling and thought. There is a kind of double bind involved with Wordsworth's idea of the causation here: writing is portrayed as both extremely "unpleasant" (physically and emotionally), yet it is necessary as a form of "self-defence." Against what? And which is the cause and which the effect? Does the writing cause the apparent illness, or is the illness making the writing physically difficult? His terms are extreme and his syntax (at least in the last sentence in the passage) is not perfect, but he manages to express that at this point he is "absolutely consumed by thinking and feeling," and that the "consequence" of such obsession was giving him this bodily "pain," "uneasiness and heat." He seems to be saying, in effect, that he is trying to keep the demons away by writing, yet the writing also seems to be difficult. There will be spontaneous overflows of powerful feelings, but it will not be poetry recollected in tranquility. It will be closer to poetry recollected in anxiety.

The answer, then, cannot be that he did not find the actual physical act of writing difficult, but it was difficult physically because of *what* he was writing about and *how* he felt about it. He both profited by and suffered from a kind of inspirational writer's block. Being in Germany, being linguistically, culturally, and geographically isolated; being more or less cut off from, and even feeling rejected by, his former muse, Coleridge;[10] and being in such close quarters with his new muse and connection with his past, his sister,[11] he found himself turning inwards and towards that past.[12] He was startlingly reconnected with his hitherto unexpressed feelings of abandonment and thoughts of death. As mentioned, besides the psychosomatic manifestations that continued and became pronounced during the German period, I believe what was taking place was a form of post-traumatic stress disorder. As the *DSM-III-R* makes clear, the symptoms are "often intensified or precipitated when the person is exposed to situations or activities that resemble or symbolize the original trauma (e.g., cold snowy weather . . .)" (248). The situation that Wordsworth found himself in during (it just so happens) this extraordinarily cold winter brought back feelings associated with his particular trauma. That is, the only material at hand was himself. And in the past feelings he was opening himself up to (at least those expressed poetically), he was to discover not just his strengths and his weaknesses, but he was also getting some insight into his particular blind spots that were enigmatically stuck in time. Freud observes that a "strong experience in the present awakens in the creative writer a memory of an earlier experience (usually belonging to his childhood) from which there now proceeds a wish which finds its fulfillment in the creative work" (Freud 1989, 442). For Wordsworth, it appears that a deeply felt but unrecognized burden from the past was attempting to download itself as a result of his "strong experience in the present."[13]

The figures of isolation and the dramatized circumstances of abandonment, separation, loss, endurance, and enigmatic death, now began to underwrite his poetic concerns in very direct ways. These figures and circumstances that were before allegorized or sometimes made anecdotal and apocryphal in his earlier poetry, and in particular those poems that ended up in *Lyrical Ballads* (for example, such poems as *We Are Seven* and *The Thorn*) continued to determine most of the poetry he was about to write. But now Wordsworth's own life, his personal history, was also going to go, as it were, on the line, and the subjects of abandonment, isolation, loss, endurance, and death would rise out of these attempts to poetically reconstruct and emotionally reenact his life. (It is telling that a significant part of the written results of this autobiographical necessity, that is, the beginnings of *The Prelude*, would remain, for the most part, for his eyes only.)[14] When this material left him—when, through the process of poetry, which for Wordsworth at this time was a form of self-induced writing therapy, the openings were closed, the gaps filled, the blind spots eliminated, and the wounds healed—when the inner child had grown up and this material left him—so too would this style of poetry be left behind. Thomas McFarland rightly attributes Wordsworth's decline (or "desiccation") to a loss of "intensity of feeling" in the poetry (1992, 89–97), but he gives no particular reasons for those feelings in the first place, never mind why at a certain point they might have dried up. But it is apparent in the later poetry that the emotional intensity is missing. This may be the real reason for the apparent "decline" that has been so often noted in Wordsworth's later poetry:[15] he may have played out, resolved, or worked through the difficult subject material that sustained the kind of poetry that came to him that coldest of all winters. He did not just use this material up;[16] he came to terms with it. As I will show in a later chapter, the affirmative resolutions and independence of the *Immortality Ode* that came later, evolving as they did through difficult and determined meditation, became the turning point and end point. In the *Ode* he not only confronted himself and those "obstinate questionings" associated with "shadowy recollections," but he also at last answered them with his most powerful trope for well being: the "philosophic mind." Therapy terminated.

So what was Wordsworth thinking about that caused the simultaneous creative splurge and unusual physical discomfort? The poems and the subject material he began to write about in this, the most important and productive part of his annus mirabilis, give the answer for which we are already prepared: Wordsworth was beginning to write autobiographical verse and to make use of the lyric form for expressing unresolved feelings.

The first part of the 1799 *Prelude* was, of course, the main result of the German experience and marked Wordsworth opening up to write about his past, and this will demand that we return to it in some detail.[17] But he also wrote a number of other significant poems and fragments and made a number of beginnings during this relatively short time. Although not all of these have entered the top rank of the Wordsworth canon, many of the Goslar poems have become central to our attempt to understand the poet, and in uneasy and ingenious ways these poems begin to reveal the Wordsworthian subjects that have troubled us (as readers) as much as they seem to have troubled him (as writer). Besides the first part of the 1799 *Prelude,* Wordsworth also produced *To a Sexton, If Nature, for a favorite Child* (also known as *Matthew*), *The Fountain, The Two April Mornings, Could I the priest's consent have gained, Just as the blowing thorn began, Elegy, Remembering how thou didst beguile, Carved, Matthew, with a master's skill, Dirge, A slumber did my spirit seal, Song* ("She dwelt . . . "), *Strange fits of passion I have known, Lucy Gray, A Poet's Epitaph, Nutting, Three years she grew in sun and shower, Ruth, How sweet when crimson colours dart, Address to the Scholars of the Village School,*[18] *Written in Germany, on one of the coldest days of the Century, A Fragment* (a.k.a. *The Danish Boy*), *Ellen Irwin,* parts of *Influence of Natural Objects* (1805 *Prelude,* bk. 1, lines 452–89), and *There was a Boy* (of Winander; 1805 *Prelude,* bk. 5, lines 389–422). Wordsworth also likely wrote his fragmentary *Essay on Morals* while in Germany; this short work argues, *contra* Godwin, that all the philosophy and reason in the world cannot change our feelings, who or what we are, and what we do (Wordsworth 1974, 1:103–4). This is a important admission, and one that must have been close to his own experience. There are also a number of fragments that mark the beginning of work towards *The Prelude.*[19] In short, Goslar, despite its trying circumstances, was certainly one of the most productive periods in life. It was his *tempus hibernum mirabile*.

The poems and passages that are appropriate to look at first appear in the important letter to Coleridge quoted above and follow almost immediately the passage describing his "uneasiness and heat" (Wordsworth 1967, 235–43). It is not inappropriate to associate Wordsworth's difficult feelings with the emotional content in these texts.

The Letter to Coleridge, December 1798

The first poem to appear in the letter comes to be titled *Song,* but, as noted parenthetically above, we know it best by its first line: "She dwelt among th' untrodden ways." (Hereafter referred to as *She dwelt.*) Along with *A slumber did my spirit seal, Strange fits of passion I have known, Three years she grew in sun and shower,* and *I travelled among unknown men,* these have become known to us (but certainly not to anyone in the Wordsworth circle) as the "Lucy poems."[20] This grouping can be seen as somewhat arbitrary and misleading: *A slumber* does not mention any "Lucy" at all, while *Lucy Gray,* which obviously does, is not included in the group, despite its similar subject and corresponding date of composition; and *I travelled* was composed somewhat later (in April 1801), but gets included because Wordsworth mentioned in a letter that it was to be read after *She dwelt* (Wordsworth 1967, 333). Like the grouping of the romantic poets themselves, the Lucy grouping nevertheless remains a product of literary and historical convenience, inasmuch as it more or less points to a particular period of composition as well as an emerging subject matter—indeed, a subject matter that has challenged not just the Wordsworth business but also the business of criticism and theory in general.[21] My own view would be to group *She dwelt, A Slumber, Three years* and *Strange fits* together regardless of that thing called "Lucy." I would also include *Lucy*

Gray, since it too was written at this time, and it too hauntingly reenacts Wordsworth's troubles with the lost inner child. Better still would be to associate them within the larger grouping of poems written during the Goslar period, especially the elegies centering around the figure of Matthew.

The final version of *She dwelt* that we have with us today in many ways differs substantially from the version written out by Dorothy in the letter to Coleridge. The letter version is eight lines longer than the twelve lines Wordsworth finally settled on. The version Wordsworth settled on excludes the first and the fourth stanza, and I have put in brackets the major revisions that appear in the poem as published in the 1800 *Lyrical Ballads*.

1

My hope was one, from cities far,
    Nursed on a lonesome heath;
Her lips were red as roses are,
    Her hair a woodbine wreath.

2

She lived [dwelt] among the untrodden ways
    Beside the springs of Dove,
A maid whom there were none to praise,
    And very few to love;

3

A violet by a mossy stone
    Half-hidden from the eye!
Fair as a star when only one
    Is shining in the sky!

4

And she was graceful as the broom
    That flowers by Carron's Side;
But slow distemper checked her bloom,
    And on the Heath she died.

5

Long time before her head lay low
    Dead to the world was she:
[She *lived* unknown, and few could know
    When Lucy ceased to be;]
But now she's in her grave, and Oh!
    The difference to me!

(Wordsworth 1967, 236–37)

Dropping the first and fourth stanzas make the poem profoundly stark. Without the red lips, the wreathed hair, and gracefulness, and without the particularities of her disease, its duration, and her place of death, Lucy becomes not just "unknown," but unknowable. The revisions transform her from a living ("lived" in the second stanza above becomes the more impersonal "dwelt") being into something essential, elemental, and abstract, and thus she becomes more of a feeling or difficult idea than a particular flesh-and-blood person. Moreover, because no one else would seem to be able to know her or care about her passing from the scene, she becomes a feeling attached exclusively and emphatically to the speaker—"and Oh! / The difference to me!"

The effect of this exclusivity is not just to align Lucy with the speaker, but, more importantly, to collapse the narratorial and authorial barriers between the two: Lucy, this isolated, sensitive, unnoticed, and seldom loved young person, *is* the arrested part of Wordsworth, the Wordsworth who, with "uneasiness at . . . [his] stomach and side, with a dull pain around . . . [his] heart," is looking for the child to become the father of an undivided self. Lucy is locked into Wordsworth, and Wordsworth is looking for the key in order to liberate not her, but himself. She is the child within. Her being and growth, like the part of himself that he is just beginning to get in touch with, is crippled by isolation, separation, and guilt—and, finally, by death: his own figurative death, which is undifferentiated from and enmeshed with that of his parents, who deserted him before he had a chance to grow into a complete adult. Predictably, in the early version of the poem where Wordsworth is not blocking through the poetry of repression and abstraction, he points to the correspondent death of Lucy and himself as poet: Wordsworth opens the poem by confessing that *his* "hope," whatever that vague "hope" might be, was "Nursed on a lonesome heath," and then in the fourth stanza he says "And on the Heath she died." His nurturing and her death exist on the same plane, at the same place—the heath. A child *within* Wordsworth needs to be recovered by Wordsworth, perhaps even to be discovered *as* Wordsworth.

In this text, then, with its two appropriately conflated versions—the death of a young, idealized, forsaken child and the speaker's very personal feelings of loss, plus the "lonesome" situation of his upbringing—poetically coexist and cross over. The only story taking place here is an attempted transference, which of course suggests a desire for psychological resolution.[22] The elemental emotions in the poem strongly resist the kind of sense or meaning that narrative expression can supply, for the real story, we know, cannot be told. It can, however, be reenacted emotionally in the poem. So here we have drama without characterization; the conflict remains internal and internalized; the action takes place within the subjectivity of the speaker; and the big realization comes in the form of a strong yet inexpressible feeling that falls directly on the experience of the speaking subject: "and Oh! / The difference to *me!* "²³ Lucy is not the subject of this poem; she is the subjectivity of Wordsworth. As will be explored, this is where the originality of these poems can be located. And this is why this poem and the others in this grouping resist or at least challenge our reading of them. Upon what premises can this interpretation be based? We only have a displaced or denied feeling that desires expression.

We, like Wordsworth, cannot stop here. We, like Wordsworth, have neither found nor liberated his Lucy, his self-same Other who calls out to him from the "grave." Unlike *We Are Seven*, which, with all its dialogical defenses, attempts to confront the idea of death from a very peculiar intellectual perspective related to innocence versus experience, *She dwelt* attempts to confront death from an emotional perspective. This alone marks some progress on the part of Wordsworth as he moved towards individuation and the recovery of the whole child. But he would need more Lucy-like figures and more direct poetic access to his feelings if he was to go any further.

The letter continues with another poem, and the struggle with the same subjects is reshaped without being resolved. The only interruption between the two poems in the text of the letter is an annotation by Dorothy: "The next poem is a favorite of mine—i.e. of me Dorothy." What follows is an early version of *Strange fits of passion*.

Once more there are significant differences between the letter and the published versions. Both have seven stanzas, but in the letter version he has a final stanza (stanza 7 below) that gets dropped, while for the final, published version he adds an opening stanza (again I have put in brackets the major revisions that make up the revised version):

[Strange fits of passion I have known,
   And I will dare to tell,
But in the lover's ear alone,
   What once to me befel.]

1
Once, when my love was strong and gay,
   [When she I lov'd, was strong and gay]
And like a rose in June,
   I to her cottage bent my way,
Beneath the evening Moon.

2
Upon the moon I fix'd my eye
   All over the wide lea:

My horse trudg'd on, and we drew nigh
 Those paths so dear to me.

3

And now I've [we] reached the orchard-plot,
 And as we climbed the hill,
Towards the roof of Lucy's cot
 The moon descended still.

4

In one of those sweet dreams I slept,
 Kind nature's gentlest boon,
And all the while my eyes I kept
 On the descending moon.

5

My horse moved on; hoof after hoof
 He raised and never stopped,
When down behind the cottage roof
 At once the planet dropp'd.

6

Strange are the fancies that will slide
[What fond and wayward thoughts will slide]
 Into a lover's head,
"O mercy" to myself I cried
 If Lucy should be dead!"

7

I told her this; her laughter light
 Is ringing in my ears;
And when I think upon that night
 My eyes are dim with tears.

(Wordsworth 1967, 237–38)

As in *She dwelt*, the revised version moves towards the concerns and strange fears of the speaking subject, while drifting away from a knowable, differentiated Lucy. This is appropriate, given the thesis that the speaking subject, Wordsworth, both wants to know and face *his* fears, yet is afraid of such knowledge and emotional confrontation. Even the revision from "Once, when my love was strong and gay" to "When she I loved was strong and gay" suggests a focus that locks in on the speaker's view and object of desire rather than on the lover's well-being. And in the new opening stanza Wordsworth created for the poem, the turn is made even more towards the speaker and his recollected overflow of powerful and unusual feelings: "Strange fits of passion I have known . . ." The poem's enigmatic power hinges on the resistance for gaining insight to the speaker's apparent emotional blindness. To call them "fond," then, is to sentimentalize, even trivialize, feelings that are, at least in the first, more unrepressed, unmediated version of the poem, not at all too deep for tears.

What is striking about the final version of *Strange fits* is that now the speaker never gets to Lucy's cottage. His way (the poem, his trail of emotions) is arrested by his "wayward thoughts" of Lucy's death which inexplicably "slide" into his head. But to say they are "wayward" is not to deny the validity of these thoughts, for, as Freud would note, these kinds of daydreams are real, real in the sense of reenacting displaced feelings through imagined scenarios.[24] Rather, to say these thoughts are "wayward" is to acknowledge their arresting power in preventing our "Lover" from getting anywhere. The "wayward thoughts" stop this poem the very moment that the idea of death slides into the head of the speaker. It is unannounced and associated with unutterable fear and guilt: "'O mercy!' to myself I cried . . . " This is indeed a strange and spontaneous overflow of powerful feelings. Where do they come from? Out of what feelings and thoughts of grief did Wordsworth fashion this poem?

We are not permitted to know this revised Lucy very well, other than that she is (or was) very much alive: she "was strong and gay / And like a rose in June"—that is, healthy, happy, and, as it seems according to the metaphor, an incarnation of youthful beauty. But in the letter version we have this—and more: he arrives at her cottage; he tells her of his "Strange . . . fancies"; he hears her laugh; and he recalls, with indeterminable emotions, that night. It is not even clear whether Lucy has since died, whether she died later that night, or whether she died at all—although I must admit that for me Lucy's death (or at least the idea of her death) is the most convincing possibility, explaining why the speaker grieves over the irony of his original thoughts. We only know that the speaker's recollected emotional associations are, as mentioned, tearful and fearful.

There are five subject clusters in the final version of *Strange fits* that are problematically enmeshed with and work on each other, and therefore on us—and so they must have worked away on Wordsworth as this story evolved from the level of his affective unconscious to become manifest in his creative consciousness as a narrative lyric. The first centers around the admittedly displaced nature of the speaker's emotional state and responses—the "Strange fits of passion" and morbid "wayward thoughts" that begin and end the poem, and the open-eyed "sweet dreams" that fall into the middle of the poem. The second cluster involves the deliberate movement and determined fixation in the poem as the speaker "bent" his way and "fixed" his eye on his surroundings and then "kept" his "eyes" on the moon as the horse, knowing its way, "trudged on," never stopping, "hoof after hoof." These dramatize the waywardness that defines the first cluster while also suggesting the trancelike condition of the speaker. The third cluster simply accents Lucy's vitality; as mentioned above, it is made clear that she was very much alive. And this brings us to the next subject: Lucy's imagined death, which is a projection of the speaker's fears, especially since Lucy at the same time is portrayed as so robust. And finally, there is the subject of love that encloses the whole poem: "the lover's ear," "When she I loved," "a Lover's head"; even the way there is loved with its "paths so dear."

The last three subject clusters and the movement of *Strange fits* point to an associative process: his love/her life; her death/his fear. And these can profitably be moved around and collapsed if, as in *She dwelt*, Lucy is seen as the projected image of lost love that has been determined by death.[25] Just as the horse is locked into its destination with its uneasy rider, Wordsworth is locked into this process and the permutations of these associated subjects. But he cannot get to Lucy, that is, to feelings of love that have been lost without having been realized; in his anxiety he cannot get over the *thought* of her death and his feelings about the possibility of her death. That is, Lucy's death and the speaker's feelings are problematically enmeshed and nondifferentiated. She is, in both of these poems, a projection of his feelings of unacknowledged and unresolvable death.

If, then, we are to make an identification with Lucy, as is the fashion of many of my worthy critic-predecessors, I would say that Lucy can be none other than a projection of Wordsworth himself.[26] And so, in *Strange fits*, the narrative drama of the poem involves him moving, step by step, closer and closer to the cottage, but the mesmerizing moon, which has led him on, drops from the sky the moment he is in sight of his goal. The speaker, as Wordsworth, remains entranced in darkness, "Dead to the world," attempting to move steadily on but never getting to his destination or able to break away from the fixed image of the grave. This is the double bind: the desire to move on, to confront dreaded knowledge or feelings, and the fear of that knowledge and those feelings. In these two poems, Lucy, as Wordsworth, remains the child somewhere over the hill and beside the grave.

The other two so-called Lucy poems, *A slumber did my spirit seal* and *Three years she grew in sun and shower,* were not written out in the letter to Coleridge, but they were composed at the same time, and so it is appropriate to discuss them here, if only briefly.

A slumber is probably the most enigmatic of Wordsworth's poems. Its challenging brevity, its stark and dreamlike quality, and its oppositional structure have made it the touchstone (or target) of much critical debate, most of which has had little to do with the man and the moment that created this text.[27] But even without bringing Wordsworth into this scene of writing, we can see the poem as an abbreviated story of bereavement, of loss and death, of the speaker's silent struggle with his changed emotions:

> A slumber did my spirit seal;
>   I had no human fears:
> She seemed a thing that could not feel
>   The touch of human years.
>
> No motion has she now, no force;
>   She neither hears nor sees,
> Rolled round in earth's diurnal course
>   With rocks and stones and trees.

Once upon a time I feared nothing, and I knew someone who seemed beyond mortality. But now she is dead and buried. I now have fears. The speaker seems unable to express any feelings beyond fear. There is a tone of resignation without acceptance. All the emotions are beneath the surface, buried with the dead child within the earth. This child within the earth is inaccessible to the speaker, and this surely is the one of the reasons for the expressed feelings of hopelessness. The story is not in itself enigmatic; we know what happened—someone unexpectedly died—but we simply do not have the details of the who, what, when, where, or why. In short, it would not make a very good newspaper story. As a poem, however, it often makes for very smart criticism. As Susan Eilenberg writes, "the Lucy poems leave conspicuous room for voices other than that of the poet. They leave room particularly for the reader, who is invited to supply his interpretation in place of the story the poet refuses to tell" (1992, 110). But, in the spirit of the poems themselves, I believe we have to consider them on their own rather simple terms. This Lucy, as in *She dwelt*, simply, and quite abruptly, "ceased to be," and the speaker is noting, albeit obliquely, the difference to him. And as in *Strange fits*, we have the association of his fear and her death. So too in *Three years* is Lucy suddenly taken from the speaker, and he too is left, alone, to helplessly grieve her death without being able to accept it. The speaker imagines that Nature will do its work and look over her, but the speaker will only have "the memory of what has been / And never more will be" (lines 41–42).

Geoffrey Hartman suggests that Wordsworth's Lucy "dies at the threshold of humanization," and since she is a construct of the poet's consciousness, we should not so much emphasize Lucy's death as the "consciousness of the survivor" (1971, 157–60). I would take this observation in a different direction.

Lucy dies at the threshold of being fully expressed as a feeling of loss; and she is not just an idea in Wordsworth's frontal lobes: she resides closer to his solar plexus (where he feels the pain and the helplessness), and she represents a cluster of unresolved emotions that Wordsworth has mulled over for a long time; she is buried deep within his world; and so it is the feelings of the survivor we must emphasize. It just so happens that the cold, lonely winter in Goslar provided the negative stimulation for Wordsworth's many attempts to express his feelings. We must see him as a survivor in need of inner healing.

Mourning does not serve the purposes of the dead but of the living. Mourning is the ritualized emotion of separation and acceptance. But the Lucy poems do not quite get there. As Eilenberg notes, the Lucy poems "are abortive elegies, poems in which a man fails to detach himself from those he has lost and turn again to the living" (1992, 117). That "man," Wordsworth, apparently has not yet resolved his grief. There is separation, or the fearful thought of separation, without acceptance.

The Lucy poems circle around death and loss and the speaker's troubled emotional response. We could leave it at that, and it would be fine. That we can also attempt to see these poems as Wordsworth poeticizing his subjectivity in "self-defence" should be neither startling nor surprising. Lucy, as Wordsworth's lost inner child, keeps on beckoning, and Wordsworth keeps on approaching.

The letter continues. Responding to what Coleridge had written about skating at Ratzeburg, Dorothy says that she will now write out some lines that Wordsworth himself has been just been composing about skating. It is, she writes, "a description of William's boyish pleasures" (Wordsworth 1967, 239). The passage eventually becomes a section of the first part of the 1799 *Prelude* (lines 150–85; Wordsworth 1979, 5).[28] It could be called the first public performance of an extended passage from the *Prelude*.

The most significant feature of the passage as it relates to the thesis here is that it expresses autobiographical concerns relating directly to Wordsworth's childhood. It is quite unlike the quirky ballads with fictional characters inhabiting or wandering about the countryside of some of his earlier poetry; it is not plainly picturesque and does not take the apparently more grandly philosophical and meditational tone of *Tintern Abbey*. Instead, it recounts an event without the trappings of extended commentary. Knowing that this will become part of the 1799 *Prelude*, which was also being formulated in bits and pieces at this time, we can safely say that experiences and, more importantly, certain feelings were beginning to come back to him. The ice-skating scene represents, if one can excuse the unfortunate appropriateness of the cliché, the tip of the iceberg.

The memory is one of skating with many of his village friends, of winter days spent chasing around and playing games on the ice until the afternoons spread out against the evening sky. The recounted experience is full of playful, imaginative innocence and breath-taking pleasure. This aspect of the scene is described as completely surrounding and engulfing Wordsworth with all he saw and heard, with "resounding" and "bellowing" voices, with echoes resonating "through the darkness and cold," with the stars above "sparkling clear," and the shadows of stars below reflecting off the "polished ice." Yet it is more than just a description of a noisy pack of children. It also recalls moments of seclusion and reflection as he "retired" from the crowd into "silent bays," of recovering from dizzying himself and finding himself beside the "solitary cliffs" until "all was tranquil as a summer sea," and of noting that the "distant hills" rehearse "an alien sound / Of Melancholy." Wordsworth may situate himself in the middle of a world of busy sights and sounds, but the passage also takes the time to locate him individually among more subtle motions and emotions.[29]

This dreamlike memory is imbued with glitterings of idealism. There is, however, one significant intrusion into the magical realism of the recollection:

> And in the frosty season when the sun
> Was set, and visible for many a mile
> The cottage windows through the twilight blazed,
> I heeded not the summons: clear and loud
> The village clock tolled six. I wheeled about,
> Proud and exulting like an untired horse,
> That cares not for his home.

The one intrusion, then, which is in the opening of the passage, is the "clear and loud" call to Wordsworth from Father Time to return home, but it is "heeded not." Thus the memory of innocence threatens to be broken by the feeling of guilt for not getting *home* by six o'clock, and it is perhaps this feeling that informs the rest of the passage, and particularly the end, with its haunting feelings of melancholy, solemnity, and solitude:

> yet still the solitary cliffs
> Wheeled by me, even as if the earth had rolled
> With visible motion her diurnal round;
> Behind me did they stretch in solemn train
> Feebler and feebler, and I stood and watch'd
> Till all was tranquil as a summer sea. . . .
>
> (Wordsworth 1967, 239)

The subtle yet powerful tension in the passage is between the idealized, blissful recollection in tranquility and the melancholic, solitary feelings of guilt. And what perhaps confirms this subtle tension, or at least that Wordsworth acknowledged some negative feelings, is that for the 1805 *Prelude* he added some lines to the opening (those in italics):

> And in the frosty season, when the sun
> Was set, and visible for many a mile
> The cottage windows through the twilight blazed,
> I heeded not the summons; *happy time*
> *It was indeed for all of us, to me*
> *It was a time of rapture.* Clear and loud
> The village clock tolled six; I wheeled about
> Proud and exulting, like an untired horse
> That cares not for his home.
>
> (1805 *Prelude,* bk. 1, lines 452–60)

These added lines, forced in as they are between the refusal to heed the "visible . . . summons" of home and the "clear and loud" call of the clock to return home, must be read as a belated effort to communicate the following: *Dear Reader: Don't get me wrong; it really was a happy and rapturous time, despite whatever other feelings I had. Because I really did care for my home.* The additional thought is a rather lame addition.

So even here, when Wordsworth had unhindered access to innocent experience, to that time before his parents passed away and left him with unresolved issues centering around abandonment and loss, he could not cross over to that time without feeling guilt and placing himself in solitude. And this is borne out even more clearly in the passage Dorothy next transcribes in the letter.

In the well-known boat-stealing episode, one evening young Wordsworth takes a shepherd's skiff and then recounts his confused feelings.[30] Dorothy justifies linking it to the skating scene by stating to Coleridge, "I will give you a Lake scene of another kind. I select it from the mass of what William has written, because it may be easily detached from the rest, and because you have now a lake daily before your eyes" (Wordsworth 1967, 240). This passage also ends up in the first part of the 1799 *Prelude* (lines 89–129; Wordsworth 1979, 3–4), coming just a few lines before the skating scene.[31] And there are also more important connections between the two passages than those made by Dorothy.

Wordsworth recalls being surrounded by the landscape and by the light and sound: "the moon was up, the lake was shining clear":

> not without the voice
> Of mountain echoes did my boat move on,
> Leaving behind her still on either side
> Small circles glittering idly in the moon
> Until they melted all into one track
> Of sparkling light.
>
> (Wordsworth 1967, 240)

After rowing out some distance, a huge, gothically animated cliff takes over the scene and interrupts our rower's joyride, turning the pleasure into fear as he imagines the "thing" pursuing him.

Not unexpected but nonetheless noteworthy are the considerable similarities between the skating and rowing episodes, or at least in the way they are described. Both take place on a lake; both take place at evening; both have sparkling stars; both have surrounding cliffs; both water surfaces have reflections; both have gliding motions over the water surfaces and into the darkness, as well as more frenzied movement; both landscapes surround and engulf Wordsworth; and in both passages there is an attempted fixed gaze that tries to work through some unsteadiness or uncertainty. But there is more. There is also the imagery of solitude and the strangeness of the event as it is recalled. And both are, to borrow a phrase from the rowing episode, "act[s] of stealth / And troubled pleasure": in the rowing episode it is the stolen boat, in the skating scene it is the stolen time. Both deal with the feeling of guilt, and it is to the profound but unacknowledged feeling of guilt in the rowing scene that I shall shortly return.

But, it might be argued, would it not be natural for some guilt to be associated with these kinds of events—that is, for not coming home when one is supposed to, and for using someone's boat without permission? Yet an obvious affirmative reply to this question might not necessarily address the question of *why* these kinds of seemingly spotty or even trivial recollections should retain preeminence for Wordsworth, and *why* these particular feelings should seem to be enmeshed with and disturbing the experience. Wordsworth himself attempts to answer this in a passage that he was also composing at about this time:

> There are in our existence spots of time
> Which with distinct preeminence retain
> A fructifying virtue, whence, depressed
> By trivial occupations and the round
> Of ordinary intercourse, our minds—
> Especially the imaginative power—
> Are nourished and invisibly repaired;

> Such moments chiefly seem to have their date
> In our first childhood.

This passage too was to become part of the first part of the 1799 *Prelude* (lines 288–96). Here, as a poet, Wordsworth powerfully recognizes the "imaginative power" of such childhood memories, yet he doesn't seem to understand why such events stand up and out except as rather banal associations, and why such feelings (like those located in the present analysis) should pop into his spots. But he intuits that these recollections, triggered ("depressed") as they are by present "occupations," are also necessarily sustaining and reparative. This latter asset becomes even more clear in one slightly later revision of this passage, where "renovating virtue" is substituted for "fructifying virtue."[32] We might suggest that if, here in Germany, these recollections arose to repair or renovate, then some damage or injury seems to be implied that needed to be repaired or renovated. I do not believe, then, that these recollections came arbitrarily to Wordsworth. The cause of their onset can be found in Wordsworth's feelings then, in the condition and environment in which he found himself: having regrets about losing Alfoxden, he found himself isolated in Germany in unpleasant living conditions, unexpectedly separated from his friend and colleague Coleridge,[33] without making progress towards his expressed goals (*The Recluse* and the German language), and coupled in very close quarters with his sister; he might even have felt further disturbed and isolated thinking that the locals could have been gossiping about him and his "sister." So except for Dorothy's presence, which was a reminder of Wordsworth's family past but which may also have been a burden, these other conditions centered around loss, fear, guilt, and separation—and so did his Goslar poetry. Feelings came in aid of other feelings.

Meanwhile, back at the boat-borrowing spot of time, we see that the fear and trembling out on the lake gave way to "grave / And serious thoughts" on the way home, and these in turn later evolved into ineffable, dark, disturbing, and undetermined "thoughts" that haunted his "mind / By day, and were the trouble of my dreams." Wordsworth, in his otherwise eloquent description of this experience, resists naming the accompanying feelings that are contained by these "thoughts," but the fear turned inwards has become Giant Guilt, envisioned as "huge and mighty forms" lumbering menacingly though his conscience—"forms" that may in fact suggest an ambivalent emotional engagement with parental associations.[34] This is what Wordsworth has trouble facing up to, what gives him anxiety—and, moreover, acts as inspiration for this new kind of poetry written during the German period. The situation is similar to Wordsworth's approach to Lucy: the unknowable truth of a unknowable feeling is projected as an external thing, and the moment he gets close, it/she moves away; it/she becomes internalized and reenacted as a shapeless but indelible feeling, but it is not made cognizant. Again, it/she lies buried deep within his psyche. The paradox is that Lucy and the giant forms are, to use Wordsworth's word, "preeminent"; they resist conscious knowledge and positive emotional articulation, but they will not go away. The fear is known and the feelings of loss and isolation are expressed. Only more work will emancipate the guilt and lead to personal liberation.

As in the two Lucy poems discussed above, there is in the rowing scene a desire to know what happened, to know the fears, but there is also the fear of such confrontation: Wordsworth does not run because he is afraid, but he is afraid because he runs. Likewise, the affective power of the passage comes from this style of resistance, fear, and uncertainty. Wordsworth cannot even conjure up living images to express the "darkness," the "blank desertion," and the wayward thoughts that are being played over and over inside of him:

> no familiar shapes
> Of hourly objects, images of trees,
> Of sea, or sky, no colours of green fields . . .

Neither can we ignore that this inability to conjure up living images takes us to view the scene as overlaid with death, or at least with purgatory (as a condition of punishment) or limbo. So, as in the Lucy poems, death makes its presence not so much known as *felt*. It comes unannounced, and it borders on the irrational. Again, the feeling is real; the particular story matters only inasmuch as it lends itself to the expression of authentic feelings.

An important general pattern emerges here in Wordsworth's poetry of this period. Call it the guilt cycle. The form and the pattern may vary somewhat, but most of the constructs and the style of the process hold: the experience or the journey begins in innocence; the innocence becomes imagined or actual experience; and experience (or at least the problematically preeminent experiences that Wordsworth seems to write about) leads to fear or guilt (or both), then (sometimes) to death, then to fear and to more guilt, and then back to the experience as he tries to return to solitary innocence, to a time of pure, unthinking rapture or naïve pleasure, to, as Wordsworth might say, the untrodden ways—to where Lucy lives within. For the Lucy poems juggle innocence, fear, guilt, and the idea of death. Wordsworth feels irresistible drawn to her, yet is uncertain in his knowledge of her.

The letter to Coleridge contains one further passage of poetry. Dorothy writes: "I will now transcribe a nutting scene (I think I shall not tire you)" (Wordsworth 1967, 241). The poem came to be known as *Nutting*, and, like the other poems and passages being composed at this time, it reenacts a form of the guilt cycle just outlined above, and thus it too addresses similar enigmatic feelings. *Nutting* could have gone on to become part of *The Prelude* (like the skating and rowing episodes) and might have rightfully received the critical attention and esteem that the "spots of time" have had, but Wordsworth decided, somewhat mysteriously, to let it go off on its own.[35] Yet it is so much a spot of time.

In the notes dictated to Isabella Fenwick many years later, Wordsworth said of *Nutting*: "Written in Germany: intended as part of a poem on my own life, but struck out as not being wanted there. . . . These verses arose out of the remembrance of *feelings I had often when I was a boy* . . . " (Wordsworth 1876, 3:39; my emphasis). We can only wonder why Wordsworth did not want the poem to be associated with other verses about his life—after all, he did think very highly of *Nutting* (Moorman, 1957, 506). And so we can also only speculate about the source of those boyhood "feelings" he often had, taking them seriously, taking the anger, loss, and confusion as the expression of a young person in his solitary wanderings. But we need to go back to the opening context of *Nutting* to get to this point.

As in the rowing and skating episodes, the experience in *Nutting* is, for all appearances, commonplace. Young Wordsworth is off to the woods to gather some hazel nuts; he gets his nutting stick, finds some trees where no one has yet collected nuts, eyes his spoils, and he vigorously whacks the trees in order to collect the booty. But after his close encounter with the hazels, he also feels a little strange, "a sense of pain," about what he has done.

Elsewhere I have argued that this poem can be read as an account of repressed, adolescent (or preadolescent) sexual experience—of rape even—and that the acknowledged but confused aim of the poem is to understand his past experience and feelings (Blank 1988, 164–66). He sets off with the big stick in his hand; he sees the vaginal "nook / Unvisited" and the hazel trees "Tall and erect, with milk-white clusters hung, / A virgin scene"; he holds back, "Breathing with such suppression"; he engages in a kind of pastoral foreplay—"and with the flowers I played"; he fantasizes about a blissful orgasm—"I saw the sparkling foam"; but then he lets go and lustily acts upon his impulse:

> Then up I rose
> And dragged to earth both branch and bough with crash
> And merciless ravage, and the shady nook
> Of hazels, and the green and mossy bower,
> Deformed and sullied, patiently gave up
> Their quiet spirit . . .
>
> (Wordsworth 1967, 242)

I am not longer quite so happy with this reading's emphasis on the sexual nature of this experience, as a kind of cathartic puberty poem, but I remain committed to the idea that the poem can be read as an attempt to reenact unresolved feelings, given that there is in this text a clash between the adolescent feelings and the adult feeling about those feelings.[36] That lusty impulse I now view as something closer to anger, and anger, we know, is most often for children a reaction to fear of loss (Cochrane and Myers 1980, 26). This becomes more apparent as the passage continues, as Wordsworth now turns to examining himself rather than the scene:

>   and unless I now
> Confound my present being with the past,
> Even then, when from the bower I turned away,
> Exulting, rich beyond the wealth of kings—
> I felt a sense of pain when I beheld
> The silent trees and the intruding sky . . .
>
> (Wordsworth 1967, 242)

There is guilt running through and haunting the episode as it is described. Wordsworth cannot, in his confusion, distinguish between his projected present state and those feelings originating from the unresolved past experience. Both sets of feelings are unresolved and dislocated, and we have to draw a singularly important conclusion from this: that the "pain" is still with him. He is not sure what the "pain" is, and he is not sure where the feelings come from. The "pain" may come from the loss of innocence: something is taken away despite his material gains. We of course cannot buy the idea that aspects of nature, viz., the "silent trees and the intruding sky," are causally connected to his negative feelings. The origin is elsewhere. Trees and the sky cannot in actuality intrude—this is a projection onto the scene indicating how Wordsworth felt. The loss may be one of unselfconsciousness, and this is a kind of Fall from innocence. And in *Nutting*, as in the other poetry of this letter, that "elsewhere" is neither named nor located: it is a difference, a dimness, a vague melancholy, an unnamable darkness akin to solitude.

This is Wordsworth's big problem, and this is what the poetry emerging at Goslar is all about. This is also what makes the poetry so very interesting: it is confessional without knowing exactly what it is confessing. He cannot seem to balance the feeling of gain ("rich beyond the wealth of kings") with the feeling of "pain." It is something like the paradox of Jane Fondaesque aerobics: no pain, no gain. And, as in aerobics, it takes a while, a lot a pain, to recognize the gain. Wordsworth, too, waits. Again, the "philosophic mind" is yet to come.

As mentioned, *Nutting* reenacts a form of the guilt cycle. The boy begins in innocence, "a figure quaint," but in anticipation of and even prepared for experience. Led by "guardian spirits," he travels afar to an unvisited, pristine place where, after the joy of resistance and the fear of "expectation" work on him, he mercilessly ravages what supplies the objects of his desires. Intrusive, painful guilt follows, and the poem abruptly ends with an embarrassing gesture for a return to innocence, to that "spirit" which led him on this quest:

> —Then, dearest Maiden! move along these shades
> In gentleness of heart; with gentle hand
> Touch, for there is a spirit in the woods.

This weak reconciliation is not at all convincing, and will never do.[37] Innocence after such a fall from grace (or at least from nut-collecting decorum) cannot be reinstated *just like that*. The *"—Then"* does not follow. All of the unthinking actions, the guilt, loss, and experience, the anger and confusion, cannot be suddenly negated or countered in these rather banal three lines. There is a lot more than just gentle feeling and gentle touching moving along in these shady nooks. There is violence and pain, guilt and repression, uncertainty and regret. Out there in the woods, among the flowers and mossy stones, Wordsworth finds he has to resort to inventing an idealized, feminized, hazy presence as a significant Other, an unviolated "Maiden," to oversee and justify and perhaps balance his actions and his feelings. But the feelings themselves are the troubling object and subject of this personal quest, and are thus the center of the nutting experience: here the only significant Other can be the Self, and it may be closer to the superego than to some pastoral convention. Something was lost and discovered, and the "silent trees and intruding sky" are pointing to it, even if Wordsworth, in his confusion, cannot. They point to him, to something inside of him. That, we must conclude, was what motivated these lines, albeit an unacknowledged motivation. The poem is, after all, as Harold Bloom notes, "strong in latent content" (1971, 129). One is tempted to take this further: *Nutting* is nothing but latent content.

If this poem represents a serious allegory of Wordsworth's awakening sexuality, then, with its rather bathetic ending, it would not be inappropriate to see it as an unintentional parody of a poem about awakening sexuality. If *Nutting* is a poem that uses sexual imagery to describe an intimate encounter with Nature and developing consciousness, it is truly a troubling encounter, and we would have to question the very strange response to nature in the poem.[38] There is, at the very least, a disturbing element in the attraction to and destruction of the maternal aspects of the scene.[39] If we see the poem as an attempt to describe certain difficult and displaced feelings that belong to a certain time, feelings that center around a particular experience, then we may be getting somewhere. His hostility may have been played out on nature or aspects of the landscape, but it can only have been directed by something deeply internalized. And I am reminded of Wallace W. Douglas's clinical speculations about Wordsworth's confused temper and aggressiveness in *Nutting*—that the poem involves "infantile perceptions and interpretations of parental relations," that "the confusion also reflects much more primitive infantile fears of the loss of one or another parent to the other, or of both, in the struggle of love," and that there is, in the poem, the "need to explore, understand, and control the relations of the parents" (1968, 78–79). I would concur: loss, fear, confusion, and a pressing need to understand are at the center of this text; and for Wordsworth these feelings and needs might be indeed entangled with unresolved feelings about his parents. And there is both maternal presence (the bower womb, the forgiving spirit)[40] and a paternal authority (the phallic stick, the rebuking sky) in the poem. Yet his anger is necessarily directed at both in their conflated, hermaphroditic form: the "virgin scene," we recall, is "Tall and erect, with milk-white clusters hung." Thus "the spirit in the woods" is Wordsworth's idealized protection against what he felt and how he expressed it as a profound "sense of pain" and by uncontrollable anger, perhaps directed unknowingly against his parents. Anger is, after all, one of the necessary stages in accepting the loss of a loved one. So the good news is that at least some anger surfaces and gets expressed. But the bad news remains: Wordsworth does not articulate what the object of his anger is.[41] He still sees it as out there. He needs to see it as inside of himself.

In an earlier chapter I suggested that Wordsworth's attachment to and formulation of Nature represents an emotional gap triggered by the loss of his parents; the extreme and apparently inexplicable hostility that surfaces in *Nutting* may mark the return of the repressed.

This midwinter letter from Goslar ends with an evening picture: Dorothy hears William just coming up the stairs to where, we assume, she has been completing the letter: "He has been walking by moonlight in his fur gown and a black fur cap in which he looks like any grand Signior" (Wordsworth 1967, 242). There is a certain melancholic pride in this fantasized description of her older brother. She is clearly impressed by him. And of this group of poems in the letter? We are bound to see them *as a group*. Wordsworth would never arbitrarily throw together some inferior poetic snippets for Coleridge, of all people, to vet at his leisure. The verses would have to be the best of his representative work, they would have to be complete in some way, and they would have to contain something essential to his particular state of being. The letter continues: "William says you will preserve any verses which we have sent you, in the fear, that in travelling we may lose the copy" (243). Coleridge did not lose them, and neither did Wordsworth.

More Poetry from the Winter of Discontent

While in Germany, Wordsworth wrote much more poetry than that transcribed by Dorothy into the letter to Coleridge, and much of this new work (more than a dozen poems) was to go into the second edition of *Lyrical Ballads*. In fact, by the time of publication in January 1801, the number of poems contributed by Wordsworth had almost tripled, so that Coleridge's part, by comparison, was almost negligible.[42] *Lyrical Ballads* had really become Wordsworth's thing. From being an anonymous and rather slim one-volume publication in 1798, now Wordsworth's name went on the title page: "LYRICAL BALLADS, / WITH / OTHER POEMS. / IN TWO VOLUMES. / By W. WORDSWORTH." At this point Wordsworth the poet began to completely overshadow Coleridge the poet, and the latter henceforth turned almost exclusively to other forms of writing. In March 1801 Coleridge could write to Godwin, "The Poet is dead in me" (Coleridge 1956, 2:714). As he described his contribution to *Lyrical Ballads* in *Biographia Literaria*, "[M]y compositions, instead of forming a balance, appeared rather an interpolation of heterogeneous matter" (Coleridge 1985, 315). This is putting the issue of ownership politely. We should remember, too, that in later years, as a literary critic, Coleridge turned back to *Lyrical Ballads* in order to sternly question some of Wordsworth's poetry.[43] It is not unlikely that Coleridge was a little disappointed—maybe even slightly miffed—about how *Lyrical Ballads* had evolved. After all, it was the idea of *The Ancient Mariner* that got things started, and it was the first poem in the 1798 edition of *Lyrical Ballads*. But Wordsworth could hardly be faulted for the superabundance of poetry he was producing. And much of it was produced at Goslar.

Michael Mason, a recent editor of *Lyrical Ballads*, suggests that "the biographical bias of Wordsworthian commentary" falls short in explaining the presence of death and suffering in the poems: "In other words, we cannot assess the reliability of Wordsworth's narrators by measuring how 'close' they are to the poet himself. He simply did not use autobiographical fact in this way; he did not stick to the truth about himself when he wanted an 'I' speaker to be particularly authoritative" (Wordsworth 1992, 24). This is true, but only in a limited way. It may depend on what one means by "autobiographical fact." If it has to do with characters or places or times corresponding exactly with Wordsworth's life, then the poems of *Lyrical Ballads*—indeed, a great deal of Wordsworth's poetry—were not "close" at all to the poet's life. However, if by "autobiographical fact" one means the inner life, then I would strongly argue that in Wordsworth's poems we often do indeed get important truths about Wordsworth, and that they are very "close . . . to the poet himself." Many of the poems are, I believe, reliable indicators of Wordsworth's emotional concerns, both as he felt them and as he wrote about them. People do not necessarily carry around the facts of their outer life with them; they do, however, always carry around the facts of their inner lives. Our inner life follows us everywhere. The reason Wordsworth was poetically obsessed with strategies for exploring mourning and the feelings of loss and separation is that they were a huge, unresolved part of his inner life that continued to surface and follow him around. This in no way diminishes Wordsworth's art; rather, it humanizes it in a most profound way.

In poem after poem written in Germany, Wordsworth explores various tonal and narratological strategies to express mourning and thoughts of death. Some of this has already been seen in the Lucy poems. And we have to keep in mind that mourning is not about the dead but about the feelings of survivors, those, like Wordsworth, who felt they were left behind, abandoned. In *To a Sexton* the speaker is anxious that he be buried with and not be separated from his loved one, and that family remains be kept together. We also see this in a number of poems centering around the figure of Matthew. In *If Nature, for a favorite Child* the speaker worries that all that remains of a beloved, sensitive schoolmaster is his name inscribed on a tablet. *The Fountain* records the speaker's encounter with a friend, an old man, who bemoans the loss of his family and that there is none left to love him; the speaker offers to be as a son to the old man, but he is turned down; what is left behind can never be regained. *The Two April Mornings* is a triple mourning: the speaker records a walk with an old teacher, now dead; on that walk the old man recalled stopping beside the grave of his nine-year-old daughter some thirty years ago; he saw a fair and happy young girl there, and then he was pained that no one could take the place of his daughter.

What comes out of these poems, as well as five other short elegies written at this time,[44] is an anxiousness about death, unresolved loss, and the inability to let go of the pain. Nothing can bring back what has gone or passed away, but the speaker tries to work out how to commemorate the death. That is, in these poems the speaker struggles to bring thoughts over to those feelings in order to assuage those feelings. But despite his persistence and eloquence, his success is limited. There is very little in the way of acceptance, and the speaker often seems helpless. My angle, of course, is that this helplessness in the face of loss and death is a poetic reenactment of where Wordsworth was in his process of self-healing. Where else could it come from?

Richard Matlak suggests that some of Wordsworth's "anxiety and depression during the Goslar period" was a result of his reflections "on the series of father surrogates that had loved yet also disappointed him during his adolescence," and that these poems addressing the subject of loss and centering around the figure of Matthew were evoked by feelings associated with not being with Coleridge (Matlak 1986b, 150). While I would agree that not being with Coleridge was difficult, it was the general notion of separation that Wordsworth experienced at Goslar that called up the feelings expressed in the poetry written at the time. The feeling of separation troubled Wordsworth, not the actual absence of his friend.

Three other Goslar poems that ended up in the 1800 *Lyrical Ballads* also seem to irresistibly approach emotional conditions that were close to Wordsworth's experience: *Ruth, There was a Boy*, and *Lucy Gray*. While *Ruth* seems to go in the direction of *The Female Vagrant (Salisbury Plain)* in presenting the tragic fall of a forsaken woman, *Lucy Gray* overlaps with the Lucy poems in its more enigmatic and stark details, although the narrative is more elaborate.[45] *There was a Boy* tantalizingly hovers somewhere between an autobiographical reminiscence and the mystification of the Lucy poems.

Ruth is about loss and separation; in fact, the story recounts a double loss and separation. Both separations can be seen as being close to aspects of Wordsworth's own experience and the kind of feelings he went through. A seven-year-old child is deserted by her father, and is more or less left to her own devices to wander "over dale and hill / In thoughtless freedom bold" (5–6). This is not unlike the picture we have of Wordsworth's own early life, complete with the absent and negligent male parent, and the idea that the child is orphaned to nature's care. The "thoughtless freedom" also echoes Wordsworth's recollection of his "thoughtless youth" in *Tintern Abbey*. The pattern of separation is repeated in the adult life of Ruth. She is deserted by her husband not long after their marriage, and she is left to grieve in her loneliness. He returns to his previous vagrant, wandering ways. Ruth seems helpless in preventing the loss and in doing something to prevent her downward slide. The poem ends with the speaker's thoughts of her death and burial. There is also something close to Wordsworth's experience with Annette Vallon in the story of the young man's desertion of his lover and his subsequent aimless wanderings in nature. Even in the speaker's excuse for the young man's behavior we can detect Wordsworth saying, *What else could I do? I really did love her.* In the poem, of course, this is put into the third person:

> And yet he with no feigned delight
> Had woo'd the Maiden, day and night
> Had lov'd her, night and morn;
> What could he less than love a Maid
> Whose heart with so much nature play'd
> So kind and so forlorn?
>
> (Lines 151–56)

So in both Ruth's own sufferings (as adult and as solitary, introspective child) and in the young man's predicament we can detect Wordsworth's poetic attempt to externalize what happened to him. This kind of reenactment we could call emotional allegory.

This kind of emotional allegorizing continues in *Lucy Gray*. Lucy is a solitary child who, like the Idiot Boy, is sent to do a parent's bidding. Her job is go to the town and then to light the way home for her mother through the snowy afternoon. She is sent by her father, but on her way to town she, again, like the Idiot Boy, becomes lost; but in this poem it is in a snowstorm, and she is never found. Her footprints simply stop in the middle of a bridge, halfway, as it were, between her mother and father. The poem plays out the mystery of her disappearance by having her mythically reintegrated into the forsaken landscape:

> Yet some maintain that to this day
> She is a living Child,
> That you may see sweet Lucy Gray
> Upon the lonesome Wild.
>
> (Lines 57–60)

But her halted tracks also suggest a further kind of arrest. It is childhood's end as a child. There is no real death, only a kind of disappearing act for the solitary child making the journey to bring her mother back home. This too is her final act. Having the child stuck, forever, in the middle of the bridge, halfway between the unfulfilled needs of her parents, acts out Wordsworth's own emotional situation, both in Germany and his childhood past as he, too, is stuck between his parents. His inner child is arrested and lost somewhere out there in the lonesome landscape. Yet this lost child remains a "living" thing, defying death by residing in the memory of those who need to believe most in the survival and endurance of that child—those, that is, like Wordsworth. Of course it is true that Wordsworth heard of this story from his Dorothy:

> It was founded on a circumstance told me by my sister, of a little girl, who, not far from Halifax, in Yorkshire, was bewildered in a snow-storm. Her footsteps were tracked by her parents to the middle of the lock of a canal, and no other vestige of her, backward or forward, could be traced. The body, however, was found in the canal. (Wordsworth 1876, 3:15–16)

That Wordsworth would use this story suggests there was something in it that fit with his imaginative capabilities in Germany. That he changed the story by never presenting the dead body also suggests his need to keep this child alive, deathless—at least in his own imagination. There, in freezing snows, whether of Goslar or Halifax, we see Wordsworth and Lucy: isolated, stuck, and, for all intense purposes, dead to the world except as an imaginative, subjective construct. That is, unlike the real story, Wordsworth finds his frozen body during that German winter, though the subjectivity that embodies him is just as imaginatively lost.

Above I suggested that *There was a Boy* hangs somewhere between an autobiographical reflection and the emotional allegories reenacted in the Lucy poems. This time we have a young boy who is ten years old in the 1800 *Lyrical Ballads* version and the 1805 *Prelude*, but made to be twelve years old in the 1850 *Prelude*. In the evening, often this boy, alone, would make hooting noises to the owls, and sometimes they, in return, would answer him. And sometimes, while standing there alone in the "deep silence," waiting for the owls' response, the "voice" of the landscape would enter him unawares. He died, the speaker tells us, at age ten (or twelve), and once more we have a poem that takes up the issue of mourning, loss, and death. *There was a Boy* thus moves between elegy and lyric, but at the same time it constitutes an epitaph.

We know what Wordsworth went through as a youth (his father died when he was thirteen). If what I have just written in the previous sentence seems like an overdetermined notion to bring to the text—haphazardly tossing Wordsworth's life into the poem—we have to remember that in one of the first drafts for this text (MS JJ),[46] Wordsworth tells half of the little story in the first person. It seems, then, to have its origins as a recollection of his own Lake District childhood. Thus, for example, in the 1800 *Lyrical Ballads* version we have "Responsive to his call" (line 13) while in MS JJ we have "Responsive to my call" (line 12). The most important lines of the poem obviously have a different significance told in the first person, and below I italicize the word or words that were used in the 1800 version, and following them put in brackets the corresponding earlier MS JJ version:

> And, when it chanced
> That pauses of deep silence mock'd *his* [my] skill,
> Then, *sometimes* [often], in that silence, while *he* [I] hung
> Listening, a *gentle* [sudden] shock of mild surprize
> *Has carried* [Would carry] far into *his* [my] heart the voice
> Of mountain torrents, or the visible scene
> Would enter unawares into *his* [my] mind
> With all its solemn imagery, its rocks,
> Its woods, and that uncertain heaven, receiv'd
> Into the bosom of the steady lake.
>   (Lines 16–25 [15–24])

Here ends this MS version—or at least what we have of it.[47] In the first-person version Wordsworth recalls that the sounds of silence "often," rather than "sometimes," entered his thoughts and feelings. So too is there more immediacy when in the draft version the "shock" of the entering landscape is "sudden" rather than "gentle." In the early version, with these changes and the use of the first person, the lines are decidedly more vibrant and the speaker more startled into being.

This text is extremely precarious and filled with gaps and questions. The young boy is pictured as first of all having his presence confirmed by the hootings of the owls. Their responses, as wild "sobs" and "screams," fill the landscape with an excess of primal emotion (MS JJ, lines 12–15). The boy, as an unthinking youth, fits into and is a part of this noisy, rapturous scene. But when the owls do not return his calls, the silence preys powerfully upon his hyperanticipation: he hangs there, listening, until he hears and sees what was before always already there (the background sights and sounds). And here Wordsworth might seem to get a little confused or unclear. The sounds enter his "heart" with a "sudden shock of mild surprize," but he is "unawares"[48] that the sights enter his "mind." That is, he is aware of one but not the other. There are a few questions to be asked: Are the sounds meant to be different from the sights? If he is "unawares" that the scene enters his mind, then how can he comment on it entering him/the boy? Does he only realize in retrospect that it was entering him/the boy? Or is it that the "heart" differs from the "mind" in the way it works relative to Wordsworth's/the boy's development? I like the last question best, for it suggests that Wordsworth-as-boy operated on the emotional level of the heart but did not function with the same level of self-awareness when it came to the workings of the mind, to thought. Once more this suggests that Wordsworth breaks his life—past and present—into determinations corresponding to feeling and thought. The inner child, of course, works along feeling.

Wordsworth added seven more lines to the poem that would obviously have presented a problem if told in the first person. The boy of Winander is made to die. With this maneuver we suddenly have a speaker to mourn the loss, and so too at the end of the poem do we have the boy join the landscape out of which he tested his own presence and was startled into emotional self-consciousness:

>   near his grave
> A full half-hour together I have stood,
> Mute—for he died when he was ten years old.
>
>   (Lines 30–32)

That is, by turning this into a third-person portrait, Wordsworth is now able to give himself the narrative space to express what otherwise he might have troubled over in the first person, namely, his own thoughts of death: the ending, so to speak, of his own life. Though "mute," himself silenced by the death of the child within him, he is now able to express both how the boy felt and how he feels about how the boy felt. We are urged to picture Wordsworth, a boy, alone on the shores of Lake Windermere, attempting to commune with nature but hearing too the sad music of his own human solitude; and we are urged to picture Wordsworth calling up from his past emotional life the internalized feelings of loss, standing at the grave site—his own, or his parents'. It doesn't really matter which, for we really do not understand what our own death is until someone very close to us dies: the death of a loved one marks the consciousness of death. This is where Wordsworth's emotional life gets stuck, where his consciousness splits.

And so once again, this is a portrait of childhood's end in Paradise, and *There was a Boy* leaves both the adult speaker and the child silenced and alone at the grave. They are as one. As MS JJ makes clear, "He" is "I." The opening phrase of the poem, "There was a boy," could really be written as "There is a boy, and that boy is me," for as this text, these *texts*, make clear, the child is still there, dead but deathless, lost but not forsaken, only now he exists inside in the present rather than outside in the past. Like Lucy, he is buried deep within the adult child.

Life for the Wordsworths at Goslar had been more than dull. The physical experience was harsh and testing, and the progress in German language negligible. But the advances in Wordsworth's poetry, in the style and intensity of his poetry, were remarkable and certainly changed forever the course of his poetic interests. As Stephen Gill notes, "by the time he left Goslar a coherent 400-line poem on his early years had come into being" (1989, 161). *The Prelude*, his life project and the remaking of his life, had begun in earnest. In his poetry Wordsworth was beginning to discover certain lost or dislocated feelings by which not only his poetry profited, but also his notion of a continuous self. The reenactments continued in the other poems written or begun during the German period.

5

Home Again in Grasmere

> Home is where the heart is.
> —Pliny

Late in April 1799, William and Dorothy arrived back in England. It is not clear where they spent the two months after having left Goslar towards the end of February. Coleridge remained in Germany, in Göttingen. In March, he heard about the death of his young child, Berkely, and his wife wrote pleading that he return. In a letter to his friend in Bristol, Thomas Poole, he attempted to come to terms with his feelings about the death of his child; he quoted in full *A Slumber did my spirit seal* (Coleridge 1956, 1:478–81). The poem must have captured the experience that he was going through as he tried to make sense of little Berkely's death.

Dorothy and William paid a quick visit to Coleridge on their way back to England, but they could not persuade him to return. Coleridge wrote to his wife on 23 April:

> [H]ad I followed my impulses, I should have packed up & gone with Wordsworth and his Sister, who passed thro' & only passed thro', this place, two or three days ago.—If they burn with impatience to return to their native Country, they who are all to each other, what must *I* feel, with every thing pleasant & every thing valuable, & every thing dear to me at a distance—here, where I may truly say, my only amusement is—to labour! (484)

Coleridge was determined to complete his work, and in truth he greatly enjoyed the social and intellectual ambience at Göttingen. That he mentions how William and Dorothy were "all to each other" confirms how noticeable it was that the siblings needed to be together. Coleridge, it seems, did not have the same emotional bonding with any particular person (or place) at the time. That the brother and sister "burn[ed] with impatience" to return to England also points to how the Wordsworths must have felt in Germany. Coleridge did not return to his home until late in July.

About the time the Wordsworths were arriving back in England, Coleridge wrote to Poole again and added more about the Wordsworths' short visit and, in particular, about Wordsworth's personality and condition:

> Wordsworth & his Sister passed thro' here, as I have informed you— / I walked on with them 5 english miles, & spent a day with them. They were melancholy & hypp'd—W. was affected to tears at the thought of not being near me, wished me, of course, to live in the North of England near the Sir Frederic Vane's great Library. . . . Finally, I told him plainly, that *you* had been the man in whom *first* and in whom alone, I had felt an *anchor!* With all my other Connections I felt a dim sense of insecurity & uncertainty, terribly uncomfortable / —W. was affected to tears, very much affected; but he deemed the vicinity of a Library absolutely *necessary* to his health, nay to his existence. . . . I still think that Wordsworth will be disappointed in his expectations of relief from reading, without Society—& I think it highly probable, that where I live, there he will live, unless he should find in the North any person or persons, who can feel & understand him, can reciprocate & react on him.—My many weaknesses are of some advantage to me; they unite me more with the great mass of my fellow-beings— but dear Wordsworth appears to me to have hurtfully segregated & isolated his Being / Doubtless, his delights are more deep and sublime; / but he has likewise more hours, that prey on his flesh and blood. (Coleridge 1956, 1:490–91).

The emotional strain of the German experience on Wordsworth shows even more clearly in this expanded account. The dark feelings—"melancholy & hypp'd"—suggest that how he felt was not at all too deep for tears. (The *O.E.D.* defines "hypped" as "depressed.") That his "health" was necessarily dependent upon being close to a library also suggests his precarious condition. But Coleridge doesn't quite believe that this was all his friend needed. Wordsworth, he thinks, needs a "person or persons, who can feel & understand him, can reciprocate & react on him"; he needed people around who would unconditionally support him. This is an astute observation. Coleridge knew well enough that it was not a good thing for Wordsworth to be alone—"hurtfully segregated & isolated"—with his feelings, for he knew that Wordsworth had trouble coping with emotions associated with separation. At the end of this passage, Coleridge also alludes to the intense and lonely experience Wordsworth had in Germany, and he characterizes, rather gothically, the psychophysiological nature of Wordsworth's emotional sensitivity. It would take a little more work and significant changes in his lifestyle—and certainly more poetry—before what the cold German nights brought on could be phased out of Wordsworth's subjectivity. But change he would, and so would his poetry.

Towards the 1799 *Prelude*

As mentioned, while in Germany, Wordsworth had made a rough but determined start on a poem that we now know as *The Prelude*.[1] In this MS JJ (which decidedly moves towards what will become the first part of the 1799 *Prelude*) we have what I believe are many of the most remarkable and foundational passages of that poem, and, in writing about his childhood past, his life suddenly opened up to him in unexpected ways. I say "unexpected" for two reasons: first, the last thing that he could have foreseen was how these few hundred lines of poetic ramblings about his early years would grow to become his most obsessive life work: his poetic autobiography; second, what becomes apparent in these lines is his troubling double vision of childhood, of himself. This may have been one of the reasons for Wordsworth's need to return to writing about his life. More needs to said about this last result. The early years that Wordsworth was called back to are not, as he records them in these first jottings, just filled with feelings of "remembered joy" and "the calm / That Nature" can bestow (lines 14, 35–36).[2] There is more than just the pleasant blending of his "nurse's song" and his dreams with the gentle murmurings of the Derwent (lines 22–36). For the first direct recollections—there are four of them—give a picture of a solitary child, and the feelings of hope and joy are counterbalanced with fear and guilt.

In the first of the four we have the account of his attempt to steal raven's eggs. He hung perilously "alone / By half inch fissures in the slippery rock" (lines 59–60, 64). The feeling was of unreality, with the "loud dry wind" giving off "strange utterance," and the "sky seemed not a sky / Of earth" (lines 65–67). Yet in recalling this Wordsworth looks back in an effort to understand how it is we become a part of all we see around us. He puts it roughly here, but we know where he wants to go:

> Not with the mean & vullgar works of man
> But with high objects with eternal things
> With life & nature, purifying thus
> The elements of feeling & of thought
> And sanctifying by such disc[i]pline
> Both pain & fear untill we recognize
> A grandeur in the beatings of the heart.

(Lines 73–79)

This is indeed a remarkable and important transformation. From recollections of being utterly disconnected—alone and perched dangerously on a rock face, with feelings of unreality—he goes to a poetic discourse on being in synch with the eternal, with life and nature.

The second extended recollection in MS JJ is of robbing bird traps. Wordsworth describes anxiously hurrying from trap to trap, his heart panting with "hope & fear" as he moved among the lonely trees and crags. Sometimes he felt the "strong desire" to steal the birds that were caught in the traps of others, but then he would hear "Low breathings" and "undistinguishable sounds" pursuing him (lines 106–17). That is, he would hear the footsteps of guilt and fear. Yet again, given the reconstructed fragments of his text, it is remarkable how Wordsworth follows this with exhortations of how the "naked feelings" (line 132) of childhood connected him with the "eternal beauty" of the world around him (line 134–51).

The third episode is the boy of Winander passage, which I have discussed in the previous chapter. The fourth recollection is the boat-stealing experience. One moonlit evening, he decided to borrow (without permission) a shepherd's rowboat and take it for a ride. But as he rowed, the size and shape of a cliff suddenly overwhelmed him, and it rose up between him and sky. It became like a "living thing" that pursued him. "With trembling hands" he returned to the mooring place. For many days after he was haunted by the strange incident. He did not even know how to describe these "unknown modes of being" in his thoughts:

> There was a darkness call it solitude
> Or strange desertion no familiar shapes
> Of hourly objects images of trees
> Of sea or sky no colours of green fields
> But huge & mighty forms that do not live
> Like living men moved through my mind
> By day, and were the trouble of my dreams—
>
> (Lines 195–241)

This is a childhood state of mind ruled by absence and disfamiliarity: "call it solitude." He got there by "an act of stealth" (lines 214), which then turned, uncontrollably, into the haunting emotions of fear and guilt. There is no Nature in this obscure and dark state of mind, only colorless intimations of deathly forms. Yet once more, in the final, powerful passages of this fragment that constitutes the force behind *The Prelude*, Wordsworth moves to a completely opposite scene, to recollections of moments when he was profoundly touched by the beautiful spirit of Nature. He looks with seemingly utter clarity back to "Those beauteous colours of my early years," to

> Those hours that cannot die those lovely forms
> And sweet sensations which throw back our life
> And make our infancy a visible scene
> On which the sun is shining.
>
> (Lines 242–76)

The feelings in these two passages could hardly be more different.

So what are we to make of these, the earliest opening moves of *The Prelude,* written during the German winter? We could say that Wordsworth is confused, but it might be more useful to make the observation that, at this point, Wordsworth has two quite different visions of the past, what above I called a double vision of childhood: one that moves in and through fear and guilt and is based on particular, though somewhat confusing, remembrances; and one that seems to gather feelings of connectedness, clarity, and harmony from nonspecific recollections. One could speculate that the particular remembrances are closest to how it was, while the nonspecific commentary is how Wordsworth wished it might have been. Or it could simply be that for Wordsworth his childhood was a divided existence. Or maybe we have to distinguish between his very earliest years (infancy) and those following—his childhood. Perhaps at some point his early years are broken in two, so that we do not have a double vision at all, but two halves determined by a traumatic event. We also have to account for how Wordsworth felt when writing about these incidents, so that feelings of connectedness, clarity, and harmony are his hopeful projections onto the past. That three of the four episodes involved "acts of stealth" is also interesting. But again, taking eggs and birds and boats is perhaps not important as the attendant *and unresolved* feelings—the confusion, fear, and guilt. The surfacing of these episodes seems to have inspired the need for further examination, perhaps motivated by the desire for emotional and intellectual reconciliation. It may have once more become apparent to Wordsworth that thought needs to come to the aid of feeling. Time allowed him to transform these childhood episodes into something to meet his adult needs. Perhaps he needed to construct a mind that was lord and master of past, present, and future. And even this early he was well on his way to using emotions of the past to restorative effect:

> Nor unsubservient even to noblest ends
> Are these primordial feeling[s] how serene
> How calm those seem amid the swell
> Of human passion even yet I feel
> Their tranquilizing power
>
> (Lines 166–70)

We see here how Wordsworth would have to deal with the recollections of his past feelings. They had to be made to serve and to soothe him. If he wished to have them support and nurture him, he could not leave these feelings detached, static, and untransformed. There was no other way for the child to become father to the man.

In this, then, the earliest version of *The Prelude*, which should be viewed together with the other Goslar poetry, these episodes and the transformations are both tense and abrupt. Later, in ever-expanding versions of the poem, they are spaced out, sometimes by thousands of lines, and the intensity of the feelings and the abrupt nature of the transformations they represent are significantly softened.

Wordsworth subsequently crowded book 1 with more stark childhood memories, adding the skating, drowned-man, gibbet, and death of his father scenes to the trap-robbing, egg-stealing, and boat-borrowing episodes of MS JJ.[3] With the exception of the second and third, these episodes have already been discussed. But the drowned-man and gibbet scenes also reveal the difficulty Wordsworth had with the associated feelings of these memories. Reading them alone, without the transitional commentary Wordsworth adds, we are struck, first of all, by the indelible nature of these recalled images; second, by the attention he gives to trying to understand his feelings; and third, by the subsequent need to make some kind of sense of these memories in forming his identity.

In the drowned-man scene, Wordsworth, at age nine (though he says he is eight), with his "half-infant mind," sees across Esthwaite's lake "a heap of garments." As evening comes on, he watches for "Half an hour," but no one claims the clothes or can be seen around them. The next day a group a people show up to search the water for a body:

> At length the dead man, 'mid the beauteous scene
> Of trees and hills and water, bolt upright
> Rose with his ghastly face.

Wordsworth says he could refer to other similar "accidents" that took place out there in the rural surroundings, but he does not. They were not close to him in the same way. He writes that these were events

> that impressed my mind
> With images to which in following years
> Far other feelings were attached—with forms
> That yet exist with independent life,
> And, like archetypes, know no decay.
>
> (Bk. 1, lines 258–87)

The reason that other "accidents" were not recorded by Wordsworth must be that he was not such a direct witness. In fact, he may have been the first to take note of the pile of unattended clothing. And that he spent a "Half an hour" in solitude watching the twilight scene also suggests a kind of darkening anticipation on his behalf: he may have been the first to intuit the death. We are even reminded of the guilty anticipation he experienced when waiting for the horses to pick him up for the Christmas vacation when he father died. In this way, as possibly the first but silent witness of this death, he personalizes and internalizes the event in a unique way that cannot be shaken from his consciousness.

Although Wordsworth gives the impression of being distant from the action, it is as if he is both audience to and composer of the scene, making it his. He has looked upon the face of death, and it has sat up and looked upon him. The juxtaposition of the dead man's "ghastly face" with the surrounding "beauteous scene" must have disturbed him in ways he could not, with his "half-infant mind," understand and articulate. This is the important gap he hopes to fill. In attempting to make some kind of retrospective sense of the meaning of these "images" as they fixed upon his mind, "Far other feelings were attached," feelings, we assume, that before were neither accessible nor expressible. With time, he writes, what was before a detached image and incident now becomes part of the landscape itself, and in this way it and the associated feelings are naturalized. They are taken care of, incorporated into his own history with the passage of "following years." This is what Wordsworth needed to happen, otherwise that "ghastly face" of death would continue to haunt him and the troubling feelings would remain with him. The gap between then and now, between the event and its meaning, between the beauty and the horror, between him and the dead man, between original feelings and subsequent thoughts, would have remained open—and emotionally discomforting. And this is once more an important step for Wordsworth: a transformational moment when an unforgettable and troubling image is integrated within the larger scene, a scene, of course, that can stand as a foundation and continuation of Wordsworth's own life. In writing the poem at this moment, Wordsworth is witnessing the growth of his mind. Indeed, this was becoming his purpose: to look upon the past and see his present and intimate his future.

In subsequent versions of this passage, Wordsworth sanitized this transformation, almost as if it never took place. The emotional disturbance, the gap wherein the fear and confusion existed, is greatly played down. In these later versions he writes that even though he was just a young boy when this incident took place, he had "no vulgar fear," no "soul-debasing fear," for his "inner eye had seen / Such sights before, among the shining streams / Of faery land, the forests of romance" (1805 *Prelude*, bk. 5, lines 473–81; 1850 *Prelude*, bk. 5, lines 451–59). But it is difficult to imagine how these make-believe things could have prepared him for what he experienced. Jonathan Wordsworth finds these revised contexts of the passage completely "unconvincing," and points out that what immediately follows in the 1799 version is the famous "spots of time" passage (J. Wordsworth 1979, 578), which is a defining moment in Wordsworth's poetical—and personal—history. For here Wordsworth identifies these "moments" from "our first childhood" as having a positive function, a reparative and "fructifying virtue" (1799 *Prelude,* bk. 1, lines 288-96). Growth and maturity seem to be qualities that he can now extract or read into (or out of) these preeminent moments in the past.[4] What was once viewed as displaced is now given a foundational place. This is what he needed from such past events and associated feelings. He now has an idea of what he can make of some of his childhood feelings.

From the drowned-man episode and the "spots of time" passage, Wordsworth follows directly with the gibbet scene. The memory comes from about the age of five, likely during one of his stays at Penrith. He was horse-riding in the country with one of the family servants when he suddenly found himself separated from him. In fear he dismounted his horse and led him down a rough path to the bottom of a valley. There he came across a site where years before a man had been "hung / In irons" for murdering his wife. All that remained was the decayed "gibbet-mast" and "a long green ridge of turf . . . / Whose shape was like a grave." He left the "spot, / And reascending" saw "A naked pool" and "The beacon on the summit" of the hill. Closer to him he also saw "A girl who bore a pitcher on her head" who seemed to struggle against the "blowing wind":

> It was in truth
> An ordinary sight, but I should need
> Colours and words that are unknown to man
> To paint the visionary dreariness
> Which, while I looked all round for my lost guide,
> Did at that time invest the naked pool,
> The beacon on the lonely eminence,
> The woman and her garments vexed and tossed
> By the strong wind.
>
> (Lines 296–327)

Although the dimensions are different, the elements in this scene definitely recall *The Thorn*: in both there is a murder (at least a possible murder in *The Thorn*), a grave, a pool, a moldering wooden death marker (the thorn and the gibbet), and a windswept solitary female. Although in the case of *The Thorn* we have something like a superstitious sea captain as the narrator and in *The Prelude* we find a retrospective Wordsworth talking his way through the scene, in both there is a speaker who is disturbed by what he recounts and is unsure what to make of his response.

Here is a familiar Wordsworthian figure in familiar Wordsworthian circumstances: particularly, the solitary child confronting death; more generally, a confrontation with death. This solitary child confronting death is also the basis of the drowned-man scene, as it is also in the next and final "spots of time" passage where Wordsworth describes anxiously waiting for the horses to bring him home just before his father dies (lines 327–74). In the first chapter, I described this as a life-shaping experience and noted Wordsworth's struggle to separate his feelings of sorrow and loss from his feeling of guilt. I also noted that in describing the event, the elements in the scene came back to Wordsworth as a series of detached images, snapshots from the emotional psyche. The same can be said of the gibbet scene when, in the moment that he sees the "girl" (who has now, interestingly, become a "woman") and his feelings of being lost return to him, the snapshots of the pool, the beacon, the woman, and the wind tumble before him. The feeling expressed is that these are detached pictures, and that there is a need to somehow make a collage or connected picture out of them. My metaphor here is not altogether inappropriate, for it is Wordsworth himself who suggests the impossibility of finding "Colours and words . . . / To paint the visionary dreariness" of what took place and how he felt. In this moment do we have merely the recollected panic of a five-year-old lost boy, or do we have the emotional reenactment of an adult, not yet thirty years old, whose whole vision of childhood has been determined by the trauma of death and the circumstances of separation? Or do we have both? I believe that the significance of the recollection is that it embodies elements and feelings still problematically held within this adult child, who happens to be a poet.

Here once more is certainly the most characteristic and pervasive of all Wordsworth's reenacted scenarios: the figure of the child facing death. From a metaperspective we might put it like this: an adult portraying the figure of a child facing death. Why Wordsworth returns again and again to this one rather bare dramatic circumstance, either in the form of his own remembrances or repeatedly fictionalized in other kinds of poetic narratives, should no longer be a mystery to us: it is Wordsworth returning to the feelings he has not yet resolved out of the circumstances of his own childhood—childhood's end and the dissolution of a family.

With the arrival of the "spots of time" passages, Wordsworth continues to explore difficult and confused feelings, but now they are ostensibly based on actual memories told autobiographically. Wordsworth has begun to recognize the importance of coming to terms with past experience, despite being puzzled by much of it. That is, these recollections assume a new force, since they are not fictionalized in the same sense as most of the poems from *Lyrical Ballads* are. Wordsworth can now face them more directly, and surely this is a good thing, especially if he is to come closer to resolving them. As in *Tintern Abbey*, the poetic strategy he is beginning to discover is to give himself—create for himself—a meditative space. He can now report on the events, and then think upon and through them. He can attempt to organize his past as a continuous, meaningful structure. In most of the poems from *Lyrical Ballads*, this space and the concept of continuity is absent. He only gives, in imaginative form, the bare event, the bare emotion. The same elements—loss, separation, endurance, guilt, etc.—are still there. But the prospect of completion is absent. Think, for example, of the Lucy and the Matthew poems, where there seems to be no space for the thinking voice to enter the scene: thought does not come in aid of feeling, or if it does, there is no resolution. But now, at this moment when his most dominating life project is awakening, the circumstances in his life and his new poetic direction are ready to once again take him forward. A story begins to make itself apparent, and if we have a story, we have the possibility of an ending. Emotional denouement is what he seeks.

As Wordsworth ends the first part of the 1799 *Prelude*, he discourses upon how wonderful it is that, as a child, we fit into the world and the world into us. There was a time when, "like a bee among the flowers" (line 412), his perceptions were relatively free of any difficult emotional associations. The meaning of experience had not yet caught up with him. But even so, some associations were there,

> doomed to sleep
> Until maturer seasons called them forth
> To impregnate and to elevate the mind.
>
> (Lines 424–26)

Note how Wordsworth makes these into something that can be called forth later for greater and higher purposes. They seem to be both inspirational and sublime. The scenes from the past are in fact connected by feelings, though these feelings might be forgotten or unclear; they are, as Wordsworth writes, sleeping. But whatever the feelings are, whether "fear" or "joy," they remain the "invisible links" to the beauty of Nature (lines 432–42). Wordsworth's reason for searching into those times so often "Disowned by memory" at once becomes clear to him, and again, this is a very big deal: he says he wants "To understand" himself. He has his doubts that he will be able to do so, but at least he may be able to "make our infancy a visible scene / On which the sun is shining" (lines 442–64).

Back in the U.K.: The 1799 *Prelude*, Book 2

When the Wordsworths arrived back in England, they immediately went to Sockburn, where they stayed with the Hutchinsons until mid-December. Their own relatives would not have been interested in putting them up, nor, sadly, would Dorothy and William have wanted to stay with them. The Hutchinsons—three sisters and two brothers—ran a farm, and the Wordsworths fit in with their easy and independent ways. They had known the family for a long time. During these seven months at Sockburn, Wordsworth would complete the second book of the 1799 *Prelude* and piece it together with what he had already written in Germany. He would reflect further on the meaning of his childhood experiences. In the eldest of the sisters, Mary, Wordsworth would also find a future wife.

Wordsworth spent the first few months at Sockburn trying to work out his finances with Richard Wordsworth, Josiah Wedgewood, and Joseph Cottle. Wordsworth was concerned about how *Lyrical Ballads* had been selling, and he believed that Coleridge's *Ancient Mariner* may have been deterring some of the readers (Wordsworth 1967, 264). This may also have resulted in Wordsworth titling *Lyrical Ballads* his own, with the "OTHER POEMS," those by the still anonymous Coleridge, extraneous material.

By autumn, Coleridge expressed to Wordsworth his anxiety that his fellow poet get on with the poem to end all poems, *The Recluse*, and that he include something about the need to retain the hope expressed by the French Revolution. Coleridge added that he was "against the publication of any small poems." In a later letter he added, "I long to see what you have been doing. O let it be the tail-piece of 'The Recluse'!, for of nothing but 'The Recluse' can I hear patiently." Even a year later Coleridge was saying to a different correspondent, "W will not be diverted by any thing from the prosecution of his Great Work" (Coleridge 1956, 1:527, 538, 646). But what Wordsworth had "been doing" during the final months of 1799 was not, as Coleridge hoped, *The Recluse*. It was the second part of *The Prelude*. He was not at work on history but on his own story.

At this time Wordsworth was in bad health. Dorothy wrote to Richard in early September: "William has been unwell lately he is sadly troubled with a pain in his side" (Wordsworth 1967, 270). This was also communicated to Coleridge, who likewise reported it to Richard a week later: "I received a letter this morning a letter from William & was agitated to find that his Health is in a State which I should deem alarming." He repeated this to another correspondent, adding a further comment about his emotional state: "W. Wordsworth is ill—& seems not happy" (Coleridge 1956, 1:526–27). By November he was still afflicted, so much so that Coleridge found himself having to visit

Wordsworth. He wrote to Southey, "I was called up to the North by alarming accounts of Wordsworth's health / which, thank God! are but little more than alarms" (545). Clearly something was bothering Wordsworth, but something neither life-threatening nor physically treatable.

So instead of turning to *The Recluse* that autumn, Wordsworth returned to the poem about his childhood, and he completed a second section of *The Prelude* by about the end of the year. At the end of this period, in the last week of December, Wordsworth wrote to Coleridge: "Composition I find invariably pernicious to me" (Wordsworth 1967, 277). This is a drastic statement. His poetic efforts seemed to be taking a psychological toll. Once more: pain with gain.

That these descriptions of Wordsworth's health during his last months at Sockburn are a repeat of how he was at Goslar should not be surprising. These two periods of his life when he was composing autobiographical poetry were also periods of poor health. The aching in his side had returned. He seemed once more to be writing in "self-defence."

This autumn also had one incident that must have brought back some long-repressed feelings for Wordsworth. In the middle of October, Wordsworth's uncle, Christopher Crackanthorpe Cookson (Uncle Kit), died. This was the uncle who treated Wordsworth so very badly when he was a youth (Wordsworth 1967, 3, 8, 100). Crackanthorpe (the name is utterly Dickensian) left Dorothy £100, but William nothing. Wordsworth did not even bother to attend the funeral. Clearly he still harbored much resentment towards relatives who had treated him poorly.

If the first part of the 1799 *Prelude* can be described as largely a description of actual incidents and the attendant feelings, the second part is for the most part reflective. The first part, in fact, brings together more intense, memorable episodes than anything else Wordsworth ever wrote, containing the scenes of trap-robbing, egg-stealing, boat-stealing, skating, cardplaying, the drowned man, the gibbet, and the waiting for the horses. And originally it also included the boy of Winander passage, and it seems that his recollection of nutting was also associated with these other autobiographical remembrances.[5] For a reader, this is a great deal to take in; for a writer, it must have been a great deal to give out.

Book 2 (or "Second Part") begins by remembering those childhood days as times of endless and exhausting play. At the end of the first section he makes note of the state in which he now finds himself:

> A tranquillizing spirit presses now
> On my corporeal frame, so wide appears
> The vacancy between me and those days,

> Which yet have such self-presence in my heart
> That sometimes when I think of them I seem
> Two consciousnesses—conscious of myself,
> And of some other being.
>
> (1799 *Prelude,* bk. 2, lines 25–31)

In the introduction, I quoted these lines and noted how Wordsworth here opens up the large gap between his present adult condition and his innocent childhood past. There is more to this that connects with the other angle I have pursued in this study. That is, the gap between then and now also seems to correspond with the gap between feeling and thought. The past has left him with a kind of inscribed feelings, the "self-presence in my heart." That past is very real for him, yet the gap between himself and "those days" is "so wide." It is as if that child, who is a pure emotional and physical presence, is "some other being"; yet again, he knows that "other" so well since it resides within him. In the present, he strives to have his thinking dominate his sense of being; in the past, he existed in his feelings. The "vacancy" between the two is what he wants to fill. His poetic and personal calling is to make the "Two consciousnesses"— past and present, feeling and thought—one. Wordsworth's implicit desire, then, is to become "conscious" of just one integrated being: himself.

As book 2 continues, Wordsworth describes the various kinds of outings he took part in. He also inserts, almost apologetically, that he was "taught to feel—perhaps too much— / The self-sufficing power of solitude" (lines 76–77). This seems to be an uncomfortable confession, for solitude is such an important condition for Wordsworth. Yet we wonder how it was that he was taught *too much* to feel its power. Was it imposed on him? Did he have a choice? Who taught him this, or was it self-imposed—and if so, why? At the same time he writes that in growing up he began to perceive the important relationship between himself and his surroundings, "That sense of dim similitude which links / Our moral feelings with external forms," and how "the common range of visible things" became so "dear" to him (lines 164–65, 216). But in trying to understand how and when he changed, and in what way, he also articulates the impossibility of really knowing how "habits and desires" were formed. He does not know, but he wants to (lines 242–67).

Following is the densely elegant "infant babe" passage, which was discussed in chapter 1 in terms of Wordsworth's poeticized and deeply internalized feelings about his mother. First, Wordsworth examines the situation in general terms (bk. 2, lines 267–310). A child in its mother's arms is a fortunate being, for it does not have to worry about negotiating any kind of existential gap between himself and the world. The child's consciousness is naturally formed as "feelings" originating from his connection with his mother awaken his "mind"; thus it "spreads" to "connect him with the world." The process is at the same time nominated by Wordsworth as the birth of the "Poetic spirit," which seems to be a condition where feelings and thought interact, as one, with the world. Wordsworth makes this out as the ideal scenario. Second, Wordsworth discusses this in particular terms—that is, in terms of what happened to him (lines 310–33). But it is not an ideal scenario. Wordsworth points out that he "held mute dialogues with [his] mother's heart," but in trying to describe how his own "infant sensibility" was "Augmented and sustained," he also has to say that, for him, the "path" is "More difficult" to negotiate. The smooth transition from infancy to youth, from feeling to thought, was troubled—*is* troubled. He fears that the passage out of childhood has "broken windings" that will need "The chamois' sinews and the eagle's wing"—strength and inspiration—to see him through. How this happened becomes clear. When, as a child, his mother died, he was "left alone / Seeking this visible world, nor knowing why." He remained behind, and it was left to "Nature" to fill the gap.

We have two scenes to think about. First, we have to think of a real child, just eight years old. His primary caregiver, his mother, has suddenly died. He finds himself alone, and he has to turn to something outside of his family for support. This says much about what Wordsworth's family life must have been like. It also tell us much about the source of his most troubling emotions. Second, we have to think of a real adult, not quite thirty years old. He looks back upon his past, to probably the most traumatic event in his life: the death of his mother when he was just eight years old. Out of that trauma he has to formulate a scene of sustenance and continuity; he has to restore and repair those "broken windings" in order to discover the "path" that will take him to not just where he is, but to who he is. He has to find self-acceptance, which is another way of uniting his divided consciousness. Here he is at least facing his feelings. His greatness and recovery will be this: the source of his sorrow will also have to become the source of his power. His past will have to lead him into the future.

In the final parts of the 1799 *Prelude*, we see a youth, mainly in "utter solitude" and in "fleeting moods / Of shadowy exaltation," connecting with the objects of nature through feeling. But once more it becomes apparent that Wordsworth's efforts are needful; once more he is uncertain of the path and the source. Feelings are inside, and even objects of nature are overwhelmed by the difficulty of the inner quest:

> How shall I trace the history, where seek
> Origin of what I then have felt?
> Often in those moments such a holy calm
> Did overspread my soul that I forgot

> The agency of sight, and what I saw
> Appeared like something in myself, a dream,
> A prospect in my mind.
>
> (Bk. 2, lines 333–401)

Wordsworth's need is to know what he felt and why. And of course he needs to know how he can tell his story, which seems here to be a history of his feelings. In these youthful contemplative states, all seems to have been internalized and then turned out, so that everything is a vision of himself. This kind of visionary experience borders on a solipsistic drive, but it is checked by offering a "prospect" rather than a dead end.

As Wordsworth attempts to take his history forward in time, he looks to the struggle between his own imagination and the power of Nature, but he suggests attaining a kind of balance (lines 401–64). That is, as he sees himself mature into a seventeen year old, he describes his relationship with the world outside of himself as less self-replicating: "I conversed / With things that really are." And the final stage is to combine what he always felt was so difficult:

> From Nature and her overflowing soul
> I had received so much that all my thoughts
> Were steeped in feeling.
>
> (Lines 446–48)

Out of this Wordsworth could now come to an important point: "for in all things / I saw one life, and felt that it was joy." The vision of "one life" seems to have been promoted by the profitable integration of thought and feeling. Nature was the facilitator, or at least the facilitatory trope. But though this was an important step for Wordsworth towards healing the child within, Nature remained an external force—and voice. The power of the mind and the use of thought were not yet ready to fully to show themselves, though as *The Prelude* grew, so did the mind take over from Nature.[6] Wordsworth still troubled over leaving anything behind. He made a story in which his gain was great, but his deed was not done. To leave behind Nature and its place in his history was to leave behind those troubling feelings initially associated with Nature—that is, his mother and father. To have his mind in the place of Nature was to move towards self-sufficiency and individuation. He was now capable of moving forward in time without the feelings of his past hindering his progress.

Significantly, Wordsworth did not return to his life story until early 1804. That is, it is not until then that he evolved a strategy of poetic self-completion through his new healing trope of the mind. He then created a new view of himself, and his feelings of insecurity, uncertainty, and discontinuity were at last resolved through the process of difficult expression: the interactive discourse of emotional reenactment and contemplation. The only thing we can say that rivalled Wordsworth's determination was his eloquence. Up to that point in Wordsworth's life, the two seemed to grow together.

Longing for and Belonging at Grasmere

Perhaps the best relief from Wordsworth's silent troubles came during a walking tour he embarked upon on the last day of October 1799. Along with his favorite brother, John, and Coleridge, the first leg of the journey ended up on childhood turf, in Grasmere on 3 November, where they stayed close to a week. Coleridge was overwhelmed by the landscape and much impressed with John. He wrote to Dorothy at the end of their stay at Grasmere: "Your Br. John is one of you; a man who hath solitary usings of his own Intellect, deep in feeling, with a subtle Tact, a swift instinct of Truth & Beauty. He interests me much" (Coleridge 1956, 1:543). In the same letter, Wordsworth also wrote to Dorothy and communicated what he called a mad plan to build a lakeside cottage, but he also added: "There is a small house at Grasmere empty which perhaps we may take, and purchase furniture but of this will we speak" (Wordsworth 1967, 272). The "small house" was then referred to as the cottage at Town-End, but we now know it under the name of Dove Cottage. Today it remains the central icon of the Wordsworth industry.

By the third week of December, the brother and sister were moved in. A few days later they wrote to Coleridge and told him about their new home. They were exhausted and had colds; Dorothy had a severe toothache; and it was here that Wordsworth said that he found composition "invariably pernicious." But the overwhelming beauty of the place was also communicated (273–80). And here, at Grasmere, Dorothy's wish, made more than seven years before, to have a cottage with her brother that they could call *their own*, had finally come true (97).

The Wordsworths would stay at Dove Cottage for eight years, but even when they moved they remained in Grasmere. Wordsworth's life changed significantly while he was at Dove Cottage, and so did his poetry. He anticipated what this kind of move would mean for him as he worked on the earliest passages of *The Prelude* late in 1799: "That burthen of my own unnatural self, / The heavy weight of many a weary day" would soon be lifted: "Long months of ease and undisturbed delight / Are mine in prospect" (1805 *Prelude*; bk. 1, lines 21–29).[7] The idea was planted in advance that, at Grasmere, Wordsworth would be able to accommodate a part of himself that had hitherto pulled him down and tired him out. He felt that at Grasmere he might at last liberate himself from some of the inner burden of the past.

For Dorothy and William, moving to Grasmere was both a homecoming and a new beginning. Unlike other places they had lived together—Racedown, Alfoxden, Goslar, Sockburn—they could afford to make both an emotional and pecuniary investment at Dove Cottage. They felt connected enough that they could fix the cottage and tend to the gardening: as they wrote to Coleridge, they had plans to "enclose" their front yard "because it will make it more our own" (Wordsworth 1967, 275). They would own the furniture. In short, they had the means and arrangement to stay there for a long time. And this was an important feature of their new domestic circumstances.[8]

Wordsworth's experience of feeling settled was expressed in a poem he began a few months after arriving, in the spring of 1800. It was to be the first part of the first book of *The Recluse*, but in an expanded version we know it as a completed poem of the uncompleted large project: *Home at Grasmere*. Unlike *The Prelude*, it appears that Wordsworth made no definite plans to have it posthumously published. For Wordsworth, the poem in some ways represented his failure to get on with the job of *The Recluse* as repeatedly urged by Coleridge. Although constantly revised during his lifetime, it was not published until almost forty years after his death, and then it was not until the middle of this century that it was given any serious editorial attention. But even then it was relegated to the status of an appendix. This appendix poem printed in 1949 (Wordsworth 1949, 311–39) was the final, much revised version. Not until 1977 (Wordsworth 1977a) was the original version published (MS B). But even here there is a slight problem, for those lines that Wordsworth wrote in the spring of 1800 did not include what became the final section of MS B (lines 959–1049). These lines, likely written in January 1800 and better known as the "Prospectus" to *The Excursion* (1814), were in 1806 placed at the end of the lines written in 1800.[9]

If, then, we look at the original composition history in 1800, what we really have are two poems or, perhaps more correctly, two passages, and they are not necessarily related. One passage, written in January (lines that become the "Prospectus"), outlines the huge project that Coleridge wanted Wordsworth to get on with—*The Recluse*—and makes an invocation for inspirational endurance. The other lines, written in March and April (the bulk of *Home at Grasmere*, MS B), describe the impressions of the Wordsworths when they first came to Grasmere and contextualize some of his more difficult feelings. With the hindsight of history on our side, we know that Wordsworth would not turn much more to his philosophical-poetic discourse; instead, he would work on his own poetic discourse of self-discovery.

5 / Home Again in Grasmere

Almost the minute he arrived at Grasmere, Wordsworth must have felt the pressure to get started on his Coleridge-driven magnum opus. After all, he now had at last what he had wanted so much: a "home" with his beloved sister in the place he loved so much. There were now no excuses. Yet he apparently left off after just over seventy-five lines (MS I).[10] At the time he must have thought it a good start, and he certainly recognized that these were good lines. He names his topic (man, nature, and human life), puts his aspirations in light of Milton's poetic accomplishment, and he sees "Paradise" waiting just outside his door (lines 1–40). But he hopes that even if his "song" has to take on the darker side of human life—"ill sights," "passions ravenous," "Insult and injury and wrong and strife," "solitary anguish," and "sorrow"—"Wisdom" will guide him, so that he will "be not heartless, or forlorn" (lines 41–54). These, of course, were already significant parts of Wordsworth's experience. He invokes the "prophetic spirit" to inspire him with "foresight" so that his song will be as a beacon, "a light hung up in heaven to chear / The world in times to come." He also foresees that he may have to address more "humble matter": the individual histories of common people (lines 55–71). Finally, he makes a "prayer":

> Innocent mighty spirit, let my life
> Express the image of a better time;
> Desires more wise, and simpler manners, nurse
> My heart in genuine freedom; all pure thoughts
> Be with me, and uphold me to the end.
>
> (Lines 72–77)

Wordsworth expresses humility and the sense of precariousness here—these are expected conventions of prayer and invocation. But at the same time there is little doubt he feels empowered by his new sense of self, of self-presence and direction. That *The Recluse* remained a magnificent blueprint with only a part of its structure complete matters little.[11] It matters more how, at this time, Wordsworth was beginning to feel as he intimated a free heart and a pure mind.

Probably about a month after this, Wordsworth wrote about what his new circumstances meant to *him* at that very time and place, not to mankind. He had to contextualize at length his newfound joy, for as Thomas McFarland points out, *Home at Grasmere* is unique in the Wordsworth canon in its unequivocal expression of gladness and satisfaction (1992, 79–81). However, this observation needs to be situated in terms of the poet's personal history, and it also has to be shown that the poem does make important references to some of his past difficulties and present troubles.

Home at Grasmere opens with Wordsworth remembering being a schoolboy at Grasmere, and stopping on the side of the hill now before him to take in the beauty of the place. He remembers sighing to himself:

> What happy fortune were it here to live!
> And if I thought of dying, if a thought
> Of mortal separation could come in
> With paradise before me, here to die.
>
> (Lines 9–12)

This fictionalized childhood eloquence (for it is doubtful that young William spontaneously broke into blank verse) is more important for the adult Wordsworth than for his young self. Wordsworth may very well have stopped as a boy to gaze at the beauty of the surrounding landscape, and perhaps he did have the thought that if he were to die, he wished it to be here. In MS D, Wordsworth cleaned up the syntax and punctuation so that the childhood words were, "And happy fortune were it here to live! / And . . . here to die!" (Wordsworth 1977a, 39). For the adult Wordsworth, this recollection expressed feelings of both continuity and completion. These were important feelings for Wordsworth—and timely, too, for they began to counter the feelings of loss that dominated much of his other poetry. There was the implanted idea, a "fancy in the heart" (line 15), that he might die here, thus making his childhood daydream come true. (Wordsworth actually did die in Grasmere.) As in *Tintern Abbey*, the structure is that of a return to a spot invested with past feelings in order to evaluate his present feelings. The feeling sought is that of self-confirmation.

For Wordsworth, this is indeed a return to "paradise." In fact, he suggests that his situation is better than that in "Eden" (lines 122–28). The luxuriousness of its engulfing hills and valleys, winds and waters, sunshine and shade, meadows and woods, clouds and sky, butterflies and birds, is as Eden before the Fall. As in MS I (the first version of the "Prospectus"), where Grasmere is "Paradise" (lines 30–40), it is all innocence and beauty. His childhood hope was that this "Should be my home, this Valley be my World" (lines 17–43). And so it was. (Even in the rather cheeky announcement of his wedding a few years later, Wordsworth's place of residence was described as "the little Paradise Vale of Grasmere.")[12] As a "thought," this place was fully retained by Wordsworth. He also says that it is "a haunt / Of my affections," suggesting that emotional associations are likewise retained. In times of "joy," it made joy more joyful; in times of "sorrow," the remembrance of the place was "a gleam of light." And now, he triumphantly exclaims, it is "mine for life: dear Vale, / One of thy lowly dwellings is my home!" (lines 44–53). Wordsworth seems to be as surprised as he is happy. He is also relieved.

Yet Wordsworth now moves to a different view of the past. He acknowledges the difficulties, the many "Realities of life" (line 54) that he has had to endure. But now, home at Grasmere, he can at last declare, "I am safe":

> What once was deemed so difficult, is now
> Smooth, easy, without obstacle; what once
> Did to my blindness seem a sacrifice,
> The same is now a choice of the whole heart.
> If e'er the acceptance of such dower was deemed
> A condescension or a weak indulgence
> To a sick fancy, it is now an act
> Of reason that exultingly is mine; the distant thought
> Is fetched out of heaven in which it was.
> The unappropriated bliss hath found
> An owner, and that owner I am he.
> The Lord of this enjoyment is on Earth
> And in my breast. What wonder if I speak
> With fervour, am exalted with the thought
> Of my possessions, of my genuine wealth
> Inward and outward? What I keep, have gained,
> Shall gain, must gain, if sound be my belief
> From past and present, rightly understood,
> That in my day of childhood I was less
> The mind of Nature, less, take all in all,
> Whatever may be lost, than I am now.
> For proof behold this Valley, and behold
> Yon Cottage, where with me my Emma dwells.
>
> (Lines 74–98)

"Emma," of course, is Wordsworth's name for Dorothy, whom Wordsworth acknowledges as a "unseen" presence who accompanied him in all his movements and thoughts (lines 104–16).

This is an extraordinary passage (lines 74–98), and there is nothing quite like it in Wordsworth's poetry. Much of the syntax, with its series of short, direct clauses and sentences, is highly unusual for Wordsworth, whose sentences normally sprawl and expand. Even Wordsworth is surprised to find himself writing with such "fervour." Once more, as in *Tintern Abbey*, there is a "then" and "now" structure. But one important difference is that the Tintern Abbey revisit unfolded as a temporary confirmation of growth; this Grasmere experience is, as far as Wordsworth is concerned, permanent; the constancy of his environment will foster certainty rather than the need for further endurance. For Wordsworth, this is an important part of his emotional rehabilitation.

Much work remains to be done, and events in his household will reflect his changing self-regard, but now, at last, he has a vision of himself. He can see himself. He has the opportunity to no longer be obsessed with who he was, but by who he will be.

Wordsworth expresses that he can see clearly now all obstacles in his way. What was before a loss is now an emotional gain for "the whole heart." Now he has "reason" to rescue him from excess. He moves toward transforming the lexicon of Christian bliss into a discourse of self-empowerment and personal recovery. Wordsworth views himself more than ever as the "mind of Nature"— a difficult phrase, but perhaps in its unclarity it is a harbinger for the final transformation that Wordsworth makes in his poetic quest for individuation— namely, when he comes to see the mind as all in all, rather than Nature.

As he stands there once more, the place becomes a certain kind of feeling that goes back to an incomplete childhood:

> Embrace me, then, ye Hills, and close me in,
> Now in the clear and open day I feel
> Your guardianship; I take it to my heart;
> 'Tis like the solemn shelter of the night.

(Lines 129–32)

This place clearly represents the feeling of being parented. He wants to be held and embraced. He wants to be taken care of, to be protected from his dark fears. This is not just what he wants Grasmere to do for him. This is what, in 1800, he needed Grasmere to do and be for him. Wordsworth in Grasmere was the child returned to the safety of his home, to the home he never quite had. Wordsworth never had the opportunity to appropriately separate from home or to grow out of it. His new living circumstances now offered him the opportunity to implicitly reenact and address these issues while he felt safe, for without the feeling of safety, recovery cannot properly take place. There, with his sister and his favorite brother, John (who stayed much of the first year there), a part of family had come together. John himself expressed as much when, after having moved in with his brother and sister sometime towards the end of January, he paced "over this floor in pride . . . exulting within his noble heart that his Father's Children had once again a home together" (Wordsworth 1967, 649). Like Dorothy and William, John too seems to have been overwhelmed to have a "home together." A displaced family had reinstated itself.

For Wordsworth, Grasmere was a living landscape of regained paradise,[13] and he wished never to part from it: "'tis here, / Here as it found its way into my heart / In childhood, here as it abides by day, / By night, here only" (lines 156–59). Wordsworth knew that this might ultimately be fanciful (line 155);

there were other places just as beautiful. But for him it was real because of what it meant for him, and that is what matters. It was *here*. The sense of place in Wordsworth is always noticeable—his so-called centroversion or spot syndrome. But this was different. For Wordsworth, Grasmere represented the Mother of All Places. He does not know how to describe the "sense" of what he feels, but he does know there is

> Something that makes this individual Spot,
> This small abiding place of many men,
> A termination, and a last retreat,
> A Centre, come for wheresoe'er you will,
> A Whole without dependence or defect,
> Made for itself, and happy in itself,
> Perfect Contentment, Unity entire.
>
> (Lines 161–70)

This powerfully articulated emotional projection by Wordsworth onto Grasmere tells us what the poet has been striving for—again, what he needs: a final place, "a last retreat," "A Centre," "A Whole," happiness, "Contentment," and "Unity." But needs tell much more about the past and about deficiencies than they do about the future, and out of this list we can read what Wordsworth has not felt in any kind of continuous way: a final place, "a last retreat," "A Centre," "A Whole," happiness, "Contentment," and "Unity." This is not a "spot of time," a detached but indelible incident; it is a "Spot" that represents personal completion that goes beyond time. This too differs from the "sense sublime" in *Tintern Abbey* that connects him with "all things" (line 94–103). His new "sense" has more to do with being connected with his own sense of self that was dislocated when his parents died, leaving the child within him.

After this Wordsworth immediately reflects on how he was separated from his "Emma" and how his siblings—"a scattered brood"—were forced to go their own ways (lines 171–79). The circumstance forcing the separation was, of course, the death of the parents, though Wordsworth does not say as much. He might have gone on and said more about how and why, after the loss of the parents, "life / Remained unfixed" (line 184), but here, unfortunately, and perhaps significantly, the text is missing for seven lines (lines 185–91). There is, in this case, a literal gap in the text. Perhaps the missing lines were too strong or problematical for Wordsworth to include at this point. It is noticeable that, given the context of the passage, what Wordsworth was going to address had to do with how his "life / Remained unfixed" at a crucial time in his life.

In *Home at Grasmere* Wordsworth also writes about the three-day journey he and Dorothy made to Grasmere from Sockburn (probably December 17–20;

Reed 1967, 282–83). The way Wordsworth describes it gives the journey and their arrival epic dimensions, complete with strong supernatural elements (lines 216–77). When they left, "Bleak season was it, turbulent and bleak." They traveled on foot "through flying snows" and "long Vales," enduring the "keen breath" of "The frosty wind." But despite these hardships, they were blown forward, "like two Ships at sea": "Stern was the face of nature." Past "naked trees" and "icy brooks" they made their way. The elements of the landscape that witnessed their journey questioned their motives and destination as they traveled through the "dark domain." But the speaking elements were "moved" by these two determined and windswept figures, and they rallied around the pair. On their way they also came across a spring known as "Hart-leap Well" and three stones that commemorated an incident that took place there long ago. Wordsworth does not go into the details of the place's history here, although soon after arriving at Grasmere he will in *Hart-Leap Well*. The story is of a nobleman who chased a magnificent deer (hart) through most of a day, but, with three final leaps, it lay down and died by the spring. The nobleman placed the three stones there to pay homage to the deer's courage, and it is said that the place is cursed, so that no livestock will drink there. The Wordsworths are disturbed by the story, but they pass by "that doleful place," and, in spite of all, find "blessedness" out of the suffering endured by one of God's "poor Creatures"—something that, of course, was close to their own lives: enduring suffering in order to find blessedness. This, in fact, was the quest they were on as they made their way to happiness at Grasmere. The story commemorating the poor deer in its final resting place was in some important ways their story as well. When they at last arrive at Grasmere, the sky, like waiting parents, "faced" them "with a passionate welcoming"; the whole Vale, he writes, "Begins to love us!" This, once more, is what they needed: to be embraced at their homecoming after a lifetime of being separated from their home. Wordsworth has found himself safely delivered into the protective arms of Grasmere.

All of this makes their journey sound more like eight hundred miles than eighty, and thirty days rather than three. But, in a very real sense, their trip was epic and magical and difficult, and in the end they did reach their golden fleece or holy grail—or heaven on earth. For up until this point the thing they desired most was a home. And so for them this rather short trip really did represent the final stage of a long and difficult journey through a stormy winter, a journey that hitherto had taken much of their lives to complete. We have to imagine the kinds of emotions they experienced as these "two Ships at sea" came to their final port, just as we have to remember what they had to endure for all those years. They could now have the kind of home they never had.

As Wordsworth now looks back to the winter from his writing perspective of spring 1800, he sees the "jubilant" birds sporting above the lake (lines 277–

321). But these pleasant thoughts are interrupted by his noticing that two swans that they had watched endure the winter are no longer there to share in the "day's pleasure" (lines 322–57). This disturbs Wordsworth, because he had explicitly made them symbols for his and Dorothy's situation: "their state so much resembled ours, / . . . they a pair, / And we a solitary pair like them." Wordsworth "looked for them in vain," but he could not see them. He has fears that they may have been killed by a shepherd. This puts him out so much because, having made them a parallel pair with him and his sister in their appearance at Grasmere, what is he now to make of their disappearance and possibly death? Where are the birds? Kenneth R. Johnston (1975, 6–7) also poses this question, and he further notices that a significant portion of the poem following is taken up with this mood disturbance (but note that Johnson is using MS D as his text; I am using the earlier MS B, which is longer and has intervening lines). Johnson's point is well taken: the subject of "death and separation" and the "feeling of loss" (7) do begin to infiltrate the poem and threaten to displace what Wordsworth seems to have established so decidedly. Unlike the angle of the present study, Johnston's angle is not to contextualize this shift within the history of Wordsworth's larger emotional needs. And so what returns to Wordsworth are those very feelings and subjects (death, separation, loss) that he had thus far addressed throughout his poetic career. The fragility and precariousness of Wordsworth's blissful gains are suddenly, and even predictably, apparent. What has become of these two lonely figures? What will become of them?

Wordsworth goes on to admit that Grasmere is not, after all, a perfect place, though it is a place where "perfection absolute" can be contemplated. The security of the mind is stronger than the actual situation. There are many good people here, and here too are the incidents of human folly that occur elsewhere, but at least for those who want it, work can be found, and "extreme penury is here unknown" (lines 358–468). There is a sense of community, and in community the sense of safety.

Wordsworth proceeds to give three sketches that tell of the people who live or once lived in Grasmere.[14] The first (lines 469–532) is the story of a dalesman who loves books. His body is healthy, his mind calm. He provides a good life for his family. He is also somewhat "easy minded," and he suffers from careless thoughts. He has an affair with a young lady, and thereafter, plagued with guilt and inward suffering, he cannot face his loving family. He becomes a restless wanderer, and he finds nothing to relieve his feelings. Finally, unable to "bear the weight" of his grief and shame, he dies. The second story (lines 533–606) is of a father, a widower, who is left to parent his six daughters, none of whom have reached adulthood. The story focuses on the eldest daughter, who helps her father in the kinds of things a son might, and who also, as Wordsworth sees when he stealthily peeks into the window of their house at night, teaches her younger siblings household skills. The final tale (lines 607–45) is of a widow who tells Wordsworth about the loss of her "dead Husband." Their togetherness is manifest in a "little grove of firs" they planted in the "prime of wedlock." But Wordsworth cannot, in his own words, give equal eloquence to her story as it came from her feelings. He sees that "She is withering in her loneliness," but he nonetheless gathers some strength from what remains behind all of this: "the silent mind / Has its own treasures, and I think of these, / Love what I see, and honour humankind."

These three sketches recall many of the poems in *Lyrical Ballads*. What Wordsworth centers on are sorrow and grief, guilt and loneliness, endurance and perseverance, all revolving around absence and death. These are determining events for Wordsworth, and the dramatic elements of his stories inevitably address the notion of survival after death or desertion of loved ones—in these cases, parent and spouses. Once more, all of this is close to Wordsworth's own history and emotional experiences. We might even speculate about how two of the tales (that is, the two that, for some reason, were taken out of *Home at Grasmere* in later versions of the poem) seem to parallel in part some of Wordsworth's own experiences. In the first tale, Wordsworth may have related uncomfortably to the wandering, guilt, and suffering of the scholar-dalesman after his love affair; the story of course strongly parallels Wordsworth's affair with Annette Vallon and his own subsequent wandering and suffering. And Wordsworth's overt Peeping Tom concern with the family held together by the father after the death of the mother may hold its fascination for Wordsworth because of what might have become of his own family. That is, as he looks through the window he may be thinking: *This could have been my family after mother died. Father could have held us together the way this father has done.*

But, in 1800, the important advance comes in what Wordsworth feels he can gather not just from the landscape but from the human histories he finds around himself at Grasmere. Rather than taking these stories as passing examples of loss, Wordsworth attempts to turn them into living examples of gain; instead of weakness, he finds strength; instead of feeling alone, he and Dorothy will feel connected; instead of turning inward, they will look outside of themselves:

> No, We are not alone, we do not stand,
> My Emma, here misplaced and desolate,
> Loving what no one cares for but ourselves.
> . . . we do not tend a lamp
> Whose lustre we alone participate,
> Which is dependent on us alone . . .
>
> (Lines 646–48, 655–57)

We belong here, Wordsworth is saying, *yet we are not the center holding everything together*. Even though he is just a "Newcomer" to these parts, Wordsworth feels himself opening up: "the inward frame, / Though slowly opening, opens every day" (lines 693–95). There is now a way in.

Again, this is an extraordinarily advance upon Wordsworth's earlier inability to free himself from his feelings. And what will happen if he is "forced to cast a painful look / Upon welcome things, which unawares / Reveal themselves"?

> Not therefore is my mind
> Depressed, nor do I fear what is to come;
> But confident, enriched at every glance,
> The more I see the more is my delight.
>
> (Lines 714–17)

Wordsworth says he will no longer "fear" "unwelcome things," despite knowing that in the past uncertainty, sorrow, and solitude followed him. Now he has certainty, confidence, and a sense of community to fortify his being.

Wordsworth's newfound emotional confidence at Grasmere is a product of his sense of belonging. Even the local dogs, horses, birds, and cows will become a part of his world. He will *know* them (lines 720–52). Ever since the death of his mother, the sense of knowing a place and the feeling that he belonged somewhere have been absent, though desired, perhaps, more than anything else.

Now, as Wordsworth returns to his survey of the landscape at Grasmere, he sees in its "universal imagery" the "genial harmony" of its elements (lines 752–806). Here "solitude" cannot exist: "Society is here: / The true Community" (lines 807–18). And if what surrounds their home is at times not enough to satisfy the "insatiable mind," then the people who come to stay—like John Wordsworth ("a Stranger of our Father's house"), Coleridge, and Mary and Sara Hutchinson—will enrich their lives with hope and happiness (lines 859–74).

Wordsworth recognizes that everything has its time and place (lines 875–83), and, as we have seen, he also feels he is a part of all that surrounds him. But at the same time he recognizes something special inside of him, some "internal brightness," some "inward lustre," "Something within" that is "solely" his and "shared with none," but something that he hopes to "impart" even after he is gone (lines 884–909). The tension or contradiction here is something like that expressed in the 1802 Preface to *Lyrical Ballads*—namely, that, although the poet is a man among men, using "the very language of men," he is also special, having more "enthusiasm," "tenderness," and "knowledge" than other men; "a more comprehensive soul," "a man pleased with his own passions and volitions, and who rejoices more than other men in the spirit of life"; a man "impelled to create ["the goings-on of the Universe"] where he does not find them"; he is "affected more than other men by absent things as if they were present"; and "he has acquired a greater readiness and power in expressing what he thinks and feels" (Wordsworth 1984, 600, 603–4). This is a tall order to live up to, as is his main tenet in the Preface—that is, that the truth of human nature is to be found in elemental feelings. This is the truth he was beginning to discover by examining his own life. But here, in 1800, he is beginning to come to terms with being both a part of things and apart from them, with loss and gain; he belongs, but, as a poet, he is also unique. Wordsworth, in short, is attempting to articulate his personal life-role in *Home at Grasmere*. He wants to find his place as a person and his voice as a poet. At Grasmere he would find both.

As in *Tintern Abbey*, Wordsworth recalls his innocent childhood, with his "wild appetites and blind desires" and his attraction to "Deep pools, tall trees, black chasms, and dizzy crags." So too he recalls the workings of his vivid imagination, something he still retains, but has now tamed. If then he was like a "turbulent Stream" racing down a mountain, now he is that same stream which has increased in strength but moves "Through quiet meadows." This is a revealing metaphor. Wordsworth sees himself retaining the same substance as when he was younger but now evolving to a different formulation of that substance, one that is steadier, calmer, slower; he can retain what he once was, but now, with the depth and strength gathered in his long journey towards the sea, the path is clear, the course more deliberate, more steady. The end is in sight, the journey from the source almost complete.

Finally, Wordsworth reasons that what once "enflamed" his "infant heart,"

> the love,
> The longing, the contempt, the undaunted quest,
> These shall survive, though changed their office, these
> Shall live—it is not in their power to die.
>
> (Lines 910–52)

As mentioned earlier, in 1806 Wordsworth inserted the "Prospectus" lines at this point, thus ending the poem with them.[15] However, in the spring of 1800, Wordsworth ended instead with this kind of intimation of immortality for all that has passed through him, despite any change in the relative significance that time has imposed. This movement towards acceptance and transformation works on a personal level.

The difficult feelings expressed in *Home at Grasmere* are anything but novel for Wordsworth. But his handling of them—his acceptance of a past that will not go away but will "survive" to give him his future identity, the feeling of belonging, the vision of his own history as continuous in its gathering of inner strength—*is* something new. It surfaces in *Tintern Abbey*, and it is invoked but not played out in the 1799 *Prelude*. But in *Home at Grasmere* it now shows up with a revised feeling of self-determination. Further, in portraying Grasmere as self-sufficient and self-complete, Wordsworth is projecting his own feelings onto the green valley that spreads before him.[16] The poem may not be a success as a completed work; nor does it move unequivocally towards unconditional bliss. As Jonathan Wordsworth writes, "*Home at Grasmere* does not have a plan. It is an important poem and in many ways an impressive one, but in Wordsworth's terms it is a failure" (1980, 21). This is certainly true—to an extent. But as Wordsworth's continuing exploration and expression of his feelings, and viewed in terms of the movement towards individuation, *Home at Grasmere* is a success. It will take a little more time, but he will return to the idea that strength can be found in what has been left behind, and that sorrow and joy, loss and gain, and even past and future are relative terms, not absolutes.

For Wordsworth, the first year at Grasmere was, more than anything else, an experiment in the feeling of togetherness and belonging—a kind of born-again family. With brother John staying a great portion of 1800, and with the visits by the Coleridges and Hutchinsons, as well as many others (see Reed 1975, 55–107 passim), Dove Cottage in 1800 and 1801 became the center of an ever-expanding group (as it is today): the Wordsworth circle. As Gill puts it, "For the first time in their lives, they were really settled and drawing people to them" (1989, 184).

The year 1800 was also the year in which Wordsworth intuited the success of *Lyrical Ballads*, thus calling for a new edition acknowledging him, and only him, as the author—or as Susan Eilenberg (1992, 60–61) would call him, the sole proprietor of *Lyrical Ballads*. Coleridge, like the annotations eventually made to *The Ancient Mariner*, became a marginalized presence in the collection. Wordsworth added more poems, but besides the Preface, his most important addition was written at the end of 1800: *Michael*, a poem about family breakup, the importance of family property, and the difficulty of resolving personal loss, replaces Coleridge's *Christabel* in *Lyrical Ballads*.[17] Not long after the poem appeared, Wordsworth wrote to a friend about its main character. Michael, he writes, is "agitated by two of the most powerful affections of the human heart; the parental affection, and the love of property, *landed* property, including the feelings of inheritance, home, and personal and family independence" (Wordsworth 1967, 322). We should not be very much surprised by this. As we have seen, these are indeed the feelings and issues that Wordsworth has troubled most over: the loss of "parental affection," independence, the loss of a home, and an inheritance. Note that Wordsworth calls it the "feelings of inheritance." *Michael* would take the place of *Tintern Abbey* as the final poem in *Lyrical Ballads*. Even *The Brothers*, a poem that bridges the move to Grasmere and makes it way into the 1800 collection, is essentially about the feeling of home and return, saddled with loss and regret and the attempt to confront the past breakup of a family. Grasmere and the feelings it evoked in Wordsworth are certainly played out.

So too was 1800 a year in which some of his health problems continued (see above, pp. 72–80). As he wrote midyear, "[I]ll health has for some time rendered literary labour not advisable for me" (Wordsworth 1967, 284). He might just as well have put it the other way around: "[L]iterary labour has for some time rendered my health ill." This seems to have continued into the autumn of 1800 and through to the spring of 1801. John Wordsworth wrote at that time to Dorothy that he had concerns about his brother's condition: "I do not know what to think or say about Wm's health. I only hope he will have good spirits & bear up under the pain he may suffer as much as possible" (Ketcham 1969, 113–14), though he thought that money problems might have been the source of his brother's troubles.

In terms of literary production, 1801 was for Wordsworth quite sparse. In April, John writes to Mary Hutchinson: "I am sorry to find from my sister's Letter that Wm's health is but very indifferent & that he finds himself unable to go on with any work" (Ketcham 1969, 116). He could do little more than, at the very end of the year, approach the daunting task of *The Recluse* by making a detour to more autobiographical writing, which he did in the form of recalling his life as a university student at Cambridge.[18] The Wordsworths continued to entertain numerous visitors at their tiny cottage, and they frequently went on short trips. We also know from Dorothy's journal that William was often ill, especially towards the end of the year and into 1802 (unfortunately, the notebook for Dorothy's journal from 23 December 1800 to 9 October 1801 is missing). Coleridge too was not well throughout the year, falling under the spell of opium and Mary Hutchinson's sister, Sara ("Asra," as Coleridge encoded her name in order to distinguish her from the other Sara, his wife).

But by early 1802, Wordsworth began once more to turn to the habit of poetry, and by the summer he had completed dozens of mostly lyrical poems and ballads, though very few of them approach the intensity of those written at Alfoxden and Goslar. Most are in fact happy engagements between the poet and the subjects and stories encountered around Grasmere: butterflies, beggars, and birds. If anything, the many shorter poems written in 1802 show Wordsworth not just delighting in his surroundings but also in the composition of poetry itself. So too early in the year did he return with considerable difficulty to *The Pedlar* (that is, *The Ruined Cottage*), expanding upon his central figure. Perhaps more importantly, Wordsworth added significant material to the Preface to *Lyrical Ballads*, giving the poet special sensibilities. This is a noteworthy addition at a noteworthy time.

The feeling of stability and growth in Wordsworth's life also came in the form of his plans to wed Mary Hutchinson. They were probably engaged sometime in February 1802. At the same time, Wordsworth was corresponding with Annette Vallon and his daughter, Caroline, in all likelihood attempting to arrange a meeting and appropriate settlement. The year 1802, then, would also be a time for change and for new questions, as well as for a new determination to resolve the problem of the adult child. On the evening of 26 March, while Dorothy was getting ready for bed (D. Wordsworth 1973, 106), William wrote out a little poem with large resolve:

> My heart leaps up when I behold
>   A Rainbow in the sky:
> So was it when my life began;
> So is it now I am a Man;
> So be it when I shall grow old,
>   Or let me die!
> The Child is Father of the Man;
> And I could wish my days to be
> Bound each to each by natural piety.

Here we have Wordsworth desiring continuity between his past, present, and future—and he does so in the most extreme terms possible: if this continuity cannot be, he would prefer to "die." I would not take this seemingly desperate resolve as merely rhetorical positioning. Wordsworth needed to feel that his life—his whole life—was connected. Thus, his desire for continuity is also his fear of discontinuity. Unlike many of his earlier poems addressing the problem of how to view his childhood, in this new poem Wordsworth does not separate his child self from his adult self; neither is the "Child" relegated to the status of an unthinking or instinctual being. There is no room for it here. Instead, in this singularly important moment when he declares "the Child is Father of the Man," Wordsworth as the adult child strives to see himself as a part of, rather than apart from, what once he was.

The weight of the resolve in this seemingly simple and famous poem should not be underestimated, for Dorothy's short but revealing journal account records the difficulty her brother experienced in trying to get the poem right: "Went to bed 1/2-past 11. William very nervous—after he was in bed haunted with altering the Rainbow" (D. Wordsworth 1973, 125). Here in the "Rainbow" poem Wordsworth was working towards his most important personal achievement: to have his troubled inner child no longer denied or disconnected from who he was. But remember: this was a hope, a wish, a wonderfully articulated aspiration that haunted him. It was not a reality. There were still many profound doubts and questions, and the very next morning he articulated those in what Dorothy refers to as "part of an ode" (106). In these lines, Wordsworth notes there was a time when everything around him seemed heavenly and Edenic, but now, he writes, "The things which I have seen I now can see no more." Everywhere he looks it seems "That there hath passed away a glory from the earth." Although he can hear and see and feel the spirit of life all around him, at the same time he intuits a loss, "something that is gone." He questions: "Whither is fled the visionary gleam? / Where is it now, the glory and the dream?" Wordsworth no longer sees Nature in quite the same way. No longer does is it answer all questions; nor is it the object of all pursuits. As in *Tintern Abbey*, we get the intimation that it is elsewhere he must look: to his own feelings and faculties. He may be understanding that his responses are more important than the external objects of his gaze.

Of course all of this questioning comes from what will become the first four stanzas of the *Immortality Ode*, and this is where he seems to have left off. He may in fact have been distracted by the delivery of a load of manure for the garden (D. Wordsworth 1973, 106). Such is the bliss of country life and the fate of literary history. Two years later Wordsworth returned to these lines, which also seem to have engaged Coleridge's attention.[19] But then he would do more than just return. He would answer the questions and transform inner doubt into personal faith.

6

The *Immortality Ode:*
Back to the Future

> How does one arrive somewhere when, without knowing it, one has always been there? How does it happen that confusion turns into clarity, pain into freedom to experience feelings; that volumes of empty words turn into simple facts, the constant flight-from-self into being-with-oneself; that blindness turns into vision, deafness into hearing, indifference into empathy, ignorant crime into informed responsibility, murderous lusts into calm, clenched despair into self-protection, self-alienation into self-harmony?
> —Alice Miller, *Banished Knowledge*

In early May 1802, about five weeks after writing what would become the first four stanzas of *Immortality Ode,* Wordsworth composed a poem that attempted to consolidate inner strength and resolve. The poem was then referred to as *The Leech Gatherer*, but later renamed *Resolution and Independence.* The poem returns to an incident that had taken place in October 1800 and was recorded by Dorothy in her journal. She and William had met a decrepit old man who, as his livelihood, gathered leeches, and they talked to the old man about his history (D. Wordsworth 1973, 42). Wordsworth recast the incident in the image of his present state of being, both in the persona of the narrator—a poet-wanderer who, despite the pleasant woodland surroundings, finds himself feeling despondent, with "fears, and fancies" (line 27) flooding his mind as he thinks about the dark side of his uncertain future—as well as in the impressive figure of the leech-gatherer, an old man who has, with quiet dignity, endured hardship. The old man is also a sort of poet figure (lines 99–103) whose life-spirit and firm mind have enabled him to persevere. The drama in the poem is that the younger, rather discountenanced poet seems to need the idea of the old poet to sustain him. The very existence of the leech-gatherer allows him to focus (after a little daydreaming) on his own situation; otherwise he might fall under the spell of fear and hopelessness—of madness, even. These feelings of uncertainty, despondency, and discomposure were important to resolve. He needed to intimate a more determined and emotionally stable future for himself, and through the leech-gatherer he constructed a figure of inner strength despite severe hardship. That the poem ends so resolutely with the old man as a positive emblem is an important indicator of Wordsworth's own development.

Resolution and Independence is a poem, then, that enacts and acts upon its title, for at Grasmere this was what Wordsworth had begun to establish. The doubts and the inexplicable listlessness are still there in the disposition of the narrator, just as they are in Wordsworth's other more romantic self-portrait of the wandering poet in *Stanzas written in my Pocket-Copy of Thomson's "Castle of Indolence,"* a poem written at the same time;[1] but there is also a resolve, a determination, to get on with living a life where he feels in control and where he feels centered. He also needs to imagine a future for himself. When Wordsworth encountered the old leech-gatherer in 1800, he may have not been quite ready to transform and positively integrate the incident into the process of his self-development. Now, two years later in 1802, it appears he was ready. Predictably, the seemingly small victory celebrated in this poem, which makes a vow to "stay secure" (line 146), did not come without some effort on the part of Wordsworth, for as Dorothy records, her brother "wearied himself to death" in trying to get the poem right (D. Wordsworth 1973, 123). The feeling of security was primary to Wordsworth's needs.

Other significant events also indicate that Wordsworth's life was changing in positive directions in 1802. By late spring, Dorothy and William were reasonably hopeful that in the very near future they would be able to draw on the substantial amount of money owed to them (and their other siblings) by the late Sir James Lowther via his debt to their father (Lowther died on 24 May 1802.)[2] The other significant event was his marriage to Mary Hutchinson on the morning of 4 October. But just before the marriage, for the month of August, Dorothy and William went to France to visit Annette and Caroline, who was now nine years old. This would have been a difficult meeting, but it also would have been an important event for Wordsworth in order to clear himself of any doubts or guilt. Seeing his former lover and his daughter was the right thing to do. At any earlier time he might not have been emotionally prepared for such a meeting, since he was still carrying around many of his own problems deriving from feelings of loss, separation, and abandonment. But now, centered and secure at Grasmere, reunited with his sister, with definite financial prospects, experiencing reasonable success as a poet, and with plans to marry a woman he had grown to know well, the only items unresolved were issues from the past. Annette, Caroline, and abandonment were an important part of these issues. He was now more able to confront his feelings, rather than displace, project, or internalize them. As 1802 came to a close, never before had his life been so stable, his prospects so favorable.

In 1803, we find Wordsworth's life at Grasmere stabilized further. He made new friendships, though his relationship with Coleridge had become more uneven. Coleridge may have been a little jealous or resentful of Wordsworth's sense of peacefulness and domestic security, and perhaps he also sensed that the poetic accomplishments of his former writing partner had outstripped his own poetic accomplishments, even without much prospect of *The Recluse* ever showing itself. Coleridge's marriage was also a disaster, while Wordsworth's domestic circumstances appeared to Coleridge as enviable. In October, Coleridge wrote of Wordsworth's "Self-involution," and he spoke of seeing his friend "more & more benetted in hypochondriacal Fancies, living wholly among *Devotees*—having every the minutest Thing, almost his very Eating & Drinking, done for him by his Sister, or Wife" (Coleridge 1956, 2:1013). Such attention was in fact what Coleridge wanted. Just a few months later he could write that "his [Wordsworth's] is the happiest Family, I ever saw" (1032). Poor Coleridge. He also noticed that Wordsworth's personality was changing, so that he was "now fonder of conversation & more open" (937–38). It seems that Wordsworth was now, in 1803, able to respond to those around, rather than having his interests or attention largely turned inwards. Wordsworth seemed to be a changed man.

The year also celebrated the birth of William and Mary's first child, John, born midyear. There is little that tells us about Wordsworth's response to the birth of his son, his first child in wedlock, but if Dorothy's doting response to this new little person is anything to go on,[3] we can be quite certain that the effect was to further emotionally ground him; and, with Dorothy and Mary attending him and his son, there does not appear to have been a chance for a repeat of the negative aspects of his own upbringing. Absolute confirmation of the Lowther debt coming through at just this time would have been a great relief—and timely, too. A great burden of the past would have been removed; the shadow of the father would have at last been lifted, and the difficult memory of him finally left to rest in peace.

Wordsworth at Grasmere: first a brother, then a husband, and then a father. In all of these life roles he now seemed to be self-assured, and these life roles, at Grasmere, integrated.

While the circumstances of 1803 allowed Wordsworth to feel relatively free from anxiety and uncertainty, even to the extent of taking a six-week tour of Scotland over August and September with Dorothy, in terms of composition the poetry of that year is rather slim, especially in terms of its emotional intensity.[4] As

1804 began, it appears Wordsworth finally felt secure enough to return to those most urgent and personal questions he had posed about two years earlier in the opening gestures of the *Immortality Ode*. His gift as a poet and his strength as a person were both ready to look back to the future. Feeling and thought, as past and present, were ready to be as one.[5]

※

Certainly the most memorable critical observation ever made about the *Immortality Ode* comes from Lionel Trilling: "It is a poem about growing; some say it is a poem about growing old, but I believe it is a poem about growing up" (Trilling 1975, p.151). Trilling effectively situates the poem as part of a process in which the child strives to grow to become father of the man, in which, as I have said, the child becomes a part of rather than apart from the adult.[6] While the *Ode* has attracted a large general audience and acclaim because it touches something important inside us, for Wordsworth the poem also carried a more particular significance in terms of his own healing process. Nowhere else does Wordsworth display such breadth yet such insight; nowhere else is fear so clearly overtaken by faith. Persistent doubt is resolved by quiet, inner strength, loss is converted into gain, and thought not only overrides feeling but interpenetrates it. At the same time, the *Ode* also signals the high point of Wordsworth's poetic powers; in this way the poem is not a farewell to these powers but a simultaneous expression and acknowledgment of them.[7]

These kinds of transformations have entered our culture via the *Ode* (and art like it) as ways of describing the dynamics of the human condition, and we are touched by them; and certainly creating a poem like the *Ode* sent a clear signal to its author that his fears and aspirations were indeed very human, thus connecting him with the community of his readers as a person speaking to other persons. With the wonderful poetic positioning of the *Ode*, more than any other poem, including *Tintern Abbey*,[8] the "I" can now speak more assuredly both for Wordsworth and for us. This communicative authority is what Wordsworth discovered in the *Ode*, and what makes it such a powerful document. It is his ultimate transformational poem, but, given the structure of transformation, we have to wonder who (or what) Wordsworth became after this poem. As I have suggested a few times in this study, I believe he became less a poet (or at least the kind of poet we had come to know) and more a person—that was his own transformation. I am even tempted to pursue the idea that he became less a child and more an adult. Once you transform, you cannot, *need not*, go back to your origin in quite the same way. But what the *Ode* actually did for Wordsworth was open up his life before him in a new way. It allowed him to see his own story as a history. The evidence resides in the fact that shortly after composing the *Ode*, Wordsworth turned to writing about his own life with a new disposition: within just over a year after completing the *Ode*, Wordsworth had expanded the 1799 two-book poem about his early life and his relationship to nature into a massive, thirteen-book poem—the 1805 *Prelude*. But unlike the 1799 poem, which is remarkable for its intense poetic accounts of difficult and emotionally laden remembrances, the 1805 poem is more of a story than a reenactment. That it is a story tells us that Wordsworth no longer needed to wrestle with his inner life in the same way. In short, his inner life was no longer the same kind of problem.

In attempting to understand Wordsworth's emotional difficulties as they are reenacted in some of his poetry, we have seen how many of the issues in this study inevitably return to the dynamics and trauma of his early family life, and in particular to the confusing and disruptive feelings associated with the death of his parents before he had even reached adolescence.[9] Much later in life, when Wordsworth dictated his comments about the *Ode* to Isabella Fenwick, it was the subject of death and his problem in coming to terms with it as a child that he highlighted: "Nothing was more difficult for me in childhood than to admit the notion of death as applicable to my own being" (Wordsworth 1876, 1:194). While for all children the concept of death, especially their own death, is difficult to grasp, we have seen that Wordsworth was unfavorably predisposed to death and its attendant feelings of loss and grief. That Wordsworth singles out death is the *one* thing that was most difficult for him to deal with suggests more than just a typical response. This comment by Wordsworth also helps to contextualize a reading of the *Ode* as a poem in which he attempted to resolve that particular childhood issue with all the eloquence he could muster. That is, the acceptance of the "notion of death as applicable" to his "being" in the present is a revealing gloss on the poem and its developmental importance to the poet. That Wordsworth's grasp of reality as a child was quite literally precarious is evident in another comment related to the *Ode*: "Many times while going to school have I grasped at a wall or tree to recall myself from this abyss of idealism to the reality" (194). This is not exactly normal behavior for a child. For Wordsworth, going back to childhood in order to create a future for himself once more meant encountering death, grief, and loss—events and feelings that, if left unresolved, would destabilize aspects of his personality and behavior. The difference is that now he was ready and able to construct some notion of closure and resolution around them, whereas before his poetry inevitably left these subjects stranded, enigmatic, unresolved, equivocal.

Already familiar to us is Wordsworth's view of at least part of his childhood as life in paradise or heaven. This is confirmed once more in the 1802 stanzas to the *Ode,* in which Wordsworth recalls the time when everything seemed "Apparelled in celestial light" (line 4). Yet even though he knows that the beauty is still there in front of him and will continue to be there, something for him "hath passed away" from the earth. He calls it "glory" (line 18), but the word is almost perfect in its vagueness. There is in those first four stanzas a resolution to get rid of thoughts of "grief" and to be "strong" (lines 22–66);[10] so too is there a resolution to correspond with the perceived beauty of the living landscape. Yet three figures of solitude—"a Tree, of many one," "A single Field," and a little "Pansy"—at the same time "speak of something that is gone," and they force the same question about the passing away of "the visionary gleam" and "the glory and the dream" (lines 51–57). *Once upon a time, when I was a child, the world around me was like heaven. But now, even though I can overcome sorrowful thoughts and feelings, and I can hear and see and feel the harmonious force of life, something yet is gone.*

That "something" (line 53) Wordsworth names appears to have to do with innocence—in particular, the kind of innocence that enhances imaginative capabilities and is not cognizant of death. For without the idea of death, the world would indeed seem to be a different place and the life we live a different kind of life. One cannot but help think of the careless, green, and golden days of childhood recalled by Dylan Thomas in *Fern Hill,* where time and imagination let him play for what then seemed an eternity, though, without knowing it, he was also a chained prisoner of time. The same might be said of the *Ode* as Wordsworth wonders where the "visionary gleam" has gone. In fact, the metaphor of imprisonment used by Thomas might come from the *Ode,* when Wordsworth describes how "Shades of the prison-house begin to close / Upon the growing Boy" (lines 67–68).

As Wordsworth returns, then, to those first four 1802 stanzas in 1804, he reasons how it is that, when we are born into the world, we are without memory of a preexistent state: "Our birth is but a sleep and a forgetting" (line 58). Having opened up the possibility of such a state, Wordsworth later half apologized for having promoted the concept, maintaining that he used it mainly for poetic purposes (Wordsworth 1876, 3:195).[11] But the large concern he has is with the development of consciousness: "Heaven lies about us in our infancy!" he writes, but in passing from "Youth" to "Man" the notion of mortality takes over, and the vision of glories fades away as earthly concerns take over (lines 65–84). The little child soon conforms to and imitates the ceremonies and trappings of "Life": weddings, funerals, "business, love, or strife" (lines 85–107).

We may now be in a better position to articulate and understand Wordsworth's double view of childhood. First of all, part of childhood is close to innocence and is without consciousness of death; the child lives in a blissful state, being, as it were, closer to heaven. But then childhood is also the time when innocence is lost and the child experiences intimations of mortality; the child lives in a more anxious, uncertain state; the death of others signals his own death. Up until this point in his life, up until this point in the poem (stanza 7), Wordsworth seems to have distinguished between these two, not unlike the way he distinguishes between feeling and thought. Wordsworth, it appears, is unclear as to how to conceive of childhood, likely because his own was such a bundle of confused and often contradictory recollections and feelings, broken in two by the circumstances of his upbringing. But now, with stanza 8, halfway through the *Ode*, Wordsworth also sees the child as the "best Philosopher"—a figure who knows those "truths" the rest of us "are toiling all our lives to find" (lines 108–16). Yet Wordsworth cannot escape the feeling of loss, and once more picking up the metaphor of incarceration, he acknowledges that time will "bring the inevitable yoke" of life (lines 127). The weight of the world soon burdens us all (lines 128–29).

One further observation: The first four stanzas, the 1802 lines, all fall heavily upon "I": "I have seen . . . I have heard . . . I feel . . ." These opening stanzas thus read as a personal response to what seems to be a personal problem. But the custom of the next four stanzas (lines 5–8) is far more general, and they are without that hearing, feeling, seeing "I"/eye at their center. With the "our," "us," and "we" now introduced, we no longer hear the questioning and agonizing personal voice. To use Kübler-Ross's lexicon, it may be the emergence of a voice of bargaining, of playing loss against gain without denial or the stance of isolation. If Kübler-Ross's stages are played out, we might then expect something like a movement towards acceptance of loss, especially since the first four stanzas also tread through and end in depression. With stanza 9, there is a return to the "I," but now it is without the same kind of intensity as the first four stanzas. Furthermore, the "I" and "me" and "my" now blend in and act with the "our" and "us" and "we." The use of the second person was in fact not even part of the 1802 stanzas' rhetorical positioning: they are pure first person.

In sum, the *Ode* begins in the first person, moves to the second person, and finally integrates them—this, at least, is part of the rhetorical strategy behind the poem's power to include us in Wordsworth's process of healing. The Personal has become Universal. And so the effect is that Wordsworth's loss in the last three stanzas becomes our loss, just as his gain becomes our gain, but a better way of putting might be that Wordsworth's loss is integrated into and contextualized by a recognition of what it is to grow and change, and to acknowledge and accept the inherent "obstinate questionings" of childhood (144). The transformation of his loss into gain, of moving from denial to acceptance, is that *his* initial loss becomes *our* gain; his denial becomes our acceptance. The *Ode* contains, in short, the whole process of Wordsworth's movement towards emotional well-being, just as it gestures to include us in this mediated process. Unlike many of Wordsworth's earlier poems that take up these same subjects, the *Ode* is, in its resolution, expansive rather than eccentric; it ends by looking forwards, not backwards. Therein lies its power and its claim to popular fame.

How does this happen? Here we come to the ninth stanza, which is the turning point.

Unlike *Tintern Abbey*, which nurtures an economics of restoration, the advance the *Ode* makes in stanza 9 signals rather an economics of retention. The realization Wordsworth comes to is that nothing can bring back what was, yet something of what we were stays with us. What Wordsworth blesses is not "the simple creed / Of childhood" with its spirit of "hope"; rather, he thanks

> those obstinate questionings
> Of sense and outward things,
> Fallings from us, vanishings;
> Blank misgivings of a Creature
> Moving about in worlds not realized . . .
>
> (Lines 139–48)

It is not the happiness and freedom, the "Delight and liberty" (line 139), of childhood that must be sanctified, but rather "Those shadowy recollections," for it is these that "Are yet the fountain light of all our day, / Are yet the master light of all our seeing" (lines 152–55). This is what will guide and sustain us; this is what will "Uphold us, cherish us" (line 156). The "truths" that emanate from our "noisy years" will "perish never"; "neither listlessness, nor mad endeavour," or anything that might make us unhappy, can "abolish or destroy" what once we were (lines 156–63). And even as we grow away from childhood, moving "inland," what was a part of us and gave us intimations of immortality can always be revisited: we can see "the Children sport upon the shore" and hear "the mighty waters rolling evermore" (lines 165–70). This not just a universal metaphor for the pre-eternal sea. It is also, and perhaps primarily, Wordsworth's compounded recollection of himself, as a child, playing all those days at the lakeside. As he writes these lines, no doubt he is looking out from his cottage onto Grasmere Lake; as Moorman notes, he "enjoyed an uninterrupted view from its windows to the lake" (1957, 461). For once, Wordsworth may also be experiencing an uninterrupted view of his childhood.

This philosophy of retention, fostered by meditation, then, helps Wordsworth now to see *into* his life, and to accept both the "shadowy" and the "simple" child—to accept, that is, himself and both parts of his childhood. He can now allow the birds to sing their "joyous song" and lambs to dance, for

> Though nothing can bring back the hour
> Of splendour in the grass, of glory in the flower;
>> We will grieve not, rather find
>> Strength in what remains behind,
>> In the primal sympathy
>> Which having been must ever be,
>> In the soothing thoughts that spring
>> Out of human suffering,
>> In the faith that looks through death,
> In years that bring the philosophic mind
>
> (Lines 171–89)

Looking into "human suffering," Wordsworth has come to see "soothing thoughts"; that is, Wordsworth has now, at last, recognized that difficult feelings act as support for "soothing thoughts" and as the foundation for "the philosophic mind." Feeling and thought are no longer separated or blocked by difference or by privilege. As Alice Miller writes, "The set goal [of therapy, of emotional healing] is the recognition of one's own injuries . . . suffered in childhood" (1990b, 162). The key concept here is *recognition*, which supports and works towards Kübler-Ross's notion of acceptance. Those feelings of loss need no longer be enmeshed with or determined by grief. Wordsworth has come to recognize his childhood injuries and to acknowledge both his feelings of loss and his suffering, as well as the splendor and the glory. Wordsworth understands that he cannot go back to that time before death entered his world; instead, he will find his inner "strength" in what he can retain, knowing that he can retain it without having it pull him down or divide his consciousness. That which has been "must ever be." The child within him, the "human suffering" he has experienced, will always be there, but now he can reclaim it as a positive part of his subjective self. Now it can be a part of, rather than apart from, his growth, his adult self, his whole identity. It is the recognition and finally the acceptance of his difficult feelings that stand behind and in the greatness and power of the *Ode*, both as a personal utterance and a universal statement. It is no accident that Wordsworth is here most eloquent. Becoming a whole person is the most powerful statement any of us can ever make. Wordsworth in the *Ode* here makes it for us.

The loss of the "visionary gleam" that Wordsworth mourned over in 1802, is now, in 1804, viewed as something that no longer solicits grief, knowing that endurance and continuity will be found in "what remains behind." Indeed, "nothing can bring back" the "glory and the dream" (57), but even in loss "faith" can be found.

Finally, as Wordsworth comes to the end of the *Ode*, he thanks

> the human heart by which we live,
> Thanks to its tenderness, its joys, and fears,
> To me the meanest flower that blows can give
> Thoughts that do often lie too deep for tears.
>
> (Lines 203–7)

"To me"—this is what it comes down to: *"To me."* This is what matters. The 1802 stanzas leave off with a solitary little flower speaking of "something that is gone" (lines 53–54), and it represents loss and incapacitating or questioning feelings. The 1804 poem ends—subtly, quietly—with the same tiny figure but a completely different feeling: no longer does even the "meanest flower" call up questions of discontinuity and a range of difficult emotions. Self-reflection no longer means being stuck in those feelings. The ability to feel and to respond is now a connecting strength. The ending of the *Ode* may appear a little confusing, or at least tautological in its reasoning, for in one way it seems that Wordsworth is suggesting that the ability to feel can cause thoughts that go beyond feeling. Instead, we should recognize in it Wordsworth's quiet but determined attempt to fuse feeling and thought in the spirit of self-acceptance, for without such acceptance he cannot become a whole person who can look both forwards and backwards, into the world and into himself, without fear or loss or guilt.

How is it that Wordsworth was able to discover and resolve the emotional problems that were set in his early years? Years—and much inwardly searching poetry—do bring the "philosophic mind," and living circumstances can become more favorable; these do figure in Wordsworth's healing. But in the *Ode* we see a continuation of the meditation process that began in *Tintern Abbey*, remembering that such a process is conducive to healing (Chopra 1991, 143–45). One of the *Ode*'s bottom lines, then, is I-Am. When Wordsworth can say this, the Who-I-Was can cease to make life difficult, and the Who-I-Will-Be can become an article of faith. The figure of the difficult, lost child virtually disappears from Wordsworth's poetry after this point, and this itself must be an irrefutable indicator of how he changes. The child no longer calls out for help and attention, because he has now been heard and answered, though it took many years and much poetry for this to come about. That Wordsworth is at the same time liberated from his past and his troubling feelings is also indicated in the commitment with which he immediately turns to writing about the rest of his life: as mentioned, early 1804 saw Wordsworth suddenly expand the two-book 1799 *Prelude* to five books, and then to a thirteen-book version, completed by May 1805. Clearly now he felt he could trace his history, including aspects of his recovery, without being pulled into or becoming stuck in it. Not all of what he wrote about is completely self-assured and perfectly insightful, nor, as we have seen, is it inclusive, but what he did evolve was a determined sense of self and self-history. He discovered, in effect, that there is life after childhood. To quote Miller once again: "To encounter one's own history not only puts an end to the blindness hitherto displayed toward the child within oneself but also reduces the blockage of thought and feeling" (1990b, 38). This in an uncanny way calls up how Coleridge's description of Wordsworth at the beginning of 1804, as "the only man who has effected a compleat and constant synthesis of Thought & Feeling and combined them with Poetic Forms...." (Coleridge 1956, 2:1034). And so this is where we leave Wordsworth, with his thoughts and feelings unblocked and synthesized, and with, as it were, his history before him.

The *Ode* could be situated in such a way as to represent the break in Wordsworth's adult life between his early and middle years. Some might even see the completion of the poem as a break between the early and late Wordsworth. So too could 1804 be called on to locate the beginning of his so-called decline. But Wordsworth did not experience a decline. His life went on in very profitable and fulfilling ways. It is just that much of his poetry written before 1804 contains certain elements, certain feelings and problems, that evolved out of his individual history and subjectivity and that he had to work through. There can be, in my opinion, no other reason to account for what we find in much of that early poetry, and what we do not find in his later poetry. Those feelings and problems—and the way they are written about—fade out of his poetry written after 1804. But we should not let the loss of a certain kind of poet overshadow the birth of a healthy person.

I would prefer to see 1804 and the *Ode* in terms of passage, growth, or process. No doubt Wordsworth's circumstances changed significantly after coming to Grasmere. Yet he remained a poet, just, of course, as he remained a person. But he became a changed poet, just as he became a changed person. The relationship between the two—and the reasons for it—is what this study has attempted to examine. That his poetry after 1804 loses much of its emotional intensity is clear; but as Wordsworth went to so much great pain to tell us, that which has "been must ever be."

When Wordsworth discovered something about his own inner healing, he also touched something within all of us. And so, in the end, we return to where this story began, with the universal that springs forth from the personal, to the child within all of us.

APPENDIX A

Wordsworth as the Lost Child

In her model of the dysfunctional family, Sharon Wegscheider (1981) identifies four kinds of roles or character types that develop in children from such families. One of these she calls the *lost child*. What we know of Wordsworth's character (reflected in his poetry and otherwise) fits within this type. The question as to whether or not Wordsworth's family could be called "dysfunctional" may be moot. What is clear is that his family life was unsettled and fractured, and that there were major problems for Wordsworth; that he called himself a moody and violent child is cause for examination. (None of the other three types remotely resemble Wordsworth.)

Below is an adaptation of Wegscheider by Covington and Beckett (1988, 81–82), showing "some of the more common positive and negative residues of the old childhood roles":

LOST CHILD

POSITIVE	NEGATIVE
creative, imaginative	lonely, isolated, withdrawn
well-developed skills	lacks social skills
hobbyist	feels invisible, excluded
well-read	can be obsessed with self
spiritually developed	low self-esteem, distorted self-image
resourceful	sad, depressed
enjoys solitude	mistrusts, blames others
can work independently, alone	has difficulty connecting with others
nonconformist	fears reality
good manual dexterity	fantasizes life away
good listener	inactive, indecisive

Keep in mind that this is neither an inclusive nor exclusive list. As Covington and Beckett note, "People may drift in and out of their childhood roles at different times, depending on the quality of their lives at particular times" (82). Certainly most of these traits of the "lost child" correspond with Wordsworth's profile at different periods in his life. In these terms, then, the thesis of this study is that Wordsworth drifted in and out of this particular childhood role (i.e., that of the "lost child"), and that this drifting in and out manifested itself in the particular emotive and imaginative qualities in much of his early poetry. The figure of the lost child is everywhere in that poetry.

APPENDIX B

Wordsworth, Trauma, and the Poetry of Dissociation

Two related areas have, at last, and relatively recently, become more understood in psychiatry and clinical psychology, and both of these have figured in this study of Wordsworth and his poetry: trauma and dissociation. In fact, many personality disorders and dysfunctional behaviors are beginning to be seen almost exclusively in terms of trauma and dissociation.

I have suggested that Wordsworth's early poetry often creatively enacts his particular emotional difficulties, and that these difficulties arise from the clearly traumatic nature of his childhood—specifically, the sudden death of his parents at a relatively early stage in his life (compounded by the subsequent breaking up of his family after the death of his mother, preceded by his father's workaholism and difficulty with grief, his abusive grandparents, and the emotionally exhaustive two decades in clearing up his inheritance). What must be brought forward more directly is the relationship between trauma and dissociation. Trauma, or "psychic trauma," may be the easier to understand:

> Psychic trauma occurs when a sudden, unexpected, overwhelmingly intense blow or series of blows assaults the person from outside. Traumatic events are external, but they quickly become incorporated into the mind. A person probably will not become fully traumatized unless he or she feels utterly helpless during the event or events. (Terr 1990, 8)

This description clearly fits with Wordsworth's circumstances, including the helplessness. But dissociation as a behavioral manifestation of childhood trauma is not so well known. Here I would call upon the extensive work by John N. Briere (most of which is cited in Briere 1992).

So what is dissociation? Briere defines it as *"a defensive disruption in the normally occurring connections among feelings, thoughts, behavior, and memories, consciously or unconsciously invoked in order to reduce psychological distress"* (1992, 36; his emphasis). An individual will dissociate "in order to lessen the sometimes overwhelming anxiety and pain associated with complete awareness of traumatic events" (37).

What does dissociation look like? Dissociation looks something like daydreaming—a temporary "spacing out," so to speak, or even something like an out-of-body experience where the individual withdraws inwardly and sometimes views past personal experiences; it is usually a momentary disengagement or detachment from the present, often in the presence of stress or other difficult feelings or associations (37–39). All of us do this, but dissociation works along a continuum: those who have suffered unresolved trauma dissociate most frequently and most deeply, simply because it is a necessary defensive behavior to protect consciousness from having to deal with the attendant confusion and anxiety.

Sometimes Wordsworth produces what I would call *poetry of dissociation*. He enters or unannounced comes to a past scene or experience (often ultimately associated with death, guilt, loss, or separation), and while operating from within that recovered memory, a disruption surfaces; subsequently, Wordsworth, as (to put a term to it) *poetherapist*, makes an attempt to connect the feelings and the thoughts that surface. In other words, Wordsworth, quite remarkably, sometimes uses his poetry (or his poetry uses him) to examine his own dissociative spots of time and their origins—or at least the feelings attending those recalled events. Wordsworth's creativity habit is, as he describes it himself in the 1800 Preface to *Lyrical Ballads*, a process of deep, dissociative contemplation that suddenly brings forth "powerful feelings." This process of recollection was not easy for Wordsworth, and, as we have seen, his health record surrounding his periods of intense composition reflects the depth, difficulty, and determination of his efforts to poetically locate himself, *his* self. Wordsworth often found himself engaged in the process of memory recovery because he had so much trouble remembering, so much trouble putting together the pieces of his mind and emotional life. So too are there many particular moments in the poetry when Wordsworth describes a kind of "gaze" that can transform the moment, or, as in *The Brothers*, a gaze that in difficulty looks through the present to images from the past.

Lenore Terr, a psychiatrist and expert on childhood trauma, puts it this way: "A traumatic event, because it remains so well-impressed in the child victim's mind, may appear later in all sorts of guises—both symptomatic and creative" (Terr 1990, 25). Indeed, as I have tried to show, Wordsworth had all kinds of creative guises and voices through which he expressed his own childhood trauma and unresolved feelings. Terr goes on to say this: "An artist's old trauma may create a "theme," permeating his lifetime actions as well as his creative product. . . . On a few rare occasions, adults will give such eloquent words to their terrors from childhood that we can better grasp how traumatized children feel" (36). Some of Wordsworth's poetry constitutes a thematics of trauma and, I believe, one of those "few rare occasions" of eloquence. Unfortunately, we have not always been reading his eloquence in this way. I hope this study has offered such a possibility.

APPENDIX C

Wordsworth, Recovery, and Writing

I have attempted to show that one course of Wordsworth's life had to do with attempted recovery from unresolved trauma, and that this is reflected in some of his poetry. Appendix B reflects back upon this study and gestures that trauma indeed figures importantly in Wordsworth's story and in his poetry. As the story of psychotherapy itself evolves, trauma, more than anything else, is beginning to be seen as central to most personality disorders. Again, I could call upon Terr (1990) to support this. But I should also point to Judith Lewis Herman's landmark study, *Trauma and Recovery*. Herman holds that recovery from trauma unfolds in three stages: 1) establishment of safety, 2) remembrance and mourning, and 3) reconnection with ordinary life (1992, 155–213).

Most of the poetry discussed in this study was written in, and from, the second stage—from the position of remembrance and mourning. This is where Wordsworth was in the early part of his adult life. Herman writes that in this stage, "the survivor tells the story of the trauma" (175). This work of "reconstruction" actually transforms the memory: "[T]he ultimate goal," Herman says, "is to put the story, including the imagery, into words" (177). When, after much emotionally painful therapeutic work, the facts or details of the trauma finally surface and are faced, then the individual can move forward towards that reconnection with ordinary life. Now, Wordsworth did not have a therapist to guide him through this process, but he did have a growing support group who were sympathetic to his needs; and he was able to find a means to express himself so that he was able to bring thought over to feeling, cognition over to emotion, the intellectual over to the phenomenological. At the end of this stage of remembrance and mourning he could write about himself with the kind of authority that suggests recovery or well-being. As discussed in chapter 5, Wordsworth's move to Grasmere in 1800 can clearly be seen as the beginning of his reconnection with ordinary life: he was settled in home territory, he was beginning to receive success and recognition as a poet, he was with his sister, his finances began to look positive, he appeared to have come to some kind of understanding of his French connection (he went to France in 1802), and by 1803 he was married and had a child. In settling down he had settled inwards. The adult child was growing up.

As Herman writes, "[R]econnection is about the task of creating a future" (196). "Helplessness and isolation are the core experiences of psychological trauma.

Empowerment and reconnection are the core experiences of recovery" (197). Looking at Wordsworth's poetry of loss, death, loneliness, endurance, grief, and guilt, we do indeed see helplessness and isolation in multiple guises, figures, and voices. Looking at the *Immortality Ode*, just as certainly we see empowerment and reconnection: intimations of immortality can only be about "the task of creating a future." The *Ode* remains, in my view, the most powerful literary work about recovery in the English language. It is a personal statement of universal hope.

Notes

Introduction. "The hiding places of my power"

1. A relatively early examination of the Preface evaluating W's desire for a poetry that could, despite language, get through to "truth," is made by Roger Sharrock (in Jones and Tydeman 1972). He quite rightly notes that there is, in the Preface, "a radical pessimism about poetry's capacity for recording experience" (158), while at the same time there is a desire on W's part to find "words which can convey the object or experience as nakedly as possible, the words of the original participants in the action" (161). This, says Sharrock, is W's "linguistic crisis" (161); and he is right: it was critical for W to believe and trust in a language that would allow him to cut through where others' styles of poetry fell short.

2. See W. J. B. Owen (1969, 65) for a discussion of W's theory of poetry as expressive in a more literary and historical context. My use of "expressive" here has to do with W's desire (and belief) that his poetry could communicate real feelings and thoughts without the artifice of language stifling the content.

3. Writes Miles: "Reading the *Lyrical Ballads* and the *Prelude*, I was oppressed by a constant insistence on what seemed to be considered the stuff of life in so many words—hope, joy, fears, tears, laughter, moods, affections, passions, and all the other labeled responses in terms of names of emotions" (1942, 4). I am less "oppressed" than impressed by such insistence.

4. W's use of the Fall as a structural image is discussed by Jonathan Wordsworth (1982, esp. 231–78).

5. The 1805 *Prelude*, bk. 2, lines 1–33; 1850 *Prelude*, bk. 2, lines 1–33 (Wordsworth 1979, 66–67).

6. Bateson in important ways subscribes to the view of W to which I am sympathetic. He notes the "recurrent pattern of crisis, psychological disintegration, and gradual convalescence" and the heroic "private struggles towards psychic integration," and that "the personal quest was not so much for a sensuous reality as for emotional reality"; however, I do not go along with the idea that the onset of W's "personal crisis" is related to the poet's "tragic discovery that he and his sister [Dorothy] were passionately in love with each other" (1954, 199–201). Even if W and his sister were "passionately in love" (and one has to admit they were extremely close), reasons must be given for

such a situation, and those reasons would have to go back to the family circumstances. I do not believe that much of the poetry can be read profitably with Dorothy in mind.

7. See note 15, chapter 4, below.

8. The idea of the inner child as a therapeutic concept has been around for a number of years (see, for example, Mills and Crowley 1986, Whitfield 1987), and has especially been used with much success in self-help groups (for example, in the Adult Children of Alcoholics Program). The idea gained much popular usage in the work of John Bradshaw (1990; 1988a; 1988b) and M. Scott Peck (1978). Perhaps its earliest popularity came from the work of Eric Berne (1964) and W. Hugh Missildine (1964). One important spin-off from the concept of the inner child is family systems theory, which sees the emotional development of an individual as necessarily within the context of the family. In the next chapter I hope to bring some family systems thinking to aspects of W's own development. Perhaps some of the attention to the idea of the child within can be traced back to Carl Jung's notion of the child archetype. For an anthology of writings on the inner child, see Abrams (1990).

9. This, in fact, is close to the idea behind McFarland's (1992) study that W's greatness is founded upon expressing intensity of feeling. McFarland does not, however, say much about how this happened. Nonetheless, his reading of the texts is convincing.

10. See Miller (1986; 1990a; 1990b; 1990c; 1990d).

11. These days when talking about children in crisis, therapists often refer to *acting out*—that is, to various overt behaviors that point to the emotional disturbances. There is also the *acting in* child, who shows his or her emotional pain in less overt ways, by, for example, withdrawing or being depressed (Cochrane and Myers 1980, 12). W's poetry is, I believe, the result of an adult child who, in his poetry, imaginatively acts out because in real life he tends to act in. Of course this idea is premised with the same view (and metaphor) of behavior that is promoted by Alice Miller.

12. For a example of New Historicism's overreading, see McFarland's critique (1992, 1–33) of Levinson (1986).

13. There is a long-running critical history examining the content and compositional circumstances connecting Coleridge's *Ode* and W's *Intimations Ode*. See, for example, McFarland (1981, 74–77), Teichman (1971), Meyer (1950), and Smith (1935). We might note too that in one letter version of Coleridge's *Ode*, W is the addressee; in other versions it is "Sara" and "Lady."

14. This general style of therapy is called cognitive-behavioral, where cognitions stand between, as it were, feelings and behavior. The belief is that, in this process of therapy, irrational thoughts can, over time, be replaced by reasonable thoughts. For a survey and description of this psychotherapy, see Dryden and Golden (1986). Unlike so-called humanistic approaches to therapy that are mainly expressive, cognitive-behavioral approaches generally maintain that emotions and behavior result from thought (or cognitive variables), and, thus, to facilitate change in the individual, the therapist must change the client's thoughts. The problem, of course, is deciding which comes first: the feeling or the thought. This is W's territory, for he often attempted to have thoughts override, as it were, feelings, but because of the depth, intensity, and sometimes

confusing nature of his feelings, it took much work to come to a time when his cognitions could integrate and accept his emotions.

15. Elisabeth Kübler-Ross's extraordinarily important work on stages of accepting death is useful here: she points to five stages: denial, anger, bargaining, depression, and acceptance. See the opening of chapter 2, below, for fuller description of these.

16. For example, one of W's important earlier biographers, William Knight (1889), had access to Dorothy's journals, which mention over and over again W's health problems, but he decided to edit this out (D. Wordsworth 1973, viii). Later biographies have also underplayed or ignored the significance of W's health.

17. Paul D. Sheats reminds us that W "inherited a subjective bias from his age.... For a young and enthusiastic minstrel of the 1780's the true voice of feeling was a profoundly introspective voice" (1973, 9–10).

18. I am thinking of a sentence in H. G. Schenk's investigation of European romanticism, when, in considering Nietzsche's example, he writes: "It is hard to avoid the impression that at this stage psychological introspection and religious remorse have become inextricably interwoven" (1966, 245).

19. Of course here I am thinking of Geoffrey Hartman's famous essay, "Romanticism and Anti-Self-Consciousness" ([1962] 1993), which theorizes upon the way romantic poetry moves towards various forms of naïveté.

20. I say psychophysiologically because when we experience an emotion, or when we have a feeling, our bodies react; when we are worried our stomachs may churn and our heads may ache; when we are nervous our mouths may go dry; when we tell a lie our skin may sweat (so that a lie detector may pick it up); when we are anxious our heart rate may increase.

21. Much of this theory has been put upon the Lucy poems. See below, chapter 4, notes 21 and 27, for some of these discussions.

22. It is in the work on personality by psychologist Gordon Allport that the differences between nomothetic and idiographic views become clear. Whereas the nomothetic approach looks towards general laws and principles in order to understand the traits of large numbers of people, the idiographic approach looks at the individual's uniqueness (see, for example, Allport 1961; 1966).

23. Bialostosky points out that in Paul de Man's reading of W, "the private sphere of personal memory" and "the world of history" are put against each other (1992, 160). These are actually quotations from de Man (1984, 55).

24. In Blank (1988, 3–4; 1991, 3–5).

Chapter 1. The Adult Child

1. W's letter is primarily aimed at James Currie's *Life and Work of Robert Burns* (Edinburgh 1815). But in the *Burns* letter W also has a go at the *Edinburgh Review*, and at Francis Jeffrey in particular, who had recently negatively reviewed W's *Excursion* and *The White Doe of Rhylstone*. This tit-for-tat was picked up by John Wilson in

Notes to Chapter 1

Blackwood's Edinburgh Magazine 1 (June 1817): 265: "It is not Robert Burns for whom he [W.] feels,—it is William Wordsworth."

2. As W writes to Sir George Beaumont in 1808, "I wish either to be considered as a Teacher, or as nothing" (Wordsworth 1969, 195).

3. I am referring to the notes dictated to Isabella Fenwick in 1843 and published in Wordsworth (1857) and Wordsworth (1876). There is also the *Memoir* put together by the poet's nephew, Christopher Wordsworth, in 1851. For Mary Wordsworth's letters regarding the *Memoir*, see Wordsworth (1993, 278–93). Onorato (1971) uses *The Prelude* to frame the character of W. The extent to which *The Prelude* can be used as reliable commentary on W's life is a long-running debate: for example, while Legouis (1897) uses the poem to support an understanding of W, Meyer (1943) points out that *The Prelude* is an untrustworthy representation of the poet. What has to be balanced is how W describes events and emotions with how he originally experienced those events and emotions.

4. Meyer suggests that W was the "victim" of "maladjustment and emotional immaturity" and that his early adult years can be characterized by "a long and painful effort to adjust unruly emotions and presuppositions to a world which he found to be more hostile than friendly" (1943, 5). This emphasis on the emotional reality in W's poetry fits into the general thesis of this present study.

5. For example, Heffernan glosses the boat-stealing episode in *The Prelude* as strongly suggesting "the genesis of the Oedipal desire: the wish to possess the mother and dispossess the father"; citing Frosch's (1985) conjectures, Heffernan also believes that, in the boy of Winander passage from *The Prelude*, young W holding his hands up to hoot to the owls is "like a breast," all originating from a regressive oral stage and the desire to repudiate this "infantile instinct" (1988, 259, 269–70). This is simply too ingenious, and obviously theory-driven. The same kinds of creatively improbable conjectures are made in the name of the father. Heffernan on the boat-stealing scene again: the boy "sees the cliff as his father's phallus, as the father's rigid interdiction [pun intended?] of the boy's desire to invade the mother's womb" (260).

6. Onorato puts it this way via a discussion of *Tintern Abbey:* after the death of the mother, in the solitude at Hawkshead, W "began gradually and preconsciously projecting into Nature his sense of the mother, finding again in that way aspects of the lost relationship with her" (1971, 72). Barbara Schapiro also notes the relationship between W's mother and the idea of Nature, but she notes "the aggressiveness and destructiveness directed toward Nature or the mother," and she disagrees with Onorato: "The motivating force of his poetry is not to recapture the lost mother but to fortify the self in relation to her. . . ." (1983, 94).

7. The editors of Wordsworth (1979) call the treatment dealt out by the Cooksons "petty tyrannies" (164 n. 9). For these young children trying to grow up, they would be anything but "petty." One of the best indications of the bad situation at Penrith is Dorothy's 1787 letters to Jane Pollard. I will examine this is more detail later in the chapter.

8. De Selincourt suggests, quite correctly and politely, I believe, that the father was "not, perhaps, the type of man who finds it easy to enter into the life of his children" (1933, 3–4).

Notes to Chapter 1

9. For example, on 24 June 1802, W writes to Richard: "You seem to speak to me as if you were speaking to a child: this is very unbecoming on your part. . . ." (Wordsworth 1967, 371).

10. Here I would agree with William A. Gordon (1972), who, in an essay examining W's ambivalent feelings about his father in *The Borderers*, also concludes that the anger and resentment over the inheritance transfers from Lowther to the father: "To the conscious mind of William Wordsworth, the fault no doubt was Lonsdale's, but the unconscious significance could very well have been linked to his father, who was, from the infantile point of view, triply at fault. He failed to defend his mother from her death; he abandoned the child by his death; and he failed to protect the sustenance which the inheritance signified to Wordsworth's later life" (74).

11. For W's interests in Lonsdale's politics, see Wells (1940) and Douglas (1948).

12. The dating of *The Vale of Esthwaite* is uncertain, but it was likely spread over 1786 to 1788 (Reed 1967, 18–19). The passage is lines 418–37.

13. Bateson gets particular over the poem's motivation, suggesting that, as the result of a broken relationship, it displays "a temporarily disorganized personality," and that the production is both schizoid and cathartic (1954, 111).

14. In the two-part *Prelude* (from which I will be quoting) these are from bk. 1, lines 327–74; in the 1805 *Prelude*, bk. 11, lines 344–388; in the 1850 *Prelude*, bk. 12, lines 287–335 (Wordsworth 1979, 9–11, 434–37).

15. Richard E. Brantley (1974) suggests that the source of the guilt and the need for punishment in this passage have a dimension of Evangelicalism (especially via John Wesley), in which W was immersed.

16. Alan Bewell describes this episode as a "radical reshaping of the conventional crossroads narrative," where the witch is displaced by the poet who discovers his imaginative powers (1989, 180–3). Following Leslie Brisman (1978, 314–18), he also suggests the event has strong oedipal overtones.

17. Bateson writes that the father's "death was certainly not the emotional disaster for the children that his wife's had been," and that the absence of other poetical references to his father (there are just two) suggest "a confession of indifference" (1954, 50–1). I would hold quite the opposite: the father's thin presence suggests the inability of W to come to terms with the loss. The loss of one's father, whether liked or hated, whether distant or close, is never an indifferent affair. The death of a close father is in some ways easier to accept than death of a distant father, since in the case of the former, one's feelings are bound to be clearer or more realized. There is something to take from it, and to hold on to. In the case of the distant or difficult father, there can often be the feeling of guilt, regret, or unfinished business.

18. Following a different line of argument than the one put forth here, but coming to a similar conclusion, consider what M. D. Faber writes about romanticism in general via a discussion of W and *The Prelude* in particular: "The natural world replaces the social order as the substitute for the lost parental object" (1991, 444). This attempt to replace the "lost parental object" with Nature is what *The Prelude* and some of W's other poetry comes to be about, and W's idea of the father, like that of the mother, and like the return of the repressed, stands behind this. Schapiro writes that for W, nature is

"the source of both dread and joy," and that the angry, destructive, and aggressive feelings in Wordsworth's poetry are "directed as much toward the father as toward the mother" (1983, 98, 99).

19. Onorato can add to this: "In his experience of fixated growth Wordsworth is not free to identify himself strongly with the father, whose own early death when Wordsworth was thirteen made the difficult psychic circumstance of the boy even more precarious. Circumstantially excluded from many of the normal experiences of identification from boyhood to manhood, Wordsworth discovered, adapted, and invented the role of the Poet, his personal fiction" (1971, 179). Onorato makes the connection between poetry and father without considering the evidence I use here. W needed poetry to grow up, just as one would normally use a parent to negotiate passage to adulthood. Moorman writes that for W, the father's death was not important "so much because he felt intense personal affection for his father, as because it set in motion imaginative experiences that helped forward his creative powers" (1957, 68).

20. Friedman (1979): "For him [W] to strike out against an established social order may well have been unconsciously perceived by him as striking out against the authority of his father, still alive in his timeless unconscious, though dead since 1793" (295).

21. Matlak (1987b) makes the further observation that W's history with male figures is the history of abandonment and loss, with "the trauma of the father's death at its center" (392).

22. See, too, Townsend (1966). The letters written about John's death are easily the most emotional written by W. John's death seems to have represented the end of what kept the siblings together: "the set is now broken" (Wordsworth 1967, 540).

23. Even W. W. Douglas's study, which to its credit attempts to get close to "the pattern of Wordsworth's responses to the exigencies of living" and to "the pattern of his emotional experience," after considering the evidence misses the point: "On the whole, John and Ann Wordsworth must have [sic] accounted very satisfactory parents. There is no reason to suppose that John Wordsworth was not in every external way a kind and affectionate father to his children. Nor is it likely that Ann Wordsworth did not exercise a great and, in many ways, satisfying care for her children" (1968, 10, 66–67).

24. Bateson's comment is all the more disturbing given other statements he makes that various circumstances contributed to W's character—e.g., see note 29, below.

25. For a more detailed analysis of Shelley's estimation of W, see Blank (1988).

26. Reed (1967); see esp. 41–42 n. 2, 46–47 n. 3, 49 n. 4.

27. Even in 1805, Dorothy records her regrets about being taken from her family life. Things changed desperately for her after the death of her mother, as they must have for her siblings: "[F]or six years (the interval between my Mother's Death and his [her father]) I was never once at home, never was for a single moment under my Father's Roof after her Death, which I cannot think of without regret for many causes. . . ." (Wordsworth 1967, 663).

28. When I speak of co-dependency here, I mean it in the sense described by Bradshaw (1990), when one individual's feelings and sense of identity are overenmeshed with someone else: "Co-dependence is fostered in unhealthy family systems," and

people who are co-dependent are "dependent on something outside of themselves in order to have an identity"; "Co-dependent behavior indicates that the person's childhood needs were unmet. . . ." (9). This was obviously the case with Dorothy, and it demonstrates that, like W, she too carried the burden of the past, of the lost inner child, within her. For example, many entries in her journals suggest she did not know what or how to feel—independently. In her letters and journals she was sometimes beside herself in wanting to be with W, and, as her letters to Jane Pollard show, she was absolutely enraptured by her brother's personality or behavior. No one, to date, has used the co-dependent model to describe Dorothy's behavior. The insanity she experienced in her later life, as well as the idiosyncratic aspects of her character, might, I believe, be attributed to her troubled personal history (see Fadem 1978). See note 31, below.

29. As Bateson notes, the "early miseries" of the young W children "help to explain the passionate attachment that he [W] felt not only for Dorothy but also for his brother John" (1954, 53). For some other discussions of the incest issue, see Kroeber (1974), Matlak (1978a), and Reiman (1978). The most striking primary source to demonstrate the closeness of W and Dorothy comes in her journal entry describing W's marriage day, and especially those parts of the entry she erased (see D. Wordsworth 1973, 154).

30. McFarland, citing this same passage from *Esthwaite*, suggests, quite rightly, that "Dorothy bore within her relationship to him [W] the most important relationship of all, that to his departed mother" (1992, 84–85). Mary Moorman in the introduction to Dorothy's journal writes that "The relationship between these two was as intimate, perhaps, as the relation between brother and sister can be" (D. Wordsworth 1973, xix). I also think that the closeness of Dorothy and W, and their feelings of being isolated from their family, is reenacted in the figures of Emily and Francis in *The White Doe of Rylstone*.

31. Besides not apparently developing any sexual relationships with men (she seems to have rejected all advances by men), and besides her overzealous preoccupation with W, I am thinking of the kind of extreme emotional responses she had (see, for example, De Quincey 1970, 199–201). She is always seen as childlike, suggesting that somehow her emotional development was stifled or arrested. She also stammered. From the late 1820s until her death she suffered from what De Quincey called "nervous depression" (205). Mary Moorman believes that Dorothy's illness was not from any "emotional distress" but from arteriosclerosis (D. Wordsworth 1973, xix n. 1; see too Gittings and Manton 1985, 282–83). Again, I would not rule out the possibility that her illness was psychogenic in its onset. When she reverts to a kind of childlike state in her prolonged illness, there is the suggestion that her past is coming back with a kind of vengeance. See Fadem (1978), Brownstein (1973), and Hardwick (1974, 152) for a discussion of some of these issues.

32. For the importance of Taylor for W, see the 1805 *Prelude,* bk. 10, lines 492–510.

33. For example, in December 1791, Dorothy writes: "I have, during the whole of this Summer, without being absolutely ill, been less able to support any Fatigue and been more troubled with Headache that I ever remember to have been, I have of late

had an extreme Weariness in my limbs after the most trifling exertions such as going up stairs, &c; I think, however that all my Complaints are not leaving me; I am at present taking medicine; a thing so rare with me that I can hardly reconcile myself to the Idea of its Necessity while I cannot, in fact, say that I am ill" (Wordsworth 1967, 64). Again, this sounds like depression rather than an organic illness. Another example: in the Grasmere journal, after a few days her loneliness and melancholia become manifest as headaches (D. Wordsworth 1973, 19–20). Her co-dependence on W can best be summed up by her in four words: "No letter, no William" (23). Yet W did not seem to be very sympathetic to Dorothy in these moments. She records her anxiety about Coleridge in November 1801, "I was melancholy and could not talk, but at last I eased my heart by weeping—nervous blubbering says William. It is not so" (D. Wordsworth 1973. 57). When W was away from her, she often felt much distress; for example, in her journal she writes, "I slept in Wm's bed, and I slept badly, for my thoughts were full of William" (91).

34. Moorman in a footnote to this entry notes that the words "and melancholy" were erased, suggesting, perhaps, that she wanted to keep the more psychological side out of the picture of W.

35. Coleridge's strong psychological bent is apparent throughout his work. See Coburn's introduction to Coleridge (1951) for an overview of how Coleridge's views on just about everything are grounded in a psychological perspective.

36. See Coleridge (1951, 67); Miall (1991, 36). Coleridge may have picked up the term from contemporary work, since his use of the word appeared in his unpublished essay "On the Passions."

37. The *DSM-III-R* (1987) is the final word for the medical profession on mental disorders. For the section on somatoform disorders, see its pages 255–67.

38. See Lipowski (1990) for a discussion of the strong relationship between somatization and depression.

39. Again, I defer to the *DSM-III-R* (1987, 247–51) for the outline of this disorder.

40. As Dorothy describes W's plans in early December 1791: "William is, I hope, by this time arrived at Orleans, where he means to pass the Winter for the Purpose of learning the French Language which will qualify him for the office of travelling Companion to some young Gentleman if he can get recommended. . . ." (Wordsworth 1967, 66).

41. For the original discussions of W's amorous French connection, see Harper (1921) and Legouis (1922). Thus it took seventy years for the affair to become public knowledge.

42. W visited Annette and Caroline in 1802, 1820, and 1837. He also provided a modest yearly allowance, beginning in about 1815. There is also the possibility that he saw Annette and his newborn child in the autumn of 1793 (Moorman 1957, 238–42; Gill 1989, 77–80). If so, this would have been an extraordinarily dangerous trip, given that foreigners were being arrested, and some of them executed. If he did see her, he once more had to leave under duress. Many years later, he told Thomas Carlyle that he witnessed an execution in Paris in 1793 (Reed 1967, 147 n. 14). Financial support of Caroline continued to be a problem at least up until the 1830s. See Wordsworth (1993,

275–77) for a letter from Annette to Dorothy (2 April 1835) expressing the legal difficulties of continuing support.

43. This expectation is expressed in a letter that Annette wrote to W three months after the birth of Caroline: "O my beloved, soon it [my heart] will be stirred when I shall say to her: 'Caroline, in a month, in a fortnight, in a week, you are going to see the most beloved of men, the most tender of men'" (Moorman 1957, 180).

44. Commentators include Bateson (1954, 88), Moorman (1957, 182), Gill (1989, 66), and Onorato (1971, 323–32). More theoretically inclined assessments include Caruth (1987), Spivak (1981), and Jacobus (1984). Liu (1982) and Galperin (1989) place the story within the discourse of the Revolution. For some (e.g., Erdman 1978, 15; Sheats 1973, 75–76), like me, W's attitude towards and feeling about the Revolution are completely paralleled by and enmeshed with his love affair. The story was cut from the 1850 *Prelude*. W records that the story of the two lovers was told to him while in France by his mentor of the time, Michel Beaupuy, his "patriot friend" (1805 *Prelude*, bk. 9, line 554); but W also reported that he had heard the story "from the mouth of a French lady, who had been an eye and ear to all that was done and said" (Wordsworth 1926, 572). W's confusion in this may be deliberate.

45. Unlike Gill, who believes that W's experiences with Annette do not demand "inclusion in an account of the growth of a poet's mind" (1991, 79), I do. In fact, they are central. Unfortunately, W could not bring himself to face the emotions and the incident directly in *The Prelude*.

46. The six sonnets written in Calais are *Calais, August 1802*, *Composed by the Sea-Side, near Calais*, *It is a beauteous Evening, calm and free*, *To Toussaint L'Ouverture*, *To a Friend, Composed near Calais*, and *Calais, August 15th, 1802* (Reed 1975, 190; Wordsworth 1984, 708–9).

47. The most striking element in *The Borderers*, W's only drama, is the character of Rivers, or, as he was also called, Oswald. W wrote a detailed psychological justification of Rivers (Wordsworth 1974, 1:76–80 and Wordsworth 1982), an extreme character who, in W's description, might perhaps be seen as a projection of W's conflicting feelings about Annette and his personal situation, and as having a relation to the tale of Julia and Vaudracour (Moorman 1957, 304–5). *The Borderers* will be discussed in more detail in the next chapter.

48. Onorato in a similar way notes that W's "account of France" enigmatically calls up the image of the angry and passionate child (1971, 349–50).

49. See Appendix A for the characteristics of the "lost child."

50. The child was son of Basil Montagu. The mother had died, and the child had lived in difficult circumstances with the father in London. It seems the father could hardly take care of himself (Wordsworth 1967, 146–47 n. 4; Moorman 1957, 260–61). As Moorman writes, W "hated to see children unhappy" (266), knowing perhaps too well what that felt like.

51. For example, Reed calls it a "moral crisis" (1967, 141).

52. Jonathan Wordsworth also suggests that, at the end of the "crisis period," in spring 1796, W may have had a nervous breakdown, and that this may have been related to the denial of emotions he came across in Godwin's *Political Justice*

(1982, 296). This is a good point. For W, emotions were central to his interpreting of experience.

Chapter 2. The Poet's Progress: Early Struggles, Early Gains

1. For a complete history of these texts, see Wordsworth (1975, 3–18).

2. As Sheats puts it, *Salisbury Plain* contains "Wordsworth's first attempt to place the trauma of separation and loss in a chronological perspective, his first history of an individual mind," and the female vagrant tale especially draws on W's feelings and experience (1973, 86–89).

3. W opens the 1799 *Prelude* by establishing the origin of his own history with the flowing of the Derwent.

4. Galperin suggests that *Salisbury Plain* and other works written before 1797 were "not as crucial to [W's] overall development" as the poems that went into and followed the 1798 *Lyrical Ballads* (1989, 10); as I hope to explain, this is not so in the case of *Salisbury Plain*.

5. W wrote that Raisley Calvert had "confidence on his part that I had powers and attainments which might be of use to mankind" (Wordsworth 1967, 546).

6. De Quincey calculated that W walked about "175 to 180,000 English miles" during his lifetime (De Quincey 1970, 135).

7. See the introduction to Wordsworth (1982) for the complete MS history.

8. But note that *The Borderers* also has a critical history that connects it with political and historical concerns. See, for example, Purington (1992), Erdman (1978), and Sharrock (1964). R. F. Storch perhaps comes closer to my interest in and view of the play, as he sees it as a radically unselfconscious work that intensely expresses conflated social and psychic energies; it also anticipates W's later work (Storch 1969). But Storch does not account for the origin and nature of those psychic energies. Liu (1989, 301–3) reviews some the critical approaches to *The Borderers* and divides them into two camps: those putting it into the context of "the philosophy of self as moral philosophy, and those that apply nineteenth- and twentieth-century contexts to inflect it as philosophy of mind or psychology" (301). The text certainly can be read through either or both of these approaches, but both of them, like Liu's own very intelligent reading, keep the reader away from the expressive power of the play that originates in W's particular subjectivity. Liu's generalized sense of family also needs W's particular sense of family; that is, we need W's history as least as much as social history.

9. In early versions of the play, this character is called Rivers and Danby. Later he is called Oswald.

10. See Wordsworth (1979a, 3–35) for the details of *The Ruined Cottage*'s MS history. MS D is the text in Wordsworth (1984). For the Dove Cottage MSS equivalent numbers, see Wordsworth (1979a, x–xii). I will be using Wordsworth (1979a) for my quotations from MSS. B and E.

11. Some of the parallels can be seen the footnotes in Wordsworth (1979a, 392, 394, 398, 402, 410).

12. Here, for example, we can count Jonathan Wordsworth (1969) and M. H. Abrams (1974).

13. Here, among others, we find Neil H. Hertz (1967), Geoffrey Hartman (1971), Reeve Parker (1972), Peter J. Manning (1976), Philip Cohen (1978), and Evan Radcliffe (1984). F. W. Bateson in a review of J. Wordsworth (1969) says that he prefers *The Ruined Cottage* without the Pedlar's history and philosophy: "Margaret's sufferings and the mystical musings of the loquacious pedlar do not mix" (Bateson 1969). Perhaps observations like those of William H. Galperin (1984), that there are really two kinds of poems (*The Pedlar* and *The Ruined Cottage*) with their own evolving views or aims is fairer than the idea of good poem or bad poem. The difference in evaluation may be, as is hinted at by Galperin, ideological (what do we want out of a romantic poem?); it may also have to do with W's continuing movement towards speaking for himself rather than through a distancing rhetoric. Galperin correctly notes that what remains as the foundation of the poem is subjectivism (360–61). Parker's observation that "The strength of Wordsworth's poem lies in his resourcefulness in projecting his manifest personal and psychological involvement through complex artistic structure" (90) is correct, but Parker is interested in the "artistic structure," not the "psychological involvement."

14. Government security officials believed for a while that the residents of Alfoxden were French and that they were mapping out the area for a possible French invasion. A spy was sent to the area to check on them. That one of their friends at this time was John Thewall, a well-known radical, did not help: see Meyer (1950–51), Moorman (1957, 327–32), and Roe (1988, 248–62).

15. In this letter, W writes that he has already completed thirteen hundred lines of this poem. These lines are actually made up of *The Ruined Cottage*, *The Old Cumberland Beggar*, *A Night Piece*, and some lines describing a meeting with an old soldier (Johnston 1984, 5–6). *The Excursion* was the only part of *The Recluse* published during W's life. *The Prelude* was to be a kind of preface for *The Recluse*.

16. See Coleridge (1956, 1:399–400, 402–3, 411–12); Wordsworth (1967, 219–20).

17. One could never deny that these poems also contain social and political commentary, that they can be situated within their own historical circumstances. See Parrish (1973) for such an analysis of *Lyrical Ballads*. Much critical energy has been spent on the originality of the poems in *Lyrical Ballads*. While some critics (e.g., Mayo 1954) have claimed that the poems are not unlike other poems written during the time, others (e.g., Jordan 1976, Gravil 1982) have said the poems constitute an important break from or radical innovation out of the popular literature and the tradition. For a quick summary of some of these positions, see Patrick Campbell (1991).

18. This passage is in *Zoomonia*, 2:359; reprinted in Wordsworth (1992, 385–86).

19. As Averill (1980, 155–56) points out, the section in *Zoonomia* in which W found the tale has to do with the psychological effects of internalizing disturbing emotions and ideas. W must have known about this material earlier, or at least heard about it. W would have found this material relevant, given his own state of health.

20. The attempt by W to create a particular kind of narrator who, as he describes it

in his *Note to "The Thorn"* (Wordsworth 1984, 591–92), is wordy, repetitive, and somewhat simple, has been the subject of much critical debate. See, for example, Parrish (1957), Ashton (1972), Priestman (1975), Owen (1977), Thomas (1978), and Christensen (1980). For the questioning voice of the narrator in the poem, see Wolfson (1979, 553–58). As my discussion will make clear, I am interested in the poem in a way that is described by Albert S. Gerard: "Wordsworth's purpose in placing the story of Martha Ray on the lips of a narrator was partly to hide the autobiographical character of the emotions described in the poem" (1972, 228). In fact, the reader will see that the interest throughout this study is to examine the "autobiographical character of the emotions described" in W's poetry. Coleridge argued that the voice behind *The Thorn* and W's other poems from *Lyrical Ballads* is necessarily W's (see Coleridge's *Biographia Literaria*, chap. 17; in particular, Coleridge 1985, 339–42). The nature of Coleridge's response to the poem is covered in Christensen (1980).

21. When in *The Thorn* W writes that the mosses were determined to "drag it [the thorn] to the ground" (line 20), we recall that in *The Ruined Cottage* the weeds "dragged the rose . . . /And bent it to the earth" (lines 314–17).

22. The couplet—"I've measured it from side to side: / 'Tis three feet long, and two feet wide" (lines 32–33)—has a long history of critical commentary, most of which condemns the lines for poor style and bathetic substance. For recent commentary on this, see Sheats (1991), who suggests that W's use of the lines has indirect ideological significance in confronting his audience's sensibility.

23. Michael Kirkham (1974) writes that the "obscurely 'impressive' scene raised to consciousness and focussed certain associated images and feelings; thus, although the story of the deserted mother could be termed an 'invention', the meanings latent in it were, rather, the *discoveries* of introspection" (67). This is correct. What needs to be explained is what feelings were "raised," and why.

24. Campbell and Mueschke (1933) suggest that *The Thorn* reflects W's "personal experience" and "continues to betray his emotional excitement over the situation of the seduced and abandoned mother" (23–26).

25. After 1815, *The Mad Mother* was retitled *Her Eyes are Wild*. As in *The Thorn* and *The Idiot Boy*, the male parent in *The Mad Mother* is absent. W was familiar with the feeling of the absent father in his own life. Moorman makes a very interesting and valid point that "No doubt the thought of Annette and his own desertion of her, and of his unknown child, gave to these poems, and to many to many others, a sharpness of realism that they would not otherwise have possessed"; and she even notes "a similarity between the language of some of the stanzas of *The Mad Mother* and that of Annette's letters" (1957, 385).

26. Jacobus (1976, 101) writes that the debate in these poems is between "intuitive and rational thought," but it seems clear that the debate ultimately comes down to how thought can contain feeling and how each influences the other.

27. See, too, Bialostosky (1982, 234–36) for some commentary that places the poem in the context of "a father's ambivalence toward his son and a son's toward his father" (236). My point is to note the sources of such ambivalence, which is grounded on such feelings of love and trust.

28. Hartman (1971, 145) notices this too ("The girl was the same age as Wordsworth was when his mother died"), and he adds that it was at this time W began to project his maternal needs on nature. Actually, W was one month shy of his eighth birthday when his mother died.

29. And here the reader can consult Mayo (1954), Jacobus (1976), and Gravil (1982).

Chapter 3. *Tintern Abbey* Revisited; or, Aching Joys and Healing Thoughts

1. The guidebook was William Gilpin's *Observations on the River Wye* (1781). See Kenneth R. Johnston (1983) for an explanation of how W used Gilpin. See also Wesling (1970, 25).

2. Cottle in turn very shortly sold the rights to the volume to J. & A. Arch, a London firm. For publication details of *Lyrical Ballads,* see Daniels (1938) and Foxon (1954).

3. Of course, there are other levels on which *Tintern Abbey* operates, although I would insist that the personal, subjective level is primary. I nevertheless value Kenneth Johnston's (1983) observations, which take note of the "socio-political tensions" of the poem. See too Levinson (1986, 14–57), Brinkley (1985), McGann (1983, 85–88), and Liu (1989, 215–17, 579–80). A part of the argument working through this camp has to do with whether the sociopolitical dimension of *Tintern Abbey* is conspicuous by its absence, or if this dimension is subtle and subversive. The poem does mention, after all, "plots of cottage ground," "pastoral farms," "vagrant dwellers," the isolation felt in "towns and cities," "acts / Of kindness," "the fever of the world," and even the "still, sad music of humanity." And yes, W does not mention the pollution and other problems of the time and place in his poem. But I would argue that these are not central to what W at this time in his life needed to poetically engage. His political and social commentaries are often sidelined by the more pressing needs of his troubled inner life. That *Tintern Abbey* is perceived as not taking on the role of reform or critique in a more direct or determined way says more about what the criticism wants than what W needed. So when Levinson writes that in *Tintern Abbey* the "primary poetic action is the suppression of the social" (37), could a reader likewise go to an overtly social poem and suggest that the primary poetic action is the suppression of the personal? Here I would refer the reader to the introduction, to my idea of process criticism: the means should justify the end.

4. Eilenberg uses this same concept of life insurance in discussing how W viewed the legacy of his poems as they reflected on him as a person and how his poetry represented for him immortality (1992, 207–8).

5. Holistic models of healing are gaining increasing credibility in the medical profession, but it is a difficult fight against a training regimen that views individuals with a mechanized model that treats mind and body separately. Hence the division of medicine and psychiatry, though even most of psychiatry treats individuals with a chemical model. See, for example, Chopra (1987; 1991; 1991a) and Greenwood and Nunn

(1992) for examples of medical practitioners encouraging a holistic model. W's evolving holistic model that emerges in *Tintern Abbey*, in which mind and matter, individual and nature, are as one, is important aspect of his struggle towards well-being.

6. The structure and logic of the question in fact come from William James (brother of Henry), one of the pioneers of modern psychology. In his essay "What is an Emotion?" (written in 1884), he theorizes that the model is wrong that suggests that perception of something leads to an emotional response, which in turn is then given bodily or physical expression. James suggests quite a different order: "My thesis on the contrary is that the bodily changes follow directly the PERCEPTION of the exciting fact, and that our feeling of the same changes as they occur IS the emotion." Thus, he writes, "we feel sorry because we cry, angry because we strike, afraid because we are sorry, angry, or fearful, as the case may be" (James 1977, 2). For a useful essay suggesting other similarities between James and W involving perception, memory, and consciousness, and even James's indebtedness to W, see Ferrantello (1991).

7. Coleridge quotes two lines from *Tintern Abbey* in his notebook, early 1801, and comments:

> —and the deep power of joy
> We see into the *Life* of Things—
> i.e.—By deep feeling we make our *Ideas dim*—& this is what we mean by our Life—ourselves. I think of the Wall—it is before me, a distinct Image—here. I necessarily thing of the *Idea* & the Thinking as two distinct and opposite Things. Now [let me] think of *myself*—of the thinking Being—the Idea becomes dim whatever it be—so dim that I know not what it is the Feeling is deep & steading—and this I call I—the identifying the Percipient & the Perceived—. (Coleridge 1957, vol. 1, entry 921)

Relevant to the present discussion is that Coleridge, like W, was interested in the relationship between thinking and feeling. Coleridge suggests that feeling is what sustains self-presence. This has to be put beside what W does in *Tintern Abbey*.

8. The meditational quality of *Tintern Abbey* has not gone unnoticed by Isobel Armstrong, who writes that "it is a reflective poem, meditating on experience and meditating on the experience of meditation, but it is also reflexive in the sense that it turns back on itself and absorbs and constructs out of its past forms, releasing new possibilities" (1978, 276). For a uncluttered and ranging description of how W uses the meditational act to discover the depth of the self found in suffering, and how that conception of a deep self has redemptive and unifying effects, see Jean Hall (1991, 44–63). Hall also relates W's meditational activity to the poet's need for growth (114). The idea of change is central in *Tintern Abbey*. Because Max Byrd sees this change as "inner and psychological rather than outward and physical," he prefers to call it "metamorphosis" or "self-transformation" (Byrd 1983, 24, 26).

9. The idea of change is central in *Tintern Abbey*. Because Max Byrd sees this change as "inner and psychological rather than outward and physical," he prefers to call it "metamorphosis" or "self-transformation" (Byrd 1983, 24, 26).

10. McNulty (1981, 98–99) theorizes that W is not writing about five years ago, but seven years ago, when W may have travelled by the area of the Wye with his friend, Robert Jones. McNulty says this would account for the happy side of the recollection in the passage from *Tintern Abbey*. But I do not see W's self-portrayal as happy, anyway.

11. This may be a moot point if one believes that feelings or emotions are a category of instincts.

12. As Alan Richardson writes about Dorothy's presence at this point in *Tintern Abbey*, "Wordsworth treasures in his sister not the representative of humanity but the reflection of his former self" (1985, 745). This idea of how W uses Dorothy is taken in a different direction by Marlon B. Ross, who suggests that Dorothy in *Tintern Abbey* fits W's pattern of rendering female figures as static and unable to progress; it is often his voice of masculine subjectivity that dispossesses these female figures (1986, 406). I would put it differently: these texts (including *Tintern Abbey*) exhibit W's needs, not those of his fictionalized female subjects, and often this is done at the expense of giving a life to these female figures.

13. Fadem again: "She [Dorothy] is the embodiment of the essential passions that informed his [W's] childhood and the omnipresent corrective to his own inescapable—and indeed necessary—thoughtfulness" (1978, 25). I especially like here the idea that Dorothy represents W's emotional life, for in *Tintern Abbey* W wants to have his newfound thoughtfulness help Dorothy when she is down and out, while he also wants to hold on to, yet go beyond, her. Thus she represents his past and his emotional life. Fadem also anticipates the idea running through my argument: "What Wordsworth searches for and finds so elusive is a via media between feeling and thought" (25); "'Tintern Abbey' is the first of Wordsworth's poems to explore fully the antipodes of intense feeling and mature thoughtfulness" (27).

14. For a interesting analysis of Dorothy's silence in the presence of W's revered authority (and W's influence on George Eliot's formulation of the same situation), see Homans (1981). Homans poses an interesting question: "What does it mean to follow instructions given not for the sake of the student [e.g., Dorothy] but for the sake of the teacher [W]?" (224). The point is a good one, for in *Tintern Abbey* the presence of Dorothy is important for W, but his words can be seen to be for himself, for his sake and his survival.

15. It can be argued that Dorothy is indeed used by W in *Tintern Abbey*. As McGavran notes, "Dorothy remains for him [W], like the abbey itself, a part of the landscape to which he has turned a blind man's eye," yet he consigns "her to nature and to a lower adolescent stage of identity and creativity, so that he may continue to behold in her what he was once (line 120) but has now, he insists, outgrown" (1990, 335–36).

16. McNulty (1981) suggests that *Tintern Abbey* follows the impromptu pattern of an ode. But see Richard Matlak's (1986) view of the poem as following the Ciceronian pattern of argumentation.

17. See Foster (1986) for an expanded version of *Tintern Abbey* as a scene of writing.

Chapter 4. Down and Out in Germany: Writing in Self-Defense

1. The allusion here is to the lines in Milton's *Paradise Lost* where Satan says, "The mind is its own place, and in itself / Can make a heaven of hell, a hell of heaven" (bk. 1, lines 254–55). W raises these stakes considerably in the *Prelude*, where he notes not only the creative will and imaginative power of the mind, but also that the mind is in itself a "divine" thing of beauty. W, as one of the "Prophets of Nature," will teach

> how the mind of man becomes
> A thousand times more beautiful than the earth
> On which he dwells, above this frame of things
> . . . .
> In beauty exalted, as it is itself
> Of substance and of fabric more divine.
>
> (1805 *Prelude*, bk. 13, lines 442–52)

In Shelley's comic critique of W, *Peter Bell the Third* (1819), he notes that in his own age there are those who "believe their minds are given / To make this ugly Hell a Heaven" (Shelley 1977, 333; lines 244–45). For an examination of this aspect of satanism in romantic literature, see Thorslev (1963). Establishing his mind as a *place* of powerful tranquility was paramount in W's poetic striving for individuation.

2. Bateson correctly notices that for W, "The sense of touch, consciously and almost desperately appealed to, provided the one effective means of return to the objective world" (1954, 179). W's precarious hold on reality is expressed in his note on the *Immortality Ode* that describes his condition as a schoolboy: "Many times while going to school have I grasped at a wall or tree to recall myself from this abyss of idealism to the reality" (Wordsworth 1876, 3:194).

3. Topophilia in W's poetry is discussed in Seamon (1984). In its vaguest sense it refers to a "love of place," but it involves the emotional bond that an individual has to a place or an environment. Seamon completely leaves out reasons for W's attachment to places.

4. Geoffrey Hartman borrows the term "centroversion" from Jung. It has to do with the mind's movement towards "the haunting-and-haunted spot" (Hartman 1971, xii). In his "Retrospect 1971" for *Wordsworth's Poetry 1787–1814* (the book was originally published in 1964), Hartman claims to have followed "Wordsworth's self-interpretations as closely as possible," and he claims to have traced these "self-interpretations" in W's "obsession with place." But while Hartman finds that W "rediscovered the religious (and romance) motif of numinous places," thus leading to a humanizing of the imagination as it engages "spots" in nature, he admits that he does not follow "Wordsworth's doubts, revisions, and vacillations" (xi–xiii)—that is, in terms of the present book, he does not pursue the poet's particular history of trauma and need for a poetry that in many ways amounts to a talking therapy. W's desire for apocalypse was internally driven and internally directed. But in the "Retrospect" Hartman did realize

that he might have paid more attention to the lack of assurance and decisiveness in the poetry, the peculiar corruptness in W's texts; and Hartman believes that W, who perhaps "never did emerge to an assured sense of self," carried in his poetry the suggestion of "a vital schizophrenia or decentering expressive of so much in personal growth" (1971, xvii).

5. I openly borrow the phrase "sense of history" from Alan Liu's impressive study *Wordsworth: The Sense of History* (1989); and I purposely put it up against "sense of self," not just to prioritize and privilege the latter, but to collapse the differences between the two. Like Liu, I believe that W's poetry after about 1786 changed radically from a poetics of the picturesque, which is an untroubling poetics of outward affirmation and presence, to one of inward denial and absence. But my study must necessary prefigure Liu's, for Liu situates W's poetic moments of insight and blindness somewhere along the axes of Napoleon and the French Revolution, while for me the "world" in W, the big realizations, the attempted discovery of a particular, individual subjectivity, collect around events and feelings that traumatically separated him from his family system and the meaning of his childhood existence, thus leaving W with two separated and almost irreconcilable lives: an Edenic, innocent youth, and a fallen, troubled adolescence that stretched into adulthood. The determining axes, then, for W, were marked by the death of his parents and by a problematical adolescence. The gap opened up by the two separated lives was to be filled with W's most powerful trope for restoration and recompense, a trope suggesting both nurturing and parenthood: Mother Nature. What I see is that, for Wordsworth, Napoleon and the French Revolution reenacted the structure and significance of these previous, more personal moments, and hence their significance for W—and for Liu. Liu's big thesis remains: that Wordsworth denied history; but again, the prefigurative history that Wordsworth denied was his own history. Or in other words: the object of denial in W's discourses, the shadowy presences, were not primarily repressive engagements with, say, Napoleon, the French Revolution, or the economics of writing; the object of denial remained the self in history rather than the history in the self. The objects of reality for all of us are primarily familial and subjective (given that the self is constructed within the family), and we defend, create, displace, and deny other forms of reality in the name of the family. This perspective as it relates to W and the French Revolution is mentioned by M. D. Faber, who sees W's French crisis in *The Prelude* as an expression of the "ambivalence he underwent in the course of his own infancy." Instead of getting to "the root of his conflict," says Faber, "he stays at the surface, dealing with purely political issues" (1991, 443).

6. Stephen Gill rightly notes that W "spent a lifetime looking for 'authority' in poetry that is essentially exploratory of what he does know and trust" (1989, 145–46).

7. *The Prelude* may have been dedicated and addressed to Coleridge, but it can also be read as an apology to Coleridge for not getting on with the greater job. Coleridge, of course, could never complete his own magnum opus.

8. As Anthony Conran notes, the "first thing that must strike us is a quite clear disintegration of one style—that of *Lyrical Ballads* and *Peter Bell*—and the gradual reaching of perfection of another" in the Goslar poems: what Conran calls "narrative

genre-pieces" (1969, 158–59). Conran also notes "the loneliness and self-questioning of Goslar" (158), and that the new poetry "is stylized and simplified to one moment only: the challenge is always the loss, and usually the death of a loved one, either fancied or in fact" (161). With these new poems "the testing of maturity began in earnest" (161). This is all quite correct, but Conran does not say why this change comes about, or how it might be contextualized within W's poetic-personal development.

9. Coleridge's friend was Thomas Poole, and he wrote to Coleridge in October 1798 that it was better that he be where *"pure German"* was being spoken.

10. Richard Matlak: "After the blissful experience of Alfoxden, being separated from Coleridge was disheartening, but being rejected by him at Göttingen threatened Wordsworth's vocational dignity and identity" (1978b, 391).

11. Writes Richard Holmes about W's state and circumstances at this time and his desire to move off with his sister: "Less explicit, perhaps, was Wordsworth's desire to be completely alone with Dorothy, who ever since the Tintern Abbey expedition had become something like her brother's Muse, magically holding open the gateway back into the Cumberland childhood" (1990, 209–10).

12. Moorman sums up the Goslar situation this way: "Circumstances favoured this blessed retreat into the past" (1957, 421). The problematical word here is "blessed," for this "retreat" caused a great deal of psychosomatic pain for W. The kind of poetry he wrote during this period does not suggest the "tranquil restoration" that had become his goal. But to Moorman's credit she does note the following about the onset of W's psychosomatic illness at this time: "At what point the uncomfortable symptoms became associated with the act of writing we do not know, but certainly from the German time onwards they have to be reckoned with as an enemy against which Wordsworth wages a continual and very courageous and exacting warfare" (416). This important observation has not received appropriate treatment. Moorman lets it go by; this study does not.

13. The phrasing in this sentence and the context of writing as a means of unconscious healing crosses over to a sentence in Alice Miller's *Thou Shalt Not Be Aware*. Miller here is writing about a book by Charlotte Vale Allen that describes Allen's abusive childhood: "She says that it was writing this autobiography that finally released her from the terrible burden of her past" (Miller 1986, 320). As we shall see, W, too, in the German winter, was beginning to write autobiography in an attempt to release himself from the burden of the past.

14. That *The Prelude* (the title was not W's) never got published during his own lifetime is remarkable and significant. (For W and his circle, it was generally known as "the Poem to Coleridge.") It had been in publishable form (that is, as a fair copy or equivalent) at least three times between 1799 and 1850, the last date being the year of his death. For example, in the preface to the edition of 1814, he says that *The Prelude* "has long been finished" (Wordsworth 1936, 589). W was not one to keep his poetry away from the public. He must have known that it was superior poetry, and he must have thought about the literary impact it would have. But he kept it away, tinkering and tampering—and in some ways un-writing it. The general consensus is that W's revisions are, as Jonathan Wordsworth notes, "for the worse" (1979, 567). The question

has to be asked: What was it about this personal poem that demanded he keep it out of the public domain?

15. Reasons for the so-called decline are not just varied but also denied. Perhaps "decline" is the wrong term. His poetry does not slide downhill into mediocrity. Nor can we say that he suddenly began to write bad poetry. W always wrote fine poetry, all the way from the very early loco-descriptive sketches through to the kind of Christian poetry he wrote in his later years. But his poetry does change, and we have to account not just for the kinds of changes but also for the reason(s) for the changes. For the best recent treatment of the decline theory and the poetry of W's later career, see Galperin (1989) and Gravil (1983). Earlier examinations include Batho (1933), Sperry (1935), Strout (1940), Burton (1942), Hamilton (1963), and Groom (1966). E. L. McAdam Jr. (1962) correlates W's decline with the death of Wordsworth's brother, John, in 1805. Reiman (1978) writes that W's "decline as a poet can be directly traced to the resolution, one by one, of the conflicts within him—one of the strongest of which arose from the mixed feelings . . . toward his sister" (144). See too Rylestone (1991) for a reading of the "Ecclesiastical Sonnets" that establishes them as central to W's achievement.

16. Willard Sperry (1935) suggests that W simply ran out of interesting material—memories of childhood, in particular.

17. While in Germany, W drafted most of the first part of the 1799 *Prelude*. The idea for and structure of part two can also be traced to MSS from the German period. For information regarding the composition and MS history of the 1799 *Prelude* see Wordsworth (1979, 507–8, 512–15), and Jonathan Wordsworth and Steven Gill (1973).

18. Mark L. Reed believes that because of its "common subject matter and the fact that most of W's Goslar work was based on his childhood, that *Address* was a Goslar poem, and the other five [Matthew poems] were probably Goslar poems, or at least German" (1967, 256n.).

19. These are printed in Wordsworth (1979, 485–94).

20. Hartman (1971) notes that the Lucy poems take up "the theme of separation" and are "Wordsworth's nearest approach to *personal* myth" (157; my emphasis). He is right, up to a point, and it is appropriate to see that the poems center not on the death of Lucy but on the "consciousness of the survivor" (160)—that is, on W's feelings as a survivor of some form of death or feelings associated with death. But Hartman also writes this about the Lucy poems: "Unusually little is known about their genesis. They seem to have sprung up independently, during that German winter of 1799, the thought of England fastening on Wordsworth's heart" (157). My point is that the general "thought of England" is simply an insufficient motivator or a sufficient reason for this kind of subject material to spring up. Richard Matlak (1986b) also sees separation, along with death and chastisement, as central to the Lucy poems as well as to the Goslar poetry in general. He sees the Lucy poems as revealing W's "ambivalence towards Dorothy" (149) by her presence in Goslar.

21. Spencer Hall concludes that the Lucy lyrics "do share common features—tonal, thematic, conceptual, imaginative, verbal, metrical—which set them apart from other poems by Wordsworth" (1971, 162). For the use of these poems to make critical and theoretical points, see, for example, Caraher (1991), Graff (1990, 168–69), J. Hillis

Miller (1990, 174–79), Hartman (1977), Holland (1976), and Hirsch (1967). Hirsch (227–29, 238–40) brings together readings of W's *A Slumber* by Cleanth Brooks (1951, 736) and F. W. Bateson (1950, 33, 80–81) and makes the point that interpreters must "establish the most probable context" (239). This would involve "a deliberate reconstruction of the author's subjective stance to the extent that this stance is relevant to the text at hand" (238). It should be clear to any reader of the present book that I like this idea, since I am emphasizing the "subjective stance" in examining a particular context for a particular author at a particular time in particular texts. Thus Hirsch approves more of Bateson's reading, which bridges W's relevant attitudes with those expressed in the text. But Hirsch also makes it clear that one must be aware that the experience in the text does not necessarily express the author's subjectivity. See, too, note 27, below.

22. In the case of *She dwelt*, I have just said that the situation is "attempted and unconscious." The idea is that these poems take the place of a kind of therapy, but there is not a differentiated analyst (speaker) and analysand (subject). But the point of the poem is clear enough. To quote Freud: "What are transferences? They are the new editions or facsimiles of the impulses and phantasies which are aroused and made conscious during the process of the analysis; but they have this peculiarity, which is characteristic for their species, that they replace some earlier person by the person of the physician. To put it another way: a whole series of psychological experiences are revived, not as belonging to the past, but as applying to the person of the physician at the present moment" (from *Fragment of an Analysis of a Case of Hysteria ['Dora']*, in Freud 1989, 234).

23. In a very close reading of *She dwelt*, Roger L. Slakey writes that "the drama of the situation is clearly the speaker's, not the girl's," and that the ending on "me" confirms that the speaker becomes "trapped in his own feelings, unable to express himself further": "It points rather to a mere state of being," and not to an emotional realization; the poem's "reflection leads not to release but to abyss" (1972, 630, 636, 637).

24. John Price, in a psychoanalytic reading of *Strange fits*, recalls Freud's observations that often patients' disclaimers about irrelevant or haphazard associations point in fact to the importance of what is disclaimed (1974, 362 and n. 1). W seems to want to dismiss his random thoughts about Lucy's death as simply "fond and wayward." We, of course, should not.

25. J. M. Hawthorn asks the question "Why does Lucy die?" and answers that "her death allows the lover to detach his image of her from a changing reality, to enjoy the satisfaction of an emotional relationship for a supremely private sort, with the independence and freedom of practical uninvolvement" (1971, 77).

26. See Herbert Hartman (1934) for early indentifications of Lucy, which include, among others, a Gypsy child, Annette Vallon, and Mary Hutchinson. For one of the best studies of the Lucy poems and their origination in the Goslar period, see Matlak (1978a). However, Matlak, following Bateson (1954, 151–54) and ultimately the rather haphazard statement made by Coleridge ("Most probably, in some gloomier moment he had fancied the moment in which his Sister might die"—Coleridge 1956, 1:479), sees Lucy as the projected feelings of deep ambivalence that W had for Dorothy during the stay in Goslar: "Wordsworth both loved Dorothy and wished to be rid of her,

because of the serious inconvenience of her presence, and the Lucy poems formed an expression of this ambivalence" (46). Bateson centers more on possible incest between the siblings. For a more sensible revisionary view of the relationship between Dorothy and W, see Reiman (1978), who views Wordsworth's "mixed feelings" (144) about his sister as significant in motivating some of his most interesting poetry. See too Price (1974) for a confirmation of the incest theme as it manifests itself in *Strange fits*. I would agree that Dorothy's absence would have made a difference to W's stay in Germany, but only inasmuch as the feelings of isolation would have manifest themselves in a different way. Matlak sees "the entire Goslar experience as a distortion of emotional reality" (62), but I would see it as an attempt by W's creative unconscious to clarify, not distort, some of W's deepest and most difficult emotions.

27. See Hirsch (1967, 181, 227–30), Brooks (1951, 736), Holland (1976), Hillis Miller (1978), Phelan (1981, 91–97), M. H. Abrams (in Eaves and Fischer 1986, 143–58), and Miller again (in Eaves and Fischer 1986, 101–11), de Man (1983, 223–26), and LaCapra (1989, 113–16). See, too, note 21, above.

28. In the 1805 *Prelude* this is bk. 1, lines 452–89; in the 1850 version, bk. 1, lines 425–63 (see Wordsworth 1979, 52–55). This passage was also extracted and put into a poem called *Influence of Natural Objects in Calling Forth and Strengthening the Imagination in Boyhood and Early Youth (from an unpublished poem)* and was published in *The Friend*, 28 December 1809 (Wordsworth 1936, 70–71).

29. J. Douglas Kneale in examining the sounds of nature in W—"all these whisperings, murmurings, utterings, prattlings, breathings and echoings"—notes correctly that "the haunting voice of nature is also sometimes a usurping voice." Of the skating passage in particular Kneale writes: in "the uncanny extravagance of the mountain echoes . . . that take up the voices of the skaters and return them frighteningly, there is always the sense of a recurrent 'alien sound' . . . unable to harmonize perfectly with the human voice" (1988, 83). I also perceive this uncanniness, fear, and disharmony, but I see it as a feeling, an emotional projection that reveals an uncertain subjectivity.

30. It is often called the boat-stealing episode, but this is somewhat misleading. More properly, it might be referred to as the boat-borrowing episode, for, as Onorato notes, "Surely, the boy intended to return the boat. . . ." (1971, 271).

31. In the 1805 version this is bk. 1, lines 372–426; in the 1850 version, bk. 1, lines 357–400 (see Wordsworth 1979, 48–51). Onorato makes a good point about the boat-stealing episode that can also be applied to the skating episode: "Wordsworth wished to write of it before there was a *Prelude* and a theory of growth to 'explain' it" (1971, 268). In other words, while in Germany this "mass" of detached experiences and feelings was emerging before Wordsworth could evolve a narrative strategy in which to place these experiences and feelings.

32. The nine lines of the 1799 "spots of time" passage become twenty-one in the 1805 version and seventeen in the 1850 version (Wordsworth 1979, 428–31). The "virtue" that the "spots" have in the 1805 version is that they can uplift us, and they are associated with the belief that they originate from those incidents where "the mind / Is lord and master, and that outward sense / Is but the obedient servant of her will." The revision suggests that W is attempting to fashion some kind of control over his feel-

ings. This marks, to say the least, an extraordinary and complicated leap for W: it can be read as both a sideways gesture towards understanding those problematical feelings and an attempt to suppress them with the powerful trope of the mind. W was driven to make the mind its own place (see note 1, above), even if it meant displacing other forms of subjectivity, viz., feelings. W would also come to displace the power of nature with the power of the mind in order to emotionally liberate himself.

33. Matlak notes that some of "Wordsworth's anxiety" at Goslar was the result of "the end of his blissful residence with Coleridge at Alfoxden and the likelihood that the creative experience of that year might never again be attained" (Matlak 1978a, 47). Indeed, the record shows the important bonding between the two poets. Again Matlak: "[H]aving experienced the excitement of Coleridge's presence, Wordsworth could hardly do without it" (50). Moorman notes that the Alfoxden period can be characterized by W discovering an authenticity in his poetic voice, something we can view as characteristically "Wordsworthian" (1957, 357). Writes Gill: "At the end of the Alfoxden year the Wordsworths were in a limbo of expectation" (1989, 151). In regard to the writing of the Lucy poems, Hall points to the conditions in Goslar as causally related to the kinds of poems composed there, but he only says that it was a "frustrating" and "problematical winter" (1971, 161). I am trying to point why this might be.

34. Barbara Schapiro: "The [rowing] incident, as an externalization of the boy's ambivalent relations with the parent imagoes (the cliffs suggest a paternal as well as maternal retaliation), results in the deep sense of inner disruption with which he concludes." Schapiro adds that she sees the same "emotional dynamics" in the skating scene (1983, 105).

35. *Nutting* eventually gets classified by W as one of the "Poems of the Imagination." For the dating and MS history of *Nutting,* see Reed (1967, 331–32).

36. I defer to what Alice Miller writes about this kind of experience: "At puberty, adolescents are often taken totally by surprize by the intensity of their true feelings. . . ." (1990c, 107). This is certainly the case in *Nutting,* and thus the poem can read as a surprised response to the intensity of the feelings.

37. David Perkins sums up the end of *Nutting* just as bluntly: "[T]he last three lines are a mistake," he says, and this is an example of where "Wordsworth interferes with a poetic success"; this is characteristic of W's "imperious temptation to find a moral in his experience and to state it" (1964, 185–86). Douglass H. Thomson has also noticed in even the drafts of *Nutting* "the difficulty Wordsworth experienced in reconciling the past moment with his mature vision" (1979, 294). See too Thomson's essay for a detailed explication of the earliest drafts of *Nutting* (and in particular Dove Cottage MS 16, which addresses a "Lucy") and for the relationship they have to the Lucy poems and published version of *Nutting.* Bigley's (1991) essay on *Nutting* profitably brings out the important problem of voices and feelings in the poem. For an analysis of the poem that explores the textual significance of the sister figure, that is, the "Maiden," see Crawford (1992).

38. See, for example, Perkins (1959, 14–16) and Ferry (1959, 22–28), who, according to Grob (1962), see "the metaphor of sexual violation" in *Nutting* as a way to intensify "our response to the act of desecration" (828). Grob, however, sees that the

metaphor is used to "draw ethical implications from the experience and raise the poem from the aesthetic to the moral level" (828).

39. Shapiro points out that the description in the poem "betrays a primitive oral greed as well as oedipal feelings toward the mother" (1983, 106). This in turn suggests that in *Nutting* W wants more of his mother and a return to her nurturing embrace, but that he is also angry at her, perhaps because of her premature loss—a kind of undesired weaning.

40. I take the bower/womb association from James W. Pipkin (1978, 14), who sees *Nutting* (like the "spots of time" passages) as a rites of initiation poem in which Wordsworth attempts to become "aware of the divine history immanent in his own life" (19).

41. W had more than one version of *Nutting*. I would go along with William Heath's conclusions: "My claim is that in the versions of 'Nutting' (and in the Lucy poems and appropriate passages of *The Prelude*) Wordsworth was experimenting with notions of truth and contending realities, and that he was discovering in those experiments ways in which he could make of a scene, a place, what the psychologist D. W. Winnicott might call 'potential space' needed for creative growth" (1973, 93). What W also needed out of these poetic experiments with past realities was personal growth.

42. See Wordsworth (1992, 359–61; 1965, 1–4) for a complete listing of the 1798 and 1800 poems.

43. Coleridge particularly examines Wordsworth's poetry in chapter 17 of the *Biographia Literaria*, but see too chapters 14 and 18–20.

44. The elegies I am referring to are *Could I the priest's consent have gained*, *Just as the blowing thorn began*, *Remembering how thou didst beguile*, *Carved, Matthew with a master's skill*, and *Dirge* ("I bring ye little noisy crew"). These are all printed in Wordsworth (1984, 142–47), and are sometimes associated with other "Matthew" poems. Along with the other short poems just briefly discussed, these may have been the first poems W wrote while in Germany.

45. Writes Eilenberg about the relationship between *Lucy Gray* and the other Lucy poems: "'Lucy Gray' supplies an etiology for the ghostly melancholy of the central Lucy poems; it tells a story about what it is like to look for a girl who has fallen out of the text and thereby eluded interpretation" (1992, 113). If *Lucy Gray* tells the story about the difficulty of interpretation, I believe the difficulty is in interpreting W's use of this story as a commentary on his own emotional status.

46. This is transcribed in Wordsworth (1979, 492).

47. A version of *The Boy of Winander (There was a Boy)* must have been written in the first part of W's stay in Germany. He sent a copy of the poem to Coleridge at Ratzeburg probably in late November or early December, for Coleridge recorded his "pleasure" in reading the poem and how a couple of the lines were unmistakably Wordsworthian (Coleridge 1956, 1:452–53). However, we do not know how much or what version W sent.

48. Steven Lukits (1988) examines W's use of the word "unawares," and suggests an intertextual connection with *The Rime of the Ancient Mariner* and *Resolution and*

Independence. More interesting from the perspective of the present study, Lukits suggests that in poems like *The Boy of Winander* (including the "spots of time" passages) there is a "metaphor collision of unforgettable feelings and remembered images. The poems which he writes about these experiences of life place the feelings and images of the past within the grip of his present passions" (159). He adds that when writing *The Boy of Winander*, W "was beset with doubts about his poetic self-confidence" (159). That is, the poem is more than just a recollection; it is also a projection.

Chapter 5. Home Again in Grasmere

1. W had earlier written some unrelated passages that would end up in *The Prelude*, but with these he had no developed plan for an autobiographical poem (see Reed 1967, 29–30).

2. The text I am quoting here is the reading text of MS JJ in Wordsworth (1977, 123–30).

3. For the compositional ordering of book 1, see Wordsworth (1977, 3–26) and Reed (1967, 29–31, 333–36).

4. It could be argued that there are almost twenty "spots of time" passages, though I find that the episodes in the 1799 *Prelude* provide the most clear examples. The characteristics of the spots of time passages have been recognized for some time. Jonathan Bishop (1959), for example, noted that they have much in common, including the emergence of a solitary figure, the circumstance of darkness, and overtones of guilt. Bishop, it so happens, also notes that the passages "are not impersonal, but private," and that these "groups of memories" tell "of the fears, curiosities, and guilt of childhood"; further, he notes that the greater *Prelude* contains the process of "self-analysis" (58–60). With these observations I would concur.

5. Recall again what W wrote about *Nutting*: "Written in Germany: intended as part of poem on my own life, but struck out as not being wanted there" (Wordsworth 1876, 3:39).

6. As Sybil S. Eakin (1973) suggests, "Wordsworth's original intention, when the spots of time episodes were part of the two-part *Prelude*, was to vindicate an education by nature; his determination at this time was wholly at odds with the notion that the mind could be 'lord and master'" (391).

7. As the editors of Wordsworth note (Wordsworth 1979, 30 n. 6), lines 1–54 of the 1805 *Prelude* likely date from November 1799. See, too, Finch (1970a).

8. For a thorough examination of the sense of domesticity at Grasmere and how it related to the division of labor and value of writing in the household (differing for W and Dorothy), see Heinzelman (1988).

9. Although dating the earliest composition of *Home at Grasmere* is extremely difficult and sometimes speculative (see Wordsworth 1977a, 8–22), Jonathan Wordsworth (1980) makes a solid case that most of MS B was composed in 1800, and in particular, in March and April. This is the version I will be using. It is also in Wordsworth

(1984) and J. Wordsworth (1982, 390–415). Finch (1970) extends the dating of MS B from 1800–1806. But again, it appears that most of the MS B version was written in the spring of 1800, and then slightly revised in 1806 with a slightly expanded "Prospectus" added.

10. A reading text of MS I is in Jonathan Wordsworth (1980, 388–90). I will be quoting from this text. See Wordsworth (1977a, 255–63) for photographs and transcriptions of MS I.

11. Here, of course, I am thinking of W's own building metaphor in describing *The Recluse*, from his preface to *The Excursion* (Wordsworth 1936, 589).

12. W's wedding announcement appeared in the *Morning Post* for 9 October 1802 and is printed in Moorman (1957, 574–75). The author of the announcement is not known, though it may have been Coleridge in a puckish mood.

13. Here I allude and pay homage to not just Milton but to Jonathan Wordsworth's careful analysis of lines 1–667 of *Home at Grasmere*, entitled "Paradise Regained" (J. Wordsworth 1982, 114–32). As Jonathan Wordsworth notes, while W is Adam, he is also Moses come to the promised land (115).

14. Two of these tales, significantly revised and put into the mouth of the Pastor, were later placed in book 6 of *The Excursion* (lines 1079–1191).

15. He also added six lines as a transition (MS B, lines 953–58).

16. Here I am thinking of the important observation Karl Kroeber makes when he says that, in W's portrayal of the valley, the "self-completeness" and "self-unified" nature of the place is so very important: "The self-sufficing unity of being which the poet holds forth as a human ideal is naturalistically embodied in the form and condition of Grasmere Vale" (1974, 133). I have taken this one step further: the self-sufficing unity of being that W holds forth is a personal ideal.

17. Unfortunately, one complete passage of *Michael* was omitted in the printing of the 1800 *Lyrical Ballads* (actually, it was not until January 1801 that the second edition appeared). I will add here too what Eilenberg writes about *Michael:* that it "exhibits a guilty anxiety on the subject of the heir" (1992, 93). This might be brought to W's feelings regarding his own father and his legacy.

18. The passage he wrote at the end of 1801 is bk. 3, lines 1–167, of the 1805 *Prelude*. W's recollection of Cambridge suggests ambivalent feelings: on the one hand, his relatives had great expectations, and this gave W anxiety; on the other hand, he also felt free to spread his thoughts and feelings to all that he beheld and to examine those thoughts and feelings.

19. For an examination of how W's Rainbow poem and the four stanzas challenged Coleridge, resulting in Coleridge's *Dejection: An Ode* and continuing in W's *Resolution and Independence*, see Smith (1935), Meyer (1950), McFarland (1981, 74–7). This poetic dialogue between the two poets was further complicated by Coleridge's poem *The Mad Monk*, which predates W's first four stanzas of the *Immortality Ode* and clearly predicts some of the *Ode*'s lines (Moorman 1957, 529–30; Holmes 1990, 279–80, 318). But there is also the suggestion that W may have in part authored *The Mad Monk:* see Parrish and Erdman (1960).

Chapter 6. The *Immortality Ode:* Back to the Future

1. The first four stanzas of this poem describe W's condition in general terms, complete with mysterious illness, while the last three stanzas describe Coleridge. According to Dorothy's journal for 9 May, W worked on the two poems on the same day (D. Wordsworth 1973, 123).

2. For a more complete discussion of this, see above, pages 55–58.

3. See, for example, Wordsworth (1967, 395–97, 404, 415).

4. See Reed (1975, 33–36) for an indication of what W worked on for the year. The trip to Scotland is commemorated both in *Dorothy's Recollections of a Tour in Scotland A.D. 1803* and W's group of poems entitled *Memorials of a Tour in Scotland, 1803* (Wordsworth 1936, 225–36).

5. As Frederick Kirchhoff notes, the 1802 stanzas suggest that W is "trapped in a pattern of simple alternation between past and present, external and internal moods. He is able only to differentiate," not assimilate (1986, 121–22). Kirchhoff further suggests that in the *Ode* W comes to accept and even admire "the condition of his own childhood" (124), and Kirchhoff also recognizes that W's accomplishment is psychological rather than intellectual, though there is also in the *Ode* a realization of poetic powers and after the *Ode* a falling off of these powers. With all of this I would generally concur, but these observations cry out to be contextualized within W's career and personal growth.

6. For an analysis of Trilling's assessment of the *Ode,* see Robinson (1981) and Vendler (1978).

7. In this I would agree with Trilling, who sees the *Ode* as W's "dedication to new powers" (1975, 151). Vendler's critique of Trilling is interesting here, as she dismisses his moral approach. She believes that, among other things, the *Ode* "represents the acquisition of the power of metaphor," and that W's achievement was to come up with a poetic language that attempts to unify, synthesize, and mediate the two languages and consciousness of childhood and adulthood (1978, 84–86).

8. One of the reasons why *Tintern Abbey* is much less a universal statement is that it situates itself in such a particularized way, including the presence of a certain sister.

9. Again, I would refer to Don Johnson (1988, esp. 287–94). Johnson is keen to point out the division in W's life as determined by the death of W's parents and the difficulty surrounding mourning.

10. The "timely utterance" (line 23) that gives him relief is normally considered to be either *My heart leaps up* or *Resolution and Independence*. But see Hartman (1987, 152–62) for a more discursive analysis of the possibilities of what the "timely utterance" might refer to.

11. McFarland (1982, 62) rightly calls W's use of the preexistent state a "Platonic fiction," likely borrowed from Coleridge. But for an analysis of the *Ode* that takes W's argument for the immortality of the soul less naturalistically, see Anya Taylor (1986).

Works Cited

Abrams, Jeremy, ed. 1990. *Reclaiming the Inner Child*. Los Angeles: Jeremy P. Tarcher.
Abrams, M. H., ed. 1974. *The Norton Anthology of English Literature*. Vol. 2. New York: W. W. Norton.
Allport, Gordon W. 1961. *Pattern and Growth in Personality*. New York: Holt, Rinehart and Winston.
———. 1966. "Traits Revisited." *American Psychologist* 21:1–9.
Armstrong, Isobel. 1978. "'Tintern Abbey': From Augustan to Romantic." In *Augustan Worlds*, edited by J. C. Hilson et al., 261–79. Leicester, England: Leicester University Press.
Ashton, Thomas L. 1972. "'The Thorn': Wordsworth's Insensitive Plant." *Huntington Library Quarterly* 35:171–87.
Averill, James, H. 1976. "Suffering and Calm in Wordsworth's Early Poetry." *PMLA* 91:223–34.
———. 1980. *Wordsworth and Poetry of Human Suffering*. Ithaca: Cornell University Press.
Bateson, F. W. 1950. *English Poetry: A Critical Introduction*. London: Longman.
———. 1954. *Wordsworth: A Re-interpretation*. London: Longman.
———. 1969. "Cottage Restored." *New Statesman,* 22 August 1969, 246–47.
Batho, Edith C. 1933. *The Later Wordsworth*. Cambridge: Cambridge University Press.
Beckett, J. V. 1981. *Coal and Tobacco: The Lowthers and the Economic Development of West Cumberland, 1660–1760*. Cambridge: Cambridge University Press.
Berne, Eric. 1964. *Games People Play*. New York: Ballantine.
Bewell, Alan. 1989. *Wordsworth and the Enlightenment: Nature, Man, and Society in the Experimental Poetry*. New Haven: Yale University Press.
Bialostosky, Don H. 1982. "Narrative Irony and the Pleasure Principle in 'Anecdote for Fathers' and 'We Are Seven.'" *JEGP* 81:227–43.
———. 1992. *Wordsworth, Dialogics, and the Practice of Criticism*. Cambridge: Cambridge University Press.
Bigley, Bruce. 1991. "Multiple Voices in 'Nutting': The Urbane Wordsworth." *Philological Quarterly* 70:433–52.

Bishop, Jonathan. 1959. "Wordsworth and the 'Spots of Time.'" *ELH* 26:45–65.

Blank, G. Kim. 1988. *Wordsworth's Influence on Shelley: A Study of Poetic Authority*. London: Macmillan.

———, ed. 1991. *The New Shelley: Later Twentieth-Century Views*. London: Macmillan.

Bloom, Harold. 1971. *The Visionary Company: A Reading of Romantic Poetry*. Ithaca: Cornell University Press.

Bonsall, Brian. 1960. *Sir James Lowther and Cumberland and the Westmorland Elections*. Manchester, England: Manchester University Press.

Bradshaw, John. 1988a. *Bradshaw On: The Family*. Deerfield Beach, Fla.: Health Communications.

———. 1988b. *Healing the Shame that Binds You*. Deerfield Beach, Fla.: Health Communications.

———. 1990. *Homecoming: Reclaiming and Championing your Inner Child*. New York: Bantam Books.

Brantley, Richard E. 1974. "Spiritual Maturity and Wordsworth's 1783 Christmas Vacation." *Studies in English Literature: 1500–1900* 14: 479–87.

Briere, John N. 1992. *Child Abuse Trauma: Theory and Treatment of the Lasting Effects*. London: Sage.

Brinkley, Robert A. 1985. "Vagrant and Hermit: Milton and the Politics of 'Tintern Abbey.'" *The Wordsworth Circle* 16:126–33.

Brisman, Leslie. 1978. *Romantic Origins*. Ithaca: Cornell University Press.

Brooks, Cleanth. 1951. "Irony as a Principle of Structure." In *Literary Opinion in America*, edited by M. D. Zabel. New York: Harper.

Brownstein, Rachel Mayer. 1973. "The Private Life: Dorothy Wordsworth's Journals." *Modern Language Quarterly* 34:48–63.

Burton, Mary E. 1942. *The One Wordsworth*. Chapel Hill: University of North Carolina Press.

Byrd, Max. 1983. "Metamorphosis and *Tintern Abbey:* Two Notes." *Modern Philology* 81:24–37.

Campbell, Joseph. 1988. *The Power of Myth*. With Bill Moyers. New York: Doubleday.

Campbell, O. J., and P. Mueschke. 1933. "Wordsworth's Aesthetic Development, 1795–1802." *Essays and Studies in English and Comparative Literature* 10:23–26.

Campbell, Patrick. 1991. *Wordsworth and Coleridge: Lyrical Ballads: Critical Perspectives*. London: Macmillan.

Caraher, Brian G. 1991. *Wordsworth's "Slumber" and the Problematics of Reading*. University Park: Pennsylvania State University Press.

Caruth, Cathy. 1985. "Past Recognition: Narrative Origins in Wordsworth and Freud." *MLN* 100:935–48.

———. 1987. "'Unknown Causes': Poetic Effects." *Diacritics* 17, no. 4:78–85.

Chopra, Deepak, M.D. 1987. *Creating Health: How to Wake up the Body's Intelligence.* Boston: Houghton Mifflin.

———. 1991. *Unconditional Life: Discovering the Power to Fulfill Your Dreams.* New York: Bantam Books.

———. 1991a. *Perfect Health: The Complete Mind/Body Guide.* New York: Harmony.

Christensen, Jerome. 1980. "Wordsworth's Misery, Coleridge"s Woe: Reading "The Thorn.'" *Papers on Language and Literature* 16:268–86.

Cochrane, Carmie Thrasher, and David Voit Meyers. 1980. *Children in Crisis.* London: Sage.

Cohen, Philip. 1978. "Narrative and Persuasion in *The Ruined Cottage.*" *Journal of Narrative Technique* 8:185–99.

Coleridge, Samuel Taylor. 1951. *Enquiring Spirit: A New Presentation of Coleridge from his Published and Unpublished Prose Writings.* Edited by Kathleen Coburn. London: Routledge & Kegan Paul.

———. 1956. *Collected Letters of Samuel Taylor Coleridge.* Vol. 1. Edited by Earl Leslie Griggs. Oxford: Clarendon.

———. 1957. *The Notebooks of Samuel Taylor Coleridge, 1794–1804.* Vol. 1. Edited by Kathleen Coburn. London: Routledge & Kegan Paul.

———. 1959. *Collected Letters of Samuel Taylor Coleridge.* Vol. 3. Edited by Earl Leslie Griggs. Oxford: Clarendon.

———. 1985. *Samuel Taylor Coleridge.* Edited by H. J. Jackson. Oxford: Oxford University Press.

Conran, Anthony. 1969. "The Goslar Lyrics." In *Wordsworth's Mind and Art,* edited by A. W. Thomson, 157–80. Edinburgh: Oliver and Boyd.

Covington, Stephanie, and Liana Beckett. 1988. *Leaving the Enchanted Forest: The Path from Relationship Addiction to Intimacy.* San Francisco: Harper and Row.

Crawford, Rachel. 1992. "The Structure of the Sororal in Wordsworth's 'Nutting.'" *Studies in Romanticism* 31:197–211.

Danby, John F. 1960. *The Simple Wordsworth: Studies in the Poems, 1797–1807.* London: Routledge and Kegan Paul.

Daniels, R. W. 1938. "The Publication of 'Lyrical Ballads.'" *Modern Language Review* 33:406–10.

Dann, Joanne. 1980. "Some Notes on the Relationship between the Wordsworth and Lowther Families." *The Wordsworth Circle* 11:80–82.

de Man, Paul. 1983. *Blindness and Insight: Essays in the Rhetoric of Contemporary Criticism.* London: Methuen.

———. 1984. *The Rhetoric of Romanticism.* New York: Columbia University Press.

De Quincey, Thomas. 1970. *Recollections of the Lakes and the Poets.* Edited by David Wright. Harmondsworth, England: Penguin Books.

De Selincourt, Ernest. 1933. *Dorothy Wordsworth: A Biography.* Oxford: Clarendon.

Douglas, Wallace W. 1948. "Wordsworth in Politics: The Westmoreland Election of 1818." *MLN* 63:437–49.

———. 1968. *Wordsworth: The Construction of a Personality*. Kent, Ohio: Kent State University Press.

Dryden, Windy, and William Golden, eds. 1986. *Cognitive-Behavioural Approaches to Psychotherapy*. London: Harper and Row.

DSM-III-R. 1987. *Diagnostic and Statistical Manual of Mental Disorders*. 3d ed. rev. Washington, D.C.: American Psychiatric Association.

Eakin, Sybil S. 1973. "The Spots of Time in Early Versions of *The Prelude*." *Studies in Romanticism* 12:389–405.

Eaves, Morris, and Michael Fischer, eds. 1986. *Romanticism and Contemporary Criticism*. Ithaca: Cornell University Press.

Eilenberg, Susan. 1992. *Strange Power of Speech: Wordsworth, Coleridge, and Literary Possession*. Oxford: Oxford University Press.

Ellis, David. 1985. *Wordsworth, Freud, and the Spots of Time: Interpretations in "The Prelude."* Cambridge: Cambridge University Press.

Erdman, David V. 1978. "Wordsworth as Heartsworth; or, Was Regicide the Prophetic Ground of Those Moral Questions." In *The Evidence of the Imagination: Studies of Interactions between Life and Art in English Romantic Literature*, edited by Donald H. Reiman et al., 12–41. New York: New York University Press.

Faber, M. D. 1991. "Imagination and the Unconscious: A Critique of the Neo-Romantic Program." *Psychoanalytic Review* 78, no. 3:437–57.

Fadem, Richard. 1978. "Dorothy Wordsworth: A View from 'Tintern Abbey.'" *The Wordsworth Circle* 9:17–32.

Ferrantello, Donna. 1991. "'The Picture of the Mind Revives Again': Perception in William James' Psychology and 'Tintern Abbey.'" *The Wordsworth Circle* 22:131–35.

Ferry, David. 1959. *The Limits of Mortality: An Essay on Wordsworth's Major Poems*. Middletown, Conn: Wesleyan University Press.

Finch, John Alban. 1970. "On the Dating of *Home at Grasmere:* A New Approach." In *Bicentenary Wordsworth Studies*, edited by Jonathan Wordsworth, 14–28. Ithaca: Cornell University Press.

———. 1970a. "Wordsworth's Two-Handed Engine." In *Bicentenary Wordsworth Studies*, edited by Jonathan Wordsworth, 1–13. Ithaca: Cornell University Press.

Foster, Mark. 1986. "'Tintern Abbey' and Wordsworth's Scene of Writing." *Studies in Romanticism* 25:75–95.

Foxon, D. F. 1954. "The Printing of *Lyrical Ballads*." *The Library*, 5th ser., 9:221–41.

Freud, Sigmund. 1989. *The Freud Reader*. Edited by Peter Gay. New York: W. W. Norton.

Friedman, Michael H. 1979. *The Making of a Tory Humanist: Wordsworth and the Idea of Community*. New York: Columbia University Press.

Frosch, Thomas 1986. "Wordsworth and the Matrix of Romance: *The Prelude*, Book V." *CUNY English Forum* 1:179–97.

Galperin, William. 1989. *Revision and Authority in Wordsworth: The Interpretation of a Career*. Philadelphia: University of Pennsylvania Press.

Gerard, Albert S. 1972. "Of Trees and Men: The Unity of Wordsworth's 'The Thorn.'" In *Wordsworth: "Lyrical Ballads": A Casebook*, edited by Alun R. Jones and William Tydeman, 214–33. London: Macmillan.

Gill, Stephen. 1989. *William Wordsworth: A Life*. Oxford: Oxford University Press.

———. 1991. *William Wordsworth: The Prelude*. Cambridge: Cambridge University Press.

Gittings, Robert, and Jo Manton. 1985. *Dorothy Wordsworth*. Oxford: Clarendon.

Gordon, William A. 1972. "Autobiography and Identity: Wordsworth and *The Borderers*." *Tulane Studies in English* 20:71–86.

Graff, Gerald. 1990. "Determinacy/Indeterminacy." In *Critical Terms for Literary Study*, edited by Frank Lentricchia and Thomas McLaughlin, 163–76. Chicago: University of Chicago Press.

Gravil, Richard. 1982. *"Lyrical Ballads* (1798): Wordsworth as Ironist." *Critical Quarterly* 24, no. 4:39–57.

———. 1983. "Wordsworth's Last Retreat." *Charles Lamb Bulletin* 43:54–91.

Greenwood, Michael, and Peter Nunn. 1992. *Paradox and Healing: A Book about Medicine, Mythology and Transformation*. Victoria, B.C.: Paradox Publishers.

Griska, Joseph M., Jr. 1974. "Wordsworth's Mood Disturbance: A Psychoanalytic Approach to Three Poems." *Literature and Psychology* 24:144–54.

Grob, Alan. 1962. "Wordsworth's *Nutting*." *JEGP* 61:826–32.

Groom, Bernard. 1966. *The Unity of Wordsworth's Poetry*. New York: St. Martin's.

Hall, Jean. 1991. *A Mind that Feeds Upon Infinity: The Deep Self in English Romantic Poetry*. Rutherford, N.J.: Fairleigh Dickinson University Press.

Hall, Spencer. 1971. "Wordsworth's 'Lucy' Poems: Context and Meaning." *Studies in Romanticism* 10:159–75.

Hamilton, Carson C. 1963. *Wordsworth's Decline in Poetic Power: Prophet into High Priest: A Study*. New York: Exposition.

Hardwick, Elizabeth. 1974. *Seduction and Betrayal: Women and Literature*. New York: Random House.

Harper, George McLean. 1916. *William Wordsworth: His Life, Works, and Influence*. 2 vols. New York: Charles Scribner's Sons.

———. 1921. *Wordsworth's French Daughter*. Princeton: Princeton Univeristy Press.

Hartman, Geoffrey H. 1971.*Wordsworth's Poetry 1787–1814*. New Haven: Yale University Press. Originally published in 1964.

———. 1977. "A Touching Compulsion: Wordsworth and the Problem of Literary Interpretation." *Georgia Review* 21:345–61. Reprinted in Hartman 1987.

———. 1987. *The Unremarkable Wordsworth*. Minneapolis: University of Minnesota Press.

———. 1993. "Romanticism and Anti-Self-Consciousness." In *Romanticism,* edited by Cynthia Chase, 43–54. New York: Longman. Originally published in *Centennial Review* 6 (1962): 553–65.

Hartman, Herbert. 1934. "Wordsworth's Lucy Poems." *PMLA* 49:132–42.

Havens, Raymond Dexter. 1941. *The Mind of a Poet: A Study of Wordsworth's Thought*. Baltimore: Johns Hopkins University Press.

Hawthorn, J. M. 1971. "The strange deaths of Sally, Ann, Lucy and others . . ." *Trivium* 6:70–80.

Hayden, Donald E. 1983. *Wordsworth's Walking Tour of 1790*. Tulsa, Okla.: University of Tulsa Press.

Haydon, Benjamin Robert. 1960. *The Diary of Benjamin Robert Haydon*. Vol. 2. Edited by Willard Bissell Pope. Cambridge: Harvard University Press.

Hazlitt, William. 1932. *The Complete Works of William Hazlitt*. Vol. 11. Edited by P. P. Howe. London: J. M. Dent and Sons.

Heath, William W. 1973. "Wordsworth's Experiments with Truth." *The Wordsworth Circle* 4:87–98.

Heffernan, James A. W. 1988. "The Presence of the Absent Mother in Wordsworth's *Prelude*." *Studies in Romanticism* 27:253–72.

Heinicke, Christoph, M. 1973. "Parental Depravation in Early Childhood: A Predisposition to Later Development?" In *Separation and Depression,* edited by John Paul Scott and Edward C. Senay, 141–60. Washington, D.C.: American Association for the Advancement of Science.

Heinzelman, Kurt. 1988. "The Cult of Domesticity: Dorothy and William at Grasmere." In *Romanticism and Feminism,* edited by Anne K Mellor, 52–78. Bloomington: Indiana University Press.

Herman, Judith Lewis. 1992. *Trauma and Recovery*. New York: Basic Books.

Hertz, Neil H. 1967. "Wordsworth and the Tears of Adam." *Studies in Romanticism* 7:15–33.

Hirsch, E. D., Jr. 1967. *Validity in Interpretation*. New Haven: Yale University Press.

Holland, Norman N. 1976. "Literary Interpretation and Three Phases of Psychoanalysis." *Critical Inquiry* 3:221–33.

Holmes, Richard. 1990. *Coleridge: Early Visions*. London: Penguin.

Homans, Margaret. 1981. "Eliot, Wordsworth, and the Scenes of the Sisters' Instruction." *Critical Inquiry* 8:223–41.

Jacobus, Mary. 1976. *Tradition and Experiment in Wordsworth's "Lyrical Ballads" (1798)*. Oxford: Clarendon.

———. 1984. "The Law of/and Gender: Genre Theory and *The Prelude*." *Diacritics* 14, no. 4:47–57.

James, John W., and Frank Cherry. 1989. *The Grief Recovery Handbook: A Step-by-Step Program for Moving Beyond Loss.* New York: Harper and Row.

James, William. 1977. *What is an Emotion?* In *Theatre Papers*, 1st ser., edited by Peter Hulton. Devon, England: Department of Theatre, Dartington College of Arts. Originally published in *Mind* 9 (1884): 188–205.

Johnson, Don. 1988. "The Grief Behind the Spots of Time." *American Imago* 45:287–307.

Johnston, Kenneth R. 1975. "'Home at Grasmere': Reclusive Song." *Studies in Romanticism* 14:1–28.

———. 1983. "The Politics of *Tintern Abbey*." *The Wordsworth Circle* 14:6–14.

———. 1984. *Wordsworth and "The Recluse."* New Haven: Yale University Press.

Jones, Alun R., and William Tydeman, eds. 1972. *Wordsworth: "Lyrical Ballads": A Casebook.* London: Macmillan.

Jones, Mark. 1991. "Interpretation in Wordsworth and the Provocation Theory of Romantic Literature." *Studies in Romanticism* 30:565–604.

Jordan, J. E. 1976. *Why the Lyrical Ballads?* Berkeley: University of California Press.

Keats, John. 1975. *Letters of John Keats.* Edited by Robert Gittings. Oxford: Oxford University Press.

Ketcham, Carl H., ed. 1969. *The Letters of John Wordsworth.* Ithaca: Cornell University Press

Kirchhoff, Frederick. 1986. "Reconstruction of the Self in Wordsworth's 'Ode: Intimations of Immortality From Recollections of Early Childhood.'" In *Narcissism and the Text: Studies in Literature and the Psychology of the Self*, edited by Lynne Layton and Barbara Ann Schapiro, 116–27. New York: New York University Press.

Kirkham, Michael. 1974. "Innocence and Experience in Wordsworth's 'The Thorn.'" *Ariel* 5:66–80

Kneale, J. Douglas. 1988. *Monumental Writing: Aspects of Rhetoric in Wordsworth's Poetry.* Lincoln: University of Nebraska Press.

Knight, William. 1889. *The Life of William Wordsworth.* 3 vols. Edinburgh: William Paterson.

Kramer, Lawrence. 1986. "Victorian Sexuality and 'Tintern Abbey.'" *Victorian Poetry* 24:399–410.

Kroeber, Karl 1974. "*Home at Grasmere:* Ecological Holiness." *PMLA* 89:132–41.

Kübler-Ross, Elisabeth. 1970. *On Death and Dying.* New York: Macmillan.

LaCapra, Dominick. 1989. "The Temporality of Rhetoric." In *Soundings in Critical Theory.* Ithaca: Cornell University Press.

Leavis, F. R. 1971. "Wordsworth: The Creative Conditions." In *Twentieth-Century Literature in Retrospect*, edited by Reuben A. Brower, 323–41. Cambridge: Harvard University Press.

———. 1972. *Revaluation: Tradition and Development in English Poetry.* Harmondsworth, England: Penguin. Originally published in 1936.

Legouis, Emile. 1897. *The Early Life of William Wordsworth, 1770–1798.* Translated into English by J. W. Matthews. London: Dent. Originally published in French in 1896 as *La Jeunesse de Wordsworth, 1770–1798.*

———. 1922. *William Wordsworth and Annette Vallon.* London: E. P. Dutton.

Levinson, Marjorie. 1986. *Wordsworth's Great Period Poems: Four Essays.* Cambridge: Cambridge University Press.

Lipowski, Zbigniew J. 1990. "Somatization and Depression." *Psychosomatics* 31:13–21

Liu, Alan. 1982. "'Shapeless Eagerness': The Genre of Revolution in Books 9–10 of *The Prelude.*" *MLQ* 43:3–28.

———. 1989. *Wordsworth: The Sense of History.* Stanford, Calif.: Stanford University Press.

Lukits, Steven. 1988. "Wordsworth Unawares: The Boy of Winander, the Poet, and the Mariner." *The Wordsworth Circle* 19:156–60.

MacGillivray, James R. 1930. "Wordsworth in France." *TLS,* 12 June, 496.

Manning, Peter. 1976. "Wordsworth, Margaret, and the Pedlar." *Studies in Romanticism* 15:195–220.

———. 1983. "Reading Wordsworth's Revisions: Othello and the Drowned Man." *Studies in Romanticism* 22:3–28.

Matlak, Richard E. 1978a. "Wordsworth's Lucy Poems in Psychobiographical Context." *PMLA* 93:46–65.

———. 1978b. "The Men in Wordsworth's Life." *The Wordsworth Circle* 9:391–97.

———. 1986. "Classical Argument and Romantic Persuasion in 'Tintern Abbey.'" *Studies in Romanticism* 25:97–129.

———. 1986b. "A Psychobiographical Approach to Wordsworth's Goslar Poetry." In *Approaches to Teaching Wordsworth's Poetry,* edited by Spencer Hall and Jonathan Ramsey, 147–52. New York: MLA.

Mayo, Robert. 1954. "The Contemporaneity of the *Lyrical Ballads.*" *PMLA* 69:486–522.

Mazzeno, Laurence W. 1977. "Of Fathers, Children, and Poets: Wordsworth's 'Anecdote for Fathers.'" *Psychocultural Review* 1:421–33.

McAdam, E. L., Jr. 1962. "Wordsworth's Shipwreck." *PMLA* 77:240–47.

McFarland, Thomas. 1981. *Romanticism and the Forms of Ruin: Wordsworth, Coleridge, and the Modalities of Fragmentation.* Princeton: Princeton University Press.

———. 1982. "Wordsworth's Best Philosopher." *The Wordsworth Circle* 13:59–68.

———. 1992. *William Wordsworth: Intensity and Achievement.* Oxford: Clarendon.

McGann, Jerome J. 1983. *The Romantic Ideology: A Critical Investigation.* Chicago: University of Chicago Press.

McGavran, James Holt, Jr. 1990. "Xanadu, Somersetshire, and the Banks of the Wye: A Study of Romantic Androgyny." *Papers on Language and Literature* 26: 334–45.

McNulty, John. Bard. 1945. "Wordsworth's Tour of the Wye: 1798." *Modern Language Notes* 60:291–95.

———. 1981. "Self-Awareness in the Making of 'Tintern Abbey.'" *The Wordsworth Circle* 12:97–100.

Meyer, George Wilbur. 1943. *Wordsworth's Formative Years*. Ann Arbor: University of Michigan Press.

———. 1950. "*Resolution and Independence*: Wordsworth's Answer to Coleridge's *Dejection: An Ode*." *Tulane Studies in English* 2:49–74.

———. 1950–51. "Wordsworth and the Spy Hunt." *American Scholar* 20:50–56.

Miall, David S. 1991. "Coleridge on Emotion: Experience into Theory." *The Wordsworth Circle* 22:35–47.

Miles, Josephine. 1942. *Wordsworth and the Vocabulary of Emotion*. New York: Octagon Books. Reprinted 1965.

Miller, Alice. 1986. *Thou Shalt Not Be Aware: Society's Betrayal of the Child*. Translated by Hildegarde Hannum and Hunter Hannum. New York: Meridian. Originally published in German in 1981.

———.1990a. *The Untouched Key: Tracing Childhood Trauma in Creativity and Destructiveness*. Translated by Hildegarde Hannum and Hunter Hannum. New York: Doubleday. Originally published in German in 1988.

———.1990b. *Banished Knowledge: Facing Childhood Injuries*. Translated by Leila Vennewitz. New York: Doubleday. Originally published in German in 1988.

———.1990c. *For Your Own Good: Hidden Cruelty in Child-Rearing and the Roots of Violence*. Translated by Hildegarde Hannum and Hunter Hannum. New York: Noonday. Originally published in German in 1980.

———.1990d. *The Drama of the Gifted Child*. Translated by Ruth Ward. New York: Basic Books. Originally published in Germany in 1979; originally published in English as *Prisoners of Childhood*.

Miller, J. Hillis. 1978. "On Edge: The Crossways of Contemporary Criticism." *Bulletin of the American Academy of Arts and Sciences* 32:13–32. Reprinted in Eaves and Fischer 1986, 96–111.

———. 1990. "Narrative." In *Critical Terms for Literary Study*, edited by Frank Lentricchia and Thomas McLaughlin, 66–79. Chicago: University of Chicago Press.

Mills, Joyce C., and Richard J. Crowley. 1986. *Therapeutic Metaphors for Children and the Child Within*. New York: Brunner/Mazel.

Missildine, W. Hugh. 1964. *Your Inner Child of the Past*. New York: Pocket Books.

Moorman, Mary. 1957. *William Wordsworth: A Biography: The Early Years, 1770–1803*. Oxford: Oxford University Press.

———. 1965. *William Wordsworth: A Biography: The Later Years, 1803–1850*. Oxford: Oxford University Press.

Onorato, Richard J. 1971. *The Character of the Poet: Wordsworth in "The Prelude."* Princeton: Princeton University Press.

Osborn, Marijane. 1976. "Wordsworth's *Borderers* and the Landscape of Penrith." *Transactions of the Cumberland and Westmorland Antiquarian and Archaeological Society* 76:144–58.

Owen, W. J. B. 1969. *Wordsworth as Critic.* Toronto: University of Toronto Press.

———. 1977. "'The Thorn' and the Poet's Intention." *The Wordsworth Circle* 8:3–17.

Page, Judith W. 1988. "'The weight of too much liberty': Genre and Gender in Wordsworth's Calais Sonnets." *Criticism* 30:189–203.

Parker, Reeve. 1972. "'Finer Distance': The Narrative Art of Wordsworth's 'The Wanderer.'" *English Literary History* 39:87–111.

Parrish, Stephen Maxfield. 1957. "'The Thorn': Wordsworth's Dramatic Monologue." *ELH* 24:153–63.

———. 1973. *The Art of the Lyrical Ballads.* Cambridge: Harvard University Press.

Parrish, Stephen Maxfield, and David Erdman. 1960. "Who Wrote *The Mad Monk*? A Debate." *Bulletin of the New York Public Library* 64:209–37.

Peck, M. Scott. 1978. *The Road Less Travelled.* New York: Simon and Schuster.

Perkins, David. 1959. *The Quest for Permanence: The Symbolism in Wordsworth, Shelley and Keats.* Cambridge: Harvard University Press.

———. 1964. *Wordsworth and Poetry of Sincerity.* Cambridge: Harvard University Press.

Phelan, James. 1981. *Worlds from Words: A Theory of Language in Fiction.* Chicago: University of Chicago Press.

Pipkin, James W. 1978. "Wordsworth's 'Nutting' and Rites of Initiation." *Interpretations: Studies in Language and Literature* 10:11–20.

Price, John. 1974. "Wordsworth's *Lucy.*" *American Imago* 31:360–77.

Priestman, Donald G. 1975. "Superstition and Imagination: Complementary Faculties of Wordsworth's Narrator in 'The Thorn.'" *Journal of Narrative Techniques* 5:196–207.

Purington, Marjean D. 1992. "Wordsworth's *The Borderers* and the Ideology of Revolution." *The Wordsworth Circle* 23:97–108.

Radcliffe, Evan. 1984. "'In Dreams Begin Responsibility': Wordsworth's Ruined Cottage Story." *Studies in Romanticism* 23:101–19.

Read, Herbert. 1930. *Wordsworth: The Clark Lectures, 1929–30.* London: Jonathan Cape.

Reed, Mark L. 1967. *Wordsworth: The Chronology of the Early Years, 1770–1799.* Cambridge: Harvard University Press.

———. 1975. *Wordsworth: The Chronology of the Middle Years, 1800–1815.* Cambridge: Harvard University Press.

Reiman, Donald H. 1978. "Poetry of Familiarity: Wordsworth, Dorothy, and Mary Hutchinson." In *The Evidence of the Imagination: Studies of Interactions between*

Life and Art in English Romantic Literature, edited by Donald H. Reiman et al., 142–77. New York: New York University Press.

Richardson, Alan. 1985. "The Dangers of Sympathy: Sibling Incest in English Romantic Poetry." *Studies in English Literature* 25:737–54.

Ricks, Christopher. 1987. "William Wordsworth 2: 'A sinking inwards into ourselves from thought to thought.'" In *The Force of Poetry*. Oxford: Oxford University Press.

Robinson, Jeffrey C. 1981. "The Immortality Ode: Lionel Trilling and Helen Vendler." *The Wordsworth Circle* 12:64–70.

———. 1987. *Radical Literary Education: A Classroom Experiment with Wordsworth's "Ode."* Madison: University of Wisconsin Press.

Roe, Nicolas. 1988. *Wordsworth and Coleridge: The Radical Years*. New York: Oxford University Press.

Ross, Marlon B. 1986. "Naturalizing Gender: Woman's Place in Wordsworth's Ideological Landscape." *ELH* 53:391–410.

Rylestone, Anne L. 1991. *Prophetic Memory in Wordsworth's Ecclesiastical Sonnets*. Carbondale: Southern Illinois University Press.

Schapiro, Barbara A. 1983. *The Romantic Mother: Narcissistic Patterns in Romantic Poetry*. Baltimore: Johns Hopkins University Press.

Schenk, H. G. 1966. *The Mind of the European Romantics: An Essay in Cultural History*. New York: Frederick Ungar.

Seamon, David. 1984. "Emotional Experience of the Environment." *American Behavioral Scientist* 27, no. 6:757–770.

Sharrock, Roger. 1964. "*The Borderers*: Wordsworth on the Moral Frontier." *Durham University Journal* 25:170–83.

Sheats, Paul D. 1973. *The Making of Wordsworth's Poetry, 1785–1798*. Cambridge: Harvard University Press.

———. 1991. "'Tis Three Feet Long, and Two Feet Wide': Wordsworth's 'Thorn' and the Politics of Bathos." *The Wordsworth Circle* 22:92–100.

Shelley, Percy Bysshe 1977. *Shelley's Poetry and Prose*. Edited by Donald H. Reiman and Sharon B. Powers. New York: W. W. Norton.

Slakey, Roger L. 1972. "At Zero: A Reading of Wordsworth's 'She dwelt among the Untrodden Ways.'" *Studies in English Literature 1500–1900* 12:629–38.

Smith, Fred M. 1935. "The Relation of Coleridge"'s 'Ode to Dejection' to Wordsworth's 'Ode on Intimations of Immortality.'" *PMLA* 50:222–34.

Sperry, Willard. 1935. *Wordsworth's Anti-Climax*. Cambridge: Harvard University Press.

Spivak, Gayatri Chakravorty. 1981. "Sex and History in *The Prelude* 1805." *Texas Studies in Literature and Language* 23:324–60.

Stoddard, Eve Walsh. 1980. "*The Borderers:* A Critique of Both Reason and Feeling as Moral Agents." *The Wordsworth Circle* 11:93–97.

Storch, R. F. 1969. "Wordsworth's *The Borderers*: The Poet as Anthropologist." *Journal of English Literary History* 36:340–60.

Strout, A. L. 1940. "Wordsworth's Desiccation." *Modern Language Review* 35:162–72.

Swann, Karen. 1991. "Suffering and Sensation in *The Ruined Cottage*." *PMLA* 106:83–95.

Taylor, Anya. 1986. "Religious Readings of the Immortality Ode." *SEL* 26:633–44.

Teichman, Milton. 1971. "Wordsworth's Two Replies to Coleridge's 'Dejection: An Ode.'" *PMLA* 86:982–89.

Terr, Lenore. 1990. *Too Scared to Cry: How Trauma Affects Children . . . and Ultimately Us All*. New York: Basic Books.

Thomas, Gordon K. 1978. "Coleridge Stuck on 'The Thorn.'" *The Wordsworth Circle* 9:379:81.

Thomson, Douglass H. 1979. "Wordsworth's Lucy of 'Nutting.'" *Studies in Romanticism* 18:287–98.

Thorslev, Peter L., Jr. 1963. "The Romantic Mind is its Own Place." *Comparative Literature* 15:250–68.

Townsend, R. C. 1966. "John Wordsworth and His Brother's Poetic Development." *PMLA* 81:70–78.

Trilling, Lionel. 1975. "The Immortality Ode." In *English Romantic Poets: Modern Essays in Criticism*, edited by M. H. Abrams, 149–69. Oxford: Oxford University Press.

Vendler, Helen. 1978. "Lionel Trilling and the *Immortality Ode*." *Salmagundi* 41:66–86.

Wahl, Charles William, ed. 1964. *New Dimensions in Psychosomatic Medicine*. Boston: Little, Brown.

Wegscheider, Sharon. 1981. *Another Chance: Hope and Health for the Alcoholic Family*. Palo Alto, Calif.: Science and Behavior Books.

Wells, J. E. 1940. "Wordsworth and De Quincey in Westmorland Politics, 1818." *PMLA* 55:1080–1128.

Wesling, Donald. 1970. *Wordsworth and the Adequacy of Landscape*. New York: Barnes and Noble.

Whitfield, Charles L. 1987. *Healing the Child Within*. Deerfield Beach, Fla.: Health Communications.

Wolfson, Susan J. 1979. "The Speaker as Questioner in *Lyrical Ballads*." *Journal of English and Germanic Philology* 77:546–68.

———. 1988. "Dorothy Wordsworth in Conversation with William." In *Romanticism and Feminism*, edited by Anne K. Mellor, 139–66. Bloomington: Indiana University Press.

Woodring, Carl. 1968. *Wordsworth*. Cambridge: Harvard University Press.

Wordsworth, Christopher. 1851. *Memoirs of William Wordsworth, Poet-Laureate, D.C.L.* 2 vols. London: Edward Moxon.

Wordsworth, Dorothy. 1973. *Journals of Dorothy Wordsworth.* Edited by Mary Moorman. Oxford: Oxford University Press.

Wordsworth, Gordon G. 1920. "The Boyhood of Wordsworth." *Cornhill Magazine* 121:410–20.

Wordsworth, Jonathan. 1969. *The Music of Humanity: A Critical Study of Wordsworth's "Ruined Cottage."* New York: Harper and Row.

———. 1979. "The Two-Part *Prelude* of 1799." In Wordsworth 1979, 567–85. Originally printed in *The Cornell Library Journal* 11 (Spring 1970): 3–24.

———. 1980. "On Man, on Nature, and on Human Life." *Review of English Studies* 31:17–29.

———. 1982. *William Wordsworth: The Borders of Vision.* Oxford: Clarendon.

Wordsworth, Jonathan, and Steven Gill. 1973. "The Two-Part *Prelude* of 1798–9." *JEGP* 72:503–25.

Wordsworth, William. 1857. *The Poetical Works of Wordsworth.* 6 vols. London: Moxon.

———. 1876. *The Prose Works of William Wordsworth.* 3 vols. Edited by Alexander B. Grosart. London: Moxon.

———. 1926. *The Prelude, or Growth of a Poet's Mind.* Edited by Ernest de Selincourt. London: Humphrey Milford/Oxford University Press.

———. 1936. *Wordsworth: Poetical Works.* Edited by Thomas Hutchinson, revised by Ernest de Selincourt. Oxford: Oxford University Press.

———. 1940. *The Poetical Works of William Wordsworth: Poems Written in Youth; Poems Referring to the Period of Childhood.* Edited by Ernest de Selincourt. Oxford: Clarendon.

———. 1949. *The Poetical Works of William Wordsworth: The Excursion; The Recluse, Part I, Book I.* Edited by Ernest de Selincourt and Helen Darbishire. Oxford: Clarendon.

———. 1965. *Lyrical Ballads.* Edited by R. L. Brett and A. R. Jones. London: Methuen.

———. 1967. *The Letters of William and Dorothy Wordsworth: The Early Years, 1787–1805* 2d ed. Edited by Ernest de Selincourt, revised by Chester L. Shaver. Oxford: Clarendon.

———. 1969. *The Letters of William and Dorothy Wordsworth: The Middle Years, Part 1, 1806–1811.* Edited by Ernest de Selincourt, revised by Mary Moorman. Oxford: Clarendon.

———. 1974. *The Prose Works of William Wordsworth.* 3 vols. Edited by W. J. B. Owen and Jane Worthington Smyser. Oxford: Clarendon.

———. 1975. *The Salisbury Plain Poems of William Wordsworth.* Edited by Stephen Gill. Ithaca: Cornell University Press.

———. 1977. *The Prelude, 1798–1799.* Edited by Stephen Parrish. Ithaca: Cornell University Press.

———. 1977a. *Home at Grasmere*. Edited by Beth Darlington. Ithaca: Cornell University Press.

———. 1979. *The Prelude 1799, 1805, 1850*. Edited by Jonathan Wordsworth, M. H. Abrams, and Stephen Gill. New York: W. W. Norton.

———. 1979a. *"The Ruined Cottage" and "The Pedlar."* Edited by James Butler. Ithaca: Cornell University Press.

———. 1982. *The Borderers*. Edited by Robert Osborn. Ithaca: Cornell University Press.

———. 1984. *Wordsworth*. Edited by Stephen Gill. Oxford: Oxford University Press.

———. 1988. *The Letters of William and Dorothy Wordsworth: The Later Years, Part IV, 1840–1853*. Edited by Alan G. Hill. Oxford: Clarendon.

———. 1992. *Lyrical Ballads*. Edited by Michael Mason. London: Longman.

———. 1993. *The Letters of William and Dorothy Wordsworth: A Supplement of New Letters*. Edited by Alan G. Hill. Oxford: Clarendon.

Zeig, Jeffrey K., ed. 1982. *Ericksonian Approaches to Hypnosis and Psychotherapy*. New York: Brunner/Mazel.

Index

Abandonment, 27, 48, 60, 62, 65, 80–88, 89, 92, 93, 97, 105, 116–18, 122, 140, 147, 159, 206
Abuse, 79; emotional, 54, 68–70
Acceptance, 29, 30, 34–35, 38, 53, 65, 91–92, 106, 122, 127, 134, 138, 156, 157, 200–201, 211, 213. *See also* Self-acceptance
Adult child, 22, 122, 173, 182; definition of, 11
Alfoxden, 73, 109, 112–13, 114, 123, 125, 126, 140, 141, 142, 143, 161, 190, 202
Allport, Gordon, 15
Anger, 31, 53, 54, 69, 70, 91–92, 163–66
Anxiety, 20, 23, 31, 57, 60, 61, 66, 72, 79, 94, 128, 146, 168, 207, 218
Art, 16
Averill, James H., 111

Bargaining, 91
Bateson, F. W., 24, 35, 67
Beattie, James, 58
Beaumont, Sir George, 42, 73, 76
Bereavement. *See* Loss
Bialostosky, Don H., 10, 36
Blake, William, 20
Bloom, Harold, 165
Bradshaw, John, 38
Briere, John M., 218

Bristol, 125–26, 174
Burns, Robert, 41
Butler, James, 105, 108
Byron, George Gordon, Lord: *Don Juan*, 33

Calvert, Raisley, 95, 97
Calvert, William, 93
Cambridge, 202
Campbell, Joseph, 24
Centroversion, 141, 195
Chester, John, 144
Childhood, 11, 20, 62, 118, 212, 215. *See also* Wordsworth, William: and childhood
Chopra, Deepak, 132
Cockermouth, 47, 68
Co-dependency, 70–71
Coleridge, Berkeley, 174
Coleridge, Samuel Taylor, 29, 31, 50, 52, 67, 73, 75, 77, 78–79, 97, 99, 102–4, 112–13, 125, 138, 139, 141–42, 143–47, 149–50, 159, 161–62, 166, 167, 168–69, 184–85, 189, 191, 199, 201, 204, 207. Works: *Biographia Literaria*, 167; *Christabel*, 112, 201, 202; *Dejection: An Ode*, 29; *The Nightingale: A Conversation Poem*, 125; *Osorio*, 103; *The Rime of the Ancient Mariner*, 112, 167, 184, 201
Coleridge, Sara, 113, 202

Collins, William, 58
Communicative authority, 208
Cooksons (WW's grandparents): Christopher Crackanthorpe, 70, 185. *See also* Penrith
Cottle, Joseph, 97, 103, 125, 126, 184
Cowper, William, 58
Criticism: bottom-up, 36; idiographic, 37; nomothetic, 37; overdetermined, 16, 28; process, 37; top-down, 36, 37

Dandby, J. F., 118
Dann, Joanne, 56
Darwin, Erasmus: *Zoonomia*, 114
Death, 26, 27, 48, 60, 63, 91–92, 97, 99, 105, 107, 116, 117–18, 122, 123, 124, 147, 151–52, 154–57, 162, 167–68, 170, 173, 180, 182, 187, 209–11, 213, 221; of Wordsworth's parents, 30, 42, 47–48, 53, 54, 57–59, 65, 151, 186–87, 195, 197, 198, 209, 218, 219
Deconstruction, 28
Denial, 29, 31, 32, 53, 91, 106, 122, 134, 138, 211
Depression, 26, 31, 79, 91–92, 98, 175, 211
De Quincey, Thomas, 42, 56, 80, 93
de Selincourt, Ernest, 85–86, 113
Despondency, 206
Dialogical: defenses, 152; voice, 39
Dissociation, 46, 72, 102, 142, 218–19; poetry of, 219
Douglas, Wallace W., 35, 166
Dove Cottage, 189–90, 201
Durckheim, Karlfried Graf, 24

Economics: of restoration, 212; of retention, 212
Egotism: Wordsworth's, 26, 67
Eilenberg, Susan, 156–57
Ellis, David, 35
Emotional: confidence, 199; denouement, 183; dislocation, 141; projection, 195; rehabilitation, 193; well-being, 212
Endurance, 9, 23, 31, 53, 66, 100, 107, 114, 117–18, 124, 143, 147, 170, 193, 196, 198, 205, 213, 221
Erickson, Milton, 36
Existential gap, 186

Family, 11, 34, 35, 67, 71; displaced, 194; dysfunctional, 216–17; romance, 64, 87; systems theory, 56
Fear, 9, 23, 26, 29, 88, 99, 111, 119, 133, 154–56, 161–62, 166, 176, 177–78, 180, 183, 197, 203, 206, 208, 214
Feeling and thought, 11, 20, 15, 19, 22, 23–25, 28, 38, 40, 44, 49, 52, 80, 96, 107, 111, 113, 120, 121, 122, 123, 127–31, 134, 136–37, 146, 155, 172, 178, 183, 186–88, 208, 210–12, 214, 215, 220
Feelings: dislocated, 173; expressing, 21; originating in childhood, 11; understanding, 130; unresolved, 11, 20–21, 23, 54, 59, 77, 122, 142, 148, 157, 164, 166, 168, 178, 209, 219; and words 19
Fenwick, Isabella, 163, 209
Fonda, Jane, 164
France, 64, 80–88, 90, 92, 93, 97, 98, 101, 118, 145, 220
French Revolution, 81, 88–89, 92, 184
Freud, Sigmund, 16, 17, 29, 32, 147, 154; and screen memories, 21,
Friedman, Michael H., 35, 64

Germany. *See* Goslar
Gill, Stephen, 41, 45, 48, 56, 83, 87, 173, 201
Godwin, William, 36, 90, 97, 149, 167
Goethe, Johann Wolfgang von, 33
Gordon, William, 59
Goslar (Germany), 62, 74, 76, 113, 125,

138–39, 140–73, 174–76, 184, 185, 190, 202
Göttingen, 144
Grasmere, 23, 42, 73, 74, 80, 189–91, 195–97, 202–3, 206–7, 215, 220; Grasmere Lake, 212
Gray, Thomas, 58
Grief and grieving, 9, 23, 29, 31, 48, 59, 66, 88, 91, 105–8, 110, 111, 120, 143, 154, 157, 198, 209, 213, 218, 221
Guilt, 9, 29, 31, 48, 60, 61–64, 66, 71, 84, 99, 100, 115, 118, 124, 128, 142, 151, 158–62, 164–65, 176, 177–78, 182, 197, 198, 206, 214, 219, 221
Guilt cycle, 162, 163–65

Halifax, 170
Hamburg, 144
Harper, George McLean, 41
Hartley, David, 46, 78
Hartman, Geoffrey, 29–30, 32, 124, 125, 156–57
Havens, R. D., 54
Hawkshead, 72
Haydon, Benjamin Robert, 67, 68
Hazlitt, William, 18, 39, 67
Healing, 24, 26, 30, 95, 100, 129, 131–32, 137, 138, , 139, 157, 188, 208, 211, 214, 215
Heath, William, 20–21
Heinroth, Johann Christian, 79
Helplessness, 26, 31, 102, 111, 168
Herman, Judith Lewis, 220–21
History, 35, 39
Holistic, 135 ; model, 130, healing, 131–32
Hope, 26, 53, 96, 97, 102
Hutchinson, Mary, 77, 88, 105, 112, 184, 199, 202, 203, 206, 207; and family, 184, 201
Hutchinson, Sara, 202

Incest, 71

Individuation, 10, 127, 128, 152, 188, 194, 201. *See also* Sense of self: individuated
Inner child, 11, 21, 91, 122, 204; healing of, 188; lost, 26, 72, 132, 143, 147, 150, 151, 157, 170, 172
Intensity, 10, 26, 68, 114, 117, 141, 148, 173, 179, 207, 209, 215
Isolation, 151, 162, 211

Jacobus, Mary, 117, 118
Johnson, Don, 55
Johnston, Kenneth R., 197
Jones, Mark, 36
Jones, Robert, 93

Keats, John, 32, 59, 67, 138
Kübler-Ross, Elisabeth, 63–64, 91–92, 211, 213

Lake District, 47, 132
Lamb, Charles, 67
Language, 17–22, 28, 38 44
Leavis, F. R., 39–40, 104, 109–10
Lessing, Gotthold Ephraim, 144
Literary criticism, 27–28
London, 93, 125
Loneliness, 27, 48, 52, 55, 111, 133, 198, 221
Lonsdale, Lord. *See* Lowther, Sir James
Loss, 9, 22, 23, 27, 29, 30, 31, 54–55, 58, 60, 61–65, 66, 69, 72, 84, 88, 89, 91, 97, 102, 107–8, 117, 120, 122, 124, 128, 136, 137, 143, 147, 156–57, 159, 161–66, 168, 169, 182, 194, 195, 197, 200, 201–2, 204, 208, 209, 211, 211–14, 219, 221
Louis XVI, 81, 92
Lowther, Sir James, 55–58, 60, 206
Lowther, Sir William, 57–58

Mason, Michael, 167
Mathews, William, 94
Matlak, Richard E., 35, 64–65, 168–69

Mazzeno, Lawrence, 59, 122
McFarland, Thomas, 10, 20, 48, 65, 147–48, 191
McGavran, James Holt, Jr., 128
Meditation, 26, 123, 132, 135, 147, 157, 183, 212, 214
Memory, 20–21, 44, 69
Meyer, George Wilbur, 35, 44
Miller, Alice, 23, 27, 29, 32, 41, 63–64, 80, 100, 205, 213, 215
Milton, John, 11, 32, 64, 109, 140, 191
Montagu, Basil, 98, 120, 125
Moorman, Mary, 41, 54, 56, 57, 58, 59, 81–83, 99, 212
Mourning, 157, 168, 220. *See also* Loss

Napoleon, 82
Nature, 15, 23, 25, 47, 49–55, 62–63, 101, 105, 108, 128, 132–37, 156, 164, 166, 173, 176, 177, 183, 187–88, 194, 204
Nervous breakdown, 90, 93, 101
Nether Stowey, 103, 112, 125
New Historicism, 28

Onorato, Richard J., 26, 28, 35, 37, 65, 86

Page, Judith W., 87–88
Pain, 26, 136, 168
Parrish, Stephen, 116–17, 118
Penrith, 48, 54, 68–71, 72, 94, 99, 181, 218
Personal, the, 37; for Wordsworth, 15–16, 19, 30, 38
Poetic affect, 28
Pollard, Jane, 57, 69, 70, 93
Poole, Thomas, 78, 174–75
Post-traumatic stress disorder, 79, 147
Process Criticism, 37
Psychoanalysis, 16, 27
Psychoanalytic criticism, 29, 37
Psychobiographical approach, 35
Psychogenic health problems, 72–80, 92, 175. *See also* Psychosomatic; Wordsworth, William: health
Psychology, 16, 21, 24, 101, 107, 124, 130, 151, 218
Psychosomapoetics, 77
Psychosomatic, 31, 79, 115, 142, 147. *See also* Psychogenic health problems
Psychotherapy. *See* Therapy

Racedown, 33, 89, 95, 98–103, 111–12, 125, 142, 190
Ratzeburg, 144, 157
Read, Herbert, 104
Recovery, 26, 29, 40, 45, 66, 88, 102, 106, 127, 137, 141, 152, 194; and writing, 220–21
Reed, Mark L., 41, 68, 99
Reenactment, 11, 27, 28, 29, 31, 37, 39, 45, 46, 50, 53, 54, 60, 66, 79, 80, 83–84, 89, 99, 105, 111, 116, 117–18, 121, 124, 129, 142, 143, 146, 150, 151, 154, 162, 164, 168, 173, 182, 189, 194, 209; as emotional allegory, 170–71
Reil, J. Christian, 79
Repression, 29, 30, 31, 151, 165, 166
Ricks, Christopher, 10
Robespierre, Isidore Maximilien de, 81
Robinson, Henry Crabb, 67
Roethke, Theodore, 140

Salisbury Plains, 93, 95
Saussure, Ferdinand de, 43
Schapiro, Barbara, 48
Schiller, Johann Christoph Friedrich von, 103
Scotland, 207
Security, 206
Self, 165, adult/child, 203; acceptance, 15, 23, 27, 187, 214; awareness, 172; change, 38; completion, 188; confirmation, 192; defense, 157; determination, 201; development,

206; discovery, 136, 190; empowerment, 194; examination, 49, 124, 131, 142; exploration, 27; healing, 168; inner, 16; projection, 68; recognition, 23; splitting, 22; sufficiency, 188; and transformation, 136, 206; undivided, 151. *See also* Sense of self; Subjectivity
Sense of self, 11, 21, 34, 95, 141, 215; individuated, 66, 130. *See also* Individuation
Separation, 9, 48, 50, 65, 97, 124, 142, 143, 147, 157, 161, 168–69, 175, 182, 195, 197, 206, 219
Shakespeare, William, 64, 95, 103
Sheats, Paul, 86, 99
Shelley, Percy Bysshe, 138; *Peter Bell the Third*, 67–68
Sockburn, 184, 185, 190, 195
Solipsistic drive, 188
Solitude, 51–52, 62–63, 66–67, 108–9, 117, 122, 129, 158–60, 164, 173, 186, 199, 210
Somatoform disorders, 79. *See also* Psychogenic health problems
Sorrow, 23, 26, 30, 31, 58, 99, 105, 128, 182, 187, 198, 199, 201
Southey, William, 97, 103, 185
Spenser, Edmund, 64
Spivak, Gayatri Chakravorty, 83, 87
Spot(s) of time, 62, 64, 133, 142, 160–62, 163, 177–83, 185, 219
Spot syndrome, 102, 195
Subjectivity, 11, 24, 27, 29, 32, 33, 34, 36, 37, 38, 39, 42, 44, 49–50, 52, 65, 72, 107, 124, 145, 151–52, 170–71, 176, 215; displaced, 141; radical, 28; self, 34–35, 39, 97, 114, 117, 121, 127, 142, 213; and self-defense, 157; subjective authority, 142
Suicide, 48, 69
Superego, 165
Switzerland, 81, 93

Taylor, William, 72
Tempus hibernum mirabile, 149
Terr, Lenore, 219, 220
Therapy, 21, 27, 30, 36, 44, 80, 137, 213, 220; poetry as therapeutic, 26, 100, 147
Thomas, Dylan: *Fern Hill*, 210
Thought and feeling. *See* Feeling
Tintern, 126
Tintern Abbey, 93
Topophilia, 141
Transference, 137, 151
Transformational poetry, 15, 23, 40, 96, 101, 137–38, 180, 194, 206, 208–9, 211
Trauma, 11, 21, 27, 30, 31, 51, 63, 66, 72, 79, 96, 98, 102, 142, 147, 178, 182, 187, 209, 218–19, 220
Trilling, Lionel, 24, 28, 208
Tyson, Ann, 72
Tyson, Hugh, 72

Universal, the: for Wordsworth, 15–16, 19, 38

Vallon, Annette, 32, 80–88, 100, 169, 198, 203, 206–7

Wales, 89, 93, 98, 126
Wedgewood, Josiah, 73, 184
Wegscheider, Sharon, 216–17
Wilson, John, 119
Windermere, Lake, 173
Woodring, Carl, 16, 56, 101
Wordsworth, Ann (mother of WW), 47–55, 66, 68, 71, 91–92, 118, 122, 124, 128, 134, 136, 166, 186–88, 198, 199, 218
Wordsworth, Anne–Caroline (daughter of WW), 81, 93, 118, 203, 206–7
Wordsworth, Christopher (brother of WW), 47, 69, 145
Wordsworth, Christopher (nephew of WW): *Memoirs*, 64

Wordsworth, Dorothy (sister of WW), 42, 47, 48, 52, 56, 69–71, 72–78, 89, 92–93, 97, 98, 101, 103, 105, 106–7, 112, 116–17, 125, 126, 129, 136–38, 143–45, 147, 150, 152, 150, 157, 159, 161, 166, 167, 170, 174–75, 184–85, 189–90, 191, 193, 194, 195–97, 202–4, 205–7

Wordsworth, John (brother of WW), 47, 65, 69, 189, 194, 199, 201, 202,

Wordsworth, John (father of WW), 47, 48, 55–65, 66, 68, 71, 91–92, 109, 118, 122, 124, 128, 134, 166, 179, 180, 182, 188, 194, 198, 207, 218

Wordsworth, John (son of WW), 207

Wordsworth, Jonathan, 181, 201

Wordsworth, Mary (wife of WW). *See* Hutchinson, Mary

Wordsworth, Richard (brother of WW), 47, 57, 73, 92–93, 185

Wordsworth, William: and autobiography, 41–44; and childhood, 11, 20–21, 22, 24–26, 50–52, 62, 108, 141; 157–58, 163, 169, 170, 171, 176–89, 184–86, 192, 194, 195, 200, 203, 209–14, 216–17, 218 (*see also* Penrith); and composition, 26 (*see also* Writing); decline, 24, 65, 80, 147–48, 215; health, 42, 45, 47, 72–80, 88, 94–95, 106–7, 142, 145–48, 175, 184, 202, 219 (*see also* Psychogenic health problems; Psychosomatic); natural language, 18; as teacher, 38, 42; as poetherapist, 219

Poetry: *Address to the Scholars of the Village School,* 148; *Anecdote for Fathers Shewing how the Art of Lying may be Taught,* 120–21; *The Borderers,* 59, 87, 99–101, 103, 104, 124; *The Brothers,* 202, 219; Calais sonnets, 87–88; *Carved, Matthew . . . ,* 148; *The Complaint of a Forsaken Indian Woman,* 120; *Could I the priest's consent have gained,* 148; *Descriptive Sketches,* 81, 93; *Dirge,* 148; Ecclesiastical sonnets, 48; *Elegy,* 148; *Ellen Irwin,* 149; *An Evening Walk,* 93; *The Excursion,* 83, 100, 106, 110, 190; *Expostulation and Reply,* 123; *The Female Vagrant,* 95, 168; *The Fountain,* 148, 168; *A Fragment,* 149; *Goody Blake and Harry Gill: A True Story,* 114–16, 120; *Guilt and Sorrow,* 95; *Heart–Leap Well,* 196; *Home at Grasmere,* 190–201; *How sweet when crimson colours dart,* 148; *The Idiot Boy,* 112, 118–20, 170; *If Nature, for a favorite Child,* 148, 168; *Imitation of Juvenal,* 57; *Immortality Ode,* 24, 26, 51, 80, 143, 148, 204, 205–15, 221; *Influence of Natural Objects,* 148; *I travelled among unknown men,* 149; *Just as the blowing thorn began,* 148; *The Last of the Flock,* 123; *The Leech Gatherer* (see *Resolution and Independence*); *Lines left upon a Seat in a Yew–tree,* 33, 101–2; *Lines Written at a Small Distance from my House,* 120; *Lines written in Early Spring,* 120; *Lucy Gray,* 148, 149–50, 169, 170; Lucy poems, 38, 149–57, 162, 168–69; *Lyrical Ballads,* 20, 21, 30, 59, 112–24, 125, 138–39, 143, 147, 150, 167–68, 171, 183, 184, 198, 201, 219; *The Mad Mother,* 120; *Michael,* 31, 201–2; *Nutting,* 25, 31, 148, 162–66; *The Pedlar,* 106–10, 203 (see also *The Ruined Cottage*); *A Poet's Epitaph,* 148; 1799 *Prelude,* 22, 49–52, 55, 62–63, 108, 124, 133, 143, 147, 148, 157–61, 163, 173, 176–89, 201, 209, 215; 1805 *Prelude,* 25–26, 33, 38, 42–43, 44, 53–54, 58, 60, 66, 81, 83–87 (the tale of Vaudracour and

Julia), 88–90, 92, 95, 97–98, 101, 109, 112, 126, 142, 149, 159, 171, 180, 189, 201, 209, 215; 1850 *Prelude*, 50, 85; *The Recluse*, 39, 44, 112–13, 161, 184–85, 190, 191, 202, 207; *Resolution and Independence*, 77, 108, 205–6; *The Ruined Cottage*, 77, 104–11, 115, 124, 142; *Ruth*, 148, 169–70; *Salisbury Plain*, 83, 95–97, 99, 124; *She dwelt among th' untrodden ways*, 149–52, 153, 156; *She was a Phantom of delight*, 53; *Simon Lee, the Old Huntsman*, 123; *A slumber did my spirit seal*, 148, 149, 155–57; *Song* (see *She dwelt among th' untrodden ways*); *Strange fits of passion . . .* , 148, 152–56; *The Tables Turned*, 123; *There was a Boy* (of Winnander), 149, 169, 171–73; *Three years she grew . . .* , 148, 149; *The Thorn*, 83, 112. 116–18, 120, 147, 181; *Tintern Abbey*, 26, 78, 80, 124, 125–39, 141, 157, 169, 183, 192, 193, 195, 200, 201, 204, 208, 212, 214; *To a Sexton*, 148, 168; *Stanzas written in my Pocket-Copy of Thompson's "Castle of Indolence,"* 206; *The Two April Mornings*, 148, 168; *The Vale of Esthwaite*, 58, 60, 71; *We Are Seven*, 120–22, 147, 152; *Written in Germany, on one of the coldest days of the Century*, 145, 149

   Prose: *Appendix to the Preface*, 18; *Autobiographical Memoranda*, 48, 66, 68–69; *Essay on Morals*, 149; *Essay, Supplementary to the Preface*, 19; *Essays upon Epitaphs, III*, 19; *Letter to a Friend of Robert Burns*, 41; Note to *The Thorn*, 19–20; Preface to *Lyrical Ballads*, 16, 17–18, 105, 115, 199–200, 201, 203

Writing, 46, 97, 100; as reenactment, 142 and self–defense, 73, 76, 140, 146, 157, 185; and self–discovery, 138; as therapy, 30, 147, 219, 220–21; and Wordsworth's health, 72–80, 145–48, 185

Wye Valley, 125–25

Yarmouth, 144

OHIO UNIVERSITY LIBRARY
Please return this book as soon as you have
finished it. In order to avoid a fine it must
be returned by the date stamped be-